Praise for

1923

"Mark Williams Jones's *1923* is scary stuff. The fever broke, but the disease remained. In time, the Nazis reorganized, and Germany's patriots stood by to provide cover to purge the enemies at home: the democrat, the socialist, the Jew. It was a homespun crusade that destroyed all law and overturned all order. Jones's book asks where we are today—at the end of the troubles, or at the beginning?"

—Peter Fritzsche, author of
Hitler's First Hundred Days

"*1923* is a gripping account of interwar Germany's *annus horribilis*— the year when French invasion, hyperinflation, and Hitler's 'Beer Hall Putsch' shook the young republic. Thoroughly researched and beautifully written, Jones's story of a democracy under terrible pressure is a warning for our times."

—Alexander Watson, author of *Ring of Steel*

"Drawing upon a wealth of primary source material, Jones takes us deep into the crisis year of 1923. His fascinating insights into the emotions and experiences of people whose lives were touched by it shows powerfully that there was nothing inevitable about the survival of Germany's young democracy in 1923—nor about its death a decade later. As modern democracies today once again face existential challenges, Jones's book is a timely reminder it is within our hands whether we fight to uphold them or allow them to collapse."

—Katja Hoyer, author of *Beyond the Wall*

"A crisp and methodical chronicle of the year Germany went wrong. Jones traces the eruption in a deftly detailed and convincing narrative. His vivid history of Germany in 1923 is a timely alert to the dangers of repetition."

—Nicholas Shakespeare, author of
Six Minutes in May

1923

Also by Mark William Jones

Founding Weimar: Violence and
the German Revolution of 1918–19

1923

*The Crisis of German Democracy
in the Year of Hitler's Putsch*

MARK WILLIAM JONES

BASIC BOOKS

New York

Basic Books
Hachette Book Group
1290 Avenue of the Americas, New York, NY 10104
www.basicbooks.com

Printed in the United States of America

Originally published in 2023 in Great Britain by Basic Books UK,
an imprint of John Murray Press, an Hachette UK company
First US Edition: August 2023

Published by Basic Books, an imprint of Hachette Book Group, Inc. The Basic Books name
and logo is a trademark of the Hachette Book Group.

The Hachette Speakers Bureau provides a wide range of authors for speaking events. To find
out more, go to hachettespeakersbureau.com or email HachetteSpeakers@hbgusa.com.

Basic Books copies may be purchased in bulk for business, educational, or promotional use.
For information, please contact your local bookseller or Hachette Book Group Special
Markets Department at special.markets@hbgusa.com.

The publisher is not responsible for websites (or their content) that are not owned by the
publisher.

Maps drawn by Barking Dog Art
Typeset in Janson Text LT Std by Palimpsest Book Production Ltd, Falkirk, Stirlingshire
Library of Congress Control Number: 2023932410

ISBNs: 9781541600201 (hardcover), 9781541600218 (ebook)

LSC-C

Printing 1, 2023

For Ulrike

Contents

PART IV: Autumn and Winter 1923

German Political Parties in 1923

Bavarian People's Party (BVP) (Gustav Ritter von Kahr's party)
A conservative Christian party with its headquarters in the southern German state of Bavaria that represented Bavarian Catholicism. It was more conservative than the German Catholic Centre Party and strongly opposed to Berlin's influence upon the state of Bavaria. It was firmly opposed to the political left.

Catholic Centre Party (Centre Party) (Joseph Wirth's party)
A centre-right party that represented German Catholics. More liberal than the Bavarian People's Party, it supported Weimar democracy and was willing to form coalitions with the Social Democratic Party of Germany.

Communist Party of Germany (KPD) (August Thalheimer's party)
A national Communist party committed to the destruction of capitalism and Weimar democracy, and their replacement with a Communist system of government allied with, and inspired by, Bolshevik Russia.

German Democratic Party (DDP) (Walther Rathenau's party)
A national liberal party that represented middle- and upper-class voters. It supported Weimar democracy and was willing to form coalitions with the Social Democratic Party of Germany.

German National People's Party (DNVP) (Karl Helfferich's party)

A national conservative and antisemitic party that vehemently opposed the existence of Weimar democracy and wanted to see the return of the monarchy to Germany. It was firmly opposed to the political left.

German People's Party (DVP) (Gustav Stresemann's party)

A national conservative party that was closely aligned to the interests of big business. It was opposed to the political left and strongly divided upon the issue of whether it could participate in coalition governments with the Social Democratic Party of Germany.

National Socialist German Workers' Party (NSDAP; Nazi) (Adolf Hitler's party)

A strongly antisemitic party determined to destroy Weimar democracy. It opposed all international political co-operation and blamed 'Jews' and 'socialists' for the creation of the Weimar Republic. Its leadership and members consistently glorified violence. Largely based in Bavaria, it was a growing force during 1923.

Social Democratic Party of Germany (SPD) (Friedrich Ebert's party)

The largest political party in Germany in 1923, it represented the working class. Of all the political parties it did the most to establish democracy in Germany. It was divided between a moderate, centre-left core and a left-wing that included members prepared to co-operate with the Communist Party of Germany.

Maps

Weimar Germany in 1923

Baltic Sea

EAST PRUSSIA

POLAND

N
W   E
S

■Berlin

•Frankfurt
an der Oder

Meissen
•Dresden
·n• •Pirna

Breslau •

SAXONY

CZECHOSLOVAKIA

| 0 | 25 | 50 | 75 | 100 miles |
| 0 | 25 | 50 | 75 | 100 km |

AUSTRIA

▦   Belgian zone of occupied Rhineland
▨   Ruhr, occupied by France and Belgium
      since January 1923
▧   British zone of occupied Rhineland
▤   Saarland, occupied by France
▨   French zone of occupied Rhineland

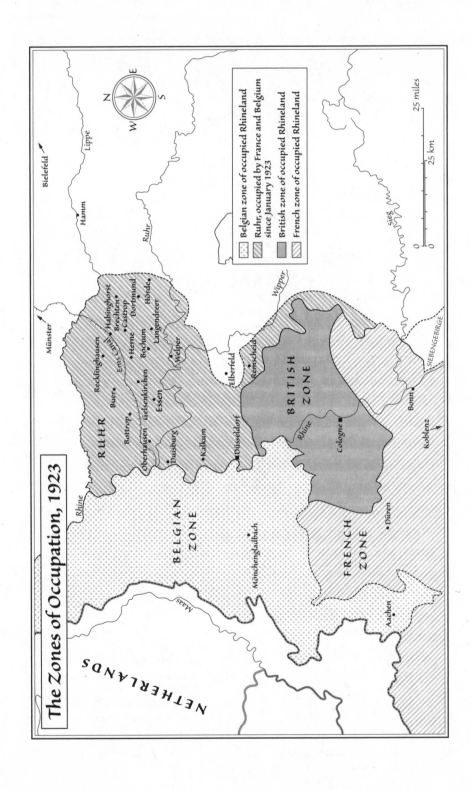

The Zones of Occupation, 1923

Belgian zone of occupied Rhineland

Ruhr, occupied by France and Belgium since January 1923

British zone of occupied Rhineland

French zone of occupied Rhineland

NETHERLANDS

RUHR

BELGIAN ZONE

BRITISH ZONE

FRENCH ZONE

25 miles

25 km

Lippe

Bielefeld

Hamm

Münster

Recklinghausen

Habinghorst

Brechten

Castrop

Dortmund

Hörde

Herne

Ems Canal

Langendreer

Bochum

Welper

Buer

Gelsenkirchen

Battrop

Oberhausen

Essen

Duisburg

Kalkum

Düsseldorf

Rhine

Mönchengladbach

Maas

Aachen

Elberfeld

Remscheid

Wipper

Rhine

Cologne

Düren

Bonn

Koblenz

Sieg

SIEBENGEBIRGE

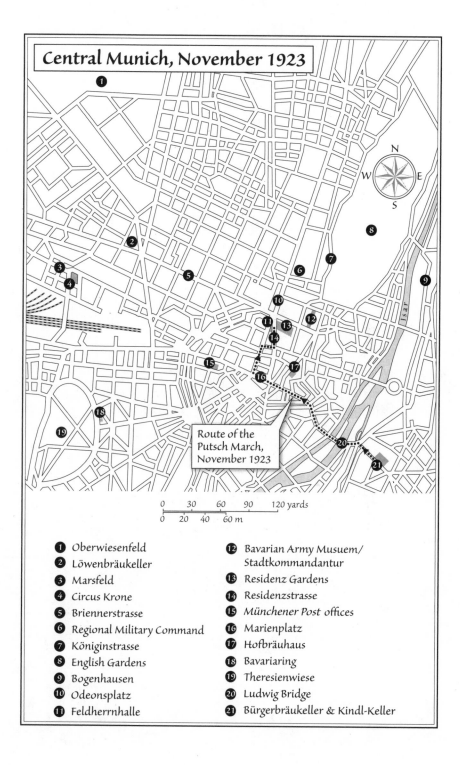

Central Munich, November 1923

N
W E
S

Isar

Route of the
Putsch March,
November 1923

```
0    30    60    90    120 yards
0   20   40   60 m
```

1. Oberwiesenfeld
2. Löwenbräukeller
3. Marsfeld
4. Circus Krone
5. Briennerstrasse
6. Regional Military Command
7. Königinstrasse
8. English Gardens
9. Bogenhausen
10. Odeonsplatz
11. Feldherrnhalle
12. Bavarian Army Musuem/ Stadtkommandantur
13. Residenz Gardens
14. Residenzstrasse
15. Münchener Post offices
16. Marienplatz
17. Hofbräuhaus
18. Bavariaring
19. Theresienwiese
20. Ludwig Bridge
21. Bürgerbräukeller & Kindl-Keller

Introduction: Germany 1923 –
The Democracy That Did Not Die

At close to midday on Friday, 9 November 1923, around two thousand armed Nazis set off marching in military formation through the centre of Munich. They were there, in the capital city of the southern German state of Bavaria, to seize political power and, in their minds, to use extreme violence to cleanse Germany of the democratic Weimar Republic that had wrongly governed their country since the end of the First World War.

At the back of the procession, a heavy machine gun was perched on top of an armoured car. In front of it, marchers – mostly young men – carried rifles, pistols and light machine guns. At the very front of the procession, their leader stood apart. It was Adolf Hitler, then aged thirty-four. While everyone else was wearing some kind of military or paramilitary uniform, he was dressed in civilian clothing, holding a Browning pistol in his hand. The only Nazis ahead of him were the armed bearers of swastika flags.

Hitler's plans were already settled. Just a few feet away from him, one of his key strategists, the fifty-year-old regional court judge Baron Theodor von der Pfordten, had a document in his pocket. It was the draft constitution that the leaders of the march wanted to implement. If they had taken control of the state that day, their authoritarian regime would have immediately built concentration camps and carried out the mass execution of everyone who had opposed the Nazis politically since November 1918. Germany's Jews – around 1 per cent of the population at this time – were to be targeted specifically: all Jewish civil servants were to be immediately dismissed and their property seized. Any Jew who failed to comply with the new regime's demands was to be executed, as was any non-Jewish German who tried to help or protect them.

There was no doubt about what Hitler would do once in power. The question, rather, was whether the violence promised by Hitler and his followers in the SA, the Nazi party's paramilitary wing, and other like-minded paramilitary organizations, would be sufficient to defeat the democratic ideal that the people could choose their government, regardless of the wishes and desires of those most prepared to use force.

The issue remains troubling to this day: how did Weimar Germany, a largely progressive modern country, where, in January 1919, 75 per cent of the electorate supported parties that were in favour of liberal democracy, so quickly turn into a brutal dictatorship that was, in the disturbing yet accurate words of philosopher Hannah Arendt, dedicated to the 'industrial production of corpses'? In 1923, though, democracy won. Theodor von der Pfordten's November 1923 constitution never came to pass – he was shot dead by the Bavarian Landespolizei shortly after the Nazis commenced their march. His constitution has nearly disappeared from memory.

The Bavarian Landespolizei had been sent to the Odeonsplatz in central Munich to protect the institutions of the Bavarian state in the face of the threat posed by the marchers. Just seconds after the police and marchers faced off against each other, both sides started shooting. It lasted for one or two minutes. When it was over, twelve putschists were dead, mostly young men who were at the very front of the march alongside Hitler and von der Pfordten, who was the oldest person to die. Four policemen lost their lives, as did a waiter who came out of a nearby restaurant to watch what was going on. This was a significant loss of life in a city in peacetime, but in a century defined by political violence, it is hard to imagine that the putsch would feature on anyone's list of major massacres. The reason the body count was so low was because, for all the Nazis' bravado about how they would use force to overthrow the state, once the firing started, they fled.

Hitler survived the hail of bullets by only a fraction of an inch.

As the marchers faced up to the police, he had linked arms with the former diplomat Max Erwin von Scheubner-Richter. When the first shots were fired, they dived to take cover. As he fell, Hitler dislocated his shoulder. Scheubner-Richter came off worse: he was shot dead. Had the bullet that killed him veered just inches to the right, Hitler's name would today be as little known as Scheubner-Richter's.

Amid the confusion, Hitler quickly fled the square. Taking shelter in a side street, he was intercepted by a Nazi-supporting doctor, who organized a car which took him out of Munich and into hiding. Two days later he was arrested by the police. His attempt to take control of the state had lasted barely twenty hours. Ten years later, he would return to the same spot as German chancellor or prime minister.

In 1923, the democratic republic that Hitler wanted to destroy had only existed for five years. At the end of the First World War in November 1918, large crowds demanding peace and democracy had gathered in German towns and cities. On 9 November 1918, when the wave of protest reached the centre of Berlin, the Social Democratic politician Philipp Scheidemann declared Germany a republic just hours after the Kaiser abdicated. The first elections were held on 19 January 1919, and across the following months Germany's pro-democratic political parties debated the contents of the new constitution, which came into force on 11 August 1919. This sought to institutionalize political compromise and protect Germans from the dangers of excessive capitalism. Most of the debates about the constitution's contents were held in the town of Weimar, located midway between Germany's more liberal north and its mostly conservative south. Ever since, even though it legally retained the name of the German Reich, this incarnation of the state has been known as the Weimar Republic.

Like the United States today, Weimar Germany was a federal state system with political power split between the national capital of Berlin and the capitals of the regional states. The north-German state of Prussia was by far the largest of the German states. It was home to 60 per cent of the Republic's sixty-three million citizens and governed at the regional level by the pro-republican Social Democrats, who used their power to strengthen democracy. The second largest state was in the German south: Bavaria. With 11 per cent of the population, it quickly became the capital of the German conservative anti-republican backlash. Many of the political and cultural conservatives who gathered there hoped to see the return of the German monarchies, including the return of the Bavarian king, who had fled on 8 November 1918. They fundamentally opposed the ideal of democracy and saw its destruction as the first point on a journey that would end with the avenging of Germany's defeat at the end of the First World War.

In 1919, when Weimar's constitution came into force, Hitler was still a political nobody. An Austrian citizen, he had fought in the First World War as part of the Bavarian Army. When the war ended in November 1918, unlike the overwhelming majority of soldiers, he did not want to return home for Christmas because he had no home to go to. In the words of historian Thomas Weber, the army was his 'replacement family'. Launching his political career, at first he addressed only small audiences, but by 1921 he was known as a beer hall demagogue, the leader of a fringe political group that was a meeting place for disgruntled men who wanted to shout abuse about their political opponents and threaten them with violence. That fringe group was the Nazi Party, or more formally the National Socialist German Workers' Party (NSDAP). It was one of many right-wing sects where opponents of democracy gathered to talk about its destruction.[1]

Hitler's success in this arena was largely down to his performance as a speaker and his growing mastery of the art of beer hall demagoguery. In his speeches he unleashed abuse on Jews and Socialists, whom he blamed for all of Germany's ills, then sipped his beer and observed the crowd's reactions to his words. When they cheered loudly, he knew he had scored a winning point and would repeat it, time and again. Gradually, through trial and error, he learnt how to speak to disgruntled men and, over time, women too.

The year 1923 was to be Hitler's breakthrough year. On 8 November 1922, when one politician spoke his name in the

Bavarian parliament, suggesting that he could be the next Bavarian minister-president, the idea was met with roars of laughter. But in the following months, Hitler's successes overwhelmed those who had wanted to laugh him off. At the end of 1922, his party had around eight thousand members spread across some hundred branches, mostly in Bavaria. By the eve of the putsch, party membership had increased to about fifty thousand. Hitler owed his success to his promise of national and individual salvation for everyone who followed him, making no secret of his desire for violence, regularly threatening his enemies with death. His opponents started to notice him too. After one particularly violent rhetorical outburst, Alwin Saenger, a lawyer and Social Democratic member of the Bavarian parliament, who had previously been beaten up by anti-semites after they mistakenly identified him as a Jew, publicly called him a 'psychopath'.[2]

But on the political right assessments such as Saenger's carried little weight. Hitler could incite hatred and call for the destruction of the Weimar Republic because many of Bavaria's leaders, including key figures in the police and judiciary, believed that fundamentally he was on the right side of history. As the number of his followers started to increase, they even began to share a stage with Hitler, helping to make him attractive to upper- and middle-class voters who might otherwise have been put off by his lower-class origins.

By the autumn of 1923, many Bavarian conservatives shared Hitler's view that the time had come to strike against the republic; they simply disagreed with him about the tactics and timing necessary to do so. When Hitler chose to launch his coup on 8 November, they abandoned him, calculating that the putschists would not have the support they needed to take power in Berlin. The Nazi leader never forgot their betrayal. The man Hitler felt held greatest responsibility, Gustav Ritter von Kahr, an anti-republican conservative member of the Bavarian People's Party, was murdered by the Nazis in July 1934.

Kahr's murder, during the so-called 'Night of the Long Knives', when the Nazis murdered several of their own party members as well as settling scores with older enemies, was a key moment in the process by which the Nazi dictatorship was established. On 30 January 1933, Hitler was appointed chancellor. This marked the end of the first phase of the creation of an authoritarian regime in Germany, which had already begun the previous summer, when pro-democratic parties were forced out of power in Prussia. Once Hitler was appointed chancellor, he began what he called the 'national revolution'. By the time he returned to Munich on 9 November 1933 for the tenth anniversary of his failed putsch, his regime had already started to implement some of von der Pfordten's ideas. Hitler's men of violence had terrorized into submission all who opposed the Nazis' rule, while he and his propagandists had gained millions of new supporters for Nazism. But it was only at the end of the summer of 1934, following the death of retired general Paul von Hindenburg, the man who appointed Hitler as chancellor and had been first elected president of the Weimar Republic in 1925 and re-elected in 1932, that Hitler became the single undisputed leader of the Germans, the *Führer*, the fulcrum of all political decision-making for the remainder of the Third Reich.

But in the weeks after the failure of the putsch in November 1923, such a future seemed unlikely. As they looked back on Hitler's breakthrough year, most German supporters of democracy thought that they would never hear his name again. One influential liberal journalist, Erich Dombrowski, even predicted that in the future people would not understand the violence and hatred of the times that he lived in.[3]

German democrats were optimistic because their favoured political system had survived. Alongside the Hitler putsch, the state had navigated challenges including the military occupation of Weimar Germany's industrial heartland by the French and Belgians, as well as national and international humiliation as its currency collapsed, leading to financial chaos and mass unemployment.

When these multiple and overlapping crises reached their climax in late autumn 1923, many people feared that the year would end with a civil war between Communists and Nazis, or between the north and the south, or both. Others feared that regions in the west would break away from Germany. The French government would have been delighted by such a turn of events. It hoped to see the establishment of a small pro-French state that would help to protect them from any future act of German aggression. It called this state the Republic of the Rhineland.

These were the challenges that Weimar's pro-democratic political leaders faced over the course of 1923. They did so in the knowledge that their lives were on the line. At the high point of the crisis, the most influential political defender of the democratic system, Gustav Stresemann, warned that if the Nazis ever made it to Berlin, he would prefer to be shot at his desk rather than take flight to try to defend the democracy from elsewhere. Stresemann's defence of Weimar democracy was aided by the decision-making of Friedrich Ebert, the first president of the Weimar Republic, another politician who faced down death threats throughout the year. Weimar's constitution contained emergency powers for use in a time of crisis. In 1923, Ebert used them to help save democracy; in 1933 Paul von Hindenburg used them to destroy it.[4]

The spiral of crises began on 11 January 1923, when France's prime minister, Raymond Poincaré, tried to solve a complex web of political problems that had dominated European international relations since the end of the First World War by militarily occupying the Ruhr district, Germany's industrial heartland. Poincaré claimed that the soldiers were there to obtain reparations in kind after Germany had failed to keep up with the payments that were a requirement of the Versailles Treaty, which successive German governments had argued were unreasonable. In the first instance, Poincaré told the world that his soldiers were there to obtain coal from the Ruhr's mines.

The Versailles Treaty limited the size of Germany's army, so the German government lacked the military capacity to turn to its military to oppose the occupation. Instead, led by Chancellor Wilhelm Cuno, a conservative businessman who had become chancellor the previous November, it declared that Germans would 'passively resist' the occupation. The mines and factories of the Ruhr shut down. German workers and civil servants refused to comply with the occupiers' demands. German railway workers refused to move trains. The French occupiers soon realized that they would not get the coal they wanted, and the invasion devolved into a contest that would continue until one side decided to back down. Germany held the weaker cards: passive resistance didn't just mean refusing to comply with the demands of the French and Belgians in the Ruhr, it also meant turning off Germany's industrial heartland for as long as the occupiers remained there. That meant a massive blow to state revenues, as well as the threat of unrest if the workers of the Ruhr went unpaid. The solution to both problems was to print money. Germany's politicians and central bankers intended to use new notes to cover the cost of passive resistance. Initially, it was assumed that this campaign would only last for a couple of weeks and that the central bankers would use financial tricks to support the value of the German mark on the international exchange markets, including using the country's financial reserves to buy up German currency and prevent a fall in its value. At first this high-risk strategy appeared to be working. Up until April, the fall in the value of the mark remained at a manageable level. But it quickly became clear that Germany would face financial ruin if it tried to keep it going into the summer.[5]

But that is exactly what Germany's leaders tried to do. After four months of sacrifice they thought that it was better to abandon the currency than to lose the Ruhr. That decision set the stage in the summer of 1923 for the worst financial crisis that Germany had ever faced. The German leadership knew that this was a bad choice. But they hoped that a mixture of further financial tricks, including increasingly rapid supplies of new money, could maintain some kind of functioning economy. They also hoped that at some point during the year international opinion would recognize that Germany was a victim of French aggression and that the ensuing pressure on France would bring an end to the occupation.

The idea that Germany might lose the Ruhr for ever was a realistic one. Over the course of 1923, as the costs of the occupation mounted, France's goals became increasingly hardline. The idea of splitting the Ruhr off permanently from Germany became more attractive to Poincaré. The French and Belgians controlled access to the region, often stopping exit and entry from the area as punishment for the conduct of the German population. To overcome the opposition of German railway workers, the French even created a new company to replace the national rail company, the Reichsbahn, in the Ruhr. In an era when the rail network was a crucial piece of national infrastructure, this was a clearly hostile move. At moments of high tension, they also used German civilians as human shields on trains in the Ruhr.

By the summer, the continued printing of new notes had transformed 1923 into the year of the zeros, launching Weimar Germany into the greatest period of runaway hyperinflation the world had ever seen. At its climax in the autumn, money, one of the most important organizational features of human interaction, as well as something that shapes humans' sense of self-worth in relation to others, had ceased to function. The German world had been turned upside down.[6]

But not everyone was losing as a result. Some speculators used the rapid changes in the value of money to make massive profits. Others bought up the assets of their struggling rivals. When the winners displayed their new wealth, they created resentment. In this political and economic climate, the backlash against the republic grew in strength and more and more people blamed Germany's Jewish minority for everything that had gone wrong.

The scale of these problems might have finished off the Weimar Republic. But in 1923 it held together. Pro-democratic political leaders fought back to save their constitution and their democracy. Just as the Nazis' 1923 putsch ended in failure, in the autumn the German Communists' plans to seize power were abandoned, the armed separatist groups that wanted to break away from Germany to become independent foundered and French imperialist plans to take control of German territory failed. In 1923, the Germany currency died, but, despite the various forces out to destroy it, Weimar democracy did not.

It survived because the coalition of forces that supported democracy in Germany, including liberals, social democrats and conservative centrists, despite the fundamental differences between their political beliefs, all understood that the democratic system was worth protecting; that it was something that had to be supported and defended against attack from extremists of every kind.

Their victory in 1923 is important. At a time when established democracies risk becoming authoritarian regimes, there has been no shortage of new historical work being carried out on the end of the Weimar Republic. This book offers a wider view of Weimar's fate. The history of the German state in 1923 shows us how a republic can survive in the face of multiple threats. Its continuation over the course of the year and the key role played by supporters of democracy in key offices offer an important contrast with the actions of the leaders who killed the republic in 1932–3. The political leadership offered by pro-democratic politicians in 1923 shows us what can happen when leaders make the right choices.

In the winter of 1918–19, with the backing of the vast majority of the electorate, the opposition the democratic leaders had faced as they created the republic was weak: conservatives had been discredited by defeat in war and Communists did not have sufficient support beyond a small number of working-class hotspots. That situation had changed by the summer and autumn of 1923, when many people were on their knees due to the greatest financial crisis that the world had ever seen. The backlash against the republic grew in strength, and maintaining support for the democratic system in the face of its armed and violent opponents became far harder. But in the end, Germany's democrats could stand up to that challenge because, even though the democratic political system had only existed in Germany since 1919, the ideals of democracy ran much deeper – a point that we have often missed because of our interest in identifying the long-term origins of Nazism.

This is one of the most frightening lessons of this book. The Weimar Republic was able to see out the 1923 crises because of the strength of its culture of democracy, but after that culture was consistently eroded from the political right and the extreme left, it was no longer powerful enough to survive the challenges which began to be felt in Germany the year after the world economic crisis began in 1929. The contrast between the outcomes of the 1923 and 1930–2 crises offers a powerful reminder that even strong democracies, if they are continually undermined from within, may eventually collapse into authoritarianism.

Taking its place in the large body of historical work about the Weimar Republic and the rise of Nazism, this book lowers the microscope to examine individual conflicts and to ask how they relate to the bigger developments taking place at the national and international levels. The individual acts of violence that it analyses are not anecdotal; they are the heart of what made the overlapping crises of 1923 so powerful. The killing of civilians or the rape of German women by French and Belgian soldiers, the anger caused by foreign bayonets being on show in public spaces, the appeals to nationalism, the feeling that a neighbour or relative was profiteering from the collapse of the currency while one's own family suffered, the radical language of Hitler and the antisemitic violence of his followers and sympathizers: these were issues that powered the crisis year. They are what made political mobilization in Germany in 1923 the source of so much anger and emotion. If we do not understand that anger and emotion, we will never understand what mobilizes people to support extremes in times of crisis.[7]

PART I

1922 and the Coming of the Crisis Year

I

German Democracy Fights Back

The nurse Helene Kaiser was the first person to reach them. She had been waiting at a tram stop on her way to work at Berlin's Charité hospital, when instinctively she had thrown herself to the ground, startled by a quick succession of sounds that were out of place in the Grunewald, one of the city's quietest and most expensive suburbs: the roar of a car engine, the screeching of tyres and then what sounded, implausibly, like a short burst of machine-gun fire and the dull thud of a grenade. As she lay on the ground listening, she heard one car accelerate away, while another rolled to a stop, and then silence. She had seen little, and said later that she had thought that a gunman had hidden himself in the bushes opposite the car.

Whether there was a gunman or not, she was compelled to help, to try to save lives, even if it meant risking her own. She got up and ran towards the car, an expensive NAG cabriolet with red wheels. Its top was down and a small fire burned in the back. In the driver's seat, a man, Josef Prozeller, sat uninjured but shaken. Behind him another man was lying on his side. He had been shot. There was so much blood flowing from his face and limbs that a pool was forming.

First, Nurse Kaiser put out the fire that had been caused by the grenade. Then she took the injured man in her arms and held him tightly, trying to stop his bleeding while screaming at Prozeller, 'Quick, quick, get us to a doctor.' But it was too late. The injured man died in her arms as Prozeller drove. He had been hit a total of five times. The autopsy revealed that the first shot had already been enough to kill him.

The date was 24 June 1922 and the dead man was Walther Rathenau, Germany's fifty-five-year-old foreign minister. He had been shot dead by a former naval officer and student named Erwin Kern. Kern's friend Hermann Fischer had thrown the grenade. Their car was driven by Ernst Werner Techow. Between them, they had just carried out one of the most important political assassinations of the decade in Europe. Eight years earlier, in July 1914, assassins had shot dead Archduke Franz Ferdinand of Austria, triggering a chain of events that plunged the continent into war. In June 1922, Kern and Fischer were part of a plan to achieve something similar: by assassinating the foreign minister, they hoped to stir up a crisis that would end with the collapse of the republic itself.[1]

Kern and Fischer were young men from respectable families who had been radicalized by Germany's defeat in the First World War. They were members of the country's first right-wing terrorist network, the Organization Consul, which was founded in 1920 by Hermann Ehrhardt, a former naval officer. Ehrhardt had particular grounds for hating the republic and its representatives. The revolution that created the Weimar Republic in November 1918 started when German sailors and stokers raised the red flag over the navy's ships in the docks at their home ports of Kiel and Wilhelmshaven on the north German coast. Officers like Ehrhardt were determined to take revenge. In the winter of 1918–19, they founded three top-heavy officers' divisions known as the Marine Brigades. One was commanded by Ehrhardt and named after him. During the revolutionary upheavals of 1919, they fought against left-wing rebels, before turning against the Weimar Republic itself in the spring of 1920 in a quickly defeated anti-republican putsch. In its aftermath, Ehrhardt went into hiding and founded the Organization Consul to continue the struggle under ground. Its shadowy existence was helped by the creation of fake companies, and the use of false addresses and secret codewords. Any form of betrayal among the organization's membership was punishable by death. Their cat-and-mouse game with the state was helped by their many sympathizers in the police and judiciary.

The Organization Consul's leadership hoped that when the time came, its heavily armed secret network would emerge either to fight against the state and bring down the republic, or to join forces with the under-strength Reichswehr and avenge the defeat of November 1918. In August 1921, it carried out its first high-profile murder: two former members of the Marine Brigades tracked down ex-finance minister Matthias Erzberger, who had signed the armistice of November 1918 and voted for the Versailles Treaty, and murdered him while he was walking in the woods on holiday in south-western Germany. In early 1922, Kern and Fischer carried out their first daring terrorist operation together: they led a raid to free the former submarine officers Ludwig Dithmar and John Boldt from prison in Leipzig. Dithmar and Boldt had been sentenced to four years' imprisonment by a German court, at the behest of the victorious allies in summer 1921, for opening fire upon survivors of the Canadian hospital ship *Llandovery Castle*, which had been sunk off the coast of Ireland on 27 June 1918.

In the summer of 1922, the Organization Consul intended to undertake a campaign of high-profile assassinations. There was a logic to its violence: it hoped that by murdering politicians who symbolized the new German democracy it would provoke the working class into an insurrection and that in the ensuing chaos it would have another chance to overthrow the republic. On 4 June, two of its members came close to killing Philipp Scheidemann, one of the highest-profile Social Democratic politicians in the early Weimar Republic. Scheidemann was out walking with his daughter when the two men ran towards him, spraying poisonous gas as they went. The fifty-seven-year-old drew his pistol and opened fire on his assailants. His shots missed but the sight of the gun was enough to scare them off. The assault left Scheidemann unconscious and seriously ill, although he would make a full recovery. The failure of this attack added to the pressure facing Kern and Fischer just under three weeks later: the leadership of the Organization Consul could not tolerate another setback.

When they arrived in Berlin in early June 1922, they had contemplated a variety of plans for assassinating Rathenau. One involved shooting him with revolvers in the street in central Berlin. But they ruled out this idea, fearing it left them with little hope of escaping.

After weighing their options, Fischer and Kern concluded that a drive-by shooting would be best. Studying Rathenau's movements revealed that he was most vulnerable during the drive from his home in Grunewald to the Foreign Ministry in central Berlin. Rathenau regularly took the same route, followed a predictable schedule and relied only on a single driver; he had refused extra police protection. After practising shooting from a moving vehicle in woods near Berlin, Fischer and Kern discovered that if they used handguns there was a chance that they might miss. Rather than take that risk, they picked up a machine gun they had left hidden with the leader of the ultra-nationalist and antisemitic Deutschvölkischer Schutz- und Trutzbund in Schwerin.[2]

By the night of 23 June, Kern, Fischer and their driver, Techow, sat together in a safe house in Schmargendorf in Berlin that belonged to Richard Schütt. They were joined there by Techow's seventeen-year-old younger brother, Hans Gerd, who was still at school, and his schoolfriend Willi Günther, who had helped them find this hideout just a short distance from Rathenau's home.

The next morning the older Techow discovered a snag. He later claimed that there was a problem with the large six-seater Mercedes that they had borrowed for the attack and that he had had to spend a couple of hours working under its bonnet. Whatever the case, they were running late, and by 10 a.m. they weren't even sure they would manage to set out that day. But shortly before 10.30, Techow was finally ready to drive. Before they left, Günther hid the machine gun in the car while Fischer fitted it with fake number plates. Techow and Günther drove the car out of the garage, while Fischer and Kern discreetly walked a short distance away so that they could be picked up nearby. Günther's job was to make sure that none of their neighbours would see Kern and Fischer drive away. Once Techow picked them up, he got out of the car and returned to the garage. Once they had taken up their places in the back of the Mercedes, Kern and Fischer changed into brand-new long leather jackets with leather caps of the kind worn by racing drivers in the 1920s that left only the oval of their faces showing.[3]

A few minutes later, they pulled into a side road close to Rathenau's villa. There they waited, their eyes fixed on the Königsallee, until Prozeller drove past in the dark-grey cabriolet. As usual, Rathenau was sitting in the back seat on the left of the vehicle and smoking his morning cigar. Techow began the pursuit.

A group of builders and the local postman had the best view of what followed. They noticed a slow-moving car in the middle of the street followed by a large six-seater that was catching up with it. Both vehicles had their hoods down. As the first car slowed to take a curve in the road, it suddenly swerved to the right and the second car's engine roared as it moved to overtake it. Then time seemed to stand still. A man sitting in the back left of the Mercedes stood up and opened fire on Rathenau. This was Kern. As he sat down, Fischer stood up and threw a hand grenade which then exploded in the back of the minister's car.[4]

As soon as the grenade exploded, Techow hit the accelerator and the trio made their escape. The assassins had no reason to panic. Some witnesses had run after the car, but no one had managed to keep sight of it as it passed through the twists and turns of the roads in this part of Berlin – one of the reasons why they had chosen this location for the assassination in the first place. Kern and Fischer took off their leather jackets and dumped the murder weapon. 'We shot Rathenau!' they rejoiced. Techow then dropped them off in the Hohenzollern-damm, from where they headed into central Berlin while he drove back to the garage, where Günther was waiting. As he hid the car he enthusiastically reported: 'The plan worked. Rathenau is dead.'[5]

Later that afternoon, as the shock of Rathenau's murder resonated across Germany, the trio of Kern, Fischer and Techow met openly in the centre of Berlin, where they visited the city's zoo, unafraid that anyone would identify them. The following night they stayed with Kern's aunt in Steglitz in the south-west of the city. They told her that they had come to Berlin to try to find a job for Fischer. On 26 June, they went rowing on the lakes at Wannsee, and on 27 June, they left the German capital.

In the meantime, one of the biggest police investigations in the history of Berlin was under way. Within an hour of the shooting, the chief of police, Bernhard Weiss, had arrived at the murder scene, accompanied by the head of the political police, the equivalent of today's domestic intelligence services, and countless detectives. They would spare no expense in the hunt for the killers, issuing a 1-million-mark reward for information. Yet despite the many witnesses, at first all that was known about the suspects was that they were three young men aged between twenty and twenty-five, and wearing a 'grey uniform'. And unlike modern terrorist groups, the Organization Consul issued no statement claiming responsibility for its actions. False leads overwhelmed the investigators, and the car remained hidden away in the garage. For a few days it looked as if Techow, Fischer and Kern had got away with one of the most spectacular political murders of the 1920s.[6]

But, on 26 June, a student told the police that he had heard a young man in Berlin boasting to a group of students about the Rathenau murder. The police tracked the teenager down and arrested him – it was Willi Günther. Under interrogation he lost his nerve and confessed. The investigation had its first and most important breakthrough.

Weiss and his team of officers now knew the killers' identities. On 27 June, they located the car and arrested Techow's younger brother Hans Gerd. At first, they kept this sensational news secret, still hoping to find Techow, Kern and Fischer in hiding in Berlin. But once they were certain that the chief suspects had left the capital, they circulated wanted posters widely. On 28 June, the trio were officially announced as fugitives from justice, their names broadcast across Germany.[7]

Techow's uncle, Erwin Behrens, was a well-connected figure in German industrial circles. The day before the names were published, Techow had turned up at Behrens's estate close to Frankfurt an der Oder, some 80 kilometres to the east of Berlin. When Behrens read his nephew's name in the newspaper, he made a discreet call to the police. Even though Techow was a chief suspect for a crime that could end with the death penalty, Behrens handed him in, later admitting that he considered giving his nephew a pistol and telling him to commit suicide in nearby woods.[8]

More arrests followed. Of the original group that had helped the three young men carry out the murder, almost all were arrested within a few weeks. Only Kern and Fischer remained free, in hiding in north Germany, searching for ways to get help from members of Ehrhardt's Organization Consul or other like-minded opponents of Weimar democracy, but unsure who could be trusted.

The noose was tightening. On 7 July, while they were staying under false names in a guesthouse at Lenzen, a small town on the river Elbe about halfway between Berlin and Hamburg, someone reported to the police that the Rathenau murderers had been spotted there. Kern and Fischer were eating nearby when officers began searching their guesthouse, and took flight on their bicycles with the police in pursuit. Just seconds before the ferry that crossed the Elbe pulled away from the quay, they jumped on board. The boat was too far out by the time the officers giving chase reached the quay.

Kern and Fischer had escaped and now decided to head south, using hikers' maps to avoid the main routes, cycling by night and lying low by day. They wanted to get to Bavaria and link up with other members of the Organization Consul, who would help them cross over the border with Austria and escape punishment, as Matthias Erzberger's killers had done the year before.[9]

They travelled 300 kilometres south of Lenzen to a town called Rudelsburg an der Saale. There, a committed supporter of the Organization Consul named Hans Wilhelm Stein lived in the medieval Saaleck Castle. Once Stein had put Kern and Fischer up in the castle, he set off on his own 430-kilometre journey south to Munich, to link up with the Organization Consul leadership and make a plan for Kern and Fischer's escape. But before leaving Rudelsburg, Stein told some locals that he was going away. When the same locals spotted a light that Kern and Fischer had left on in the castle, they started to wonder who might be there. From a distance, they observed the occupants and recognized them thanks to the wanted posters.

This time there was no escape. When the local police arrived in the courtyard, Kern and Fischer barricaded themselves inside the building with guns at the ready. But the shootout was over before it started. Kern stood at the highest window of the tower, ready to take aim at the officers in the courtyard below. Before he could fire, a policeman took aim and shot five times, hitting Kern in the head. Fischer frantically tried to save his friend, but there was nothing that he could do: Kern was dead. As the police took cover outside, Fischer carried his friend's body to one of the two single beds where they had been sleeping. He lay down on the other, drew a pistol and committed suicide.[10]

For the republic's most ardent opponents, Kern and Fischer were national heroes. They were buried side by side in a graveyard near the castle where they lost their lives. At their joint funeral, Kern's coffin was draped in the Imperial German Navy's war flag and Fischer's in the black, white and red flag of the former empire. To mark her son's death at the funeral, Kern's mother sang the 'Ehrhardt Song', the song of the II Marine Brigade, which ends with the refrain 'Get the Jews out of Germany'. Students from Jena reportedly fought over the right to carry their coffins. Once the Nazis were in power in 1933, the pair's heroic status increased even further. On the anniversary of their deaths, their graves were opened and their coffins moved to a newly decorated resting place at the centre of the graveyard. This time their coffins were lowered into the ground covered by a single flag bearing a swastika. Heinrich Himmler, the head of the SS, the elite Nazi force that ran the concentration camp system in the Third Reich and later took responsibility for organizing the Holocaust, and Ernst Röhm, the head of the SA, as well as Ehrhardt himself, were among those in attendance. Kern's sister described the memorial services in their presence as 'unforgettable'.[11]

Rathenau's murder brought the political battle between supporters and opponents of Weimar democracy into the open. The shots that were fired did not just kill Rathenau: they announced that the far right's war on the republic might be about to enter a new and more aggressive phase. They were a bold statement that the opponents of liberal democracy believed that they could gun down the representatives of the state in broad daylight in the streets of the capital. They came at a time when the language of politics had already reached fever pitch. On the afternoon of 23 June 1922, just hours before he was murdered, Rathenau and the German chancellor, Joseph Wirth, the man who appointed Rathenau as foreign minister, had been subjected to a verbal tirade in the chamber of the German Reichstag by Karl Helfferich, the leader of the opposition conservative-nationalist and antisemitic German National People's Party (DNVP), one of the most important anti-democratic political parties in the early Weimar Republic. Helfferich claimed that Wirth's government was responsible for a trail of misery and suicide, and demanded that they face trial for treason. Implicitly, he suggested that they deserved the death sentence.

Helfferich's words left his enemies and supporters alike in tumult. While like-minded opponents of Weimar democracy cheered him on, his opponents on the political left and in the centre shouted abuse at him. As he listened in the press gallery, the liberal journalist Erich Dombrowski thought that the Reichstag had become 'a madhouse'. He wondered if it would not make more sense for all of the deputies simply to leave the chamber for the duration of such a spectacle, leaving Helfferich to foam at the mouth on his own. But Helfferich got the audience he wanted. By the time the session ended in the early evening, the newspapers on the political right were ready to celebrate his outpouring. Those on the left simply called him a 'provocateur'.[12]

Rathenau knew how dangerous demagogues like Helfferich and his conservative allies really were. He knew that their affectations of conservative respectability were hollow. And as the highest-profile German Jew in government at the time in the Weimar Republic, he knew exactly how antisemitism worked. In late 1921, he had warned that the way the populists repeatedly targeted the less well-educated sections of society with misinformation and lies would eventually hurt Germany. At this time, he pleaded with politicians of all parties to remember their duty to shape a civilized debate and warned them that if their way of doing politics ended up dividing the country even further, they would not be able to wash their hands of responsibility afterwards.

On 24 June 1922, the Reichstag had barely come to terms with the aggression of Helfferich's speech the previous day when the news arrived that Rathenau had been murdered. Deputies accused one another of failing to defend democracy. Many blamed Helfferich personally for the murder. Pro-republican politicians and journalists accused him of using language that led young men to carry out such violence. Even normally reserved politicians announced that it was time to treat Helfferich as if he were a 'villain and murderer'. But not everyone condemned him. One newspaper reported that a politician on the right brought a wreath of oak leaves, the military symbol of victory, bearing an anti-republican symbol into the chamber and called Helfferich 'the defender of German honour!'[13]

In the aftermath of the murder, liberal supporters of German democracy focused on the relationship between right-wing anti-republican political slogans and speeches and the act of violence. Georg Bernhard, the editor-in-chief of the *Vossische Zeitung*, called Helfferich 'the misfortune of Germany' and 'the most unpleasant type of German nationalist demagogue'. Theodor Wolff, the editor of the liberal *Berliner Tageblatt*, one of the keenest observers of political life in Germany during the 1920s, agreed: 'We don't like to accuse whole circles where the act of an individual is involved,' he wrote, 'but here the blame is so clear, the responsibility so obvious, that it is impossible not to bring charges or to attempt to disguise the blatant truth' that men like Helfferich were responsible. Wolff was especially annoyed with politicians and journalists of the right whom he accused of accepting the pollution of political discourse because it increased their support base.[14]

When the Reichstag session finally began shortly after 3 p.m. on 24 June, Rathenau's chair was occupied by a bouquet of white roses. Wirth warned that a terrible poison had been spread through Germany.[15] Rathenau's murder wasn't just a political assassination, it was an assault on the republic itself: 'First, the leaders of the republic fall, then the republic itself.' As he spoke, he was interrupted by jeers warning him that he would be next.

But the murder did not produce the violent uprising that the Organization Consul's leaders had hoped for. Instead, Germany's pro-democratic forces mobilized. They seized the moment to protect and re-establish the democratic values upon which their republic had been founded.

During the night following Rathenau's murder, the Reichstag met again. The first president of the republic, the Social Democrat Friedrich Ebert, one of the founding fathers of Weimar democracy, turned to the constitutional powers that allowed him to put through emergency legislation in times of crisis. He introduced a presidential order that banned anti-republican political activities, including assemblies and associations, and introduced new fines and prison sentences for anyone who insulted the republic or damaged its symbols, including the black, red and gold flag, which was hated by conservative nationalists. This first step was followed by the Law for the Protection of the Republic, which was passed on 21 July 1922. This ordered the imprisonment of anyone who conspired against past or present rulers of the republic and, above all, instituted a new State Court for the Defence of the Republic. The new court would consist of seven judges. Three would be members of the highest state court, the Reichsgericht, appointed by the court's president. They would sit alongside a further four judges, who would be chosen by the president of the republic. This quartet would not have to be serving judges but could be lay individuals, selected because of their political loyalty to the republican government.

These measures were an admission that, until this point in time, the justice system in Weimar Germany had been blatantly politically biased, with right-wing judges, who had been appointed under the monarchy that had been destroyed by the revolution in 1918, letting right-wing crimes go unpunished or with only minimal punishment. The new court was supposed to put a stop to that. It also had the power to instruct other agencies to initiate investigations or to launch them itself. This was an important point: while supporters of the republic welcomed the law as the minimum requirement to protect democracy, it put the republic's court on a collision course with the sovereignty of the federal German states, especially the conservative government of Bavaria.

The latter immediately resisted the incursion of a court of the republic into matters of justice on its own territory – it was no coincidence that the secret headquarters of the Organization Consul were in Munich. Just a day after the presidential order had come into existence, a Communist member of the Reichstag predicted: 'This weak government will not succeed in enforcing its will in Bavaria.' He criticized the government's response to Rathenau's murder, observing pointedly that there had been similar speeches after the murder of Matthias Erzberger, who had been gunned down by members of the Organization Consul the previous year:

> You've heard enough of all these words to make you vomit. It is high time for action to begin. Words alone will not frighten the bandits. You must show your teeth to these beasts, to show that you are ready to bite, or they will not back down.[16]

✦

In death Rathenau had achieved what he could not in life: he was recognized as a great German. His murder served as a rallying point for the republic. The day after his death, large crowds marched on central Berlin, demonstrating in the large square in front of the Reichstag. The largest protests took place on 27 June 1922, to coincide with a specially choreographed funeral ceremony that was held inside the Reichstag building. The powerful German congress of trade unions, the ADGB, declared a national strike to allow workers to join in public acts of mourning and to show their support for the republic. In the Ruhr, where miners' shifts did not allow for a half-day strike, workers downed their tools for twenty-four hours. They were joined by employees of the Prussian and German governments, who were also told to stop working to mark the occasion – a rare moment of solidarity in a society plagued by the division between organized labour and the state. In addition to the three major parties of the left, the Social Democratic Party, the Independent Socialist Party and the Communist Party, the middle-class German Democratic Party, Rathenau's own party, called on its supporters to take to the streets. Of the major pro-republican parties, only Wirth's Catholic Centre Party did not join the protest.[17]

It is difficult to say with certainty just how many people partici-pated in the demonstrations. When he looked back on them at the end of the 1920s, the author and diplomat Harry Graf Kessler, one of Rathenau's first biographers, estimated that in Berlin alone more than a million people were in the streets. He may have exaggerated the size of the crowds, but there is no doubt about their historical significance: this was one of the largest pro-republican demonstra-tions to take place in Germany before Hitler was appointed chancellor in January 1933. That support gave Ebert and Wirth the authority they needed to defend the republic and refound its authority. Arguably, the support expressed for the republic in the aftermath of Rathenau's death represented the high point of repub-lican political power in the 1920s.[18]

In Berlin, despite pouring rain, crowds thronged around the Reichstag, where Rathenau's coffin was brought into the chamber and placed in the president's gallery. All around the chamber there were black banners with black, red and gold ribbons. The Reichswehr provided the parade of honour and the State Opera the music. The service began with Beethoven's Coriolan Overture. Ebert spoke on behalf of the nation. Standing beside Rathenau's coffin, he lamented the loss of one of Germany's most talented servants:

> The bullets of cowardly murderers hurled him from his path. But this wicked act was not just aimed at Rathenau alone, but at all of Germany. This bloody act was directed against the German Republic, and against the idea of democracy, of which Dr Walther Rathenau was a staunch defender and champion.

In strong language that defined support for democracy as part of the essence of Germanness, Ebert added that the perpetrators of the murder were 'no longer a part of the German Nation'.[19]

Adolf Korell spoke on behalf of Rathenau's German Democratic Party. His words and the public support for Rathenau suggested that the republic was finally about to turn its back on the antisemitism of the political right and accept that Jews could belong to the German nation:

> Rathenau is *also a murdered Jew* and therefore a victim of those so-called ideas of racial purity. Before Rathenau's coffin, let us vow to finally forgo the word 'national' if it is only for the good of one party. We willingly extend our hands to everyone who wants to protect and build the German Republic.

The funeral offered an opportunity to set politics aside and avow loyalty to the republic. It gave conservative organizations like the Reichswehr, which had failed to prove its loyalty to democracy during the Kapp Putsch in Berlin in March 1920, a chance to show that they would protect the republic and join in its ceremonial life. It was a statement about the authority of pro-republican rulers to govern Germany unchallenged by the anti-democratic forces of the political right. It was a moment when the murderers and anti-semites could be condemned as not belonging to the German nation. Beyond Berlin, countless more Germans demonstrated across the country. In the view of the representatives of the largest political parties, the people behind the murder and those who supported them belonged to the worst part of the country's past and had no place in its democratic future.

Helfferich's party went on the defensive. It issued a statement that firmly rejected all attempts to associate its members with the murder. It called the accusation 'outrageous, unproven and unjustifiable'. The party leadership stated that it had nothing to do with the murder and that it was intent on bringing the republic to an end legally.[20]

Denial of responsibility wasn't the only response on the political far right, of course. There were plenty of examples of people who were openly pleased with the news of Rathenau's death.[21] Echoing Helfferich's claims that his party's honour had been insulted by the reactions to the murder, some opponents of Weimar democracy turned events on their head and claimed that Germany's conservatives were now under threat. One leading antisemitic publicist, Ernst Graf zu Reventlow, even claimed that the reaction to the murder showed that there was a deliberate attempt to use this event to destroy what he called 'Germans' ability to fight back against "the Jews"'.[22]

Just over two weeks after the murder, an article in one of the most important Jewish newspapers in Weimar Germany, the *CV-Zeitung*, argued that Rathenau's murder had finally made it clear just how antisemitic Germany had become since the end of the First World War. It remarked: 'How often did we listen to people telling us, "Your picture is too dark. Things are not half so bad."'[23] It was only after Rathenau's murder, it argued, that even the most optimistic observers could see that they were living through a moment of increasing antisemitism. The examples it provided included antisemitic political language that called the foreign minister a 'Jewish rascal', accusations that there was a Jewish conspiracy to destroy Germany, and an upsurge in suggestions that Jews committed ritual murder and paedophilia. The Central Association of German Jews described these accusations as the staple diet of the 'pogrom press', a reference to newspapers like the *Völkischer Beobachter* (belonging to the Nazi Party) and the conservative national *Deutsche Zeitung*. The *CV-Zeitung*, the association's paper, listed violent crimes committed against Jews in the recent past and noted that, in all of these cases, the state prosecutors had failed to take action against the accused. In the summer of 1922, it called for urgent increases in support for educational measures to tackle antisemitism, lamenting that many existing initiatives had fallen short of their goal because of an absence of people and funding.[24]

Yet educational measures would have had little impact on the membership of the Organization Consul. Its members were virulently antisemitic from its very beginnings. Before anyone had heard of Adolf Hitler, the men in Ehrhardt's Marine Brigade blamed Jews for the November Revolution of 1918–19 and even talked about killing Jews. Heinrich Tillessen and Heinrich Schulz, who murdered Matthias Erzberger, were both ardent antisemites. It did not matter to them that Erzberger was actually Catholic. Tillessen was certain that Erzberger was secretly Jewish and that his real name was 'Herzberger'. He developed this belief from reading the antisemitic publications of a right-wing publishing company, Hammer Verlag, one of the worst echo chambers of the early 1920s. Schulz called Rathenau 'the most hated man' in his circle. When he returned to Germany in 1933 from the exile into which he had fled after the murder of Erzberger, Schulz joined the SS, where he climbed to the rank of Lieutenant Colonel and helped to plan the Holocaust.[25]

Such beliefs are an important reminder that the anti-democratic politics of the Weimar Republic were racist politics: the forces that wanted to destroy the democratic republic believed that their nation-state should be racially pure and feared the presence of Jews like Rathenau in positions of power and influence. However, it is important to remember that these groups, even if strong and gaining support, were still in the minority. Ebert's comments at Rathenau's funeral and the large number who mourned him were more reflective of public opinion than anything that was said by people like Helfferich. When he spoke, Ebert's words had authority.

But the political attempt to re-establish the republic's political legitimacy and regain the support that had been lost since the constitution came into force in August 1919 was not to last. Within six months, the strengthening of democratic political cultures that might have followed in the wake of Rathenau's murder had unravelled. Within a year, the republic had been weakened even further. It faced too many challenges simultaneously for its pro-democratic leadership to maintain the defence of the republic that began in the aftermath of the murder. In the following months, the Weimar Republic was made dizzy by nationalist mobilization, invasion and inflation. These crises distracted its founders from strengthening their democracy and fighting back against the far right's racist violence. On the first anniversary of Rathenau's murder, the ceremonies that were held to remember him were smaller and less powerful than those that had occurred in the immediate aftermath of his death. In the summer of 1922, the French government didn't see the democratic mobilization that followed Rathenau's murder, it only saw the murderers and assumed that they represented the true Germany. This left the French increasingly convinced that the politics of strength were the only way to deal with their neighbour.

2

The Future of French Power

Joseph Wirth, the chancellor at the time of Rathenau's murder, didn't just need to re-establish the republic's authority in the summer of 1922. He needed to strengthen his own political power. Even within his own party, Wirth's position was not at all secure. He was the leader of the Catholic Centre Party, which governed with the support of the 'godless' Social Democrats. His political vulnerability was worsened by the frequency with which the office of chancellor changed hands. Since the start of the Weimar Republic, five men had held the position. The biggest challenge for Wirth, as it had been for his predecessors, was Weimar Germany's foreign relations.[1]

The starting point was the Versailles Treaty: the treaty between Germany and the victor states of the First World War that was signed in June 1919 and provided the legal basis of the new international order. When its terms and conditions were first published in Germany in May 1919, supporters of all political parties were furious, with many thinking that it treated Germany like a colony.[2]

Rather than sign the treaty, the first Weimar government with an electoral mandate chose to resign. That decision allowed its leader, the Social Democrat Philipp Scheidemann, to criticize the treaty aggressively and make it even harder for his successor to accept it. Scheidemann's place was taken by the Social Democrat Gustav Bauer, who recognized that the defeated nation had no choice but to sign or face invasion, occupation and an even worse peace. After taking on the burden of accepting its terms, Bauer managed to remain chancellor until the spring of 1920, before his government collapsed in the aftermath of the Kapp Putsch, a short-lived right-wing attempt to use violence to destroy the republic that failed in the face of mass opposition. Bauer's was followed by two governments that stayed in office for a combined total of just over a year.

Wirth's predecessor as chancellor was Constantin Fehrenbach, the first member of the Catholic Centre Party to hold the office. In May 1921, Fehrenbach resigned following the publication of what became known as the London Ultimatum, an announcement by the victorious Allied governments about an issue that perpetually tormented the rotating cast at the helm of the Weimar Republic: reparations.[3]

Two years after the first publication of the Versailles Treaty, the London Ultimatum announced for the first time the figure that the Allied governments thought that Germany should pay: 132 billion goldmarks (German currency backed by the value of gold). The first half of the annual interest charge, 2 billion goldmarks, was to be handed over within twenty-five days.[4]

The enormity of the figure shocked Germany. The most destructive fighting of the First World War had taken place on French soil, leaving an area that was roughly the size of the Netherlands completely destroyed. For liberally minded Germans like Rathenau, there was no question that Germany, Europe's largest economy, should pay something towards the cost of its reconstruction. But nobody assented to the figure that the Allies suggested in the London Ultimatum. Rather than accept these terms, Fehrenbach resigned, leading to Wirth's appointment as chancellor. Instead of trying to force the Allies to alter their goals, Wirth developed a strategy that came to be known as 'fulfilment'. It was based on the idea that the best way to obtain concessions from the victorious Allies was to try to do as much as possible to meet their demands, while proving that the demands themselves were unreasonable. It was a policy that pleased neither the Allies nor Wirth's nationalist critics. For more than a year, his government followed this course, facing hostile criticism from the German right without obtaining any significant benefits from the Allies.[5]

After he became chancellor in 1921, Wirth personally convinced

Rathenau to turn his back on his career as a millionaire industrialist and join him on the political front line. It was the first time that Rathenau, whose father had founded the company AEG and helped to bring electric lighting to Germany, had been offered a position in the cabinet. He took a few days to accept. As one of Germany's highest-profile Jews, he was fully aware of the antisemitic backlash that awaited him, describing the decision as the 'most difficult' of his life. But in the end his sense of duty was too great. From May to October 1921, he held the position of minister for reconstruction and in January 1922, following another cabinet shake-up, Wirth made him German foreign minister – the eighth holder of the position since the republic's foundation. He was one of only two German Jews to hold ministerial positions in the Weimar Republic and the only one to hold the position of foreign minister.[6]

On Easter Sunday, 16 April 1922, just over two months before his death, Rathenau was in the Italian province of Liguria, about 30 kilometres to the south-east of Genoa. From inside a nearby restaurant, a small group of German diplomats were watching him. He hadn't slept much the previous night and, after spending the morning mostly in silence, he was pacing up and down. He now faced the greatest moment of personal and political pressure in his short career as a government minister, with Germany's future place in the international system hanging in the balance.[7]

Rathenau had gone to Italy to lead the German delegation at the 1922 Genoa Conference for Economic and Financial Reconstruction. This major conference which brought together thirty-four countries and which is now largely forgotten was organized at the behest of the British prime minister, David Lloyd George. It initially appeared to be good news for Germany: it was the first time that the Allied Supreme Council, the body created by the victors of the First World War to manage their victory, invited Europe's two 'rogue states', Weimar Germany and Bolshevik Russia, to an international conference and gave them the status of equal participants. It looked like Wirth and Rathenau's policy of fulfilment was finally starting to work – at least at first.[8]

Lloyd George, one of the 'Big Three' leaders at the 1919 Paris Peace Conference alongside the French prime minister, Georges Clemenceau, and the American president, Woodrow Wilson, wanted the conference to be the starting point for a new era of international relations and European reconstruction. He intended the Genoa Conference to end with the reopening of trade between western Europe and Bolshevik Russia as a key step in restoring prosperity to the continent as a whole. He had chosen Italy as the venue in the hope of inducing the Italian government to support him in any diplomatic clashes with the French – and with the possible side benefit of allowing him to spend time with his lover and future wife, Frances Stevenson. Fundamentally, he hoped that the Genoa Conference would show just how far the continent had come since the heated days of the Paris Conference and the signing of the Versailles Treaty in 1919.[9]

When the conference began on 10 April, Italian prime minister Luigi Facta promised that by the time it ended there would no longer be 'friends and enemies, victors and vanquished'. Lloyd George was equally optimistic. He promised that the 'greatest gathering of European nations' would deliver a real and lasting peace. But as Rathenau walked on the beach in Liguria a week later, that initial optimism felt like something from the distant past.[10]

From the beginning of the conference, Lloyd George's major concern was the French. Britain and France had been allies during the First World War. But since their shared moment of victory in November 1918, their governments had clashed over a range of issues. Resolving those disagreements not only meant potentially prioritizing French interests above German ones, it might also involve delivering a crippling financial blow to Weimar democracy, as Rathenau well knew.

One of Lloyd George's major preoccupations was finding common ground with the French in their dealings with Lenin's Russia. In the wake of the Russian Revolution, when Lenin openly set out to overthrow capitalism and smash capitalist states, the empire-states of western Europe agreed that their only option was to destroy Bolshevism first. After Lenin's Bolsheviks failed to spread their revolution westwards, Lloyd George's previously hardline policies towards Lenin's Russia began to thaw, while successive French governments remained firmly opposed to any concessions to the Bolsheviks, not out of principled opposition to their violence or ideology, but because of debt. Lenin's February 1918 repudiation of tsarist Russia's international debts had erased the savings of one million French bondholders. Though Britain and Germany had since signed limited trade agreements with Russia, no French government could tolerate any concessions that would continue to leave it out of pocket.[11]

Lloyd George's planned conference raised considerable alarm in Paris, but France nonetheless agreed to participate, provided it was understood that nothing that had been agreed at Versailles could be changed. Lloyd George accepted the French terms at a meeting of the Allied Supreme Council in Cannes in January 1922. He did so because it was the only way that he could get the French to agree to allow the conference to take place. But the difference between France's goals and those of Britain, Russia and Germany, all of whom wanted to see changes to the order established at and since Versailles, put the leaders of each of these states on a collision course.[12]

To reinforce their opposition, the French sent their minister for justice, Louis Barthou, to Cannes, whereas every other country sent either its prime minister or foreign minister or both – a calculated snub. Even worse, Barthou was a well-known hardliner. He had previously been minister for war, and he was still chair of the Reparations Commission, the body set up by the Allies to manage Germany's payments to them. Germany could expect no sympathy from him and Barthou made his views clear from the very start. Just minutes after Lloyd George and Facta began the conference with optimistic appeals for the creation of a new European order, Barthou warned that Genoa was not a 'court of appeal' and criticized the 'vain language' of some of the politicians present – a direct allusion to the colourful speeches of Lloyd George and Facta.[13]

Things deteriorated further when Barthou flew off the handle in response to a speech by the Soviet representative. The people's commissar for foreign affairs, Georgy Chicherin, was both the first representative of the Soviet Union to speak at an international conference of states and a veteran revolutionary. Chicherin called upon everyone present to abandon the agreement made at Cannes and to transform the Genoa Conference into a much broader discussion that would cover issues like debt reduction, redistribution of wealth and collective disarmament. Barthou interrupted to lecture everyone present that Chicherin had overstepped the mark. It took the combined intervention of Lloyd George and Facta to stop Barthou from speaking further and to bring the undiplomatic scene to an end. To overcome their mutual hostility, soon after, Lloyd George invited the French and Russian delegations to private talks in the Villa d'Albertis, a beautiful Renaissance palace overlooking the city of Genoa which an Italian aristocrat had provided as a base for the British delegation for the duration of the conference.[14]

For Rathenau and Wirth, the prospect of private negotiations between Britain, France and Russia was especially worrying. Rumours began to circulate that the meetings were really about finding a way to solve Russia's debt obligations to France by making the Germans pay. At the 1919 Paris Peace Conference, the victors had been adamant that Germany should pay reparations to them. But they were also certain that they did not want Germany to pay anything to Lenin's Russia. To solve this dilemma, the Versailles Treaty permitted the Allies to determine when and how much reparations Germany would have to pay to Russia at a future date – which would be set once the anti-Bolshevik and pro-capitalist Whites won the Russian Civil War. The possibility now loomed that these legal mechanisms were being seriously discussed as a solution to the problem of how to finance Russian reconstruction.[15]

Excluded from the meetings, Rathenau feared that Paris and London were coming up with a plan to make Germany pay reparations to Russia so that Russia could repay its outstanding debts to France. In this scenario, France's and Russia's need for money would trump Weimar democracy's need for political legitimacy. If this came to pass, Rathenau would return to Germany in infamy as the Jewish foreign minister who had added the cost of Russia's wartime and pre-war debts to Germany's reparations bill. In his private letters to Lilli, the young wife of one of the AEG board members with whom he had a close relationship, he described having a crushing weight on his shoulders. Rathenau knew that if the worst came to pass at the conference, he would surely pay for it with his life.[16]

Rathenau's fears were made worse by Lloyd George's refusal to meet face to face with the German delegation during the first week of the conference. Rathenau could only think that Lloyd George must be up to something. Earlier that spring, the Russians had twice offered Rathenau a treaty that would legally rule out future reparations claims against Germany. Rathenau had refused on the grounds that a new Russian-German treaty would rupture his relationship with Lloyd George. But now finding himself sidelined by the British and facing a potentially unsustainable financial burden, he began to reconsider his earlier haste.[17]

On Good Friday, 14 April 1922, the German delegation was briefed on the progress of the talks in Lloyd George's villa. An Italian intermediary warned that the Russians, British and French had made good progress and were close to a deal. This news left Germany's diplomatic representatives desperate. They saw only one option. It took Rathenau all of Saturday to accept that this was the best course of action, but that evening he instructed Baron Ago von Maltzan, a leading German diplomat with excellent connections with the Russian delegation, to make contact with them.

After dinner, Rathenau returned to his hotel and waited in the lobby. To his amazement, Chicherin's answer came at 1 a.m.: the Russians wanted to talk. Rathenau was to travel to their hotel as early as possible the next morning.

Operating in the dark, the Germans debated what the next day might bring. While Rathenau was still in his pyjamas, a small group of diplomats, as well as Chancellor Wirth, crowded into his hotel room to discuss their options. Wirth and Maltzan were determined to go ahead with the talks. But others remained suspicious. If Chicherin really was close to a deal with the British and the French, why did he want urgently to meet the Germans?

The next morning tensions increased further. After breakfast the German delegation finally received the message that they had wanted to hear for over a week. A UK diplomat told them that Lloyd George would meet Rathenau that day. By the time he got the message, however, the German foreign minister was already on his way to meet the Russian delegation, which was staying in a hotel in Santa Margherita, 30 kilometres down the coast from Genoa.

Rathenau now faced a new dilemma. If he turned around and went to meet Lloyd George first, an offended Chicherin might take Russia's offer off the table. Rathenau had no idea if the British were already aware of what he was up to and feared that their invitation might be a deliberate ploy to scupper Germany's plans to reach an agreement with the Russians first. All he was certain of was that Genoa was teeming with spies.

Torn, pacing up and down the beach, he had to make a gut decision. After a few more minutes on his own, he headed back to the restaurant to meet the Russians. He had decided that it was too late to reverse the process that had brought them to this point. To the diplomats huddled around him, he announced: 'The wine has been poured, it is time to drink it.'

Minutes later, the German delegation arrived at the Russians' hotel. Even though both sides had draft treaties ready from their previous negotiations, it still took them the entire afternoon to agree on the final details. But there was no going back. Shortly after 6 p.m., Rathenau signed a German–Russian agreement that became known as the Treaty of Rapallo.[18]

It was a stunning moment in twentieth-century international relations: Germany and Russia had reached agreement outside the frameworks created by the powerful victor states of the First World War. For the others at the Genoa Conference, it represented an unforgivable betrayal. Lloyd George's conference was meant to bring Weimar Germany back into the fold of Western liberal nations, not end with it signing a new treaty with Bolshevik Russia. An American observer at the conference wrote home that he felt like a bomb had just exploded. The British foreign secretary called it 'a gratuitous insult'.[19]

The shock caused by the Rapallo Treaty can be difficult to grasp. After all, the deal between Chicherin and Rathenau was quite limited. They agreed to restore diplomatic relations between Germany and Russia, an agreement that would soon be replicated by states across western Europe. They also agreed that neither side would make reparations demands upon the other, thus ending the prospect of transfers from Germany, via Russia, to France. Additional terms included agreement on the resumption of trade and permission for German companies to work in Russian oil and gas fields. There was also a secret military agreement that foresaw a limited amount of sharing of military technologies and some active planning to escape the conditions of the Versailles Treaty. This was possibly a stepping-stone to greater co-operation, but it was on such a minor scale that it offered little threat to France, which at this time had the strongest army in Europe.

However, the explicit contents of the treaty mattered less than the psychology of when and how it was signed. Most of those in Genoa thought that the First World War had been caused by the dangers of secret diplomacy and international alliances. Rapallo looked like a return to that world. To a continent struggling to come to terms with the millions of deaths caused by the war, it felt as though Germany and Russia were backsliding towards disaster.

For the British prime minister, the treaty was a major personal failure. One observer described Lloyd George as literally 'hopping mad' when he was first told about it. His first words were: 'Impossible, surely such a thing could not happen.' Then he raged at 'damn German stupidity'. Many commentators expected that the conference would now collapse. But three days after the Rapallo Treaty was signed, Lloyd George held a painful press conference where he announced that it would continue. As punishment, German representatives would be excluded from participation in the commission dealing with future relations with Russia. They also received a critical letter, warning them that they had stepped out of line.[20]

As early as the summer of 1919, Lloyd George had been fully aware that a final peace treaty that was too harsh on Germany could push it towards the Russians. That was one of the reasons he had resisted French demands to punish Germany even more during the Paris Peace Conference. But at Genoa he simply couldn't conceive that holding private negotiations with the French in his villa might lead to a Soviet-German treaty. It was a failure of political imagination of the gravest order.

Lloyd George's shock was also caused by something that commentators and historians speculated about for decades but which we now know with absolute certainty: the rumours that the negotiations in the Villa d'Albertis were close to reaching the kind of agreement Rathenau feared were entirely untrue. Barthou remained deeply mistrustful of the Russians and was more interested in arguing about the recent past than forging an agreement. As for Chicherin, he had gone to Genoa to obtain recognition and respect for Russian sovereignty, and had no intention of accepting an agreement that would consign Russia to the status of a colony whose mineral resources belonged to Britain and France. When Lloyd George's delegation finally contacted the Germans to invite them to meet, he had no hidden agenda and Rathenau had no reason to fear. Lloyd George simply wanted to discuss what was going to happen next.[21]

Five weeks after the Rapallo debacle, on 19 May 1922, the Genoa Conference ended without agreement. It was obvious that Lloyd George's great plans for European reconstruction had failed. At its final plenary session, Rathenau brought Germany's contribution to a close with a memorable speech that warned of the persistent dangers of the war's legacy:

The current state of the world is not peace, but a state similar to war; in any case, it is not perfect peace. Unfortunately, in the individual countries public opinion has not been demobilized. The remnants of war propaganda circulate still, and poison the atmosphere.

After this, he finished his address in Italian, quoting the fourteenth-century poet Petrarch, one of the most important figures in the European Renaissance: 'I go calling out: Peace, peace, peace!'[22]

Even Barthou was impressed. For Rathenau's first biographer, the cosmopolitan Harry Graf Kessler, the speech represented a triumph for Rathenau and for Germany. Kessler, who was in Genoa for the duration of these events, suggested that by the end of the conference Rathenau had repaired the damage that Rapallo had done to Anglo-German relations. He even argued that, by bringing Germany and Britain closer together, the conference was ultimately a triumph for Rathenau. Yet although Rathenau's words went down well in the final session, they were just as meaningless as Lloyd George's and Facta's on the opening day. The armies of the First World War may have been demobilized, but minds were not. The Rapallo Treaty had contributed to Genoa's failure, and trust between nations remained broken.[23]

It was a crucial moment in the history of the Weimar Republic. Instead of coming away from Genoa with closer relations with Britain and France, Rathenau and Wirth returned home even more isolated than before. The French were furious and considered the Rapallo Treaty as dangerous as a declaration of war.[24]

Eight days after the treaty became public knowledge, French prime minister Raymond Poincaré went to Bar-le-Duc to deliver France's reply. This was the town where Poincaré had grown up, and he remembered well the years from 1871 to 1874 when it was occupied by the Germans, with the last German soldiers only leaving after France had paid all of its reparations to Germany following its defeat in the war of 1870–1. The town also held a special place in the French experience of the First World War. In 1916, when the fate of France depended upon the ability of the fortress of Verdun to hold out against a massive German assault that aimed to 'bleed the French white', the only French supply route to Verdun started at Bar-le-Duc.[25]

Standing in such a symbolically important location, Poincaré announced that France would deal with Germany unilaterally in the future. Fed up with the pace at which it was paying reparations, Poincaré simply could not ignore the emergence of a new

Russian-German partnership and the widespread expectation in France that the Rapallo Treaty was the starting point for a German-Russian alliance.

It was a crucial turning point in French policy towards Germany. Even though Poincaré was a hardliner, since his appointment as prime minister in January 1922, he had done little to suggest that his policies in government would live up to the rhetoric that he had used in opposition. The Rapallo Treaty changed that. It brought France closer to unilateral action against Germany, while crucially removing the brakes on French aggression that had been in place because of British opposition to such a move.

The Weimar Republic's future international relations with the victor states would now depend on whatever action the French government decided to take next. The fate of German democracy depended on the mood of Raymond Poincaré. Throughout the summer he remained enraged that the Germans had reached an agreement with Russia, while continuing to delay reparations payments to France. As each month passed, he grew more determined to put French boots on the ground in the Ruhr to make the Germans pay.

But as 1922 came to an end, the threat of a French invasion was only the beginning of Weimar democracy's anxieties. In October 1922, the political system that would eventually destroy German democracy in 1933 came to power in a European state for the first time. That month, Italy's Fascists provided all European nationalist opponents of liberal democracy with a blueprint for its destruction. It was a seismic moment for the continent's future.

3

The Fascist Moment

Benito Mussolini was a short man with a bald head and darting eyes. When he founded the Italian Fascist Party in 1919, it was widely predicted that Italy's Socialists were on the verge of taking power. But by the summer of 1922, the Fascist movement, whose representatives had received fewer than five thousand votes in the Italian elections of November 1919, was strong enough to threaten the existence of Italy's limited parliamentary democracy. And by the autumn of that same year, by becoming the continent's first Fascist head of government, he had changed the course of European history for ever.[1]

Mussolini's stronghold was in the Italian north, where his first supporters had started the Fascists' campaign of violence in 1919 by seeking out fights with Socialists in the streets, often attacking them when the Socialists flew red flags. As the Fascist movement grew, its supporters looked down on the Italian capital of Rome as an Italian swamp whose corrupt elite was destroying Italy. When the time came, Mussolini promised that Italy's fascists would lead a 'March on Rome' and create a 'new Italy' that would restore the nation and the capital to the greatness of the ancient Romans, whose power had conquered most of Europe.

For observers trying to predict the course Italian politics would take in the summer of 1922, the threat posed by Mussolini was hard to gauge. He was well known as a speaker who used bombastic, exaggerated rhetoric. But as summer turned to autumn, the rumours of an impending Fascist move against the state grew louder. At the same time, there was a shift in the rhetoric of Mussolini and the Fascist leadership. They toned down their calls for the creation of an Italian republic and stressed their movement's loyalty to the king and the Italian army, hoping thereby to convince the military that it would be wrong to open fire on their 'brothers' in the Fascist movement.

Fortunately for Mussolini, even with the looming threat of a Fascist coup d'état, there was no consensus among his political opponents about how to deal with him. Even though the Fascist movement was based on violence, and its members had previously murdered elected members of the Italian parliament, many among Italy's political elite considered a Mussolini government to be a lesser evil than the threat of a country led by the Socialist left.[2]

In mid-October, Mussolini gave four men the task of planning the Fascists' power seizure. The plan they came up with involved five stages. First, the Fascists would mobilize their armed supporters across Italy and take control of public buildings, especially police headquarters and prefectures, and shut down communications, including the post, the telegraph system and railways. In the second stage, the most experienced and best fighters would assemble in towns within striking distance of Rome. They would then issue an ultimatum demanding that Mussolini be given power. In the event that their demand was rejected, the armed Fascists were to force their way into Rome, seize government buildings and keep fighting until all resistance was defeated. In the event that they were forced back out of Rome, their plan foresaw the establishment of a rival Fascist government in central Italy, whence they would continue the fight until victory was theirs. It was nothing short of a recipe for civil war.[3]

Though the details of Mussolini's plans remained under wraps, the reality was that what was coming was an open secret. On 26 October, the prime minister, Luigi Facta, and the minister of the interior warned Italy's prefects that a Fascist insurrection was about to take place and instructed them to prepare to resist it with force. General Pugliese, the army commander in charge of defending Rome, got ready to stop the Fascists' armed *squadristi*, the infamous Black Shirts. But in a sign of what was to come, Facta's government was unable to reach agreement about the necessity of immediately introducing martial law in advance of the Fascists' assault on the state. On 27 October, the Fascists made their move. The first occupations occurred in the cities of Cremona, in the Italian north, as well as in Pisa and Siena, both of which were within striking distance of Rome. During the night of 27–8 October, there were further mobilizations as Fascists occupied key buildings across Italy. In most cases, there was no real resistance or serious blood-letting: both the armed Fascists and the police and prefects charged with defending the state held their fire to see what would happen next.[4]

In Rome, in the early hours of the morning of 28 October, Facta's government unanimously declared a state of siege that was to come into force at midday. For a few brief hours, it looked like the government was going to demand that the army and police use force to put down the Fascist insurrection. But just hours after the plans were agreed, the Italian King Vittorio Emanuele refused to sign the order. Without his backing, the army would not open fire on the *squadristi*. It was a decisive moment in European history. Vittorio Emanuele opened the door to the Fascist coup d'état.

The king's reasons for doing so have never been fully explained. Few European royal families allow historians to consult their archives freely, even today. The most likely explanation is that he came to believe that the price of trying to stop the Fascists by force would be higher than that of allowing them to proceed. He didn't want to be responsible for starting a full-blown civil war. It is also possible that he feared for his place on the throne. If he signed the order and the Fascists won, he perhaps thought that they would remove him from office as a punishment for supporting their opponents, especially as there may have already been a deal behind the scenes to replace him with another member of the Italian royal family. What we can say with more certainty is that if he had signed the order and sent the army out to defend the institutions of the state, there is little doubt that the Fascists would have been routed. Even if the army contained officers and men who sympathized with Mussolini and the Fascists, their discipline and loyalty to the king would have been enough to allow them to open fire. By failing to take that step, Vittorio Emanuele opened the door for other Europeans to dream that the next Fascist government would be in their country.

Once Facta's emergency measures were rescinded, the forces of the state stood down and allowed the Fascists to behave as though they were now in power. At the local level, the Fascist squads claimed victory, entering municipal buildings in many towns, raising their flags and cheering the dawn of a new era. In Rome, Facta resigned. Vittorio Emanuele's first choice to replace him was former prime minister Antonio Salandra, the veteran politician who had taken the decision for Italy to enter the First World War in May 1915. But Salandra was too weak politically to rule on his own. He suggested that the king should ask Mussolini to join him in a coalition government, which would be under Salandra's leadership. When Mussolini refused this offer outright, Vittorio Emanuele concluded that there was no alternative but to offer the position of prime minister to Mussolini.

Mussolini received the news on 29 October 1922, but he was in no rush to accept the king's capitulation. When his forces first mobilized at the start of the coup, he had barricaded himself into his Milan offices, planning to stay as far away from the action as possible. Even after the king sent his message, Mussolini took his time. He wanted to enter the capital only after his armed men had marched into Rome, to make it look like they had used force to seize power, in spite of the reality that General Pugliese had opened the gates of the city to them once the king's order was known. Mussolini's trick worked: the images of armed men marching into Rome solidified the powerfully enduring myth that the *squadristi* had marched on Rome and seized power. It left an important legacy: from this point on, the Fascists' glorification of violence included the idea that they could only take over the state through an act of aggression, real or imagined.

In Italy, Mussolini's appointment set in motion the end of the liberal state. In the coming months, supported by a mass movement accompanied by violence, Mussolini pursued the destruction of the opposition. Some enemies were eradicated almost at once, while other rival power centres, including the monarchy, were allowed to remain in existence so long as they did not openly challenge the regime. Mussolini's Fascist dictatorship would hold firm for almost twenty-five years.

The news of Mussolini's appointment sent shockwaves around the world. The 'March on Rome' now represented a frightening statement about how Fascist strongmen could proceed to seize power. Just five years after Lenin's Bolsheviks had begun their campaign of violence to take control of the territories of the former Russian Empire, Fascism offered a second alternative to liberal democracy.[5]

In Germany, Mussolini's victory represented a major propaganda victory for Hitler. A parliamentary democracy that had been on the victorious side of the First World War had been defeated. Italy's Socialist left had been unable to stop Mussolini's Fascists from taking control of the state. In the wake of Mussolini's appointment, Hitler now commanded the attention of the German press. In the Social Democratic Party's flagship newspaper *Vorwärts*, Hitler was mentioned only twice in the two calendar months before the 'March on Rome'. By contrast, in November and December 1922, following Mussolini's appointment, he was the subject of no fewer than twenty-six articles.[6]

Above all else, Mussolini's example fuelled Nazi self-confidence. A week after Mussolini's appointment, Hermann Esser, the editor of the Nazis' most important newspaper, the *Völkischer Beobachter*, spoke in Munich's Hofbräuhaus beer hall. He told the rally:

What a group of courageous men were able to do in Italy, we can also do in Bavaria. We also have a man like Italy's Mussolini. His name is Adolf Hitler. The parliamentary swindle must be brought to an end . . . in its place must come a national dictatorship.[7]

Supporters of Weimar democracy got the message. On 16 November, the newspaper of the Central Association of German Jews, the *CV-Zeitung*, quoted Esser's words on its front page in an article warning of the threat that the German 'Fascists' posed to both Germany's Jews and the German fatherland. They warned that the example of Mussolini was likely to trigger a battle between rival right-wing groups in Germany: after all, at this time, Hitler was just one of many anti-democratic politicians aspiring to become the German Mussolini. The *CV-Zeitung* feared that this battle would encourage rival speakers to become increasingly radical in a battle to outdo one another and assume leadership over the entire far right. It warned that they were intent upon unleashing pogroms in Germany, and that the ensuing chaos would end with the creation of a German dictatorship. It lamented, moreover, that Hitler could glorify violence and call for the overthrow of the state without serious challenge from the state powers.[8]

In October 1922, German Jews weren't just despondent because of Hitler's growing prominence. They were also disappointed by the trial of thirteen young men charged with participation in, or supporting, the murder of Walther Rathenau. Held in Leipzig's spectacular neo-Renaissance Supreme Court building, opened as a symbol of German judicial independence in 1895, it was the first opportunity that the newly created State Court for the Defence of the Republic had had to demonstrate its ability to administer republican justice. Its performance on this occasion would leave many disappointed.

The trial began on 3 October 1922. On the first day of the trial, the courtroom, which had capacity for seven hundred people, was overflowing. But the crowds that gathered weren't made up solely of supporters of democracy. Its opponents also gathered. Some wore emblems that identified them as supporters of Hitler, while others let their views be known by joining in the Nazi chant of 'Heil' whenever the police vans passed through the streets to carry the accused to and from the court. The police guarding the prisoners and protecting the court were nervous. There were rumours, which they took seriously, that an underground group, perhaps even the Organization Consul, would try to use force to free the accused.

When he was led into the courtroom on the first day of the trial,

Ernst Werner Techow's face was pale. He had good reason to be fearful. Weimar Germany may have been a liberal democracy with a progressive constitution, but it retained the death penalty – administered by guillotine, the noose or the axe. It was a fate that many people wanted for Techow. When he took the stand for the first time, he admitted that he was a member of the Organization Consul but claimed that it had had nothing to do with the murder. He emphasized instead that Erwin Kern, 'this fanatic' – and who was now dead, of course – was the driving force behind everything that the group of men had done. He told the judges: 'I was under his influence and I couldn't go back.' Techow's unconvincing testimony was followed by similar performances by the other accused.[9]

The coverage was divided across the partisan press. On the first day of the trial, one reporter for the pro-republican *Berliner Tageblatt* said that listening to the defendants speaking left observers wondering if Rathenau and Erzberger had been murdered at all.[10] Another commentator thought that the defendants had 'learnt nothing so thoroughly as lying'. Yet the anti-republican nationalist and conservative press published articles that defended the accused and repeatedly suggested that they were simply 'good boys' who had become involved in something that they didn't really understand.[11]

Having initially suggested that the trial would be a display of republican justice, the correspondent for the *Vorwärts* newspaper grew increasingly frustrated with the proceedings. It quickly became clear to him that the court was not going to go after the politicians, journalists and financiers who gave life to what he called the many-headed 'Murder Hydra'. As his frustration increased, he demanded: 'We need to find out who are the masterminds pulling the strings, we already know the puppets.' But few were listening.[12]

On the final day of the trial, Techow was visibly pale. Ludwig Ebermayer, the sixty-four-year-old senior state attorney who had served as the chief prosecutor in a series of high-profile political cases at the start of the Weimar Republic, had demanded that Techow face the death penalty. But the judges found him guilty only of being an 'accessory to murder' and sentenced him to fifteen years' imprisonment and ten years' 'loss of civil rights'. Not only had he escaped the death penalty, Techow would not even face lifelong imprisonment for his crimes. Realizing his good fortune, he enthusiastically thanked his defence lawyers and looked with gratitude towards the president of the court.[13]

The judges were even more lenient with the other conspirators. Willi Günther was given eight years' imprisonment, while five others received sentences that they had already completed as a result of being held in custody for the duration of the trial. A further three defendants were found not guilty. One of the guilty, Ernst von Salomon, would start writing a novel about his experiences with the gang while he was imprisoned. When *The Outlaws* was first published in 1930, it would be the start of his career as one of twentieth-century Germany's best-selling right-wing authors.[14]

Judge Alfred Hagens, who chaired the proceedings, justified the court's sentencing on the final day. He stated that the case in Leipzig was against the 'young helpers and tools' and said that it was impossible not to have 'a certain compassion for them'. Hagens blamed antisemitism for the murder, which was certainly true, but in this instance the focus on antisemitism was also a convenient way of ignoring the need for the judges to examine the organization behind the murderers. It was also a way of suggesting that antisemitism was something that could be fixed through education, rather than an unchallengeable belief that provided a structural framework for German opponents of democracy.

Few commentators were genuinely satisfied with the outcome. The Social Democratic *Vorwärts* noted that the first trial at the State Court for the Defence of the Republic was 'not the republican act that one had expected'. On the political right, the sentences were condemned as excessive. The ultra-nationalist *Deutsche-Zeitung* thought that the Techow brothers were 'children, who belonged in the reformatory', and described their sentences as 'downright monstrous'. Another ultra-nationalist newspaper, the *Deutsche Tageszeitung* argued that the outcome of the trial had shown beyond all doubt that accusations that the nationalist right were responsible for creating the climate in which the murder could take place were entirely false. For the newspaper that served as the voice of German Jews, the *CV-Zeitung*, the most important lesson offered by the Rathenau trial was that it was absolutely necessary to 'eliminate the spirit that gave birth to the attacks'. There could be no safety for German Jews, it warned, until the 'spirit of hatred and slander that is found every day in the antisemitic press' was eradicated.[15]

The best that could be said of the outcome was that it was at least an improvement on the behaviour of the reactionary courts of the past which had not even convicted right-wing killers. But the trial did not deliver a warning to any organized group on the right or the left that the institutions of the state and its ministers were untouchable. It did not send a message about the state's legal power to prosecute those who used violence against it. And it did not demonstrate a determination to prosecute antisemitism. In the end it amounted to both a political and a judicial failure.

As the trial took place, across Germany, nationalist and antisemitic speakers with either formal ties to the Nazi Party or growing sympathies with its goals repeatedly asserted false claims about Rathenau and Jewish influence upon Germany. One of the most notable such firebrands was a thirty-one-year-old female Nazi named Andrea Ellendt.[16] Like the leader of the Organization Consul, Hermann Ehrhardt, Ellendt's anti-democratic radicalism had its origins in the German navy during the First World War. Her husband, a naval officer, was killed during the fighting, and at the end of the war she began her political career when she joined the right-wing and strongly antisemitic Deutschvölkischer Schutz- und Trutzbund (German Nationalist Protection and Defiance Federation) in Munich. Tall and thin, she kept her hair tied back and tucked away under a striking hat shaped like the steel helmets that German soldiers wore during the First World War. Observers of her speeches noted that her habit of wearing a long dark raincoat or leather jacket, which she tightened at her waist with a wide leather belt, helped her to stand out.

By the summer of 1922, Ellendt was based in Kitzingen, a town with around ten thousand residents in the wine-producing region of Mainfranken in northern Bavaria, about 250 kilometres north of Munich, where her speeches regularly filled the town's largest venues. From there, she travelled to nearby towns and villages where, in the words of the newspaper of the Central Association of German Jews, the *CV-Zeitung*, she 'sowed her poisonous seeds and claims that the government and its republic were solely responsible for the present misery'.

Her increasing popularity was a product of the economic crisis of 1922 and in particular the collapse in agricultural prices that left many rural families facing ruin. Though we often associate the fall of Weimar with the economic crises of 1923 and 1930–2, it is a mistake to forget that the economy became dysfunctional much earlier. Economic problems were caused by a decade of inflation that began in August 1914, when the German government took the decision to finance the First World War by issuing bonds to German citizens that would be repaid when Germany was victorious. After the defeat in 1918, the value of the German currency continued to decline, and the agricultural sector was hit particularly badly.

On the day of Rathenau's murder, 24 June 1922, 1 US dollar was worth around 330 German marks. Just over a hundred days later, at the start of the trial of the gang that killed him, the cost had risen to 1,800 marks. This was not even close to the worst of the hyperinflation that would almost destroy the Weimar Republic in 1923, but the effects were bad enough to draw crowds to listen to the speeches of Nazis like Ellendt. On top of the fall in the value of the German currency, the 1922 harvest had been poor. This worsened the situation facing farmers, many of whom were angry because they had to sell their products for less than they had spent on seed and fertilizer since the start of the year. For them, Ellendt offered a simple and straightforward explanation for who was to blame: 'racketeers', 'usurers', 'profiteers', 'Jews'.[17]

But Ellendt wasn't just a popular preacher who targeted minorities, she was an early representative of Fascist politics in rural Germany. Even before the term was widely used, she had her own company of Stormtroopers or assault troops. As she traversed the wine-growing region, she was followed by around fifty to eighty men armed with clubs and knuckle-dusters and led by a swastika flag-bearer. When she spoke publicly, her followers' job was to intimidate anyone who interrupted her. If any Jews were present, they forced them to leave. After she finished speaking, she sent her troops off on rampages through clusters of 'Jewish streets' in small towns or villages, where they chanted, 'Jews out, string them up!'[18]

Ellendt's case should have served as a perfect example of the way that the Law for the Protection of the Republic could be used to defend the Weimar constitution and punish those calling for violence against it. But there was no will to create such examples, especially in Bavaria. Just as the court in Leipzig was failing to demonstrate the power of democracy against Rathenau's killers at the national level, her ability to continue anti-republican agitation in local communities in northern Bavaria was making a mockery of the new law. In some places, where attempts to ban her from speaking were made, she used a simple legal trick to get around them. She redefined the gatherings as 'private meetings', open only to members of the newly founded 'Association of Listeners of Ellendt'. A membership card was made available to attendees at the entrance.

When the Central Association of German Jews protested against her antisemitism, the district president to whom they addressed their concerns advised them to ignore her speeches. He warned them to avoid doing anything 'that might particularly nourish the current antisemitic thought, such as inappropriate behaviour towards the lectures'. Ellendt needed no such nourishment: she called the government 'criminal', 'all Jews and racketeers' or 'Jews and traitors'. She described Jews as the force behind both Russian Bolshevism and American capitalism and claimed that the 'truth' about the Jews remained unknown because 'they' controlled the press. At one meeting that was only open to women who were eighteen and older, she warned: 'Jewish doctors work against families. Judah wants to strike against Germany's unborn generations, so that they stay unborn and Judah can be victorious and rule the world' – an important reminder of how fears and experiences of miscarriage or failed conception could be made part of the antisemitic message.

Ellendt's speeches called for action. She told her audiences that they should 'hunt the government to hell'. She advised farmers not to send their produce to Berlin, where it would be used for speculation, and told them not to sell grain to Jews. She called upon Germans 'to unite and protect yourselves from Jewish power'. On one occasion, as she finished speaking, she demanded: 'The Jewish star must perish, and the cross of Christ must rise in the light of the swastika.'[19]

This language had consequences. In the autumn of 1922, the Central Association of German Jews recorded increasingly frequent attacks on Jews in public spaces in Bavaria and across Germany. In one example, it reported how two 'swastika followers' – the term it used to describe followers of Hitler – attempted to murder a Jewish businessman by trying to throw him from a moving train in Hanover. Their target survived by fighting back, pulling the emergency brake and bringing the train to a stop. While they were assaulting him, one of the perpetrators reportedly told him: 'No Jews come through here, understand that, Jewish beast!' The *CV-Zeitung* described it as 'one of the usual sort of antisemitic ethnic attacks'. In 1923, when she eventually faced trial for her antisemitic agitation, Ellendt was found not guilty. By then, the pro-democratic backlash against Fascists like Ellendt had grown muted as the republic's supporters had moved on to other national challenges. Efforts to reassert the republic's values in the wake of Rathenau's murder had run out of steam only a year later.[20]

On 14–15 October 1922, Andrea Ellendt was in the small town of Coburg, almost 300 kilometres to the north of Munich, where she was a speaker at the 'German Day', a weekend-long nationalist rally organized by the Deutschvölkischer Schutz- und Trutzbund to mobilize German opponents of democracy. Adolf Hitler was there too. He travelled from Munich in a train that was specially organized to bring more than five hundred Nazis to the rally. It was a shameless copy of the 'city occupations' that Mussolini's *squadristi* had undertaken during the previous eighteen months.[21]

At first it looked like their parade might pass off peacefully. Hitler's supporters paraded behind a swastika flag while a band played music. But once they caught sight of Socialist protestors who had gathered to oppose the march, the true nature of the parade quickly revealed itself. Whistles sounded and the Nazi Stormtroopers began attacking the anti-Fascist protest. When members of the working class insulted and spat at the police, the representatives of law and order took the Nazis' side.[22]

For the Nazi movement, the event became legendary. The Stormtroopers crowed that they had claimed Coburg. For the left-wing press, it was an episode of 'naked street terror'. Many middle-class observers of the violence sympathized with the Nazis, claiming that they were only defending themselves and admiring them for also attending a church service later that weekend which called for German renewal. It was exactly the kind of publicity that Hitler craved, and other newly founded local Nazi groups would emulate such actions with increasing frequency during the winter of 1922–3.[23]

The dust had barely settled on the 'German Day' at Coburg when Hitler received a further boost. On 20 October 1922, Julius Streicher, who would later become one of the Third Reich's most infamous antisemitic propagandists and be hanged for his crimes against humanity in October 1946, formally launched the Nazi Party's Nuremberg branch. It was another important milestone. Nuremberg was Bavaria's second city. Like Munich, it was home to rival anti-democratic groups, who were fighting among themselves to establish leadership in the race to overthrow the Weimar Republic. Until October 1922, Streicher was a member of the German Socialist Party, a rival group to Hitler's Nazis; both included the word 'Socialist' in their party names, even though neither was a party of the left. But Streicher had fallen out with the German Socialist Party leadership and faced financial ruin. At the start of October 1922, he approached Hitler and offered to join forces with him. If the Nazi Party paid off his debts, Streicher would bring his supporters in Nuremberg with him into Hitler's party, helping to weaken the rival German Socialist Party significantly in northern Bavaria.

Streicher's followers were part of the wave of new members that the Nazi Party attracted in late 1922. At the start of the year, Hitler's party had seventeen branches. By the end of the summer, that figure had risen to forty-six. But by the end of 1922, it had doubled once again, to around one hundred. Most were in Bavaria, but the party was starting to stretch its tentacles beyond its political heartland. The best estimates suggest that by the end of 1922 the party had around eight thousand members. Even if this is a tiny figure compared to the mass parties and pro-democratic organizations of the early Weimar Republic, there is no doubt that the final months of 1922 represent the moment when Hitler's political star first began to rise. The question at this time wasn't so much whether the Nazis would continue to grow, but rather whether Hitler would be able to maintain control over the disparate firebrands who found his movement so attractive. This is why the example of Mussolini mattered so much. Even the collection of antisemites, agitators, propagandists, ultra-nationalists, monarchists, anti-Socialists and oddballs who were drawn to Hitler and Nazism in late 1922 could see the success that Mussolini had achieved by maintaining a united Fascist front. Hitler saw it too. He realized that if he could replicate this feat the path to victory over Weimar democracy was crystal clear.

For supporters of Weimar democracy, the republic's fourth birthday, on 9 November 1922, offered little cause for celebration. Just months after the passing of new laws to defeat their opponents, the defence of the republic had grown far more challenging. The Social Democrats' newspaper, *Vorwärts*, was certain who bore the greatest responsibility for the mounting problems. An article on its front page on 9 November argued:

> The anti-revolutionary powers in Germany would never have attained such strength ... if the victors in the world war, through their capitalist policies of bankruptcy and their inability to solve

the problems of the war, had not weakened the body of the German economy, undermined the democratic republic, and paved the way for a new growth in nationalism in Germany.

It finished with the hopeful suggestion that, despite inflation, starvation, the fear of unemployment and bankruptcy, Germany 'would neither turn to suicidal Communist experiments, nor give way to Fascist adventures'.[24]

The continuing collapse of the German mark threw cold water on such hopes. On 9 November 1922, it slumped to its lowest value yet: 9,000 German marks were now needed to purchase a single US dollar – a more than twenty-sevenfold increase since June 1922. Mounting economic crisis opened the door for a multimillionaire industrialist named Hugo Stinnes to launch an assault on some of Weimar's foundational labour protections.

On the anniversary of the foundation of the Weimar Republic, Stinnes delivered a major public speech at the Reich Economic Council, charging that workers' right to an eight-hour working day, one of the most important rights established at the republic's foundation, should have no place in its future. He proposed that workers' shifts should be extended to ten to twelve hours, without additional pay. He also proposed banning workers' right to strike in sectors deemed crucial to the national economy, which, given the circumstances facing Germany, could be extended to include every major sector. Stinnes warned that if the right to strike was not banned, it would be impossible to undertake any measures to stabilize the fall in value of the German currency. That was a warning that the German central bank, the Reichsbank, was not to spend a cent of its reserves to try to increase the value of the German mark until the eight-hour working day had been abandoned.[25]

Stinnes's speech made the future of the eight-hour working day a key political battleground. Trade unions and the majority of the Social Democratic Party opposed him firmly. For them, it was critical to the republic. Responding to his claims that it was unproductive, they retorted that if men like Stinnes really wanted to make German labour more productive they should invest in plant modernization and new technology. More generally, they were furious that a man like Stinnes could get away with blaming workers for the economic slump and suggesting that punishing workers by worsening their conditions was the solution to Germany's problems.[26]

But Stinnes's agenda could not be so easily ignored. He wasn't just an extraordinarily rich industrialist, he was also a Reichstag deputy, as well as a leading member of the German People's Party, a nationalist party of the right with strong ties to industry. In the 1920 elections to the Reichstag, it had obtained just under 14 per cent of the vote, making it the fourth largest party. Not only did he enjoy direct access to President Ebert, he owned his own newspapers. In such a charged political environment, he had the means to make himself heard and to set the agenda that others had to respond to. In the winter of 1922–3, he did so with aplomb.[27]

Since Rathenau's murder, the internal politics of all of the major German parties had changed. Following the assassination, the largest pro-democratic party in the Weimar Republic, the Social Democratic Party, moved to the left. In September 1922, it merged with its former left-wing rival, the Independent Socialist Party, which had been founded in 1917 when the most radical left-wing members of the SPD quit their party because of what they perceived as the unduly conservative policies of the majority of its members. With the reunification of the SPD, the party had over one million members and 186 seats in the Reichstag, more than the combined total of its coalition partners, the liberal German Democratic Party (Rathenau's party) and the Catholic Centre Party (Wirth's party), which had 103.[28]

The three most important parties of the centre-right reacted to these developments by shifting to the right. In the summer, the German Democratic Party and the Centre Party joined with Stinnes's German People's Party to form a new anti-Socialist Working Group of the Constitutional Centre. Initially, this forum for thinking about collaboration between these groups proved useful to Wirth. It helped to secure German People's Party support for the Law for the Protection of the Republic in July 1922, and later for the extension of the term of office of President Ebert on

24 October, which required the support of two-thirds of deputies. But in the longer term its existence helped to create an unbridgeable gap between the parties on which Wirth depended for his parliamentary majority. It was only a matter of time before the German Democratic Party and the Centre Party would have to choose between maintaining their coalition with the Social Democrats or opting for a stronger formal alliance with Stinnes's German People's Party. The solution was either a break from the coalition or, if enough Social Democrats could be convinced to support the idea, a move to include Stinnes's party in a broader coalition.

Friedrich Ebert ended up making the key move. Just after his term as president was extended, he told Wirth that it was time to expand the coalition to include Stinnes's German People's Party. Ebert reasoned that Germany was going to need a strong, stable government going into the winter of 1922–3 and that, if Stinnes was included, it might help to secure more favourable treatment from the victorious Allies. By the end of the year, Wirth didn't need much convincing that his government should move further to the right. He had already told the cabinet on 23 October that it was time for a 'concentration of forces'. The question was whether the Social Democrats could tolerate the inclusion of Stinnes in a government that they nominally supported.[29]

Wirth's position had grown more tenuous since Rathenau's murder. In its immediate aftermath he had famously told the Reichstag: 'The enemy stands on the right!' But Wirth remained a politician of the moderate right, a position that left him increasingly exposed. In Bavaria, he was so disliked for his co-operation with the Social Democrats that, even though he was the leader of the Catholic Centre Party, he was not invited to attend Katholikentag ('Catholics' Day') in Munich at the end of August 1922. Munich's archbishop, Cardinal Michael von Faulhaber, who was one of the driving forces behind his exclusion, personally hated Wirth, calling him a 'statesman of the sorriest sort' and accusing him of opening 'the back door to Bolshevism in Germany'.[30]

On 13 November 1922, three days after Ebert suggested that Stinnes's German People's Party should become part of the government, a weakened Wirth secured support from both the Social Democratic Party and the German People's Party for a new diplomatic note to the Allies. Wirth also decided that he needed Stinnes's backing to make his new policy a success. Where Wirth had previously demanded that the Allies give Germany a new reparations deal before German policy-makers could do anything to try to stabilize the German mark – a policy summed up as 'first bread, then reparations' – the German government would now change course. For the first time, in the note the German government made credible suggestions that it would use the most important financial weapon available – the Reichsbank's gold – to stabilize its currency. As payback for risking the Reichsbank's gold, Wirth asked the Allies for a new three- or four-year moratorium on reparations and a new final reparations bill based on Germany's ability to pay. With these proposals under consideration, Wirth argued that they were far more likely to be successful if the German government was extended to include Stinnes and the German People's Party, which represented big business. The reunified Social Democratic Party now faced a major test.

Though some former leading members of the Independent Socialist Party supported expanding the coalition, a majority of the Social Democratic Party's Reichstag deputies opposed it. After all, Stinnes had just launched an assault on both the right to strike and the eight-hour working day. They had good reason for their opposition: the merger of the Social Democrats with the Independent Socialists left Wirth's government with a stronger majority than at any time since its formation. Wirth had also already obtained the German People's Party's support for Wirth's note to the Allies.

But Wirth's hands were tied: if he failed to expand the coalition and reassure its conservative members that he had not become a puppet controlled by the Socialist left, he knew that his days as chancellor were numbered. There was no acceptable compromise and, on 14 November 1922, Wirth resigned.[31]

A businessman, Wilhelm Cuno, became the next German chancellor. Ebert played a key role in his selection, which hinged on his achievements as general director of the Hamburg–America

Shipping Company (HAPAG). Cuno was generally recognized as having rescued the company from ruin in the aftermath of the First World War. It was a significant achievement: when Cuno took over the leadership of HAPAG after his predecessor had committed suicide, the company was facing the general challenge of the collapse in international trade with Germany as a result of the First World War, along with the particular challenge confronting the German merchant shipping sector: just as they confiscated Germany's military shipping as a prize for victory in the war, the Allies also seized its merchant fleet, arguing that even though it was civilian shipping, it had military potential. Without trading partners or ships, many people predicted that HAPAG would soon cease to exist. But Cuno managed to convince American investors to support the company and rebuild its strength.

Ebert hoped that Cuno could work the same magic with the United States government to obtain a new deal on reparations and stronger American support to stabilize the German currency. The idea was naïve but it made some political sense. At the time of Cuno's appointment, Germany was facing one of the worst winters in its modern history. Either the currency situation would continue to worsen, or stabilization measures would be introduced that might bring mass unemployment and major cutbacks to welfare and social programmes. By appointing a technocrat and politically non-aligned leader to take responsibility for these decisions, Ebert was offering the democratic parties a chance to get someone else to do the dirty work and transfer the blame to an outsider who wasn't a member of any party.

But appointing a technocrat had its risks. The French invasion of the Ruhr was just weeks away. In the face of an active threat to the existence of German democracy, Cuno would have been no one's first choice to rally popular support for the Weimar constitution. He was not the man to lead the democratic republic's resistance to a French invasion either. Even if, at first, he managed to rally Germans to respond to the occupation, he did so by taking positions that were impossible to reverse, even after they revealed themselves to be failing disastrously. If anything, on the eve of the invasion, his appointment foreshadowed the course that German politics would take in the aftermath of the invasion, when the nationalist and anti-republican right profited most from the calls to defend Germany from the French and Belgian threat.

Cuno's first speech as chancellor made this shift in rhetoric apparent when he promised that Germany would never surrender any of its territory to occupation. He had barely taken up office before that promise was tested to its absolute limits.

PART II

Winter and Spring 1923

4

The Invasion of the Ruhr

Early on 18 January 1923, the journalist Erich Dombrowski was a passenger on the overnight train from Berlin to Essen, one of the largest cities in the Ruhr district, famous as Germany's coal region. As the first light of morning started to sparkle, the region mesmerized him. Looking out of the window of the train as it passed from one town to the next, he stared at the endless towers and chimneys, and flames rising from furnaces, beneath which as many as half a million miners worked in vast underground labyrinths. There was nowhere on Earth quite like it. The highly industrialized Ruhr was so unique, Dombrowski mused, only people who had been born and raised under its rose-pink sky could truly feel at home there.[1]

Dombrowski arrived at a decisive moment for the future of Europe. Even though his employer, the capital's leading liberal newspaper, the *Berliner Tageblatt*, already had a Ruhr correspondent, Dombrowski had been sent there to report on the French and Belgian occupation of Germany's industrial heartland which had begun a week earlier. It was at once the last major military act of the First World War in western Europe, France's final attempt to use military force to secure its victory and the Weimar Republic's first truly existential crisis.

The invasion began on 11 January 1923 when three military columns – two French and one Belgian – set off from their bridgeheads around Düsseldorf and Duisburg, which were already occupied under the terms of the Treaty of Versailles. Even though they faced not a single German soldier to challenge their advance, the columns were led by mounted cavalry with their sabres drawn, followed by light artillery, tanks and soldiers with machine guns, supported by hospital cars, field kitchens, ammunition trucks and a small number of French military aeroplanes. The French appeared ready for another war.[2]

Over the next three days they occupied nearly all of the Ruhr district. The exception was Dortmund, a large city about 40 kilometres to the east of Essen, which French forces only occupied on the afternoon of 16 January as a 'punishment' for the German refusal to comply with French demands. In Bredeney, a well-off suburb of Essen, the most senior French commanders, including the head of the French occupation forces, General Jean-Marie Degoutte, took up residence in the Villa Hügel, a spectacular palace of 269 rooms built in the early 1870s by the man later known as the 'cannon king', Alfred Krupp, the founder of the Krupp steel dynasty. The rest of the force of 70,000–100,000 troops took up residence in considerably less spectacular accommodation across the region, in schools, police buildings, offices, hotels and farms, as well as in housing belonging to industry and private individuals. As they crossed the Rhine, some imagined themselves as an invasion force from the days of Louis XIV or Napoleon I, intent on conquering regions of western Germany for France.[3]

The local population responded to the occupation with extreme anger. As French soldiers marched into Essen at lunchtime on 11 January, one journalist described the entire city as being 'on its feet', with crowds lining the streets to show their displeasure despite the declaration of martial law by French forces. The Prussian police, which continued to operate, now faced the unenviable task of maintaining order. On the first day of the occupation, they managed to separate angry crowds from occupying soldiers. There were a small number of incidents when German police had to stop protestors from attacking or provoking the soldiers, but the bulk of the protests were more symbolic in nature. Groups of young people, including students, gathered to sing nationalist songs like 'The Watch on the Rhine', a patriotic war song about protecting the Rhine from French invasion. By nightfall on the first day of the invasion, there was no record of any shots being fired or of any loss of life. The French armoured car that had taken up position in the square in front of Essen's town hall at midday had been intimidating, but by evening it had withdrawn.[4]

The situation changed on 15 January. That evening a German teenager was shot dead by the French military in Bochum, a mining town about halfway between Essen and Dortmund, which had been occupied by the French the previous day. In the same incident a woman was shot in the stomach and a man in the leg, though both survived. The gunfire occurred after a group of young people, some of whom were allegedly members of the Bismarck League, gathered to sing nationalist songs, including a well-known soldiers' song, which contained the words: 'We want a victorious triumph over France'. As they passed through the Königsallee close to a French post at the railway headquarters building, the French guard opened fire. Of the twenty-five French soldiers present, most fired blank warning shots intended merely to scare the crowd and force it to disperse. But at least one and possibly more fired live shots. Whether this was deliberate was never established.[5]

News of the fatality brought the anger in the city to boiling point. Across the Ruhr, crowds formed and marched through the streets singing patriotic songs. To the north of Essen, in Buer, the French military commander announced that any person who failed to stop instantly when instructed to do so by French soldiers would be fired upon with live ammunition. On 18 January, the occupiers banned the singing of 'The Watch on the Rhine' and the German national anthem. They also banned performances of Friedrich Schiller's play *William Tell*, whose central story of heroic resistance to a foreign occupier was deemed too provocative in the circumstances.[6]

The dead teenager's funeral was a significant event. President Ebert sent a telegram of condolence and his office helped to co-ordinate financial donations to the victim's family. *Vorwärts* declared that there was blood on Poincaré's hands. It argued that it didn't matter whether the demonstrators had provoked the French soldiers by singing, or whether they had been juvenile and 'foolish'. What mattered was that the soldiers did not fire in self-defence.[7]

A second civilian fatality occurred to the east of Bochum in the town of Langendreer on 19 January. At around 9.30 p.m., the medical orderly Franz Kowalski was walking from the Kaiserplatz to the district court building. It was dark but oil lamps lit up the area. Suddenly a shot rang out and Kowalski fell dead. Reports suggest that a French soldier had shouted at him and then immediately fired. The French commander later maintained that the soldier had complied with the rules of engagement. When Kowalski was buried on 23 January, thousands of locals, as well as national and local government representatives, schools and trade unions, attended his funeral. *Vorwärts* called it murder.[8]

In the aftermath of both deaths, German diplomats in Paris sent protest notes to the French government. The response to the first note, signed in the name of prime minister Poincaré, defended the conduct of French soldiers and warned that any threats against them would be 'ruthlessly suppressed'. There was no formal response to the second note, whose tone and content the French declared so unacceptable that they refused to receive it formally. Later, reports in French newspapers would claim falsely that the soldiers had only opened fire after the protesting crowd had fired upon them first.[9]

The deaths were the most significant acts of violence at the start of the occupation, but there were others. To the north of Bochum, in Recklinghausen, French officers attacked a group of women with horsewhips while they were attending a play. A non-fatal shooting occurred in Bochum on 24 January, when French soldiers were accused of firing upon a worker after they called on him to stop. In Cologne on 23 January, a French officer drew his pistol and fired several shots during an altercation with a German man that began when the officer insulted the man's wife; a girl otherwise uninvolved in the incident was injured. An enraged mob attacked the officer but he managed to escape. In another town, a French soldier was accused of stabbing a German civilian after they began to argue on board a train. On 23 January, a drunken German worker was sentenced to twenty days in prison and a 100,000-mark fine for insulting French soldiers by mocking their boots.[10]

From the very start of the occupation, German women and girls faced the threat of rape and sexual violence. One of the first documented cases occurred in Herne, a district to the west of Dortmund, on 19 January, when three French soldiers were accused of attempting to rape a German woman. The following day another attempted rape was reported in Bottrop, where a fifteen-year-old girl was followed by a French soldier. She was rescued by three German men who fought the soldier off and helped her home. On 31 January, a nineteen-year-old German woman was followed home by a French soldier in the small town of Annen to the south-east of Bochum. When she tried to run away he caught up with her and sexually assaulted her before she managed to fight him off and escape. In each of these cases protests were sent to the French authorities but no prosecutions followed. In Bottrop, the German police led the investigation. However, when they were unable to identify a suspect, the French military declared that the investigation had to end. In a sign of things to come, the initial French military response to allegations of sexual misconduct on the part of French troops was to question their veracity. It would not be long before sexual violence on the part of French and Belgian soldiers would become one of the most hated aspects of the occupation.[11]

French prime minister Raymond Poincaré had launched the occupation with strong parliamentary and public backing, which gave his decision legitimacy but which also made it harder to abandon the occupation once it failed to deliver on his initial goals. On 11 January 1923, as soldiers made their way into the Ruhr, in the French Chamber of Deputies the measure was approved by a margin of 476 to eighty-six – a huge vote of confidence for a politician that the British foreign secretary Lord Curzon called 'that horrid little man'. Poincaré delivered speeches claiming that France had to act to ensure that it received compensation for the devastation that its regions had suffered during the First World War and to prevent its victory being stolen from it 'bit by bit'. Meanwhile, French propaganda justified the occupation as a limited mission, as a team of French and Belgian engineers and mining experts –

formally known as MICUM (Inter-Allied Mission for Control of Factories and Mines) – set out to examine whether Germany was truly complying with their demands for payment of reparations in kind. Defending France's isolation in going ahead with the policy, Poincaré added that if the British had made a reasonable suggestion, or if the Americans had offered to cut inter-Allied debt, then France could have reduced its demands on Germany. He even added that it might not be too long before the frustrated British would join the French in the Ruhr. In any case, he was adamant that France had no choice but to act.[12]

Poincaré had made his decision to occupy the Ruhr over the course of 1922. After the signing of the Rapallo Treaty in April of that year, the French prime minister was furious. When Wirth's government sent a request for a two-year moratorium on reparations payments on 12 July 1922, Poincaré's position hardened even further. That day he asked Marshal Foch to deliver a military plan for the occupation of the Ruhr and requested him to co-ordinate the preparations. The measures that France would demand of Germany now extended to the introduction of a new German currency, as well as further financial reforms and the creation of a truly independent central bank. Until such reforms took effect, Poincaré intended to take control of 'real deposit payments' – code for the seizure of tax income, state mines and customs duties in the Rhineland. Not only did he mean to create a new customs border, turning the occupied Rhineland into a distinct economic area separate from the rest of Germany, he also proposed that France would gain majority ownership (60 per cent) of large chemical companies located to the west of the Rhine, thus taking control of most of the German chemical industry which was heavily concentrated in this region. In addition, in order to stop German delays to reparations payments to France, he wanted 26 per cent of the value of German exports to be paid in hard currency, as well as taking ownership of state-owned forests and mines on the Rhine and in the Ruhr and across Germany.[13]

At the start of August 1922, Poincaré brought a new set of hardline proposals for dealing with Germany to a meeting of Allied heads of government in London. The London negotiations ended a week later without agreement. The British cabinet described Poincaré's plan as 'ridiculous and insulting'. Even Belgium opposed it, viewing it as an obvious attempt to remove the Rhineland from Germany. When he left London, Poincaré told the French press that he did so 'empty-handed, but with his hands free'. Almost as soon as he got back to Paris, he called a special meeting of the French cabinet. It was chaired by the president, Alexandre Millerand, and both Foch and Degoutte were invited. There is no record of what was said at the meeting, but everything points towards it being the moment when the principle of occupying the Ruhr was agreed.[14]

Before France could act, however, it would not only need to craft a plan for the occupation, but would also need to make a show of having exhausted all diplomatic opportunities for co-operation. While the plan for the military occupation was being drawn up and debated, from September to December 1922 Franco-German diplomatic and business negotiations continued, though proposals were repeatedly rejected as unacceptable to France and decisions were pushed to future meetings. This continuing diplomacy has nevertheless given rise to disagreement among historians. Some put the date of Poincaré's ultimate arrival at the point of no return in September, others suggest that it wasn't until the end of November, whereas another school of thought suggests that, as the planned date for the actual occupation in January 1923 got closer, Poincaré started to get cold feet and embarked on genuine efforts to find a diplomatic solution in Brussels and London in December 1922 and January 1923.

Important as the diplomatic process may have been, the French prime minister faced a more fundamental conundrum. France's financial power had been fundamentally weakened by the costs of the First World War, yet its military power remained exceptionally strong. This disjuncture created pressure for the French leader to use the area where he had power to reinforce the area where his power was missing. Having grown up in an era when France was still a great imperial power, Poincaré faced a stark choice. He could respond to hostile acts like the Rapallo Treaty by demonstrating that French power still existed, or he could give way to Wirth and admit that France was a great power no longer. As the history of Europe's empires during the twentieth century shows clearly, it is a lot harder for politicians to admit to post-imperial powerlessness than it is for them to attempt to deliver military solutions to political and economic problems. Poincaré chose to be an imperial statesman and sent in the troops. His decision would set in motion a series of radicalizing processes that would almost destroy Weimar democracy, while fundamentally weakening France's international and economic power.

The possibility of a French invasion was well known, but when it finally occurred, Germany's political and military decision-makers had no clear plan as to how they might respond. Days before the invasion, the chief of the Reichswehr advised Cuno's government that military resistance was not an option. The only hope was to find a policy that would satisfy German nationalism at home, while presenting Germany as the victim abroad, in the hope that eventually British and American pressure might end the occupation. Cuno settled on 'passive resistance'. In order to 'resist the occupation passively', Germans in the Ruhr were to refuse to comply with the occupiers' demands, as far as was possible without engaging in physical violence. They were to continue to follow German law, which remained in force in the occupied territory.[15]

The occupation transformed Cuno from the unelected leader of a non-political technocratic government into the political focal point of a nation rallying in a time of crisis.

Amid the euphoria, the risk that passive resistance would ruin Germany economically in a matter of weeks or months was swept away on a tide of nationalist cheering. The mood was not to last, but many commentators then and since have compared the Reichstag session held on 13 January 1923 to the speech given by Kaiser Wilhelm on 4 August 1914 when he declared a political truce between all Germans that was meant to last for the duration of the war. In both 1914 and 1923, it was a hugely emotional moment: the point when the bitter political rows that had divided socialists from nationalists, Protestants from Catholics, north from south, were supposedly set aside to allow everyone to rally behind the cause of the nation at war. And for a time it worked. When it was announced in the Reichstag on 13 January 1923, the policy of passive resistance received the backing of an overwhelming majority of German deputies.[16]

Only a few politicians dissented. They tried to sound alarm bells, warning that passive resistance would lead to Germany's economic ruin and that it was better to recognize the power imbalance and concede to French demands. Their warnings would prove prescient but few were listening to them at the time. Even Gustav Stresemann, the politician who would finally end the policy on 26 September 1923 after replacing Cuno as chancellor, was initially among its most vocal supporters. On 13 January 1923, he declared France's goal to be the removal of the Rhineland from the German Empire and the acquisition of the industrial power of the Ruhr for France. He called the invasion a blatant breach of international law and demanded that Germans unite to resist it.[17]

To show that the German public was behind Cuno's government, the following day was declared a national day of mourning. For the duration of Sunday, 14 January 1923, the sale of alcohol was forbidden, flags were flown at half-mast and across Germany people were called upon to protest against the occupation. In the Königsplatz, the square in front of the Reichstag in Berlin (now known as the Platz der Republik), up to half a million people gathered for an anti-French protest that had been organized by the parties of the right and centre – the Social Democrats refused to join them. As was common practice at demonstrations of this scale, which did not have the necessary sound amplification to allow the entire audience to listen to a single speaker, eighteen different speakers addressed the crowd at separate points around the square.[18]

Stresemann spoke at the Victory Column. As he stood there on the Königsplatz in the cold of a Berlin January, before pleading for greater national unity, he told nationalist protestors that the 'formerly mighty Germany' had lost the First World War because 'we didn't remain united until our last breath'. At the end of the demonstration, the crowd roared their approval for a statement that condemned the occupation as the 'monstrous rape of the German people', and called on Germans to refuse 'to do slave labour for the peace-breakers under the shadow of their bayonets'. There were further demonstrations across Germany. In Munich, the Bavarian prime minister, Eugen von Knilling, promised that Bavaria would be loyal to Germany during the crisis and added that a day of 'righteous retribution' would soon come when a united Germany would take revenge on France. When he reflected on the demonstrations that took place that day, Cuno thought that Germans were living through a time when 'the fate of the people matters more to those people themselves than to the government'.[19]

For German supporters of Weimar democracy, the invasion created an impossible political dilemma: any move they made stood to empower the nationalist far right. From the very beginning of the occupation, German supporters of democracy knew that the anti-republican right held the advantage, having always maintained that military strength was the only way for Germany to deal with its enemies. After all of their efforts to forge a new European order based on co-operation, Germany's pro-democratic parties now faced the dilemma of how to oppose the French without empowering a new wave of anti-republican nationalism.[20]

On the 'day of mourning', Berlin's Social Democrats tried to escape this problem by organizing separate demonstrations for their party members. They argued that they could not share the same stage as several, if not all, of the speakers at the Königsplatz. At the end of January, a speaker at a rally in Berlin summed up the Social Democratic Party (SPD) leadership's dilemma:

The German workforce doesn't sing 'The Watch on the Rhine' or 'We want a victorious triumph over France', but through their discipline they will know how to counter the enemy, who are armed to the teeth, through passive resistance and, if need be, through strike action.[21]

The invasion also left Germans feeling as though they were being treated like a colony. The day after the protests, the editor of the *Berliner Tageblatt*, Theodor Wolff, called on Germans to prepare to make sacrifices and demanded order, unity and discipline. He warned that if they did not do so, Germany would be treated like a French colony. In the *Vossische Zeitung*, a liberal newspaper read by Berlin's political elite, another leading liberal commentator, Georg Bernhard, was adamant that there could be no compromises 'so long as French machine guns support martial law in Essen'. He added that France would have to choose 'the politics of the bayonet or the politics of the plough', or between 'Poincaré and Europe'. He didn't say what he thought would happen if the French stuck with Poincaré.[22]

Days after his arrival in the Ruhr, Erich Dombrowski was still dumbfounded by the sight of French soldiers. He looked at 'trains with howitzers, machine guns, vehicles, ambulances and floodlights', while 'small and large groups of French *poilus* [the French equivalent of the British term 'Tommy' or the American term 'Doughboy', the nickname given to American infantrymen during the First World War] roamed the streets'. In the trams he was astounded to see separate sections reserved for French officers, while 'the population crams and pushes into the other cars like on the Berlin metro'. One school after another was being transformed into a barracks, and he sensed the local population's bitterness worsening.[23]

On 20 January 1923, visiting the French military headquarters at Bredeney, Dombrowski marvelled at the extent of the French occupation. They had commandeered all public buildings, including all local schools, erected several checkpoints, and French army cars and trucks, as well as groups of *poilus*, were constantly coming and going. That morning, the weather was wet. In front of the town hall, which was now the French administrative headquarters, Dombrowski noticed how each time an officer entered the building, a *poilu* appeared with a mop and cleaned the floor. It would be a lot harder, he remarked, to erase the stains left by the decision to occupy the Ruhr militarily.[24]

Shortly after 10.30 a.m., Dombrowski caught sight of one of the most significant developments since the French and Belgian occupation had begun. A group of cars stopped outside the town hall. The six passengers were all important industrial figures; the most famous of them, Fritz Thyssen, the acting head of the Thyssen family business, was known across and beyond Germany. They entered the town hall accompanied by French gendarmerie, but when they came out, just five minutes later, they were under arrest. They had been detained for refusing to deliver coal and coke to the French. When they left the building, the five leading industrialists were treated like ordinary criminals, accompanied by armed French soldiers and officers. From this point on, they were known as the German 'mine owners'. Even German liberals called them 'martyrs'.[25]

Since Cuno had declared passive resistance a week earlier, the nature of the relationship between the occupiers and the population of the Ruhr had grown increasingly tense. In reality, it was a three-way affair: the French military occupiers had to deal with the German civil servants who represented the state and controlled state-owned business in the occupied region, as well as with private civilians and privately owned industry. It very quickly became apparent that the French and Belgians would not immediately achieve their stated goals. On 15 January, the day after the mass demonstrations, the German government banned the export of coal to France. On 19 January, a joint proclamation from the federal government and the state governments of Prussia, Bavaria and Hessen instructed all civil servants in the occupied region to refuse to obey the instructions of the occupation forces. They justified this on legal grounds, claiming that the occupation itself was a breach of both the Treaty of Versailles and international law. On the same day, railway workers were ordered to refuse to load coke and coal onto trains belonging to the French. On 21 January, the German Association of Iron and Steel Industrialists cancelled existing contracts and refused to pay for ore that was sent from France to Germany. This measure was intended to depress the French heavy industry sector.[26]

The French responded in turn. On 18 and 19 January, French soldiers, supported by Belgians whose policy at this stage was to follow the French lead, either occupied or surrounded Prussian state-owned mines, demanding that their works' councils resume the delivery of reparations coal. The presence of armed soldiers radicalized workers, whose opposition drew on a long tradition of working-class hostility to militarism in the Ruhr. Dombrowski witnessed a stand-off following French soldiers' threat to blow up parts of the mining machinery in the Bergmannsglück colliery in Recklinghausen if miners refused to co-operate. After they made this threat, he said, 'The anger of the working class was unlimited.'[27]

The arrests of German civilians and officials occurred in parallel. In Buer, Westerholt and parts of Gelsenkirchen, French soldiers occupied mines and arrested several directors including Oberbergrat Wilhelm Ahrens and the president of the Mining Commission in Recklinghausen, Otto Raiffeisen. They were among the first German leaders arrested. On 18 January, the president of the state tax office in Düsseldorf, Friedrich Schlutius, was arrested by the French for refusing to hand over documents to the occupation authorities. Lower-profile arrests included that of a German police officer who refused to salute a French officer on the same day. On 20 January, trade unions and the SPD demanded both the release of those arrested so far and the withdrawal of all soldiers from the mines.[28]

As much as all of these events contributed to a hardening of mentalities on both sides, the arrest of Fritz Thyssen and the other five leading industrialists hiked tensions to a new level. Thyssen had recently been elected to represent the German mining industry in talks with the French. He had sat across the table as a negotiator from the officers who had now ordered his arrest. His fate was symbolic of the fate of the occupied Ruhr: if Thyssen could be thrown in jail at the behest of the French military, then anyone in the region might share the same fate.

The actions of the mine owners had created a huge problem for the occupiers. Before the French and Belgian soldiers arrived in the Ruhr, the Rhine-Westphalian Coal Syndicate, which brought together private and state-owned mines in a single organization that together controlled 70–80 per cent of the coal supply in Germany, moved its headquarters and six hundred staff out of Essen to the German port city of Hamburg, 350 kilometres to the north. All of its records went with it in fifteen lorries. Without these records, French and Belgian engineers and mining experts had no way of showing that German mines were deliberately under-producing in order to avoid payment of reparations in kind – the formal reason given for the Ruhr occupation. They also had no way of knowing the precise details of how the German mining industry worked, which was vital if they wanted to control its production.[29]

The fate of the mine directors led to a mobilization against the occupation on a scale that no one could have predicted. Almost as soon as Fritz Thyssen had been arrested, the Thyssen general works' council threatened to cease production if he was not immediately released. By 23 January, *Vorwärts* was able to report that not a single mine whose director had been arrested was still working. The representatives of the Polish workers at the Thyssen works at Hamborn added their weight to the demands for Thyssen's release, smashing any French hopes that Polish migrant workers might side with the occupiers. The protest strikes continued for three days. The works' councils at mines owned by Hugo Stinnes, organizations that brought together labour union leaders to negotiate and often argue with management, also protested after the arrest of general director of Stinnes' mines, Walter Spindler, and joined the Thyssen workers in striking. Further support was provided by German telephone operators who refused to put through French calls, and the German post, which rejected co-operation with the French.[30]

After their arrest, Fritz Thyssen and the other industrialists were taken by car to Düsseldorf, then by train to Mainz. Along the way there were spontaneous protests at stations as their train passed through. After they were transferred to prison, their status afforded them two concessions: their hair was not cut, as was the normal practice, and they were permitted to keep their watches. Other than this, they were treated like common criminals. All their possessions were confiscated, they were placed in dirty single cells and, according to German reports, they were prevented from speaking with their defence lawyers for a full two days. They were not permitted to use the toilet on the floor of their prison but instead had to use a bucket in their cells, which was only cleaned when they received their food. It took several requests before they were eventually given soap and towels.[31]

This treatment helped turn the mine owners' imprisonment into a propaganda victory for the campaign of passive resistance. In addition to public demonstrations in the Ruhr, it produced a wave of condemnation across Germany. The Social Democratic *Vorwärts* praised the workers for showing solidarity with Fritz Thyssen, a man who had gained notoriety the previous year for his opposition to the eight-hour working day. The newspaper claimed that the protests were a reminder that there was no basis to their opponents' claims that the left had no fatherland. On 22 January, Dombrowski described telegrams and letters of support arriving at the Thyssen works from all over Germany and summed up the dilemma facing the French: they could occupy and control the region with military power, but they could not force railway workers and miners to work, and they had no mechanism to deal with the problems that would occur if the workers decided to protect the captains of industry. Cuno's message was even simpler: 'We are proud and confident that our workers, employers and officials are equally loyal to the state and nation. The more brutal the violence, the stronger our authority and hope.'[32]

A military court tried the mine owners in Mainz on 24 January 1923. While the trial was under way, large crowds of protestors gathered outside and sang nationalist songs which could be heard in the courtroom. The industrialists' chief defence lawyer, Friedrich Grimm, argued that there was no legal basis for the case. The French seizure of privately or state-owned mines, coal, coke and other materials was not supported by existing international law, the Treaty of Versailles, the agreement for the occupation of the Rhineland or French state law. As a consequence, he demanded that there should be no punishment for German individuals who refused to comply with the occupiers' demands. He warned the judges that the eyes of the world were upon them, before finishing with a piece of strongly nationalist rhetoric: 'Punish us if you think you can judge us, but we will resist, we will always resist!' While all the German lawyers at the trial contested the legality of the occupation itself, the defendants' French lawyer, Leclerc, argued that the punishment of individuals was illegal. He told the judges that 'the reputation of French justice is in jeopardy. I warn you: do not demean the judiciary in the service of military force.'[33]

After two and a quarter hours, the judges found the six men guilty of failing to carry out a requisition order, though not guilty of 'refusal to deliver coal'. Each of the accused was punished with a fine that was set at twice the value of the coal that they had refused to hand over. None of them was given a custodial sentence and at the end of the trial they were free to leave.[34]

Outside, the cars sent to convey the freed captains of industry away struggled to move through the crowds celebrating their defiance. Most of the defendants, as well as Grimm and the other lawyers, took a train north back into the occupied Ruhr. Along the way it was greeted by celebrating crowds and nationalist demonstrations. Young girls are supposed to have thrown flowers at the defendants, while elderly working-class men were reported to have had tears in their eyes. The rector of Cologne University addressed a crowd close to the city's cathedral, claiming that 'German science' had helped to defeat 'French arbitrariness'. When the train reached Düsseldorf, French soldiers blocked many of the access routes to the station. In Essen there were further celebrations. Cuno's telegram to Fritz Thyssen thanked him for his loyalty and celebrated his return from 'brutal violence'.[35]

For the occupying French, it was a public-relations disaster. The British ambassador in Berlin, Lord D'Abernon, thought that the French had 'instigated a greater degree of collaboration between the political parties and classes of Germany than could have been achieved by any other means'. The *Kölnische Zeitung* compared the arrested men to Germany's war heroes from the First World War and claimed that the case had reawakened German pride. Thyssen himself returned to Duisburg in a special train on 25 January, where he was given a hero's welcome. Large crowds waited for him throughout the night, singing 'The Watch on the Rhine' as he disembarked from his carriage. The wave of nationalism gripping the Ruhr and beyond was only growing stronger.[36]

Subsequent trials continued to translate into propaganda victories for the Germans. When Otto Raiffeisen and Friedrich Schlutius were found guilty of refusing to follow French orders, they were sentenced to one year's imprisonment with reprieve and then expelled from the occupied zone. Driven into unoccupied Germany, they were deposited at the side of an unfamiliar country road and left to fend for themselves. Protest notes sent to General Joseph Denvignes, the French chief delegate for German civil administration, accused the French of treating the deported men in a way that was beneath a 'nation of culture' and demanded that the 'former enemies' uphold the values of 'chivalry'. A few weeks later Cuno even referred to their case in a Reichstag speech. Within weeks, what began as the expulsion of a handful of individuals would end with the expulsion of tens of thousands of state employees and their families during the spring of 1923. Once expelled, officials and their families were not permitted to return to the occupied zone.[37]

Two days after the trial, in the Reichstag, Karl Helfferich, whose public criticism of Rathenau the day before his murder had drawn the ire of so many, announced that his party would 'defend our fatherland as it is'. When he said those words, even members of Rathenau's German Democratic Party applauded. It was one of several speeches that demanded an internal political truce so that the French invasion could be opposed more effectively. In response, the Social Democrat Rudolf Breitscheid announced that his party would not support such a truce. The SPD recognized that encouraging a spirit of nationalism in this way would translate into support for Germany's nationalist parties, all of which opposed or only barely tolerated the republic. That was exactly what Helfferich wanted and why it was so easy for him to declare a pause in his battle to overthrow the republic. He knew that the surge in nationalism could only benefit his style of politics. In a Reichstag speech,

Breitscheid even stated that Helfferich should personally thank Poincaré.[38]

Yet if even 'passive' resistance was still a form of nationalist mobilization, was there any means by which the SPD could oppose the French? Breitscheid called the invasion 'one of the worst conceivable attacks against German democracy and the German republic', but struggled to reframe opposition to the occupation in non-nationalist terms. Some tried to frame it as anti-imperialism or a continuation of the class struggle as the German working class resisted French capitalism. Others tried to frame it as a battle 'for the preservation of the German republic and its liberal organisations'.[39]

Poincaré cared little about German liberalism: in the short term he meant to extract timber, coke and coal from the Ruhr, and his broader goal was to weaken Germany permanently. By the end of January, he had decided that it was time to implement harsher measures. Senior German officials in the railway and postal services were to be expelled from the Ruhr and customs barriers were to be created on the eastern frontiers of the occupied region and along the bridges and ports of the Rhine. In early February, the chief of the Inter-Allied Rhineland High Commission, General Paul Tirard, was ordered to proceed with the economic separation of the Rhineland and the Ruhr from unoccupied Germany. In Munich there was one clear winner. Just days before the invasion the Bavarian prime minister, Eugen von Knilling, shared the same stage as a rabble-rouser with a growing following. His rhetoric had stumbled on a political moment that favoured it as never before. The man was Adolf Hitler.[40]

5

Hitler's First Victory

On 11 January 1923, just hours after French soldiers reached the centre of Essen, Hitler spoke before a crowd of cheering supporters in Munich, bragging that his movement had always predicted that such an invasion would come. He suggested that the Ruhr would be permanently lost. But crucially, unlike those calling for national unity and a new truce that even ardent anti-republican conservatives like Karl Helfferich supported, Hitler went on the offensive.

It was the Social Democrats who were the true enemy, he barked. The SPD had created a world in which 'every foreigner is allowed to abuse Germany with impunity'. The 'November criminals', as he called them, not the French, were the 'real enemy'. There could be no national resurrection until they were done away with. At the end of his speech, he demanded the formation of a 'revenge army', which would bring the 'criminals to account'. He warned the Social Democrat Erhard Auer, the former home secretary of Bavaria and now chairman of the Bavarian SPD and editor of the *Münchener Post*: 'The Furies are after you, you who preached "national unity", although your national solidarity was broken in Germany's darkest hour!'[1]

When Hitler spoke, he did so to a crowd who could remember the violent events that had occurred at the end of the short-lived period of Communist rule in Munich in April 1919. Estimates suggest that between six hundred and one thousand or more people were killed in Munich between 30 April and 6 May 1919 (the final figure depends upon where one draws the city boundaries). The majority were civilians, fifty-eight were soldiers on the side of the anti-Soviet forces and ninety-three were members of the Communist Red Army. As part of this bloodletting, the most notorious atrocity occurred on 30 April, when ten hostages were shot dead by members of the Red Army of the Bavarian Soviet Republic. One of them, Haila Gräfin von Westarp, was a member of the nationalist and antisemitic Thule Society. Rumours circulated that, prior to her death, she had been raped by Soviet soldiers or that she and the other victims had been brutally tortured before their murders. Other significant atrocities included the execution of fifty-three Russian prisoners of war on 2 May and the murder of twenty-one Catholic citizens in the Prinz-Georg-Palais on 6 May.[2]

The anti-Communist backlash had bequeathed a rightward tilt to Bavarian politics. By 1923, the Bavarian People's Party was the largest political party in the Bavarian Landtag, the state parliament, holding sixty-four of the 129 seats. It was strongly Catholic, but unlike the national Centre Party, which included figures like Wirth who were committed to the republic, the Bavarian People's Party was strongly monarchist, encompassing positions so pro-Bavarian that they might be considered separatist. The Bavarian People's Party looked on with interest as the street politics of the patriotic associations became more prominent in the early Weimar Republic. In Bavaria, these organizations existed either as local branches of national organizations or as entities that were unique to Bavaria. Most of them had their origins as anti-revolutionary organizations that opposed further change in 1919 and longed for the return of the monarchy. Most were also strongly nationalist and antisemitic. Of the so-called Associations for the German Race, the most important were the League of Bayern and the Reich (Bund Bayern und Reich), the Reichsflag (Reichsflagge) and the Oberland League (Bund Oberland). These were paramilitary groups that brought their members together to march, sing patriotic songs and prepare for taking revenge on the republic at an unspecified point in the future. The Nazi Party was both their ally and their rival: its paramilitary wing, the SA, wanted to co-operate with them but also to steal their members. The crucial difference between the Nazis and the other paramilitary organizations was that, at the start of 1923,

Hitler's star was rising, whereas none of the other organizations had a leader who could even start to compete with him.

When the French marched into the Ruhr, like so many others, Hitler compared the situation facing Germany there to that of a non-European colony. In his racist words: 'France rates our Germany as less than a Negro state' (the term he used was *Negerstaat*). Such racist rhetoric was hardly unprecedented in the political culture of the early Weimar Republic. Since the publication of the terms of the Versailles Treaty in May 1919, a range of German political leaders, including liberal supporters of the republic, had made similar suggestions, but with French and Belgian forces occupying the Ruhr and potentially permanently seizing its economic resources, the argument grew in importance, as similar statements by politicians and journalists who had nothing in common with Hitler in the spring of 1923 show.[3]

Cuno's day of national mourning and anti-French demonstrations on Sunday, 14 January left Hitler especially angry. In Munich, a large anti-French demonstration had been organized by the United Patriotic Associations at the Königsplatz. Hitler had intended to join the speakers there. But he later claimed that at the last minute Bavarian interior minister Franz Xaver Schweyer decided to stop him speaking to appease the French. That evening in the beer hall Hitler repeated his attacks on the 'November criminals', blaming them for the situation. The following evening at a Nazi Party meeting in the Café Neumayr, where as many as two or three hundred people were unable to find a seat due to overcrowding, he continued upon the same themes: the internal political truce that the Kaiser declared at the start of the war was the real cause of Germany's defeat in the First World War, and calls for a new truce and a national united front to oppose the 1923 occupation were rubbish.[4]

Instead of declaring a national day of mourning, Hitler claimed that the French would have really taken notice if the Germans had begun 'to hang their traitors in rows'. It was one of several 'gallows' and 'guillotine' moments in Hitler's public speaking: points in time when he asked his supporters to join him in fantasizing about killing

their opponents, calling for them to be strung up or for their heads
to roll. When he did this from the stage, his supporters called out
phrases like 'Hanging!' In one typical episode, on 18 January, he
announced:

> We know very well that if the others take the helm our heads
> will roll in the sand. But this one thing I cry: if we get to the
> helm, then woe to the others, then their heads will be the ones
> to roll! One of us will be left on the ground, the wheel will roll
> over one of us (thunderous applause)!

It was never a secret who this referred to. As Hitler stated repeatedly: the Jews are our 'common mortal enemy'. In his words: 'While
others are blowing out written and spoken protests against France,
the deadly enemy of the German race is still within the walls of
the empire and continues his subversive craft.'[5]

For the remainder of January, Hitler continued to attack the
'united front', initially letting 'passive resistance' go unmentioned.
In part this was because the term, which later became so central
to the way 1923 was remembered, took a few weeks to establish
itself. But beginning in February, as passive resistance became
established both as a practice in the Ruhr and as a war cry in
unoccupied Germany, he started to rail against it.

Everything about 'passive resistance' appalled Hitler. Pacifism or
passivity went against the very essence of his political raison d'être.
For him, there could never be an internal or external truce. Violence
was sacred to him. Already at this time, his conception of politics
was based upon having the willpower to go on the offensive, regardless of any material or strategic limitations. This conception would
remain fundamental to his decision-making for the rest of his life.
Like so much else in Hitler's thinking, its origin lies in the First
World War. He believed that if Germany's wartime rulers had
followed his maxim in 1914 instead of declaring a truce, they would
have gone on the offensive against the 'internal enemy' and the
war would never have been lost.

As the occupation of the Ruhr continued, Hitler called for

violence again and again. He promised an audience of the National Association of German Officers in the Wittelsbacher Garten in Munich on 20 February that the 'Elimination' of Germany's rulers 'would not be civil war, but justice in a criminal court'. Two weeks later, at a meeting of the SA in the Kindl-Keller beer hall in Munich, he added that 'a truly national government should whip up national passion', and that the government 'should excite the nation and fill the lampposts with hanged November traitors'. When he quoted this speech in the Bavarian state parliament in April, just a few days after Hitler's birthday, the Social Democrat Alwin Saenger called upon every politician present to ignore their party affiliations and ask themselves: were these the words of a German patriot? Saenger called it 'the stupid talk of a mentally ill person'. In times of national crisis in German history, Saenger insisted, Germans had never turned to 'psychopaths' to be their national leaders. Saenger just could not fathom that politics in Bavaria had entered a new phase of visceral hatred. He still expected reasoned argument to win out against the emotional politics of Hitler's discourse. Others were more troubled. After it included reports of Hitler's speeches that amplified his message without sufficiently criticizing it, Ludwig Holländer, a director and executive board member of the Central Association of German Jews, demanded that Jewish businesses should cease advertising with the *Münchener Neueste Nachrichten*. He called the newspaper the 'hidden central organ of the Hitler people'. It was the same conundrum that journalists face today: how can they comment on the activity of populist leaders without amplifying their message and fuelling their egos?[6]

On the weekend of 26–7 January 1923, following the model of the German Day at Coburg the previous October, the Nazis' first party convention, later described as the first Nazi Party rally, was planned to take place in Munich. The event would draw party members and supporters from all over Germany, including from parts of the Reich where the Nazi Party was banned under the Law for the Protection of the Republic, as well as from the Sudetenland and South Tyrol. On the first day of the party convention, twelve separate rallies were planned in beer halls across Munich. After Saturday night's festivities, Sunday morning was to start with a two-and-a-half-hour ceremony during which the party's flags were to be 'sworn in', a practice that mixed military tradition with political symbolism. At lunchtime, attendees were to gather in the Kindl-Keller and Hofbräuhaus beer halls for lunch and celebrations that were planned to continue into the night. Mass accommodation had been organized for all of those who travelled from outside Munich.[7]

In the weeks leading up to the rally, Nazi Party members and Stormtroopers had been involved in several violent incidents. They had torn down and destroyed the republic's flag that flew over the train station. They had organized regular protests outside luxury hotels in central Munich, including the Four Seasons, where members of the Allied commissions to Germany had stayed. In the case of the Hotel Grünwald, they had gone as far as smashing in the windows and the dining room.[8] They had held demonstrations without police permission and attacked and insulted 'dissenters' with increasing frequency. In the words of Munich's police president, Eduard Nortz, who sympathized with the Nazi movement, describing it as having a 'patriotic core' that nobody could dispute, the 'increase in passion at the public meetings of the National Socialists' had reached such a level that it had become normal for them to thunderously demand daily attacks on 'Jews and members of the Social Democratic Party'. Yet the only interference its organizers faced from the Bavarian state was that they had been refused permission to use the Königsplatz for demonstrations.[9]

That changed on 24 January, when Schweyer's Interior Ministry instructed Munich's police to ban all outdoor events that were planned as part of the party convention. That meant no marching, no parades and, crucially, no swearing in of the Nazi movement's flags. If the ban was upheld, the groups of Nazis and Stormtroopers travelling to Munich from northern Germany, South Tyrol and the Sudetenland would not be permitted to march in formation through the streets of Munich. Walking in single file or in small groups with no flags or music, surrounded by police, on their way to indoor demonstrations was no substitute. The whole point of spending hours on trains to Munich was to march through the city upon their arrival, drink and feel a sense of belonging and power. The Italian Fascists they idolized would never have tolerated such interference.[10]

When the news reached the Nazi Party offices in Munich, it was met with 'great agitation', in the words of Richard Dingeldey, who, together with Max Amann, then the party's 'Reich leader for the press', immediately went to Police President Nortz to lobby him to reverse the decision – something that Nortz could not do, as the decision rested with the Bavarian government. Nevertheless, they warned Nortz that the implementation of the ban would prove impossible: too many guests were already on their way to Munich, they claimed. Once they arrived, they would expect to be welcomed in 'a certain joyous form', including 'music and flags greeting the trains', and then to march in 'closed ranks' to their meeting places and accommodation. Dingeldey and Amann told Nortz that if they were banned from doing this, their 'bitterness' would be 'limitless'. Nortz telephoned the ministerial adviser Zeltmeier in the Ministry of the Interior. He suggested that Dingeldey and Amann go there to repeat their message to him, and Zeltmeier agreed to stay in his office until they arrived.

At this point, Hitler stormed in, 'obviously in great excitement'. He was especially angry at the way that he had found out about the ban at the 'very last hour'. In Dingeldey's words:

> He passionately expressed his indignation at the ministerial instruction that had been communicated to him, emphasized the patriotic attributes of his party, and promised that one day history would judge these petty bureaucratic harassments of his patriotic movement for freedom.

Dingeldey said that he 'kept talking himself into a frenzy'.

Nortz listened, then repeated the message he had already given Amann and Dingeldey: Hitler should go to the Bavarian Ministry of the Interior and make the same points. Gripped by furious anger,

Hitler exploded in threats. He wasn't going to do anything anymore. He had held his people, especially his Stormtroopers, under control. Now he was going to let them out to do whatever they wanted. The government could watch what would happen. He promised Nortz that his flag swearing-in was going to take place outside, whatever the circumstances. The government could bring out as many police and soldiers as they wanted. It was going to happen anyway. When the government forces opened fire to enforce the ban, Hitler would be at the front and he would be among the first to fall. But he promised Nortz that once the firing started, a 'red flood' would follow and the government would be 'finished' within two hours. They needed him more than he needed them: the resistance in the Ruhr would break down within a few weeks. Once that happened, Hitler promised, 'Then conditions will arise where the government will ask for our help, and no one shall come forward to support it.' His rant finished with a touch of Shakespeare: 'You'll see me at Philippi!'

For threatening insurrection and violence, Nortz could have had Hitler arrested on the spot. Just a week later, when these events were debated in the Bavarian parliament, Alwin Saenger demanded that Hitler should be charged with high treason. But Nortz was politically far too sympathetic to Hitler to prevent him from leaving the building that day. Instead, he advised Hitler to wait. According to Dingeldey, as this shouting match continued, Nortz told Hitler that

> one can speak about the question of demands to hold the November criminals to account. But this holding them to account could also take place in a way that would let everyone see which groups were preparing to exclude themselves from any future national uprising. When that happened it would be necessary to act against them by all means. After he heard this, Hitler told Nortz that 'none of his men would lift a foot or a finger in a national uprising until the November criminals were dealt with.' He warned him that there was 'no way that they would allow it for a second time that the people who stabbed us in the back could stay alive'.

Hitler then repeated his message to Nortz 'in short order' and left the building.[11]

Nortz informed the Bavarian government of these threats that night. The following day, after two meetings, at 1 p.m., the government took the decision to introduce a 'state of emergency' in Bavaria and ban the party convention altogether.[12]

But the decision did not last. The influential Nazi Party member Ernst Röhm came to Hitler's aid. He persuaded the state commander of the army in Bavaria, Otto von Lossow, to have a meeting with Hitler. During their encounter, Hitler promised Lossow that he would keep his men under control. Hitler and Röhm then met with former Bavarian prime minister Gustav Ritter von Kahr, who used his influence to help get the state of emergency withdrawn. Hitler was given permission to host six meetings, with certain restrictions. He also returned to Nortz, promising him that he would keep everyone under control. Nortz later remarked that it was clear that Hitler had been influenced by powerful individuals and 'that he wanted to vouch for the completely smooth running of the party congress with all his person and his honour'.

Following their meeting, Hitler knew that Nortz wasn't going to interfere even if he ignored the restrictions as soon as the party convention started. As such, he promptly did ignore them, hosting twelve meetings instead of six, and went ahead with the flag swearing-in and the march back into Munich as well. For Hitler's opponents, these events were a bitter blow.[13]

Just as Italian Fascism began with a 'war of flags', so too in Weimar the colours of the flag gave rise to violent clashes. The republic's founders chose the colours of the flag of the failed pro-democratic revolutionaries of 1848 as those of their republic: black, red and gold. This meant rejecting the old black, white and red flag of the German Empire: the Kaiser's colours. For the republic's founders, they had no place as the symbol of a state that the republic was created to replace. The Nazis faced the challenge of how to reject the republic's colours, while also pointing to the difference between them and the traditional anti-republican conservative movement – men like Hilferding, who wanted to see the monarchy and the imperial flag restored. They did this by taking the imperial flag's colours and remodelling them into a flag of their own: the black swastika in a white circle on a red ground.

This was the symbol that was being 'sworn in' at Hitler's party convention. The Munich-based goldsmith Otto Gahr, who was among the party's first members, designed the standards with Hitler's help, while the art on the standards was designed by the Munich-based embroiderer Auer. These were based on ancient Roman field standards and featured the words 'Germany, awake', taken from Dietrich Eckart's SA anthem, 'Storm Song'. The effort put into the creation of these symbols and their importance for the movement's future (by 1938, around six hundred had been made) were among the reasons that the 1923 party convention was so important to Hitler. Nazism might not have been a fully fledged political religion, but it did have aspects of religious ceremony and create a sense of community through symbols.[14]

Just two weeks before the Nazi Party convention took place, on 14 January, the centre of Munich was consumed by clashes over these very flags. On that Sunday, the trade unions organized a demonstration against the occupation of the Ruhr which overlapped with the nationalist protests. When the union demonstration ended, the workers formed a procession and began marching into the city centre carrying black, red and gold flags. In the centre of Munich, they crossed paths with the nationalists, who were appalled by the sight of the republic's colours. First came insults and shouting. When the trade unionists ended their demonstration with the cry 'Long live the republic!', it was met with boos and cries of 'Destroy it!' Nationalist demonstrators, including Nazis and supporters of the Freikorps Roßbach, an anti-republican paramilitary group that had existed since the revolution of 1918–19, charged at the republican flag-carriers, some swinging rubber batons as they did so. They tore down the flags and broke the flagpoles; according to trade unionists, the police supported them. The procession of trade unionists was forced to disperse at bayonet point, with some police officers calling them 'national traitors' and 'Jewish slaves'. For the Nazis involved, the flag wasn't just an important symbol. It was an instrument that helped them to believe that their violence had a special cleansing character.[15]

The Nazi flags were consecrated on Sunday, 28 January at the exercise fields known as the Marsfeld beside the Circus Krone, a wooden building used for various events including circus perform-ances. Two orchestras provided music. The ceremony began with one of Kaiser Wilhelm II's favourite songs, the Old Dutch prayer of thanksgiving 'We Gather Together', which was regularly performed at military displays in Imperial Germany and later during the Third Reich. As the orchestras played the presentation march, four new swastika standards were brought forward. They were black, white and red: 'on top was the swastika in a wreath, and at the end an eagle'. The flag-bearers brought the flags to the centre of the demon-stration and lowered them while the musicians played Eckart's 'Storm Song'. Hitler then called upon the assembled Stormtroopers to raise their hands and swear loyalty to the flags. In a short speech he called the republic's black, red and gold flag 'a Gessler hat' – a reference to Albrecht Gessler, a legendary fourteenth-century figure who is supposed to have forced his oppressed subjects to bow before his hat upon a flagpole, thus provoking the rebellion of Wilhelm Tell that was later popularized in the early nineteenth century, most famously by German national playwright Friedrich Schiller.

Speaking at the event, Hitler announced that the republic's flag had taken the place of Germany's once 'feared, proud flag' that was 'to us the most sacred thing'. The old flag had been torn down in November 1918. Hitler then claimed that 'another flag has flown over Germany's shame and regret', expressing his gratitude that the old imperial flag had not been 'sullied' with everything that had happened since the creation of the Weimar Republic. Then he explained that the new flag was intended for use in the 'interim period', but that it was 'a symbol of the future imperial flag, a promise not to rest until the fatherland had become free and great again'. The flag was sacred:

No one of that race, who are our enemies, and who have led us into greatest misery, no Jew, shall ever touch this flag. It shall fly ahead of us in our triumphant march across all Germany, and be the prototype for the new German national flag.[16]

When the ceremony ended, the assembled SA men began marching back towards the beer halls as planned. According to newspaper reports, there were several thousands of them, led by drummers and pipers. The procession contained four military bands and around eighty flags, with each SA section marching behind its own flag.

Two black flags stood out. One belonged to the Bund Oberland. The other was a swastika flag 'with a death's head in the middle of the cross'. The men marching behind it wore black armbands adorned with a death's head. They were the nucleus of the organization that would become the SS. Some of those marching sang a new version of the Ehrhardt Song – the song of Hermann Ehrhardt's II Marine Brigade that had been sung at the funeral of Rathenau's murderers. In place of the chorus 'They called us the Ehrhardt Brigade', they sang 'They called us Hitler's Stormtroopers.'[17]

A few days after the convention, Munich's chief of police commented that the Saturday night had been one of the quietest nights for Munich's police for a long time. His remarks were intended to justify the lifting of the state of emergency, but they are nonetheless an important part of the historical assessment of the party convention. At the end of the celebrations on the Saturday, according to press reports, speakers told the assemblies of Stormtroopers that they were to go to bed without carrying out any violence. Even Hitler's fiercest critics could not point to a significant act of violence committed by the Nazis during their party convention.

Defending his own conduct in the run-up to the lifting of the state of emergency, Nortz claimed that, even by just briefly showing its strength, the state had intimidated the Nazis into behaving. In contrast to the idea that the Nazis had Munich under their control during the convention, observers described seeing trucks of police crossing paths with trucks ferrying SA members. Nortz was adamant that, if it had been necessary, his men would have fired upon the Nazis, even as he admitted that some units had told him that they would not do so. The absence of a spectacular act of anti-state violence during the party convention was important: the Nazis had scored a 'moral' victory. Their party convention had (briefly) been banned because of the threat of violence and perhaps even a planned putsch. When there was no spectacular clash on Munich's streets during the convention, to Nazi sympathizers, the decision to ban it looked like an overreaction.

Amid all the marching, drinking and intimidation, the Nazi Party also held a traditional party assembly. It voted in favour of Hitler remaining as leader and gave him permission to choose his fellow leaders – an important stage in the cementing of the Führer cult within the party. During the Saturday night, the party meetings held in different locations in Munich also voted in favour of a single proclamation. In addition to condemning what they described as the lies that had led to the attempt to ban the party convention, they also announced a series of demands. These included the

immediate declaration of the invalidity of the peace treaty; cessation of delivery of all cash and materials; immediate currency reform; submission of a law for the protection of the fatherland; ruthless suppression of all traitors to the fatherland; immediate repeal of the protective laws; freedom for the defenders of the fatherland currently in prison; arrest of those November criminals who, as leaders, are to blame for our misfortune today; renewed demand for the accelerated intro-duction of the death penalty for usurers and smugglers.[18]

The party convention was the first victory for Hitler against the Bavarian state. By the end of January 1923, Nazi membership had risen to around twenty thousand. His leadership was what made the party stand out among the other paramilitary associations in Munich at the start of 1923. Other right-wing organizations like the League Bavaria and the Reich and the Oberland League may have had similar goals. But none of them had a Hitler at their head, using his charisma and talents as a speaker to drive it forward to the next battle.

6

The Escalation of Violence

On 2 February 1923, the shoemaker Heinrich Stockhorst was riding in a tram from Oberhausen towards Borbeck in Essen with his back towards the driver's cabin when two Belgian soldiers and a German ticket inspector began to argue. Stockhorst kept his head down and didn't turn around to look at what was happening. One of the Belgians drew his pistol and fired. The driver was hit twice but he managed to push the Belgian's gun away and the shots only grazed his arm. Stockhorst was shot dead.

The dispute had begun in unremarkable fashion: the ticket inspector refused to recognize the soldiers' coupons as valid for travel and told the driver to stop the tram so that he could force them off. But as the soldiers made their way to the front of the tram, one of them leaned into the driver's cabin and forcibly pulled the tram's accelerator, causing it to lurch forwards before suddenly stopping – the tram's safety mechanism was designed to prevent sudden changes in speed. As it did so, one of the soldiers started firing. Later, after they were arrested by the German police, the Belgians claimed that they had been fired at first. German witnesses contradicted that claim: they were adamant that no shots were fired.[1]

Stockhorst's death was part of a wider escalation of violence in February 1923. On 2 February, a school janitor named Haumann was shot at a French checkpoint in Brechten. Another man was killed on the same night after a French soldier started messing about with his revolver in a bar, causing it to discharge accidentally. On 5 February, a fourteen-year-old schoolgirl, Anna Schiffer, died after she was shot in the stomach by a French soldier at a train station in Düsseldorf. At the time, she was standing outside, looking through a glass window at French soldiers who were dancing inside a bar in the station. When he saw her, one of the soldiers raised his rifle and fired at her. Most witnesses agreed that it was an accident and that the soldier must have discharged his weapon by mistake. Her family later received the tiny sum of 150 marks in compensation from the occupation authorities.[2] A few days later in Gelsenkirchen, a police officer was shot dead by two French officers after he stopped their car when it was being driven with its lights out at night.[3]

The pattern of indiscriminate violence that began at the start of February continued for the next two months: February and March 1923 had the highest number of fatalities during the French and Belgian occupation of the Ruhr. As on so much else, French and German sources do not agree on the numbers killed. In these two months German sources suggest that fifty-eight people were killed, while a further forty-two received potentially fatal wounds caused by gunshots or bayonet strikes. Records held by the French put the figures slightly lower, but they do not dispute the basic trend: from the start of February, the occupying military became far more aggressive towards the civilian population. This increase in violence occurred in parallel with the introduction of harsher occupation measures at the behest of Poincaré and Degoutte.[4]

On 29 January, Degoutte ordered a heightened state of siege, which was followed by a ban on coal exports from the Ruhr to unoccupied Germany on 1 February. This was followed on 5 February by a new measure through which Degoutte claimed the right to overrule German legislation in the Ruhr, backtracking on an announcement made at the start of the occupation that German legislation would remain in place. By mid-February Degoutte's policies towards railway workers, police officers and civil servants had all grown harsher. He also decreed that all Germans working for the occupation authorities would be subject to military justice, making it easier for the occupiers to threaten German civil servants with 'fines, imprisonment and the expulsion of the family'. Further punitive economic measures included banning the export of all industrial products made in the Ruhr to unoccupied Germany, a severe blow to the region's manufacturing economy. On 17 February, the Germans announced countermeasures which included an order that forbade the local government from signing contracts with the occupation authorities. Public employees were also forbidden from any involvement with judicial proceedings started by the occupation forces, from publishing French or Belgian decrees, any involvement in taxation or providing any statistical information. On 18 February, Düsseldorf district president Walther Grützner, who was a member of the Social Democratic Party, was deported from the Ruhr into unoccupied Germany. A few days later, on 22 February, Degoutte ordered that if any German government minister set foot in the Ruhr, they were to face immediate arrest.[5]

As well as actual fatalities, there was a surge in non-life-threatening violence including vicious beatings of civilians with rifle butts and whips; among the victims were women, the disabled and the elderly. By mid-February, Erich Dombrowski, who continued to observe events astutely for the *Berliner Tageblatt*, described the occupier's rule as a 'tyranny' that had been created for the explicit purpose of torturing the Ruhr population into submission. The Social Democratic *Vorwärts* agreed with him, stating that the occupation had become a 'dictatorship of the riding crop and the revolver', whose goal was to 'shatter the population in body and mind'.[6]

Everywhere Dombrowski went he witnessed violence. He saw a schoolboy being brutally set upon by a group of soldiers who only stopped when a French officer intervened. He saw an elderly man punched in the face. Dombrowski thought the outbursts of violence signalled that the French had lost their nerve. In his words:

> The riding crop seemed to them the best means of instilling French culture into German men, women and children. At the slightest provocation they behaved like savages, lashed out, kicked, and shot their pistols as if they were in the Wild West.

Faced with this onslaught, Dombrowski thought that the mood of the population was now 'feverishly enraged'. He saw civilians attacking off-duty French soldiers and added that if French officers or soldiers sat visibly at the windows of cafés or restaurants it was never long before rocks were being thrown at them from a distance.[7]

When he wrote those words in mid-February, the occupation had managed to extract 60,000 tonnes of coal from the Ruhr, a meagre return compared to the nearly 2 million tonnes the French would have obtained had the occupation never occurred. But there could be no going back. Rather than admit that the occupation had not achieved its initial objectives, Poincaré dug in his heels. He was determined that his soldiers would have the time on the ground to force through French policies, regardless of the violence used. Cuno's government was equally determined that there could be no backing down on the German side. The result was an escalation in which violence became politics by other means.

This was especially the case with sexual violence on the part of the occupying troops. One of the most horrific cases occurred on 16 February, the same day that Dombrowski's words about French torture in the Ruhr appeared in print. At around 8 p.m., Josephine Malakert and her fiancé were pulling a cart with some furniture towards the Dellwig Bridge on their way to Bottrop when they were spotted by a group of six members of the occupation forces, made up of four French sailors, who were sent into the Ruhr to work on the canals and rivers, a French soldier who spoke fluent German and who was described as a translator, and a French officer. When the sailors and soldiers saw the couple in the distance, one of them fired a warning shot to tell them to stop, which they did. The sailors and translator then approached the couple and asked them for their papers. After her fiancé presented his, a soldier threatened him with a revolver and told him to leave. Malakert had no papers and was told to stay. She was then made to walk with the group along the road to Bottrop. After a few minutes one of them asked her if she would have sex with them. When she refused, they raped her repeatedly at gunpoint in a ditch. The officer was the only member of the group who did not participate actively in the rape. She later added that the first one 'came back when his comrades had finished'.[8]

We know about her ordeal because she testified to police in Bochum and gave further statements to the French gendarmerie as well as to German officials in Münster. There was some discrepancy between her statements as recorded by the different sides. The published version of her sworn statement to German investigators included the claim that her hands were tied behind her back for the duration of the rape. Records held by the French military contradict this. They also record her as having said: 'I did not defend myself, nor did I call for help. Only the man in uniform did not touch me.' In March, she apparently told German investigators in Münster:

I resisted their attempts at penetration. I wanted to scream too, but was told that if I opened my mouth I would be shot dead. The soldiers took me one after another. When one was done, the next came right up. I lay there without feeling. I still feel the heavy weight in my abdomen.[9]

In his comments on the case, Charles Auguste Jules Jacquemot, the French general in charge of the division occupying the area where the rape took place, questioned if Josephine Malakert really had been raped. He claimed that she had only pressed charges because she had been threatened by her fiancé that he would not marry her if she did not do so. Despite Jacquemot's attitude, the French investigation later charged all of the sailors with rape and the soldier with 'complicity in rape'. Two of the sailors were demoted and arrest warrants were issued for the others; however, the surviving files do not show if they were ever punished.

Although the French side did little to publicize the case or the half-hearted castigation of the perpetrators, the German Foreign Office made sure that the German population knew about the ordeal. Every French atrocity served as fresh ammunition against the occupation. But the news of every atrocity was also a reminder of the republic's weakness. The German Empire had been a great military power. From 1914 to 1918, even though they were defeated on French soil, German soldiers had protected German civilians from occupation and military violence. That memory presented a stark contrast to the republic's failure to offer any military resistance to the occupation in 1923.

Just a few weeks before Malakert's brutal rape, the Hamburg schoolteacher Luise Solmitz, who would later vote for the Nazis and celebrate Hitler's appointment as chancellor on 30 January 1933, captured her hatred of the French with the following words:

> even if we had thousands of words for repugnance, abhorrence, for not being able to understand something, it would not be enough. The only thing we can perhaps put into words, and which captures our hatred, is Kleist's 'Beat them to death! The Last Judgement will not seek your reasoning!'

Faced with the invasion, even before news of sexual violence and rape circulated among the population of unoccupied Germany, she longed for a German military response. Such longings only grew as the escalation of hatred worsened on both sides.[10]

On 7 February, French soldiers and officers went on a rampage in Recklinghausen. The trouble is supposed to have started after the French arrested German customs officers who refused to salute French officers. German accounts suggest that as soon as they were arrested, the German officers were badly beaten, triggering anti-French riots, which were said to have been led by a crowd that included off-duty German police officers. During the fighting that followed, French soldiers fought with protestors, allegedly brutally attacking them and even threatening elderly women by pointing their revolvers at them. Not long after the rioting began, French tanks rolled through the streets, forcing the crowds to disperse. But the violence did not stop there.[11]

At approximately 9 p.m., around twenty-five French officers entered the local theatre, swinging their whips and shouting, 'Out! Out!' just as a performance of Shakespeare's *King Lear* had reached the start of the fourth act. The audience panicked. The mayor of Recklinghausen, Sulpiz Hamm, later claimed that women in the audience were struck in the face with whips and that a group of French officers and soldiers were waiting outside the theatre to continue beating the audience as they took flight. Amid these scenes, a French officer is supposed to have taken to the orchestra pit and played the French national anthem, 'La Marseillaise', on the piano. French officers also forced their way into shops and arrested some shop owners while singling out others for beatings. As late as midnight, French patrols were still out in the streets preventing civilians from moving around. In response to the riots, workers in the town went on strike for twenty-four hours on 8 February. That strike led to further disturbances.[12]

In the aftermath of the rioting, the *Vorwärts* editor-in-chief, Friedrich Stampfer, travelled to Recklinghausen together with other journalists to find out what had really happened. He claimed that when he first heard reports about the behaviour of French officers and soldiers, he thought that it must have been a case of propaganda and rumour getting out of control. But after his arrival in the area, he felt like he was back in a warzone – Stampfer had fought on the Italian front during the First World War. The streets were full of French military patrols and checkpoints with barbed wire. Speaking to witnesses of the previous day's violence left him certain that there had been no exaggeration in the reports.

The origins of the rioting can be traced back to two issues that came to a head simultaneously on 6 February: the decay of relations between the German police and the French military, and the refusal to sell goods to French occupying forces. Though at the start of the occupation, soldiers had briefly cut the telephone lines to the German police headquarters, they were soon re-established and French military and German police had maintained an uneasy truce. On 3 February, after a German government order was issued forbidding German civil servants, including policemen, from saluting French officers, division general Jean-Baptiste Laignelot and police president Kurt Wiesner clashed. Wiesner argued that German law remained in place, whereas Laignelot claimed that under the terms of the Hague Conventions German officials must continue to salute the French. On 6 February, Laignelot expelled both Wiesner and his deputy. That same day, the local trade and industry union decided to forbid the sale of goods to members of the French occupation forces, and small crowds began to form to enforce the boycott. The mayor of Recklinghausen later claimed that, although French soldiers were banned from buying provisions from German shops by their own rules, in practice they had been buying enormous quantities of goods, and to the fury of the local population they had even thrown leftover bread in front of their horses.[13]

The political implications of the violence in Recklinghausen resonated for weeks. In a speech in Karlsruhe, to the south of the occupied zone, on 12 February, Friedrich Ebert called the occupation an 'unprecedented, disdainful act of violence which openly violates the peace treaty, tramples the rights of the people, and wages war with all military force against defenceless men, women and children'. Chancellor Cuno would later personally accuse Laignelot of deliberately creating a 'true regime of terror' against German civilians. According to Cuno, Laignelot told the mayor and a representative of the local police president that 'he would not shrink from the harshest measures until Recklinghausen was on its knees before him, that he was indifferent to the welfare of the population'. Cuno then accused Laignelot of unleashing the soldiers against civilians and German officers:

> Under repeated blows, the officers were thrown onto a truck
> and taken into custody. Tanks appeared in the narrow streets.
> Passers-by were mistreated and driven back and forth with kicks
> and riding crops. Women, the elderly and disabled people who
> could not escape fast enough were beaten to the ground.

Bad as they were, the events in Recklinghausen were only the beginning.[14]

At 6 a.m. on 28 February, tanks rolled into the centre of Bochum. They were supported by soldiers, armoured cars and machine-gun units. The goal of the operation was to disarm the German police. According to German press reports, as many as twenty trucks were required to transport the arrested German officers. Some were arrested in their homes, others in the police barracks. Ten days earlier there had been a similarly large raid, involving as many as twenty armoured cars at the police barracks in Essen, where the German officers had their weapons seized. In Bochum on 23 February, all the magistrates and half of the city council had been arrested. The district president sent a telegram to the mayor that condemned French violence against civilians in Bochum. For the occupiers the measures were justified: French soldiers had been attacked in Bochum and the occupying forces demanded that those behind the attacks hand themselves in. Within a week, *Vorwärts* described the ongoing military operations in Bochum as leaving the city under a 'dictatorship of terror'.[15]

The French targeting of the German police was one part of the intensification of the occupation. Another targeted the railways. These were a vital piece of infrastructure in the occupied Ruhr, essential for the movement of coke, coal and soldiers into and out of the region. That made them key to the success or failure of the campaign of passive resistance, and the French knew it. From mid-February onwards, they began to arrest and imprison senior railway officials. On 1 March, they created a new French-controlled railway company, the Régie. It was intended to eventually replace the state-owned German company in the region.

At the start of March, they also began to expel German police officers and their families. The German authorities were instructed to organize their expulsion. Families were often given only a very short period of notice before they had to leave and were only permitted to take their most valuable personal belongings with them. During their expulsion, the German Red Cross was responsible for their well-being. In Oberhausen, some policemen were briefly interned and used as 'forced labourers', enduring 'grotesque mistreatment'. In Essen, the district commander, General Fournier, to his credit agreed only partially to implement the expulsion order. From the start of the expulsions in March until at least July, his personal protection meant that German police families could remain in his district – but he was unable to offer any further challenge to his superiors and could not offer a written order against their wishes when requested to do so by the German Red Cross. When they crossed over into unoccupied Germany, refugees were received by local authorities just beyond the zone of occupation. They were entitled to compensation and given priority access to housing. Their presence became symbolic of the brutality of the occupation.[16]

Just as the expulsions started to gather pace, the French were given an additional reason for hating the German police. On 10 March, a twenty-two-year-old French lieutenant named Colpin and a forty-seven-year-old French technical officer called Joly were shot dead on the high street in Buer (today a part of Gelsenkirchen). The bullets that killed them were German-made, but it was never established with certainty who was responsible for firing them. The French were certain that the perpetrators were German and they suspected that they were German police officers, not wearing their uniforms at the time the shots were fired. German accounts rejected that accusation. One suggested that the French officers were killed by two Belgians during an argument; another alleged that Colpin and Joly lost their lives because of a row with French soldiers whom they had caught outside their quarters at the wrong time. In one of its first reports, *Vorwärts* admitted that it could not be ruled out that the perpetrators were Germans. If that was the case, it condemned them: all that they had achieved was the death of two people who bore no responsibility for the crimes of the French government, while providing the French with an excuse to carry out reprisals and worsening the situation for the population in the occupied Ruhr. Poincaré vowed to avenge the victims.[17]

French retaliation came quickly in Buer. The mayor was arrested and the town's magistrate was told that if another Frenchman was killed locally he would be immediately executed, regardless of the law. Civilians were forbidden from walking on the pavement – they were only permitted to walk in the road – and they were ordered to swing their arms while walking, with their 'inner palms' visible. After 7.30 p.m., no one was permitted to be outside and, after 10.30 p.m., all lights had to be out. Five tanks were positioned in front of the town hall. An unknown number of arrests took place and there were allegations of beating, which were later exaggerated for propaganda purposes. All cafés and shops were closed for over a week and newspapers were banned.[18]

A week after the murder, the French commander was reported as saying that their investigations had revealed that the perpetrators were members of the police. He named two Germans, Burchhoff and Wittershagen, as the chief suspects and said that they had been shot while trying to escape – a claim that was used to discredit French accounts. German accounts of the case were altogether different. According to the Wolff Telegraph Bureau (WTB), the equivalent of a Reuters report today, Burchhoff was arrested at midday on 11 March after the French were tipped off that he had been involved in the killings and was himself murdered shortly afterwards. Residents in Buer reportedly witnessed Burchhoff being dragged across the square behind the town hall by two officers and two soldiers, who hit him repeatedly with the butts of their rifles and whips. According to the report, the residents could hear 'loud, pitiful cries', before the sound of two shots suddenly rang out. Burchhoff had been shot once in the chest and once in the forehead and his skull was reportedly 'completely destroyed'. Wittershagen was supposedly dragged into a schoolyard and shot in the head. The WTB report stated that he must have been shot at close range because of the nature of his injuries and the presence of gunpowder on his face. According to the report, Burchhoff's body was so badly injured that he was unrecognizable to his closest colleagues, who were only able to identify him thanks to the ring on his finger.[19]

For the French, the murder of young Lieutenant Colpin served as a powerfully mobilizing symbol of the justice of the Ruhr occupation. He was a native of the devastated north-eastern regions of France, who had gone to the Ruhr to fight to secure the payments necessary to rebuild the region of his birth, before being shot in the back while out on patrol in a quiet German street. After his death, French propaganda portrayed him as a 'Christ-like' martyr.[20]

Two days before the French buried Colpin, German president Friedrich Ebert visited Hamm, just 30 kilometres away from Dortmund and close to the border with occupied Germany. Around six thousand invited guests crowded into a large hall to listen to his speech, while thousands more gathered outside. It was both a gesture of support for the people of the occupied Ruhr and a celebration of republican resistance. Black, red and gold flags flew both inside and outside. Ebert repeated the message that the French had long planned the invasion of the Ruhr and that the issue of coal and wood deliveries was only a smokescreen. Just as Hitler had said at the start of the occupation, he told the audience that the French were treating 'German peoples and areas like Negro colonies' and that they wanted to take control of them violently. In Ebert's words, the invasion was 'the most flagrant breach of law and morality known to modern history' and 'the most blatant and barely disguised expression of French political and economic imperialism'. He ended his speech with a plea to Germans inside the Ruhr to continue the struggle and to those outside of the occupied zones to continue to make the sacrifices necessary to support them. The highest representative of the state had thrown his weight behind the campaign of resistance. It would only take one massacre to fan the fires of hatred even further. It came when a young French officer, Lieutenant Durieux, became a French national military hero.[21]

On Saturday, 31 March 1923, Durieux led a group of soldiers into the Krupp works in Essen. Their mission was to seize vehicles for use by the French military. Initially part of a larger force, Durieux and his eleven men stayed behind after the others left. They had found five vehicles in the passenger car hall at the centre of the factory complex and were intent on taking them. Hundreds of workers quickly gathered to protest.

At around 9 a.m., in accordance with pre-existing plans in the event of the arrival of French soldiers, the Krupp factory sirens sounded the alarm. One demonstrator remembered it as an 'eerie, startling sound that chills the blood'. As the alarm continued to sound for around ninety minutes, it brought several thousand workers out to join the protest and surround the hall.[22]

Efforts to calm the situation were of little help. Members of the works' council entered the hall on no fewer than three occasions to try to negotiate an end to the stand-off. Shortly after 10 a.m., two members of the works' council, Hans Müller and Joseph Zander, were inside the hall speaking with Durieux when he ordered his soldiers to take up positions ready to fire. He told them that he would not order his men to fire provided none of the protestors attempted to enter the hall. Müller and Zander tried to convince Durieux that the only way to de-escalate the situation was for him and his men to leave. But even as the mood outside became more aggressive, the French force stood its ground. Outside the crowd was singing the German national anthem and 'We want a glorious victory over France'. At this point Zander noted that there were 'heated elements in the front of the crowd' whose presence made it harder to de-escalate the situation. Some of those outside began to distribute anti-French leaflets. The leaflets asked provocatively, 'Who will take your bread away? The French', and another ended with demands to 'strike down the "beast", the "Gallic rooster"'.[23]

Zander was so concerned by the situation that at around 10.30 a.m. he went to the headquarters and demanded that the sirens be turned off. This was intended to demonstrate to the protestors that the action was over. Another two works' council members and a Social Democratic Party city councillor also set off for Bredeney to inform the French command of the extremely dangerous situation that was unfolding in the Krupp works. Erik Reger, who at this time worked in the Krupp press office, described the mood as extremely tense. The 'howling of the sirens' was 'sinister'. But when it stopped, he thought that the silence that followed was 'even more sinister'. He later said that everyone present had a sense that something – perhaps something 'terrible' – was about to happen.[24]

Inside the hall, the silencing of the sirens did little to make Durieux and his men feel safer. The noise of the crowd could be heard even more clearly now. They could hear the singing and shouting, interrupted by the sound of stones, coal and pieces of wood raining down on the roof. They brought a machine gun up to the door, making sure that the demonstrators could see it and causing them to move backwards. But after a few moments when the crowd and the soldiers looked into each others' eyes, the French retreated back inside the hall.

Some workers were supposed to have shaken their hammers,

spades and metal pipes in the soldiers' direction, while another group of workers reportedly made it onto the roof of the hall and threw more objects towards them. Another group crowded around the back door of the hall and shook it violently. A narrow-gauge train was driven up to the back of the hall on the railway tracks that passed behind it. According to German accounts, the steam from the locomotive was then funnelled into the hall. Durieux and his men later claimed that the smoke left them incredibly anxious.

At about 11 a.m., Durieux and his men decided that it was time to leave. The exact sequence of the events that followed is heavily disputed. What is certain is that Joseph Zander, a known Communist activist in Essen who was among the members of the works' council who had tried to de-escalate the situation that morning, stood in front of the French soldiers as they came out of the hall. As he came forward, he shouted at the crowd, trying to get them to create a passage for the French to leave safely. But there was too much noise and too much confusion.

Durieux's men opened fire on the civilian crowd. Zander was among the first to fall. Later Durieux would claim that the French were about to be assaulted and that someone in the crowd fired at them first. But not a single French soldier was injured in any way that morning.

When the firing started, the protestor Johann Huth started running. Within a few seconds he had been shot in the right arm and fallen to the ground. The next day he claimed from his hospital bed that events had unfolded as follows. In the first place, Durieux and his men had come out of the hall and fired a warning shot that caused the workers to rush backwards. They were in the process of creating a passage for the French to pass, he recalled, when Durieux and his men started firing at them, even though no one had attacked them. Thirteen protestors lost their lives. Autopsies carried out by German doctors later showed that seven of them had been shot in the back. The dead included an office worker, an office apprentice, four locksmiths, other apprentices and six workers.[25]

President Ebert led the German condemnation of the killings. The 'bloodbath' left him 'full of horror'. Chancellor Cuno accused the French of killing with 'nefarious carelessness'. The population of the Ruhr, he promised, 'would not forget this heavy sacrifice of their comrades, nor would it be in vain'. Prussian minister president Otto Braun was 'full of indignation at the brutal action taken by the French intruders against defenceless workers worried about their jobs'. Düsseldorf district president Walther Grützner, who had already been deported from the occupied Ruhr, called it the 'Essen workers' massacre' and a 'mass crime of cowardice', and reminded Degoutte of the fate of the 'murdered, the seriously and lightly wounded, and the future disabled people, their widows and orphans, the women and children'.[26]

The French countered by banning the sale of newspapers and disseminating posters that blamed German factory owners for the atrocity. French propaganda even accused one protestor, who was supposed to have been wearing a swastika, of leading the demonstration at the factory. He was supposed to have swung his revolver and called out, 'We want a glorious victory over France.' Other French propaganda posters claimed that the crowd were calling out, 'Beat them to death', 'Down with them' and 'No one will escape alive', and drawing their revolvers while throwing stones and coal at the French soldiers. The Krupp works later denied that the workers included recently hired former police officers who had lost their jobs because of the French.[27]

Krupp workers protested by refusing to work on the following Tuesday and some circulated leaflets calling for violence against the French: 'Throw them down the shaft, murderers of the workers!' In one of the more reflective responses, the Social Democrats' *Vorwärts* argued that even if the workers had attacked the soldiers with stones and coal, it was still the case that not a single French soldier had been injured and that this would not have been the case if five thousand workers had truly been intent on hurting them. It added that accusations that the workers had been deliberately mobilized by the Krupp directors were an insult to the German working class. *Vorwärts* predicted that the French would produce a report into the atrocity that would say that everything occurred in line with French orders and that the workers were 'influenced' by 'agents from Berlin'. That prediction turned out to be correct: Degoutte's investigation into the incident concluded that Durieux deserved only congratulations. He had acted coolly under extreme pressure and used limited force in the face of extreme danger. He had saved French lives and, in Degoutte's view, that was all that counted.[28]

The funerals of the workers took place on 10 April, and as the dead men were buried in Essen, church bells rang in their memory across Germany. For the *Frankfurter Zeitung*, the bells were the 'cries and accusations of sixty million people who are exposed to hostile acts of violence, who are unarmed and defenceless, with nothing to oppose machine guns and tank weapons but the silent strength of their self-discipline and moral will'. French soldiers and officers were ordered to stay in their barracks and all work ceased for the duration of the funeral service. The coffins were brought from the Krupp works through the city to the cemetery of honour. The wreath from the German government was dedicated to the 'Victims who died for Freedom and Justice'.[29]

The Reichstag convened for a special memorial service, the first since Rathenau's murder. Cuno took to the lectern, just as the bells were ringing out across Berlin. He called the dead the 'Martyrs of Essen' and declared that they were symbols of all the violence committed by the French since the occupation had begun. The political consequences were clear. Cuno told the German public that passive resistance had to continue. The dead of Essen had given their lives for it. They had stood there with 'Justice' on their side, meeting the 'French murder weapons' with 'unarmed resistance'. In Cuno's words:

> How poor our words sound compared to what these martyrs to the German cause have done! It is as if their reproachful warning rings out to us from the crowd of dead, wounded and prisoners: We did all this for you so that you can live and work in freedom – and what do you do?

For him, the blame lay solely with Poincaré, whom he accused of saying not a single word of regret or showing any remorse. At the end of his speech, as the second movement of Beethoven's Seventh

Symphony was played, Cuno and Ebert went to shake the hands of the representatives of the Krupp works who had been in the Reichstag for the ceremony. [30]

The anger the atrocity inspired remained potent well into May, the same month that the most influential Krupp director, Gustav Krupp von Bohlen und Halbach, chair of the board of the Krupp company, who received special permission from the Kaiser to include the Krupp name in his aristocratic title in 1906 when he married Alfred Krupp's daughter and sole heir, was put on trial by the French for conspiring to undermine the authority of the occupation forces. Even though this was not proven, the military court condemned all of the accused. In contrast to the lenient sentences handed down to Fritz Thyssen and the mine directors at the end of January, the punishment this time was far more severe. Krupp and one other senior colleague were sentenced to fifteen years' imprisonment. Altogether, the directors and managers were sentenced to 145 years in prison and significant fines. The only lenient sentence was handed down to works' council member Hans Müller, who was given just six months. In his opening statement, the prosecutor accused the directors of Krupp of laughing as they watched the atrocity unfold, adding that it was the same 'laughter' that the French had heard from German generals as they burned down French villages during the invasion of 1914. [31]

In Germany, the news of the sentences provoked another wave of nationalist outrage. One right-wing newspaper commented that, for the French, putting Krupp behind bars was a great symbolic moment of victory: first they had occupied Essen, then a French general had taken up residence in Krupp's villa, and now Krupp himself had been thrown in jail. The German government described the judgement as

an outrageous reversal of roles in which criminals have tried their own victims and passed a sentence that is supposed to cover up the first crime with a second . . . The French judiciary has thus undisguisedly degraded itself to prostitution for French militarism.

The conservative publisher Theodor Reismann-Grone, later the Nazi mayor of Essen, wrote in his diary that the sentence 'serves to produce what we lack: hatred'.[32]

Krupp had become a symbol of French oppression, and support for Krupp, including from workers and the Social Democratic Party, was emblematic of the unified rejection of the occupation. The Krupp massacre made it harder for everyone to step back from the radical mobilization that had continued since the start of the occupation. With no powerful forces pushing for de-escalation on either side, the conflict was only going to get worse before things could get better.

7

Active Resistance

Though the accusation that the Krupp family had played a role in orchestrating the violence of Essen's bloody Sunday was never proven, there is no doubt that senior members of the Krupp family took part in orchestrating 'active resistance' against the Ruhr occupation. From January 1923, officials in the German Transport Ministry, leading figures in the Christian Trade Unions and the Essen Chamber of Commerce, as well as the chairman of the Union of German Railway Workers, Wilhelm Gutsche, senior members of the Krupp family and directors of the Krupp company helped to launch a covert campaign of economic terrorism against the occupation. Although secret, at the start, their activities also had the blessing of Chancellor Cuno. The idea was simple: every time a bomb slowed down the transport of coke and coal from the Ruhr to France, the occupation became harder to justify. They also knew that the railway network in the Ruhr could be severely disrupted by blowing up key bridges and railway junctions. This clandestine campaign of 'active resistance' was not, at least initially, intended to kill or injure the occupying forces. But it did. The railway bombers ended up blowing up trains carrying French and Belgian soldiers. They murdered Germans accused of collaborating with the occupation forces and they provided the occupiers with grounds for harsh reprisals, including using German civilians as human shields on trains in the occupied region. In the longer term, the campaign also undermined the republic. The clandestine violence of secret agents was something that the anti-republican right could glorify and celebrate. Ultimately, the anti-republican right did a better job of remembering their heroism than pro-republican forces were at remembering their victims.

Though organized by establishment figures, the campaign was carried out by operatives who belonged to the murky worlds of secret intelligence and espionage. These included experienced agents like Kurt Albert Jahnke, codenamed 'Zebu', who was given the secret title of Reich Commissioner for All Acts of Sabotage in January 1923. In 1899, Jahnke had emigrated from Germany to the United States, where he served in the Marine Corps and gained US citizenship. In 1914, he was recruited as a German agent in San Francisco. During the First World War, he spied for Germany while undertaking acts of sabotage that included placing explosives in weapons factories on US soil to hinder US arms production. Despite causing explosions, he was never caught by the American authorities and he returned to Germany in 1919.

Heinz Kölpin was another experienced agent. During and after the First World War, he ran a domestic spy network in the Ruhr which targeted left-wing radicals. This experience made him an ideal candidate for commanding operations and collecting information during the 1923 crisis. He was joined by Franz Pfeffer von Salomon and Heinz Hauenstein, former Freikorps commanders who specialized in clandestine acts of violence. An explosives expert, Pfeffer would later become the head of the Nazi's SA in 1926 as the Nazi movement came back to life in the mid-1920s. Like Pfeffer, Hauenstein was also an early supporter of Hitler's movement.[1]

As mentioned above, Jahnke's position as Reich Commissioner for All Acts of Sabotage was secret. But we know with absolute certainty that he nonetheless had direct links with the state. The minister of labour, Heinrich Brauns of the Centre Party, knew of Jahnke's position and used his ministry to provide him with funding. When the campaign started, Brauns may have even naïvely believed that he controlled Jahnke's organization in the Ruhr. Jahnke also reported to the army officer Joachim von Stülpnagel, head of Department T1 of the Troop Office in the Ministry for Defence. Jahnke's connections meant that, from early February onwards, he had sufficient authority and finance to demand that other active resistance fighters accept that he was in charge.

The operatives' headquarters were based in unoccupied Germany, formally out of reach of the French and Belgian authorities. Kölpin and Pfeffer based their organizations in Münster, 80 kilometres to the north-east of Essen, where they took charge of the Central Office North, which functioned as the regional command of the sabotage network. Hauenstein's organization was based just outside the occupied Ruhr, 5 kilometres to the south of Essen, in the town of Elberfeld. Other groups were based in cities close to the occupied zone, such as the Defence Group South-West, under the leadership of former Freikorps commander Friedrich Wilhelm Heinz, in Frankfurt. Under Jahnke's direction, they ran teams of agents in the occupied zones. By the autumn of 1923, Pfeffer claimed to have forty-two shock troops and new groups under his leadership.[2]

The contacts between these men and the leading figures who had initially called for the campaign remained secret. But they strengthened following the arrest and trial of the Krupp directors. One active resistance organization even used offices belonging to a Krupp director in Essen as a safe house and the industrial leaders made sure that they were never short of money. Pfeffer would later claim to have had 'tremendous means' to finance his operations. The state helped too: the western directorate of the Reichsbahn, which was subordinate to minister for transport Wilhelm Groener, had secret links with the sabotage teams in the occupied zone and helped the bombers identify the best locations for explosions that would cause maximum disruption to railway traffic.[3]

Even at the highest level of state politics in Berlin, not everyone knew about Jahnke and his new job title, but the campaign of active resistance had the secret blessing of the federal government. Cuno took the view that a campaign of economic terrorism was necessary to challenge the French and Belgian occupation. He also feared that if the state did not engage in any form of active resistance, ultra-nationalist war veterans and underground networks like the Organization Consul would launch their own campaigns. He preferred to lure them into a secret state-sponsored campaign rather than to let them run amok of their own accord. In a worst-case scenario, Cuno feared that active resistance could spiral out of control and end with a full-scale war between Germany and France.

This wasn't as far-fetched as it might seem. Pfeffer was particularly intent on using violence to escalate the conflict. The Central Office North, which he ran with Kölpin, considered operations that caused only 'material damage' as 'futile'. He set out to murder French soldiers, fully aware that by doing so he would force the French into reprisals that would increase the hostility of the Ruhr's population against the occupation. His plan was to use violence to create so much havoc that the occupiers had to bring more and more soldiers into the region. He also intended to launch attacks on the border between occupied and unoccupied Germany to allow his men to retreat into unoccupied Germany, so that the occupiers would face pressure to extend the zone of occupation – something that Pfeffer hoped would draw more and more people into the conflict on both sides.

Men like Pfeffer also fantasized about a single operation ending in the deaths of so many members of the occupation forces that they would respond with outright war. This violent fantasy drew on older German right-wing fantasies that Germany should have restarted the First World War in the summer of 1919 rather than sign the Versailles Treaty, even if that meant that Germany would face invasion from the superior Allies.

Pfeffer's dream was not entirely implausible. In one of his most daring operations, which began late in the evening on 1 April 1923, Easter Sunday, and continued during the night and early hours of 2 April, he mobilized as many as three hundred heavily armed men. 'Operation Wesel' consisted of a complex raid involving different groups of active resisters who co-operated for this operation, the Reichswehr and railway workers. The latter were to bring seven fully loaded trains with around 350 wagons from inside the occupied Ruhr into unoccupied Germany without the permission of the occupying powers, whose soldiers manned checkpoints on the rail network to prevent exactly this kind of breakout from occurring. Pfeffer's men went in the opposite direction to provide armed support to the railway men. On their way into the Belgian section of the occupied Ruhr, they hid in a disguised goods train that included separate carriages full of weapons supplied by the

Reichswehr in Münster. To cross into the occupied Ruhr, Pfeffer's men travelled on secondary rail routes. They got as far as the river Lippe, close to where the railway men were about to break out. It is very likely that Pfeffer hoped that the operation would end in a shootout between the Germans and the Belgians. But the gunfire never started. On at least two occasions when Belgian soldiers discovered the large German raiding party, they simply ran away. Elsewhere, as part of the railway breakout strategy, Belgian officers had been distracted by German women, most likely prostitutes, who had been instructed to keep them occupied at key points during the night.[4]

When the campaign of active resistance started, the railway system was its most important target. Initially bombs were left on the tracks to detonate as trains passed over them. This method was later replaced by bombs with timers left on trains. The campaign was part of a larger battle to control the vital rail network infrastructure.

At the onset of passive resistance in January, as many as 170,000 railway workers had refused to work for the French and Belgians.[5] As we have already seen, in March, to circumvent the refusal of German railway workers to co-operate, the occupiers created a new railway company, the Régie. Their plan was for it to eventually replace the Reichsbahn in the occupied Ruhr. By July, the occupiers had drafted in as many as fourteen thousand French and Belgian staff to run their new company. But Degoutte didn't just bring new workers into the Ruhr, he also deported German railway workers who continued to refuse to co-operate.

The expulsions took place under the threat of violence and there were frequent allegations that the expellees were deliberately humiliated by the occupying forces. The most intensive phase of deportations took place in the summer. When the Régie seized sections of the rail network, as historian Conan Fischer has shown, German employees were arrested and placed under military guard. They had only two options if they wanted to get out: either they could agree to work for the French or they faced deportation. Only a tiny minority, no more than a few hundred people, agreed to work for the French. The rest chose deportation for themselves and their families.

The figures were extraordinary. Between March and October 1923, when the campaign against the railway staff finally eased off, as many as 25,214 railway workers and 64,038 of their family members had been expelled from the Ruhr. A further 5,468 railway workers in the Ruhr had seen their homes seized. Many of the deported were forced to leave with only a few hours' notice. In some instances, other railway workers were prevented from helping the expellees. In some cases, the German Red Cross could hold small farewell ceremonies for the expelled families. But many had so little time they left their furniture and other possessions in their homes. German propaganda condemned their treatment and accused the French and Belgians of handing out excessively harsh punishments when they came before French courts. In all, over the course of the occupation, eight railway workers were killed, and a further 269 injured.[6]

The deportation of German railway workers had a significant impact on the campaign of active resistance against the rail network. In March, French officials recorded 86 attacks on the railways, followed by 56 in April, 55 in May and 62 in June. The statistics need to be considered in two ways, however. First, they included a range of incidents, many of which were not the result of the work of German saboteurs. Incidents recorded by the French as 'active resistance' could have been accidents involving individual German railway workers or other German civilians, crashes caused by poorly trained French workers, and damage caused by disgruntled French and Belgian soldiers. The occupation also halted regular maintenance work on the rail network, which led to accidents that were also classified as the result of 'active resistance'. The second consideration is that, as the frequency of attacks declined, their nature grew more intense: the agents of active resistance were choosing to undertake fewer, but more deadly, attacks.[7]

The French had numerous reasons for exaggerating the number of attacks: local commanders could thereby deflect responsibility for their failings, while at a higher level the French propaganda campaign could use the attacks to depict the Germans as a brutal enemy. The active resisters made it easy for them. On 17 April, saboteurs tried to blow up the express train from Brussels to Cologne as it crossed over the river Rur in Düren. But the bomb detonated too early, giving the train time to stop before it passed over the section of the tracks where the bomb had gone off. It was a lucky escape, especially considering that both the French secretary of defence and the Belgian minister for work were on board.

From early 1923 onwards, the active resistance fighters played a game of cat and mouse with French and Belgian intelligence operatives who used spies, bribes, arrests and torture. The German operatives were able to fight back using counterintelligence operations that set out to identify and punish traitors. Among this dirty war's victims was a man named as Sinder or Synder, a Communist who was arrested by the Essen police after providing information to the French.[8] After they learnt of his arrest, the French occupation authorities pressurized the police to release him, a practice that was common as the occupiers wanted their informants released. After he left the police administrative building, Sinder only made it as far as 100 metres, before he was shot dead in the street. Tipped off by the police in Essen, German operatives had been waiting for him. The newspapers soon named Hans Sadowski as his killer. Sadowski was a member of the Organization Heinz, a Freikorps named after its leader, Heinz Hauenstein. By May 1923, the organization claimed to have executed as many as eight people who had informed for the French.[9]

Despite German efforts to intimidate and kill collaborators, in the battle between French intelligence and German saboteurs, there is no doubt that the French were winning. One estimate suggests that as many as one-third of the five hundred men who were involved in sabotage operations had already been arrested by the French within two months of the start of the campaign. Of the sixty-one saboteurs active in the Bund Oberland, twenty-eight were discovered and arrested by the French. The French knew that large numbers in the German resistance had had experience of the fighting with the Poles over the border in Upper Silesia, so they used people from that region to infiltrate the German organizations. Other sources of intelligence included criminals and pre-existing police informants. Thanks to them, the French intelligence operation quickly discovered much about the German underground operations. They learnt from the Germans they interrogated that the saboteurs had the support of the governments of the Reich and of Bavaria. The French even knew that some operatives had had confiscated explosives returned to them in Frankfurt when German police were told the purpose of their mission.[10]

The French and Belgians also used torture to extract information from Germans after their arrest. On 14 June 1923, a four-man bomb squad were caught in possession of detonators and explosives by a Belgian patrol near railway lines in the occupied zone. After their arrest they were beaten and insulted. They were told that they would be executed immediately and forced to strip naked. In his diary, which was not written for publication, one of the arrested men compared one of his comrades' loss of teeth during their beating to the wounds that he had suffered during the First World War. The four men were later sentenced to death, but their sentences were commuted following appeal, and after their transfer to prison in Belgium they were released in November 1924.[11]

In another episode, two German telegraph workers, Langel and Steffens, were violently assaulted after they were arrested by the French and accused of engaging in sabotage against the occupiers' communication networks. Langel recalled how he was struck with 'horse whips, rubber hoses and chain whips'.

> They pulled my overcoat over my head, so that I could hardly breathe. After they let the jacket fall down again, they beat my head with the same instruments. You can still see the wounds on my head, my legs are still swollen where they hit me.

Steffens recounted the torture of being repeatedly pushed forward so that he was on the point of falling to the ground, only to be punched back upright. Then his captors hit him on the back of the head three times with a metal chain. Both Langel and Steffens suffered nervous breakdowns as a consequence of the brutality of their treatment.[12]

As the violence of the active resistance campaign worsened, the uneasy coalition of state forces in Weimar Germany that had secretly supported it began to fall apart. Forward-thinking observers could see that it was doing Weimar Germany more harm than good. The violence was only serving to justify the occupation forces' reprisals, while making it harder for the German government to appeal to the wider world for support based on the ground that Germany was the victim of French and Belgian aggression. Above all, within Germany, pro-democratic politicians could see that the campaign was emboldening the anti-republican right and that if they were not stopped soon, the Social Democrats and the government in Berlin would be their next target.

Prussian internal minister Carl Severing played a decisive role when he ended the toleration of active resistance organizations in his own state. Severing was a member of the Social Democratic Party who had grown up near Bielefeld, about 150 kilometres to the north of Essen. He had been a member of the Reichstag before the First World War, but it was only in the conflict's aftermath that he became a politician of national significance. By the time the French and Belgians occupied the Ruhr, he was already known as a powerful pro-democratic reformer in Prussia, where he was responsible for a series of measures that helped to democratize the political system in Germany's largest federal state. For his reforms to the police and judicial system, as well as his willingness to use the Law for the Protection of the Republic, the political right hated him. But like many Social Democrats, Severing was also a German nationalist. When the French and Belgians occupied the Ruhr, he initially saw no alternative but to support the campaign of passive resistance. But, like most key figures in the Prussian state government, his attitude towards the campaign of active resistance was far more mixed.

At first the police under his command in the unoccupied zone appeared to tolerate the active resistance networks operating on their territory. At the highest level, there was also some willingness to work with the active resistance fighters. On 13 March, Severing created initially five, then later eight, intelligence offices in towns in unoccupied Germany near the Ruhr. These so-called 'defence commissions' or 'defence authorities' were tasked with 'collecting news of all events beyond the lines by any means possible'. Their job included identifying Germans co-operating with the occupiers. But they weren't just observing the situation. When they decided that a German in the occupied Ruhr had got too close to the French, they worked with the active resistance teams either to lure that person out of the Ruhr into unoccupied Germany or to kidnap them. Once they were in their hands, suspects faced interrogation and prosecution.

The legal basis of this system was covered by an emergency decree, issued by President Ebert at the start of March 1923, that was so vaguely worded as to offer little protection to anyone targeted by the defence authorities. It envisaged a punishment of a life sentence or at least ten years for anyone who 'acts as a spy in economic, political or military matters, or takes in, hides or assists spies of this power during the peacetime occupation of German territory by a foreign power'.[13]

But Severing quickly changed direction, becoming a strong opponent of the campaign of active resistance. In the aftermath of 'Operation Wesel', it was clear that the active resisters' plans went far beyond the original idea of a campaign of economic terrorism. From the end of April 1923, under his leadership, the Prussian state, including the Prussian state police which answered to Severing, began to interfere directly in their operations. Severing made sure that the state support began to dry up. The active resisters found that they were no longer being secretly supplied with explosives; the officers who had previously conspired with them stopped turning up, and to make sure that no officers, police or military, continued to co-operate unofficially, all leave was suspended. As such, links to the police crumbled.

Following the instruction to turn against the active resisters, the Prussian police also started to hunt them down. They began house searches and even passed information to the French. The German

Red Cross received an order to provide no help to saboteurs on the run. The organizers of the active resistance campaign quickly realized that the state had turned against them. Just as they believed that Germany's soldiers would have been victorious in the First World War if the socialist revolution had not 'stabbed them in the back', they now thought that their campaign had been betrayed. Their bitterness increased even further when Prussian officials arrested Heinz Hauenstein in May 1923. Pfeffer thought that after they had served Germany so well, the members of his organization now faced a 'witch hunt' led by Severing.[14]

On 24 June 1923, the anniversary of the murder of Walther Rathenau, the conspirators let the Social Democrat Severing know what they thought of him. They bombed a local Social Democratic newspaper office in Münster and *Vorwärts* called the bombers 'Fascists'. It was only a matter of time before Severing's measures brought their campaign to an end.[15]

At the level of the Reich government, Cuno wasn't as fast as Severing to move against the active resisters. But over the course of May and June he also grew increasingly critical of them. It was obvious that his initial goal of controlling the resisters by channelling them into a limited campaign had backfired. In fact, the campaign of active resistance had also proven to be bad international politics: after the success of presenting Germany to the world as the victim of French aggression, bombs on train lines made it look less like an innocent victim and more like an aggressor.

Cuno's attitude hardened in the wake of the active resistance fighters' worst attack to date, which took place on 30 June 1923. The active resisters made a high-grade explosive device that was controlled by a timer and placed it either in the toilet or between the carriages on a train that was carrying Belgian soldiers on leave. As the train approached the Rhine crossing between Duisburg and Rheinhausen, the device detonated. Initial reports suggested that the explosion killed nine Belgian soldiers as well as a single train worker, and that a further forty to fifty people were injured, many of them seriously. Within a few days the number of fatalities had risen to twenty. *The Times* newspaper in London called it an 'outrage'. For the likes of Pfeffer, the only disappointment was that the bomb detonated just before the train reached the bridge. The bombers had probably hoped that the explosion would occur as the train crossed the bridge, taking it down with it.[16]

Reprisals followed swiftly. Degoutte ordered the closure of the border between occupied and unoccupied Germany for two weeks – a measure that would also reduce the food supply into the Ruhr. In Duisburg, twenty citizens were arrested and taken as hostages, and all cafés, theatres, cinemas and bars were closed until further notice. A curfew was introduced from 10 p.m. to 5 a.m. and Germans were forbidden from driving cars or other motor vehicles in the city; only French military vehicles were allowed on the roads. In Oberhausen, one measure included forcing German passengers to disembark from trams when they reached a bridge. They then had to walk across the bridge with their hands held over their heads before they were allowed back on the train on the other side.

German civilians were increasingly forced to serve as human shields for the occupiers. In the wake of the 30 June 1923 incident, the Belgians and French introduced a system of forcing prominent Germans, including businessmen, shop owners, tradespeople, newspaper editors, doctors, lawyers, churchmen, architects and civil servants, to travel on trains. They published lists of German human shields and posted them at town halls, alongside the details of the trains that they were to take. In July, in Belgian-controlled Gladbeck, up to forty-eight German human shields were forced to travel every second night on trains; after perhaps a week, their places would be taken by another group.[17]

The human shield system developed out of hostage-taking and reprisal measures that started in February 1923. In that month, the railway, telegraph and telephone networks in Recklinghausen were divided into sections, and each was allocated to a German civil servant. If anything happened in that section, the associated civil servant faced immediate arrest and imprisonment. In June, before the Duisburg train bombing, Paul Tirard, the president of the Inter-Allied Rhineland High Commission, issued an order that when undetonated explosive devices were discovered, German officials, such as commissioners of police or state prosecutors, should be required to attend the scene and remain in proximity to the bomb until it had been disarmed by a bomb disposal expert. Unsurprisingly, such measures deeply upset the German population.[18]

In Belgium, the Duisburg train bombing generated outrage. Nationalist press reports argued that the atrocity was a continuation of the violence that Germans had inflicted upon Belgians during the First World War. In Germany, press reports quickly shifted the focus away from the death and destruction towards German civilian suffering. Just a few days after the explosion, even a liberal like Erich Dombrowski stated that France's 'spirit of revenge' left the civilian population in the Ruhr facing a 'war of extermination'. In his view, Germans had to go back to ancient times to find a comparable 'regime of terror'. *Vorwärts*, however, criticized the Duisburg bombing. It pointed out that the violence had provided a propaganda victory for France and Belgium that would cause Germany to lose support internationally, including in France and Belgium. The only thing that the bombers had achieved, it argued, was to increase the suffering of the German population. The Social Democratic mouthpiece begged Chancellor Cuno to take action and 'quickly and finally make a clean sweep of those who, under a mask of nationalism, would like to blow up the passive resistance and the entire people'.[19] The lord mayor of Duisburg even told a French officer that the population sympathized with the victims and condemned the perpetrators.[20]

The train bombing left Cuno with no doubt: the campaign of active resistance had to stop. The need to act fell at a particularly inopportune time for him in early July, as he held a series of meetings with Nuncio Eugenio Pacelli, the Vatican's representative in Bavaria, who in practice was the Catholic Church's diplomatic emissary to the whole of Germany. In a letter from the Vatican, Pope Pius XI ordered Cuno to condemn the campaign of active resistance – something which drew the ire of the German press. A few days after the active resisters had bombed the Social Democratic newspaper office in Münster and blown up a Belgian troop train,

Cuno finally issued a statement from the federal government that condemned the campaign even more forcibly.[21]

Cuno's statement signalled an end to the campaign's secret state support. The last fatal attack occurred on 5 August 1923. On that day an unknown man threw a grenade at a French patrol on the Königsallee in Düsseldorf, seriously injuring seven people, of whom two later died (four of the victims were French, three were German). By then, most of the active resistance cells had been wound down.[22]

By the time the campaign of active resistance was shut down, its greatest anti-republican legacy had already been established: it had produced a symbol of the nationalist right's betrayal. His name was Albert Leo Schlageter, a twenty-eight-year-old Catholic veteran of the First World War and of the anti-revolutionary and anti-Polish military campaigns of nationalist volunteers, known as the Freikorps, when he fought in a series of important battles that were later glorified by the anti-republican right between 1919 and 1921. In the Ruhr, Schlageter had been an important figure in the campaign of active resistance. He commanded a bomb squad that was based in Essen. He was also in charge of a group of seven counterintelligence agents that existed to monitor French espionage and to strike back against their attempts to infiltrate the German campaign of active resistance.[23]

Hans Sadowski was one of his closest conspirators. It is most likely that the two were responsible for the execution of 'traitors', including the alleged informant Sinder. As far as is known, their group was only responsible for two attacks on the railways: an explosion at Hügel station near Essen on 12 March, and an explosion on a bridge on the trainline between Duisburg and Düsseldorf at Kalkum on 15 March. The second explosion was planned as one of a series of bombings that were intended to take place that night, but the others were called off due to the risk that the bombers would be caught by French military patrols operating in the area. Neither the Hügel nor the Kalkum bombing caused significant damage to the railway network and there was no loss of life as a result of either operation.[24]

On 7 April 1923, Schlageter was arrested by detectives from the French security force, the Sûreté. The cause of his arrest was debated and mythologized for years. It was alleged at the time that he was betrayed by other agents of the active resistance campaign who had a vendetta against Hauenstein's organization. These allegations even named two men, Alfred Götze and Otto Schneider, veterans of the Freikorps Roßbach, a rival organization to the Hauenstein group, as being responsible for betraying Schlageter. Additionally, untrue allegations circulated that he was personally betrayed by the Social Democratic Party's Prussian interior minister Carl Severing.[25]

Today, historians can say with reasonable certainty that it was carelessness, not conspiracy, that led to his arrest. On the morning of his arrest, he was staying under his real name at the Union Hotel in Essen. In 1928, under oath, Frau Mucke, the owner of the hotel, recalled that when he checked in that morning, Schlageter was a little drunk and in the company of a woman. That evening, a French officer came to the hotel, searching for him. When the officer arrived Schlageter was in the hotel's restaurant. After the officer went upstairs to his room, Schlageter started to make his way up the stairs where the two crossed paths. Frau Mucke claimed that when they met, Schlageter made the mistake of handing the French officer two different identity cards and that this was the initial reason for his arrest. She added that she did not think that the woman was a 'female officer of the French espionage department'. Others have speculated that she may have been a prostitute.[26]

Schlageter was taken to the building of the Essen coal syndicate and later to Werden prison. On 14 April, the French also arrested Hans Sadowski, Alois Alfred Becker and Georg Werner. Back in March, they had arrested Georg Zimmermann, Carl Bisping and Karl Max Kulmann. All seven men now faced trial together. It is almost certain that during their interrogation they were subjected to violence, although this allegation was denied by the French. On 14 April 1923, Schlageter sent letters from his prison cell to his family in Baden, asking them to send him letters of comfort and telling them that he was all right, despite the situation. He also wrote to Heinz Hauenstein, his commander in unoccupied Germany.

He told him that after his arrest it had quickly become clear to him that the French officers who had interrogated him knew everything about their plans and that it was obvious that they had been betrayed by someone in their closest circles. He called it a 'damned awful situation', adding that he was lucky not to have been executed already.[27]

Schlageter's trial took place in Düsseldorf on 8 and 9 May 1923 under the supervision of Colonel Blondel. At that time, it was not a major news story: the public's attention was focused on another Thyssen trial which was taking place in Werden and on the up-coming trial against Gustav Krupp. Schlageter and his co-accused faced trial for the formation of a criminal organization and es-pionage with the goal of preparing attacks on occupation forces or agents, as well as the bombings at Kalkum and Hügel. Schlageter and Sadowski each faced an additional charge related to a further bombing. Schlageter's legal defence was led by Robert Marx, a German of Jewish origin. The trial ended with Schlageter being found guilty and sentenced to death. In the wake of Schlageter's sentencing, German supporters of democracy found it more diffi-cult than ever to condemn the campaign of active resistance. Forced to defend Schlageter, *Vorwärts* ventured the argument that because the occupation itself was illegal, no French court had the right to sentence Germans in the Ruhr to death. In the newspaper's view, published on 12 May, if the sentence were carried out, it would constitute murder. But just as it condemned the French, *Vorwärts* attempted to warn of the dangers of active resistance and called on the government to take stronger action to suppress it. In its words: 'Only children could believe that the Franco-German conflict can be solved by means of violent terrorism.'[28]

The final decision as to whether to execute Schlageter rested with Poincaré, who signed the order in Paris on 15 May. Schlageter's legal team's appeal was rejected on the day it was filed. Schlageter's parents sent letters begging for mercy to the French prime minister, met with the queen of Sweden, a native of Baden, who promised to intervene on his behalf, and sent appeals to the Vatican to lobby the French to save Schlageter. The priest who tended to Schlageter while he was held in Düsseldorf prison, Josef Faßbender, also began to campaign to save him. In his words, Schlageter had only done what he did because 'the misfortunes of his country, which he loves with all his heart, oppressed him so much that he simply didn't know what he was doing'.[29]

But Poincaré's mind was not for turning. He wanted to send a harsh message to the population of the occupied Ruhr. With the occupation failing to deliver the results he had intended, he had been facing increasing criticism, including barbs from the conservative parliamentarian André Tardieu, who accused him of being too weak to deal with the Germans. Poincaré is supposed to have been so enraged by the accusation of weakness that he determined to see Schlageter executed.[30]

In the early hours of 26 May, prison priest Faßbender and the lawyer Paul Sengstock were allowed into Schlageter's cell as his final visitors. He was given enough time to write a final letter to his parents before Faßbender gave him communion. Schlageter was then taken to a nearby military exercise field where he was tied to a pole and, in accordance with the rules of French military executions, made to kneel before being shot at by a firing squad of twelve men. An officer then approached him and fired a so-called 'mercy shot' from a pistol at close range, to ensure that he was completely dead.

By the time he wrote his final letters and said his goodbyes, Schlageter had developed the mindset of someone who was about to be executed. He consciously used words in his last letters that he knew would resonate long after his death. His attempt to shape his own martyrdom proved successful. In his final letter to his parents and closest family, Schlageter had written: 'Now I'm about to start my last course. I will still confess and take communion. So then, see you again in the afterlife.' His last words to Faßbender were: 'Say hello to my parents, siblings and relatives, my friends, and my Germany.' These became part of the school curriculum during the Third Reich. Even before the end of the Weimar Republic, the Schlageter cult became a major political force. On Pentecost in 1931, a 27-metre-high steel cross would be erected on the spot where he had died. It was formally unveiled in front of fifty thousand people, including Cuno and members of Schlageter's family.[31]

Schlageter's execution was a tremendous blunder for the French and a huge political problem for German supporters of Weimar democracy. In June, in the Prussian parliament, the Social Democratic Party representative Richard Hauschildt condemned it on legal grounds, calling it 'a devilish act by the insurgents of French imperialism', while adding that the decision to execute Schlageter was 'from a political point of view nothing but sheer madness'. In August, the newly appointed chancellor, Gustav Stresemann, compared Poincaré's mistake to the German decision to execute British nurse Edith Cavell during the First World War, arguing that it had ignited an explosion of German nationalism. But everyone knew the major problem: Schlageter was a nationalist hero, a figure whose sacrifice could be glorified by the anti-republican right, while pro-democratic forces did not have the same repertoire of ideas about glorifying violent sacrifice in the name of democracy and their victims were quickly forgotten.[32]

The French soon realized the error: though another seven active resisters received death sentences in 1923, each had their sentences reduced to either hard labour or prison. One saboteur died in custody on the Île de Ré off the Atlantic coast of France. The rest, like the men put on trial alongside Schlageter, were released following the improvement in Franco-German relations in 1924.[33]

After his execution, Schlageter's body was taken to the Northern Cemetery in Düsseldorf where it was immediately buried. The first visitors to the freshly dug grave brought with them black, white and red wreaths. Someone erected a small wooden cross bearing the words 'Here lies Albert Leo Schlageter, a German hero'. Schlageter's remains were now an important political symbol. His former comrades, as well as members of Nazi organizations in Elberfeld, including the future Gauleiters Karl Kaufmann and Erich Koch and the future head of the SA Viktor Lutze, received permission to bring his body back to unoccupied Germany. Its first destination was Elberfeld, where a public memorial service was held in the town hall on 8 June, attended by many of the senior civil servants and politicians who had been expelled from the Ruhr, including president of the state tax office Friedrich Schlutius.[34]

The service turned into an anti-republican rally and included the participation of organizations banned under the Law for the Protection of the Republic, including the Nazis. District president Walther Grützner tried to deal with the issue by ordering the police president of Elberfeld to prevent participants in the ceremony from carrying 'black, white and red ribbons and anti-republican badges and flags'. But his order could not be enforced. Schlageter's coffin was draped in the imperial German War Flag. One former comrade of his threatened that they would have to kill him before they would be allowed to remove the black, white and red ribbons. When he half-heartedly attempted to enforce Grützner's order, the police president told some of those present that he was only following his orders and 'how he thinks as a man need not be discussed'.

When the service ended Schlageter's coffin was carried on the shoulders of members of the nationalist veterans' organization, the Steelhelmets, to the main railway station and taken by train to its burial place in Schönau in the Black Forest, where Schlageter was born. *Vorwärts* called it a 'triumphal procession through Germany', noting that the organizers were trying to create a 'mood for war'. On 10 June, Schlageter was buried in a special grave at Schönau cemetery.[35]

The dilemma of German democrats crystallized in the veneration of Schlageter, whom they had been forced to defend in spite of themselves. A martyr cult swiftly developed around Schlageter in the summer of 1923. Schlageter's last letters were published, and items that he possessed were carefully stored. Hitler's friend, the Harvard graduate Ernst Hanfstaengl, even published a tribute to Schlageter portraying him as a great German national hero.[36]

In 1933, on the tenth anniversary of Schlageter's death, a special exhibition about his life was staged and there were even plans to create a memorial museum in Berlin. He was also memorialized in statues, commemorative plaques, songs, poems, plays, portraits and hagiographies. In Freiburg, Martin Heidegger, then rector of Freiburg University, led the university's Schlageter celebration in 1933. In Nazi propaganda during the Third Reich, Düsseldorf was even called Schlageter City. Some claimed that Schlageter was the first 'soldier' of the Third Reich.

Given his legacy and the role played by the Schlageter cult in mobilizing support for the Third Reich, it is easy to forget that, although his fellow resistance fighters despised the Weimar Republic, at the time of his death Schlageter was operating in the Ruhr at the behest of at least part of the government of the Weimar Republic. However lukewarm their support may have been, the Weimar leadership had given the green light for the campaign of active resistance. Immediately after his execution, the deputy district president in Düsseldorf, Lutterbeck, condemned the execution, telling the French command there that it was a 'judicial murder' that would fill the German population and 'the rest of the cultured world with disgust and exasperation'. Chancellor Cuno immediately sent a note of condolence to Schlageter's family. Three days after the execution, on 29 May, the federal government sent a formal protest note to the French government.[37]

The Schlageter myth would become part of the history of Nazi Germany, but it is also important to remember its function in the Weimar Republic. Political myths don't exist in a vacuum, they compete with other myths to define the identity and political belief systems of national populations. This is why political leaders, whether they represent or wish to challenge the power of the state, place so much emphasis on their development. In Weimar Germany, the myths that undermined the republic included the 'stab in the back', a longing for a new national leader of the quality of Bismarck and a belief in the exceptional qualities of Hindenburg and later Hitler. German democrats and republicans did not leave these anti-republican myths unchallenged. As well as fighting for the symbols of the republic, supporters of democracy also invested in national days of commemoration. As *Time Magazine* explained to its American readers, there was a German 'fourth of July'. It was 11 August, the national holiday declared to celebrate Weimar's constitution.

In June 1923, just as the nationalists were mobilizing around Schlageter, the republicans gathered to mark the first anniversary of the murder of democratic Germany's most important martyr, Walther Rathenau. Ceremonies in his honour were held in the Reichstag and in the Foreign Office. In the Reichstag, as many as two thousand people listened to Konrad Haenisch, then district president in Wiesbaden and president of the republican Reich League, as he called for the date of Rathenau's murder, 24 June, to become a national holiday. Alongside the dates of 9 November and 11 August, he wanted it to be a pro-democratic 'Day of Struggle'. In his words: 'Because in the future the German people and their republic will not only have to work and fight, but also die if necessary.' When Rathenau's mother donated her son's villa in Grunewald to the federal government on 23 June with the instruction that the ground floor was to remain as it was while her son had lived there, Chancellor Cuno, President Ebert and interior minister Rudolf Oeser were all present for the handover. The building was to be maintained by a newly established Walther Rathenau Foundation. Accepting the gift, Oeser stated that it would be a 'duty of honour' for the Reich 'to care for and maintain the Rathenau house'.[38]

Rathenau and Schlageter now came to symbolize two different kinds of German martyr: one was a hero for the democratic republic, the other was a hero for nationalist and anti-republican Germany. For the remainder of the republic's existence, the forces that opposed it were more successful in keeping the memory of Schlageter alive than the pro-republican forces that wanted Germans to celebrate Rathenau's life and maintain the republic in his honour. Their success is a reminder that the anti-democratic forces in the republic were more comfortable with the glorification of violence than the pro-republican forces were at remembering its victims.

8

The Occupiers' Revenge

On 7 May 1923, in the town of Lütgendortmund to the west of Dortmund, the school caretaker Gustav Jeroch was up to no good. He was heading off to see a younger woman he had met through an advertisement in the lonely-hearts column of a local newspaper – she later claimed that he had promised to marry her. But Jeroch's assignation ended badly. Straying near to the railway tracks, French soldiers mistook him for a member of a clandestine group of resistance fighters. They didn't take the time to ask him questions about what he was doing there – they simply shot him dead.[1]

The soldiers were nervous. The campaign of active resistance didn't result in a large loss of life on the part of occupying troops, but the threat that they might fall to a bullet in the back or a bomb hidden on a train left them fearful and aggressive towards the civilian population. And in these circumstances, besides shooting civilians like Jeroch, some of the occupying soldiers took out their frustration on the female population of the Ruhr.

As we have seen, incidents of rape and sexual violence were already occurring at the very start of the occupation in January 1923. But even allowing for the likelihood that many victims chose not to report their assaults, the available evidence shows that the incidence of rape and sexual violence was most frequent from March to June 1922. The increase was part of the wider radicalization of the political and military conflict in the Ruhr. For some soldiers, sexual violence and rape must also have been about taking revenge on the civilian population whom the occupying soldiers accused of hiding the perpetrators of violence against them.

Rape and all forms of sexual violence are uncomfortable subjects. Even today, the words used by the victims to express the pain and terror they endured makes for viscerally striking reading. But however uncomfortable their words might make us feel, if we want to understand the escalation of violence and political anger that occurred as a consequence of the Ruhr occupation, we must read of the victims' experiences so that we can properly assess the reactions of the male officers and political leaders who were in charge of the occupation. As we will see, some of them behaved admirably, putting their own soldiers behind bars for their crimes, while others protected their own men without any consideration for German civilians. We also need to learn about the language being used to speak about rape and sexual violence so that we can understand how it was amplified and used by German propaganda to mobilize the population to support the campaign of active resistance. If we do not do so, we cannot understand how the fear of being raped or abused, or the fear that a wife or girlfriend or daughter might be taken away at a checkpoint by occupying soldiers, was a consistent part of female and male experience of the Ruhr occupation. Given that more German women and girls were raped in 1923 than French soldiers lost their lives in the Ruhr occupation, any account that ignores the subject will be wholly incomplete.[2]

Cases of rape often occurred when soldiers entered the victims' homes, or else when they targeted women and girls as they made their way through public spaces. In at least one documented case, a French railway worker attempted to rape a German girl on a train. The rapists could be groups of men or single soldiers on their own. In one case, as many as ten French soldiers and railway men assaulted a seventeen-year-old German female after they arrested her and beat the man she was with. Most of the victims were chosen arbitrarily: they were picked out in public spaces, 'arrested' and raped nearby. Some cases also occurred in formal settings, such as prisons. Maids and cleaners were also victims. Sometimes the soldiers cited a woman's appearance or behaviour as justification for their choice of victim. In the vast majority of documented cases, once the rape was over, women and girls were allowed to go. But in at least one case, a young girl was forced to stay in a French railwayman's accommodation overnight. There were also some instances of deliberately seeking out women based on the identity of their husbands. For instance, at the end of February in Recklinghausen, just as the occupying forces were preparing to disband the German police force, the wives of German police officers became targets.[3]

The ages of victims ranged in the main from girls in their early teens to women in their early forties, with a small number of cases outside this age range. In Unterrath in Düsseldorf, an eight-year-old girl was sexually assaulted on 15 October 1923. In Castrop, to the south-east of Recklinghausen, on 7 June, a French soldier attempted to rape a ten-year-old girl. Men and boys were also victims. On 12 March, French soldiers raped a miner in Recklinghausen. In the same town, on 10 June, a seventeen-year-old apprentice locksmith was sexually assaulted by a French soldier. In April 1924, a twelve-year-old boy was raped by a French sentry. A few days later, three French soldiers raped a fifteen-year-old boy in Steimel. For the rape of the twelve-year-old, the culprit was sentenced by the French military to ten years' forced labour. In the Steimel case, the soldiers were sentenced by a French military court to four months' imprisonment. They received such a mild sentence because they managed to convince the court that the boy had consented to having sex with them; the victim did not testify.[4]

There are several examples of German civilians coming to the aid of victims of attempted rape and sexual assault. When three French soldiers grabbed Frau M. on a street in Recklinghausen on 6 April, she started screaming. As soon as she heard her pleas for help, another woman rushed out of a nearby canteen, charging at the soldiers, forcing them off Frau M. and helping her to escape. In other cases, neighbours rushed to help women when they heard their screaming.[5]

Other women and girls escaped by themselves. On 4 February, two Belgian soldiers stopped a German couple in Bottrop and then led the woman away. After one of the soldiers had removed her clothing and forced her to lie on the ground, the girl, S., hit him in the face as hard as she could, causing him to lose balance momentarily and taking the chance to get up and run away. When one of the French soldiers who were about to rape the teenager Emma F. in an upstairs room let go of her for a split second, she ran to the window and jumped. She sprained her ankle when she landed, but managed to run to a nearby house. Wearing only her tights and shoes, the distraught girl banged on the door, calling for help. The family who lived there took her in, gave her clothes and later took her back to her parents.[6]

As with all incidents of sexual violence, the victims experienced these events as individual traumas. But rape and the fear of rape were part of a wider German national trauma during the occupation. German men were supposed to fight to protect 'their' women from the invader's brutality. They were not supposed to 'resist passively' while the occupying soldiers raped German women and girls. But with no realistic military alternative to passive resistance, the only option for the German side was to instrumentalize rape and sexual violence as a means of mobilizing the German population to continue to resist the occupation, while using the same subject as a means of gaining international support for Germany.

The political responses were not entirely new. During the First World War, Allied propaganda had depicted the Germans as 'Huns'. It identified them as barbarians who murdered and raped women and children during the occupation of Belgium and northern France. Some of these accusations were based on real events – German soldiers did execute civilians and commit atrocities during the First World War, particularly during the war's opening phase when million-strong armies smashed into each other and confusion reigned as urban towns with large civilian populations became battlefields. During the occupation German soldiers had also raped French and Belgian women. In 1923, German opinion leaders now reversed the propaganda that had been directed against them during the war.

But it wasn't just German propagandists who reversed the role of perpetrator and victim, as it had been during the First World

War. The French and Belgians reversed their roles too. For them, the occupation of Germany was a chance to take revenge for the rape of 'their women' between 1914 and 1918. Tellingly, even before the invasion, French soldiers' letters show that many of them fantasized that they would one day occupy Germany and rape German women. In one example from October 1916, a French sergeant recorded listening to another soldier speak openly of his desire to invade Germany 'to indulge in rape' so as to 'satisfy his excessive temperament and his just desire for reprisals'. As the French military position improved, such fantasies appear to have become more common. In a letter from November 1918, a soldier wrote: 'we are en route to the land of the Boches. Be sure that we are on our way there with strong hearts. We must fuck the German Boche animals. They have sullied ours enough. It's our turn.' Another soldier promised: 'Ah! If we ever go to Bocheland, we will make them see a few things, these fuckers, show them what we are made of, they have raped our girls and dishonoured our women, we will do the same.' In another example, a soldier wrote:

> For my part I have a stockpile of condoms because I would have too much fear of soiling myself in contact with these superb Gretchens. It looks as if they all have a sick colour, are fat and greasy and that they all smell sour; vive our little French women, so gracious, so pretty. Only they are capable of inspiring real passion in us.[7]

Once the first cases occurred in 1923, the German government began to catalogue every accusation that they received and sent formal complaints via the German Foreign Office to the French government. They also published detailed and graphic accounts of French and Belgian rapes of German women in Germany with the intention of mobilizing the German population to continue to oppose the occupation and to support the campaign of passive resistance. The Reichstag even added details to the formal records of the German parliament, making the women's voices available to all who wanted to listen to them.

The issue of race loomed large over the sexual violence, real and fictionalized, that accompanied occupation. Under the Treaty of Versailles, which came into effect in January 1920, the Rhineland was militarily occupied. The numbers of French troops in the occupied zone varied during the course of the occupation, but in the early 1920s, around one-third of them, some 25,000 men, were French colonial soldiers, often recruits from Algeria, Morocco, Senegal and Madagascar. The reasons for stationing colonial soldiers in the Rhineland have never been entirely explained. Some historians argue that it was a reward to them for their role in France's victory in the war – a way of telling them that they were truly French. Others have suggested that it was also a means of keeping non-white soldiers out of France. But in early twentieth-century Europe, when the racial superiority of white Europeans was part of the fabric of most people's social thought, it is almost certain that it was deliberately intended to insult the Germans.

After soldiers occupied Frankfurt as punishment for German military units entering the demilitarized zone following the Kapp Putsch, on 7 April 1920 a group of Moroccan soldiers at a Frankfurt machine-gun checkpoint opened fire on a crowd of protesting civilians. The impact of the firing was 'awful'. The first reports suggested that seven Germans were killed, including one child, and at least thirty injured. German accounts allege that the Moroccan soldiers used a machine gun to fire upon the crowd, many of whom had gathered there because of a rumour that the French were about to withdraw. The allegation may be true, but it may also be the case that rifle fire was mistaken for machine-gun fire by traumatized witnesses.[8]

The Frankfurt atrocity became the starting point for an orchestrated German propaganda campaign against the so-called 'Black Shame' on the Rhine. The campaigners, including state officials in the German Foreign Office and private citizens alike, accused France of breaking the unwritten rules of European civilization by putting white Europeans at the mercy of North African soldiers. French colonial soldiers were accused of raping German women and children, and of committing murder and cannibalism. To be sure, there were real cases, confirmed by French records, of French colonial soldiers raping German women in the Rhineland. But the proportion of cases carried out by North African soldiers, largely from Algeria and Morocco, was lower than that carried out by white French soldiers from France. That kind of nuance mattered little, however.

The 'Black Shame' campaign put the issue of rape in the forefront of the Germans' image of occupation. Posters and magazine covers depicted 'savage' blacks with ape-like features raping and kidnapping innocent German girls. This powerful propaganda also played a crucial part in German hatred of the Versailles Treaty. The presence of colonial soldiers on the territory of a country that still considered itself a great power humiliated Germans and reinforced the claims made by German politicians and opinion leaders that the victorious Allies were treating Germany like a colony.

During the Ruhr occupation in 1923, Jean-Marie Degoutte, who had been in charge of the Moroccans at Frankfurt, decided not to use regiments from France's colonies in the operation. He did not want to gift Germany another propaganda victory. Hence, the soldiers occupying the Ruhr were almost all white Europeans. But this did not stop Germans from continuing to use the colonial motif. The image of the black soldier raping German women, which had been so effective in mobilizing Germans against the occupation of the Rhineland, remained sufficiently powerful in 1923 for German propaganda against the occupation to still draw upon the same imagery, even if there were few North African soldiers actually stationed in the Ruhr. There were also concrete cases of colonial soldiers raping or attempting to rape German women and girls in the occupied Rhineland in 1923.[9] Fears of rape and miscegenation were an important part of the German resistance against the Ruhr occupation.[10]

Poincaré knew this was an issue he could not ignore. He was fully aware that cases of rape and sexual violence against German civilians were a fundamental part of the Franco–German contest to convince public opinion, in Britain and the United States as well as in France and Germany, that right was on their side. For that reason, every case of rape or sexual violence mattered. Poincaré made it clear to Degoutte that he wanted every single German complaint about French military conduct investigated. In one letter on this subject, sent on 10 April 1923, Poincaré complained that so far some of the investigations that had taken place had not been sufficiently thorough and the accompanying reports lacked detail. He reminded Degoutte that 'for every incident that has led to a complaint, a dossier with a carefully compiled and documented counterargument must be available'. When French investigators found that the accusations made by the German side were untrue or contestable, they were to publish substantial denials as widely as possible. In cases where French soldiers were found to have committed crimes against the population of the Ruhr, the official French policy was that their soldiers were to be brought before a court martial and should face harsh punishment.[11]

However, regardless of what the official policy was, the responses of French officers and commanders in the occupied Ruhr and the nature of sentencing before French military courts varied considerably. This is particularly clear in the cases of Frau F. and Frau Böhme.

Frau F. was raped in her home in Habinghorst at around 2 a.m. during the night of 30 April–1 May 1923. The French patrol was led by Sergeant Lapuy, who commanded six men. When they knocked on her door they had their pistols drawn and Lapuy demanded that she should let them in. He and three of his men then followed her upstairs and raped her in her bedroom. Of Lapuy she later said: 'He beat me so wildly until he was finally ready to force himself on me.' Lapuy then called in the next soldier. Frau F. tried to stand up and defend herself, but, as she later testified: 'My nerves were now so deadened that I could no longer defend myself, so that the second Frenchman (and the third and fourth) no longer caused me any pain.' Altogether, the four men raped and sexually assaulted her for around thirty minutes. When she stood up, she described awful physical and mental pain.[12]

A week later, during the night of 6–7 May, three French soldiers from the French Infantry Regiment 106 – Dromiche, Courtier and

Lambert – raped Frau Böhme during a drunken rampage in Welper, about 25 kilometres to the south of Habinghorst. The rampage started between 11 p.m. and midnight, when they started attacking Germans in the street. First, they hit a worker on the head with a 'drawn sidearm', tearing his hat in two and leaving him with a bloody wound that required stitches. Soon after, they assaulted and robbed four German men at gunpoint, hitting one of them on the head, causing him to lose consciousness briefly. They then attacked another two Germans – brothers-in-law who were on their way home from the local bar. They had been engaged in violent attacks for about an hour when the local vicar heard them making a noise outside his home shortly after midnight. He first thought that drunken youths were responsible for the disturbance and opened his window and shouted at them, threatening that he would call the police if they were not quiet. As soon as he realized that it was French soldiers, he closed the window and turned out the lights. But it was too late. As he hid in the darkness, the three soldiers walked around his house, smashing in windows. When they got to the front door, they began to kick it in. To the vicar's relief, the door held and after a few more agonizing moments, he heard them walking away towards a nearby building.[13]

For the Böhme family, the night's ordeal was only just beginning. After they left the vicar's home, the soldiers forced their way into the home of Frau S., trashing it 'like savages', shouting, 'Destroy, destroy.' Inside, one of them aimed his rifle at Frau S.'s chest, before they went into the bedroom of her twenty-two-year-old daughter. At gunpoint, they forced her to kiss one of them. But they did not do anything more to her. In his nearby apartment, a crane operator, Böhme, had heard them. He thought that they were carrying out house searches. When they banged on his door, he opened it and Dromiche and Courtier entered, while Lambert waited outside. Neither Dromiche nor Courtier said anything as Dromiche struck Böhme on the head with his sidearm, knocking him unconscious. The noise woke up his wife. She was in their bedroom with the door closed. At first, she listened as the soldiers made their way through the living room, breaking items of furniture. Then they came into the bedroom. She begged them to leave her alone. But her pleas were in vain. Courtier raped her while Dromiche stood guard over her husband. He later testified that, when he regained consciousness, he saw that Courtier was in their bedroom raping his wife but he could do nothing as he 'was held at bay by the smaller one with the bayonet'.

As Courtier raped Frau Böhme, she fainted. When she regained consciousness, in her words, she 'noticed from the wetness that the soldier had entered me completely'. Courtier and Dromiche then swapped places. As she told German court investigators, the 'horrors endured' and left her 'almost powerless'; 'this soldier broke my resistance with violence'. Once Dromiche finished, Courtier returned and raped her for a second time. This time it was even more painful. He turned 'furious' when she tried to resist him. He cursed her, grabbing and throwing her onto the bed. As she remembered, 'the soldier unbuckled his belt and caused me a lot of pain as a result'. Herr Böhme made a sworn statement to German authorities the following day. His wife had to receive medical attention for several weeks after the rape. She first gave her testimony under oath on 25 May, when a German judge and a court clerk visited her at her home. She recounted her ordeal to them in the bedroom where the crime had taken place. She was still physically unable to walk. Her psychological injuries may never have healed.[14]

In the cases of Frau F. in Habinghorst and Frau Böhme in Welper, the French military authorities immediately launched investigations and quickly discovered the identities of the perpetrators. But this is where the similarities stopped. In Habinghorst, General Douchy, the head of the 3rd Division, made a report for his commander in Dortmund that stated that it was impossible to prove that any violence had been committed towards Frau F. He claimed that an injury to her abdomen was not a result of the alleged rape. He added that there was no evidence of bruising and that rape could not have occurred because she did not defend herself. The chief accused, Sergeant Lapuy, also produced an alibi. Another soldier stated that he had been with Lapuy the entire evening and did not witness him rape anyone. This was enough for Douchy. He concluded that there was insufficient evidence to prosecute Lapuy and his men for rape. Instead, he gave Lapuy a twenty-day suspended sentence for drunken behaviour – though, tellingly, he also suggested that Lapuy take early retirement.[15]

In the case of Frau Böhme in Welper, the French military commander, General Nayral de Bourgon, was far more aggressive in his punishment of the perpetrators. Even before Frau Böhme had given her sworn testimony to the German authorities, he had put Dromiche, Lambert and Courtier, whom he later called genuine 'Apaches', who left their watch to ransack a city, before a military court on 11 May 1923. Together, the three soldiers faced six charges: abandoning their posts; aggravated assault; aggravated theft; aggravated trespass; damage to private property; and rape. For the crime of rape, Dromiche and Courtier were sentenced to twenty years' forced labour, and a further two months' imprisonment for their other crimes. The third soldier, Lambert, who stayed outside while the rape took place, was sentenced to three years' imprisonment. Nayral de Bourgon described the rapists as 'heinous'. The sentences handed down to them were among the harshest administered by the French military to French soldiers during the occupation of the Ruhr. It is not known if they served them in full.[16]

Another example of some French officers behaving responsibly occurred in Essen in March when two German teenagers, one of whom was a fifteen-year-old girl, were stopped by two French soldiers. The soldiers threatened the girl at knifepoint and forced her into a nearby field where they raped her. While they did this, the boy accompanying her went looking for help. When he came across a French patrol of six soldiers, the French captain rushed to the girl's aid. He immediately had the assailants arrested and informed his superiors that they were dealing with a case of rape. The soldiers faced an immediate punishment of fifteen days' confinement, eight of which were to be spent in a cell. However, despite this evidence, the French military court that investigated the case found the soldiers not guilty. It sided with the soldiers, who argued that they had not threatened the girl and that she had behaved in a way that enticed the soldiers.[17]

This case was a typical example of how the military justice system often ended up taking the side of the rapist. The French military often accused women of bringing forward rape accusations under pressure from their parents or husbands or of having consensual sex with French soldiers. For example, after a German woman claimed that she had been raped in a railway hut in Sterkrade, in the north of Oberhausen, on 26 February, the ensuing French investigation ruled that her father had forced her to press charges and that there had been no rape – all that had happened was that a French soldier had tried to kiss her. This ruling was made despite the fact that at least one French officer wanted to see the men placed before a court martial.[18]

While German archives contain hundreds of accusations of rape, historian Stanislas Jeannesson has shown that the French occupying authorities investigated fewer than a hundred cases, of which only around one-third ended in a sentence. The sentences that were handed down appear to have been quite arbitrary. Some rapists received between two and five years in prison. In the case of the alleged rape of an eight-year-old girl, General Simon, commander in Düsseldorf, argued that he was unable to find any information about the incident and subsequently listed a series of German rape accusations that he believed were untrue, including the alleged rape of a sixteen-year-old girl. In the case of the ten-year-old girl in Castrop on 7 June, the accused claimed that the girl had 'provocative looks'. He told military investigators that he felt worse for having left his watch than for what he did to the girl. His captain claimed that medical analysis revealed that no rape had occurred. Tellingly, however, as the accused soldier had committed previous misdemeanours, the court martial convicted him and sentenced him to three years' imprisonment.[19]

The percentage of soldiers found guilty of rape was about twice as high as that found guilty of causing the death or serious injury of German civilians, which was 15 per cent. Examples of the range of sentences in these cases include one of only three years' imprisonment for a drunken soldier who killed a German police officer, five years' imprisonment for two soldiers who beat a man to death in a public place and lifelong forced labour for a French soldier who opened fire on a café and killed three people.[20]

The French were aware of these problems. In August, a German man and his wife were in a café in Herne when a French soldier, Henri Pech, approached them. When the man tried to protect his wife, Pech stabbed him in the right shoulder with his bayonet. The man's injuries were so bad that he later died. Pech was found guilty and sentenced to just two years 'on probation'.

Even Poincaré was angry about the lenience of this sentence. As he wrote: 'The victims were harmless civilians. The soldier's actions are inexcusable and the grave consequences of those actions have had a damaging effect on public opinion, and blackened the good name and reputation of our soldiers.' He added: 'If incidents of such regrettable proportions should occur, it seems to me that a vigorous response is inevitable. Any unduly lenient measure runs the risk of being used against us by German propaganda.' Poincaré might have been annoyed at the death of a civilian and the mild punishment handed down to his killer, but as this reaction shows, his priority was the reputation of France's military, not the protection and safety of German civilians.[21]

German women and girls were not only victims of violence from the occupying forces. From February 1922 onwards, groups of German men, including organized groups known as 'Scissors Clubs', targeted women and girls whom they accused of betraying the national cause by fraternizing with French and Belgian soldiers. The Scissors Clubs' violence included cutting the hair of those they accused of being the 'darlings of the French'.

This kind of public violence drew on traditions of public shaming that had deep historical roots. In one case, after they cut off a girl's plaits, the perpetrators hung her hair in the town's marketplace. In Bottrop, two women were made to stand at the outer door of a church, where they were insulted for their behaviour. In Habinghorst-Ickern, a woman was tied to an advertising pillar, her hair covered in dye and a placard with a humiliating satirical poem hung around her neck. The act of hair-cutting was also accompanied by other forms of physical violence. Some women and girls were punched, at least one woman was thrown into a canal, and others had the windows of their homes smashed in. In one case, two teenage girls from Remscheid, which was in the zone occupied by the British, who had spent time with French soldiers in Lennep, close to the border of the occupied Ruhr, were escorted by the French military to the train at Lennep to prevent an angry mob from attacking them. But once the girls got back to Remscheid, the Scissors Club men caught up with them, cut their hair and force-marched them through the streets of the town.[22]

Other punishments included naming women in German newspapers and pamphlets that were published to oppose the occupation. Some even included sections with the title 'At the Stake', 'In the Stocks' or 'Pillory of Whores', in which 'those who had forgotten German honour' were named. In some cases, these sections included the names and addresses of women with the accusation that they 'had had dealings with or relationships with members of the foreign troops'. Other local newspapers included advertisements threatening women and girls. One read as follows: 'We hereby warn the ladies of the district [of Hattingen] not to get involved in intimate relationships with foreigners, otherwise we will proceed with severity. The Scissors Club.'[23]

The publishing of women's names was not just a private hobby – the state lent support to the practice. The staff of a censorship office in Münster were tasked with examining the truthfulness of accusations against German women in the occupied zone that it received by post before taking a decision about which names to publish. The records of its activities are not complete, but in a few weeks in the spring of 1923 it published over five thousand names.[24]

The Scissors Clubs usually consisted of young men who were sexually jealous of the French and Belgian soldiers. Rivalries with the French soldiers whom local women and girls found attractive would have happened even if the German government had invited them into the Ruhr. But there was more to the reaction. The Scissors Clubs were an expression of the way in which the occupation created a crisis of German masculine power.

In late January 1923, following the French and Belgian invasion, across Germany there was a stream of male volunteers to the Reichswehr, many of whom were from the Ruhr. These men wanted to be mobilized by the state to fight back against the French and Belgian invasion. But the policy of passive resistance left them with little scope for enacting the kind of violent 'masculine' resistance they craved. For a section of the male population in the Ruhr, this led them to take out their sense of masculine power loss on German women and girls. Just as French and Belgian soldiers used women's bodies to demonstrate their control of the Ruhr and to humiliate German men (in the most extreme cases by raping German women in front of their husbands), the males in the Scissors Clubs used female bodies to send a message about the national rejection of the French and Belgian presence in the Ruhr. The men who did this had the backing of the wider population, including other women, and those in positions of moral responsibility, including teachers and priests.

The supporters and members of the Scissors Clubs in 1923 behaved in a way that was all too similar to other military occupiers during the twentieth century. Occupation is typically a moment when the men of one nation celebrate their military subjugation of another nation by sexually 'conquering' the enemy's women. The male populations of occupied territories always respond by 'policing' the female population in order to punish collaborators – real and imagined. For the men who do this, it is a way of coming to terms with the heavy blow to their masculinity that accompanies defeat and occupation. In most cases, this powerful emotional response fuels hatreds that last longer than the occupation itself.

For the Weimar Republic, the consequences of rape and sexual violence during the occupation of the Ruhr were particularly pernicious. In November 1918, at the moment of its foundation, the equality of women with men had been declared one of the republic's key goals. In January 1919, women voted in the elections for the National Assembly that created the Weimar constitution. On 19 February 1919, the Social Democrat Marie Juchacz made German parliamentary history by becoming the first ever elected woman to speak in the German parliament. The republic's founders expected that, for giving women the vote and the promise of equality, they would be rewarded with female loyalty to the new state. But the occupation in 1923 advertised the republic's failure.

Not only was the republic incapable of protecting the bodies of its female citizens against a hostile occupier, it also sought support for the campaign of passive resistance by advertising that failure in its propaganda against the occupation. That may have made political sense, but it nonetheless contributed to the republic's loss of legitimacy and helped to create a platform for ultra-nationalists and anti-democrats to claim that they would do a better job of protecting German women. For right-wing populists and ultra-nationalists determined to destroy German democracy, it provided powerful evidence for their claim that the republic and democracy itself were somehow weak and feminine and that Germany would be better protected by a political system that placed a strongman in charge.

9

Hitler's First Defeat

On 20 April 1923, just a week after Albert Leo Schlageter was arrested by the French in the Ruhr, Adolf Hitler turned thirty-four years old in Munich. Four years earlier, when Anton Drexler had founded the German Workers' Party in January 1919, which was then renamed the Nazi Party in February 1920, Hitler had been on his own, trying to find something to replace the wartime camaraderie of the trenches. That year, on his thirtieth birthday, it is unknown if he had anyone at all, let alone any close friends or family, with whom he could celebrate the start of his third decade. In 1923, his situation was entirely different. That year, the Nazi Party, his new community of comrades, didn't just gather around him to celebrate their leader's birthday, they publicly celebrated it as a great 'breakthrough' moment in German national history: the day that the saviour of the German race was born. Later, during the Third Reich, it would become one of the most important national festivals in the Nazi calendar, a day when everything was supposed to stop to allow all Germans to celebrate the genius of their leader.

In 1923, the idea that Hitler was the saviour of the German people was still in the making. To help to create what historian Ian Kershaw has aptly described as 'the Hitler Myth', the main headline in the *Völkischer Beobachter* on Hitler's birthday praised him as 'Germany's leader' alongside a piece that compared him to Otto von Bismarck and Friedrich the Great – two of the most celebrated figures in German national history at that time. The *Völkischer Beobachter* promised that once Hitler had destroyed the Weimar Republic, his leadership would restore Germany to greatness.

Published alongside these articles was a poem by Dietrich Eckart, a racist ultra-nationalist journalist and artist, that called upon Nazi followers to 'open their hearts' to Hitler, promising them that his strength would 'scare away the night'. In the same edition of the paper, Alfred Rosenberg, who would later be hanged at Nuremberg, claimed that thanks to Hitler 'ever greater numbers of desperate people had found strength in their lives again'.[1]

As bombastic as such material may sound, it was working. Since the *Völkischer Beobachter* editor, Hermann Esser, had proclaimed Hitler the German Mussolini back in November 1922, the Nazi movement had continued to grow. On the night of his birthday, the Circus Krone, one of Munich's largest indoor venues, was overflowing as eight to nine thousand people gathered inside with thousands more outside unable to enter. Inside the hall, the atmosphere resembled a rock concert. Esser was the first warm-up speaker, followed by Anton Drexler. At 8 p.m., when Hitler took to the stage, he was greeted with wild cheering.[2]

The newspaper of German Jews, the *CV-Zeitung*, sent Artur Schweriner to report on Hitler's birthday celebrations. The Jewish journalist came away from the event filled with terror. It was obvious to him that the Nazis wanted to use violence against Germany's Jews. He even warned that they might be planning a pogrom and called on readers of the *CV-Zeitung* to get ready to protect themselves.

What stands out in particular is Schweriner's warning that the Nazis' 'will to annihilate' posed a threat to the existence of Germany's Jews. Historians have often pointed out that the verb 'annihilate' (*vernichten*) was one of Hitler's favourite words, leading to debates about when Hitler's almost constant references to the annihilation of the Jews turned from something that he said into something that he demanded that his regime did. Most of these debates focus upon Hitler's decision-making from the late 1930s up until late 1941. But as Schweriner's report emphasizes, Hitler was already publicly using this language in 1923. Hitler was allowed to say whatever he wanted and few conservatives thought twice about it. After Hitler's birthday, the German nationalist *Deutsche*

Zeitung, the newspaper of the established anti-republican conservative organization the Pan-German League, told its readers that the 'celebration of Hitler was a high point in the avalanche-like swelling of the National Socialist movement' that was taking place in Munich.[3]

Artur Schweriner had good reason to be fearful. The title of Hitler's birthday speech was 'Politics and race: Why are we antisemitic?' It contained Hitler's usual hate-filled claims that the German race would only be free when the Versailles Treaty was done away with and the 'internal enemy killed'. Hitler warned that there was no such thing as 'decent' or 'indecent Jews'. He told his supporters that this idea was just another example of the way that the Jews were 'the great master of lies' and that ultimately all Jews were Germany's 'mortal enemy'. In making this point, Hitler explicitly wanted to reject the idea that integrated German Jews like Rathenau did not pose the same threat to German culture as newly arrived Jewish emigrants from eastern Europe, who had come to Weimar Germany in increasing numbers since 1918 to flee the antisemitic violence of the Russian Civil War. Hitler was adamant that no Jew could ever really belong in Germany.

By the time of his thirty-fourth birthday, Hitler was no longer a minority figure in Bavarian politics. Even though he was not yet the leader of a major force, the rate at which his movement was attracting new members was gaining critical attention in its own right. Like many populist leaders, Hitler thrived on the condemnation he recieved. He paid attention to what was said about him and his movement and used his opponents as a source of content for his speeches. In his birthday speech, he told his followers that they should be proud that their critics tried to insult them by calling them 'loudmouths' and 'antisemites'. He lamented that too many Germans were pacifists, before threatening, 'We only know one race that we fight for, and that is our race. We may be inhumane! But when we save Germany, we will have done the greatest deed in the world.' Hitler himself admitted that his promise to use violence to remove all Jews from Germany put the Nazis 'on extreme ground'. Yet even these words were greeted with wild cheering and applause.

It wasn't just Hitler's words that gripped his audience's attention, it was the way he delivered them too. His critics described Hitler's public performances as possessing an atmosphere of terror. But for those inside his community, the events were a positive experience. His supporters interrupted his speeches by cheering, clapping and stamping their feet. When this happened, Hitler would mark the acclaim by raising his beer mug and taking a 'good swig'. But he was also often interrupted by 'laughter'. Nor were his speeches exclusively devoted to shouting and raving: Hitler could also speak quietly when he wanted. He chose to raise his voice primarily to emphasize the misdeeds of his opponents, reserving his highest decibel level for his most hated enemies: Jews and Social Democrats.

Hitler's political opponents were fully aware of what he was doing. At the start of February 1923, the *CV-Zeitung* recognized that his success was due to his ability to bring disparate and usually disunited right-wing groups together under his banner. It called him 'a man with a pronounced talent for leadership and the ability to captivate with his speeches'. A few weeks earlier, *Vorwärts*'s analysis was more straightforward: it simply called Hitler an 'apostle of hatred' (*Hetzapostel*). Another observer thought that it was the combination of his talent as a speaker, the violence of his shock troops, his hatred of German democracy and his 'excessive agitation' against 'foreigners' that drew people to him.[4]

After observing his speeches and interaction with the crowds, a reporter for the Social Democratic *Münchener Post*, which firmly opposed Hitler and the Nazis, thought that whenever Hitler said something simple and obvious, he slowed his words so as to suggest that he had just revealed something of 'great sophistication'. The writer added that as he spoke, Hitler often only used short phrases, repeatedly using the same 'keywords' to attack his opponents: 'international finance', 'Marxists', 'Jewry' and the 'November criminals' – a term that he first used in September 1922 and deployed continuously thereafter, having discovered that the crowd responded to the words' utterance with wild cheering that lasted for several minutes. The rapidity with which 'November criminals' was adopted as a term that he repeated continuously offers a reminder that, at this time in his political career, Hitler wasn't just leading the crowds as he spoke, he was learning from them: the performances were interactive, the crowds' cheers helping him to decide which phrases to use thereafter and which to drop. This mixture of inter-action, intoxication and hatred was what made his performances so powerful. He convinced his supporters that he was just like them: filled with hatred and certain that nothing could be solved until his movement created a new Germany. With words that were intended to insult Hitler, the reporter for the *Münchener Post* thought that Hitler resembled an 'entertainer', '*conférencier*' or 'beer hall speaker'.[5]

A few days after his birthday speech, the *Münchener Post* once again analysed his success and his party's attempt to portray him as some kind of 'messiah' or 'Übermensch'. The newspaper warned that Hitler's constant rhetorical 'invitation to murder, manslaughter and criminality of all kinds' was insufficient to keep his supporters together in the longer term. That is why, the newspaper argued, the Nazi movement constantly focused on the genius of its leader. The cult that was being made around Hitler, it warned, was the glue that was keeping an otherwise disparate movement together. In an early example of the belief that Germany was too educated to fall for his racist politics, it added that the people who supported Hitler were largely drawn from the less well-educated sections of society.[6]

Hitler was aware his movement was considered low class by the Bavarian establishment. That is why in the spring of 1923 he craved the support and acknowledgement of his social superiors. He enjoyed developing relations with upper-class benefactors, privately playing the role of socially awkward but politically astute rising star to their delight. But, above all, he enjoyed appearing on stage alongside his social betters, who were mesmerized by his command of his audience.

Just under two months before his birthday, on 26 February 1923, Hitler spoke at a packed beer hall. Before he started, Hermann Göring warmed the audience up with a speech of his own. A twenty-nine-year-old upper-class veteran fighter pilot who had been awarded the highest military decoration, the Pour le Mérite, Göring stood out among Hitler's entourage. He had first heard Hitler speak in October or November 1922. Later, he would write that he instantly fell for Hitler's political message, quickly becoming a regular attendee at the Café Neumann, where Hitler held weekly meetings of supporters on Monday nights. In March 1923, Hitler made Göring the head of the SA. His task was to deal with its rapidly growing membership and to strengthen its military structures. This was the starting point for Göring's Nazi career. It would later make him the second most powerful man in the Third Reich.[7]

Just weeks before Hitler made Göring head of the SA, the Reichswehr officer Ernst Röhm founded the working group of the Patriotic Fighting Associations. It brought together the SA, the Bund Oberland, the Imperial Flag Bund, the Viking League and the Fighting Association of Lower Bavaria. The group's military leader was Hermann Kriebel, a veteran of the First World War. Röhm ensured that Hitler was appointed as its political leader. *Vorwärts* called it a 'cartel'. Training was provided by the Reichswehr. Crucially, the SA was not the largest force within the new umbrella organization. It needed its street violence to make it stand out.[8]

Göring's appointment as leader occurred at the same time as the SA began its spring campaign of violence, much of which was directed at the German left and which was very similar in style to the Fascist violence that had helped bring Mussolini to power. On 1 March, the SA led an attack on the offices of the Social Democratic *Münchener Post*. The offices were protected by a two-metre-high iron door designed to keep unwanted thugs out. But it offered little protection when the assault came.

The attack was led by around two hundred 'lads', including some so-called 'refugees' from the Ruhr, who broke into the newspaper offices and vandalized several rooms. The destruction only stopped after the police arrived and arrested participants. According to reports in the Social Democratic *Vorwärts*, a female accountant was knocked to the ground after being hit with a 'heavy piece of wood'.[9]

The Stormtroopers continued their campaign of mayhem on

Saturday, 10 March, when around seven hundred of them travelled from Munich by train and trucks to Ingolstadt, a city 85 kilometres to the north of Munich. Their activities mimicked the Italian Fascists' city occupations, when truckloads of Fascists would travel from all over northern Italy to congregate in a town where their sudden numerical advantage meant that they could bully and violently intimidate their opponents. After they arrived in Ingolstadt, the SA smashed up the trade union building's windows and physically destroyed parts of it. As the rampage continued, shots were fired (probably by the Nazis) and two Social Democratic Party (SPD) supporters were injured. The rioting came to an end only with the arrival of the police.

When the SA men returned to Munich, they paraded without permission to the Marienplatz, where their day of violence finally came to an end when police reinforcements obliged them to disband. Some of the police even drew their pistols to threaten the SA men and make them disperse. According to the account in *Vorwärts*, even though they did this, there was no serious attempt on the part of the police to arrest the SA leaders.[10]

The SPD in Bavaria swiftly sought to strike back politically. On 20 March, Johannes Timm, chairman of the SPD parliamentary group, brought a motion to the constitutional committee of the Bavarian parliament. It referred directly to the events in Ingolstadt and the attack on the *Münchener Post*, and called on the Bavarian government to ban the SA and introduce stronger measures to guarantee the right to freedom of assembly, which the Stormtroopers threatened by using violence against their opponents across Bavaria. As he spoke in favour of the motion, the SPD leader, Alwin Saenger, accused the government of being in the hands of reactionary civil servants 'who are related to this movement and deeply involved with it'. He accused some of the police of helping to arm the SA and predicted that if there was no ban Bavaria would end up in a civil war.[11]

The SPD motion was supported by the German Democratic Party – Rathenau's party. That party's speaker, Pius Dirr, warned that the Stormtroopers were not just planning to attack prominent

Social Democrats like Erhard Auer, but that they would also one day come for conservatives like interior minister Franz Xaver Schweyer, who was a member of the Bavarian People's Party. But it was not enough. Timm's motion was rejected by fifteen to twelve votes. In its place, a countermotion put forward by the Bavarian People's Party was passed. It called on the government 'to monitor the paramilitary organizations closely and suppress them' if 'their aims are violence, threatening state power or endangering public order'.[12]

Just over a month later, only days after Hitler's thirty-fourth birthday, Bavaria's Social Democrats tried to have the SA banned a second time. In the debates in the parliament, Saenger repeated his warning that the SA would bring civil war to Germany and explained that rising SA violence had made it necessary for the SPD to create a self-defence organization, whose volunteers would protect their meetings from attacks by the SA's Stormtroopers. The German Democratic Party also supported an SA ban. Like the SPD, its party events had come under threat from the same source: at least one meeting of the middle-class party had requested, and received, protection from the SPD's self-defence organization. In the Bavarian parliament, the German Democratic Party's Ernst Müller-Meiningen argued that it would be a 'disgrace for democracy' if the Bavarian government did not move forcefully against the SA. 'Is the government really blind or just pretending to be blind!' he exclaimed. But the democratic parties' proposal was defeated.

Schweyer was among those who opposed it. He rejected the idea that a ban was necessary and openly expressed his admiration for the nationalist movements in Bavaria. He called them a flame that was reawakening nationalist feelings and argued that no one present could condemn them. Their 'central core', he claimed, was making 'a healthy, natural and therefore welcome appearance'.[13]

Schweyer's sympathy towards Nazism was partially based on the claim that the Nazis had to be armed to protect themselves from attacks launched by 'left-wing' radicals – a popular conservative defence of Fascist violence in Italy before Mussolini was appointed prime minister and in the Weimar Republic. He even said that the Nazis had to have the right to defend themselves. When it came to reports of police officers attending Nazi rallies, he saw no need for concern because they did so as private individuals.

For Schweyer, the real problem was the liberal press in Berlin which was spreading lies about Bavaria. At this time, when a strict application of the Law for the Protection of the Republic in Bavaria would have stopped the Nazi threat to German democracy in its tracks, Schweyer chose to blame that particular piece of legislation, which he hated, for worsening the situation. He went so far as to claim that the monarchies that Germany's republicans had destroyed in November 1918 had had no need for such a law because of the popularity of the old political system. This was not true: the imperial regime had a strict system for policing dissent and strong laws against even insulting the reputation of the monarch. Schweyer condemned the Court for the Protection of the Republic as a 'political court' and demanded that it should be done away with.[14]

But even though he did not support the SPD motion, Schweyer admitted that Hitler's movement posed some threats. He warned that their programme was dangerous for Bavaria and that their men carried out 'acts of terror' and 'acts of violence', and that the paramilitaries were guilty of 'barbarity' and 'brutality'. He also warned that the Nazi Party's 'hateful and extreme racial antisemitism was in irreconcilable contradiction to Christian morality'. But even though he acknowledged this, he did not believe that the state should suppress the Nazis. He argued that the state forces under his command had done enough. His speech was another victory for Hitler.[15]

For Bavaria's Jews, the motion's defeat was a major blow. The invasion of the Ruhr and increasing nationalism amplified the antisemitic tide that had already been on the rise. Whatever the outcome of the Ruhr crisis, one German Jewish observer predicted, German Jews would be blamed and be first in the firing line if it came to violence.[16]

In the occupied Ruhr, this was already taking place. In several locations, especially in Essen, placards were placed at street corners and on buildings close to Jewish homes and businesses, accusing the people living there of betraying the Germans by co-operating with the French. They promised the accused that they would one day face vengeance and were signed in the name of *Die Feme*, a medieval court term derived from a word meaning 'punishment' and adopted by the Organization Consul to provide legitimacy for the execution of people it considered traitors.[17]

In Bavaria, Jews faced equally terrifying threats. On 9 March 1923, the *Völkischer Beobachter* editor, Hermann Esser, gave a speech in which he claimed that the Nazis were preparing for a day of 'Settlement'. He even suggested that the threat of the mass murder of Jews could solve the Ruhr crisis. Specifically, he said that to solve the Ruhr crisis all Jews in Germany should be given twenty-four hours' notice to register at a camp to which they should bring supplies of food for eight days as well as a blanket. Any Jews who did not arrive within the given time limit were to be shot. Once all the Jews were held in camps, Esser's plan proposed sending a message to Paris: if the French did not cross back over the Rhine, 'we would be forced to transfer fifty thousand hostages to a higher power' – by which he meant murdering them. He promised that if his plan became reality, 'international capital' would demand that the French army withdraw. 'This solution', he argued, 'would be as bloodless and humane as anything.' It was only one of many antisemitic suggestions he made that the Jews were the real power behind the occupation of the Ruhr. When he threatened this act of mass violence, Esser was greeted with 'thunderous applause'. According to one sympathetic press report, Esser's plan was 'the most original point' in his speech.

Esser's threat wasn't just something that was said at a Nazi rally or a beer hall. It was recorded. This allowed the Bavarian Jewish religious communities to bring it to the attention of the Bavarian prime minister, Eugen von Knilling. On 11 March, Knilling met with three Jewish leaders, and the *CV-Zeitung* claimed Knilling listened with 'interest and sympathy'. The Bavarian Jews expressed their anxiety about increasing antisemitism. They warned against the growing number of attacks on Jewish persons and synagogues, as well as the increase in threats to Jews in political assemblies and the press. Calling for the protection of Jews' rights, the delegation demanded that Knilling take action. But no action was taken.[18]

The Nazis planned that the high point of their campaign of violence would come on 1 May 1923. The day was both the traditional workers' day and also the fourth anniversary of the city's liberation from the Bavarian Soviet Republic, the brief period in April 1918 when Communists took control of Munich. Only a few days earlier, on 26 April, a shootout between Communists and Nazis had left four wounded. Now, Munich's Social Democrats and trade unions were planning a major show of strength. They received permission from the police to march through the city in large numbers. For Hitler, their parade was a target. Three months had passed since the Nazi Party convention. Having called for violence since the start of the year, Hitler was fully aware that without a new event to keep the momentum going, he risked being thought guilty of too much talk and not enough action. Fearful of violence and under pressure from the working group, which sent an ultimatum to the prime minister, Knilling, demanding that the SPD and trade-union parade be banned, the government withdrew the left's permission to parade. In its place, the SPD and trade unions received permission to hold a large outdoor assembly on the Theresienwiese.

But even this was too much. Hitler wanted nothing less than a May Day massacre. At a meeting with other members of the working group of the Patriotic Fighting Units on 30 April, together with Göring and the leadership of the Bund Oberland, he told everyone present that his followers were too 'excited' to stop now. He wanted 'aggressive action and the use of armed force'. The government were to know that they were not the target and that Hitler and his followers would only be after the 'Reds'.[19] There were rumours that the left-wing demonstration was to be the starting point for a left-wing putsch – rumours that were probably circulated by the right to justify their own actions. But on 30 April, Lossow, concerned about a putsch from the right, refused to accede to Hitler's demands. Hitler was only granted permission to hold a small demonstration on the Oberwiesenfeld. This served as a show of strength, but it was not the event that Hitler wanted. While 25,000 workers demonstrated on the Theresienwiese, Hitler and his men were stranded far away from the action at the Oberwiesenfeld, surrounded by police. Around two thousand of them were gathered there in military formation. Every single one bore a modern infantry rifle, as well as cartridge pouches and belts. There were separate units in which all members had three hand grenades tucked under their coats and pistols. Other units had heavy and light machine guns. Behind a tree, a 12-centimetre artillery field gun stood out. It was pointed in the direction of the SPD assembly on the Theresienwiese. The Nazis also had a stockpile of handcuffs, as if preparing to take large numbers of prisoners. Göring, his Pour le Mérite pinned to his chest, was in charge. The weapons belonged to the Reichswehr, which had also provided some of them with secret training. But the Nazi demonstrators were only allowed to have them for the morning. At noon on 1 May, while Kriebel wanted to fight rather than hand back the weapons, Hitler had to tell his men that 'no man should hang his head' when they returned the weapons to the Reichswehr. At around 2 p.m., the SA men returned the weapons they had 'borrowed' that morning to the Reichswehr. They had spent the entire morning surrounded by the police.[20]

Hoping to deploy masses of men in a show of force, all that Hitler achieved was to expose his movement's total dependence on the mercy of the Reichswehr. At the end of January, the Reichswehr had come down in their favour, leaning on the Bavarian government to get the state of emergency lifted. Three months later, Lossow refused to accept Hitler's plans for violence and murder, and he was left with a damp squib.[21]

That evening Hitler put on a brave face at the Circus Krone as he lashed out in another speech against his usual opponents. But privately he was devastated. Even years later, he would describe it as one of his most significant political defeats. Some of his followers even went home before the event at the Oberwiesenfeld was over. After all, what was the point of getting into a state of hypertension, excited by the prospect of killing someone or terrified of being killed, if the man who continuously promised them a glorious future could only deliver them a chance to stand in the cold several kilometres from the enemy? In the aftermath of his first serious defeat as Nazi leader Hitler retreated to a remote village in Obersalzberg near Berchtesgaden, where he spent the following weeks in a state of depression. Later, he claimed that this was when he fell 'in love' with the region. It would remain an important place for him for the rest of his life.[22]

The events of 1 May 1923 reveal clearly that the Bavarian state had the capacity to deal with Hitler and the threat that his movement posed if its rulers wanted to. It could have done even more: Hitler had done enough on that day to be prosecuted for 'forming an armed mob'. He could also have gone to prison if he had been forced to serve the three-month suspended sentence he had received the previous year.[23]

But Hitler was ahead of the authorities. He sent them a note that included a threat that if they proceeded with the prosecution, he would create a political scandal by exposing the secret co-operation that had taken place between the Reichswehr and the paramilitary leagues, including details of the Reichswehr's plans to use the paramilitaries in a war against France. That threat was enough to convince Bavaria's minister of justice, Franz Gürtner, a member of the German National Bavarian Centre Party, to drop the case. At the start of May 1923, Bavaria's rulers were still willing to put Hitler in his place, but they did not want to take the risk of destroying him.[24]

It was the Ruhr crisis that brought Hitler back to Munich. After Schlageter was executed on 26 May 1923, there were major nationalist demonstrations across Germany in his honour. Hitler could not afford to be absent while they took place in the right-wing stronghold of Munich.

On 2 June 1923, Hermann Esser took to the stage at a Nazi rally in Munich to condemn Schlageter's execution. During his 'agitation speech' he was interrupted by Stormtroopers shouting loudly: 'Slay the treacherous dogs! Severing the pig has to go!' Just as the Nazis had blamed the 'November criminals' for the invasion of the Ruhr, Esser blamed Prussian interior minister Carl Severing for Schlageter's betrayal and execution. A few days later, the accusation was printed in the *Bergisch-Märkische Zeitung* in Elberfeld and subsequently repeated across the German press. It was the starting point for a right-wing hate campaign against Severing, which saw fears grow that he might share the same fate as Matthias Erzberger and Walther Rathenau.[25]

Men like Esser accused Severing of being responsible for the wanted poster that they falsely claimed had led to Schlageter's arrest. Once he was in French captivity, they claimed that Severing had ordered the arrest of Schlageter's commander, Heinz Hauenstein, to prevent him from leading a daring military operation to free Schlageter from his Düsseldorf prison.[26] Soon after, *Vorwärts* criticized the 'murderous rage' against Severing. Severing's role was even the subject of heated debate in the Prussian parliament on 16 and 18 June, where Schlageter was hailed as a 'national hero' who had died a martyr's death for the 'greatness of his fatherland'. In response, Severing filed a libel case against the *Bergisch-Märkische Zeitung*. When it came to court, the judges ruled that, even though the newspaper had run a story about Severing that was untrue, its editor was not deserving of punishment because he was motivated by 'national feeling'.[27]

Hitler had more success in Munich's courts in June 1923. In February, *Vorwärts* had published a report from Munich that included an accusation that the Nazi Party was funded by French espionage funds. This was based on the arrest of a Stormtrooper leader who was found to be in possession of French money. Hitler and Dietrich Eckart, then editor of the *Völkischer Beobachter*, brought a defamation case. Hitler claimed that as 'leader of the National Socialist movement' he had been defamed. Defending *Vorwärts*, the lawyer and SPD politician Alwin Saenger argued that the 'leader' had no legal basis for his claim and that Eckart had no case because the newspaper was not mentioned in the *Vorwärts* article. The district court agreed. But the Nazi leaders sought an appeal in the regional court, which sided with them.

Vorwärts was fined 40,000 marks. The same court rejected an SPD counterclaim against the *Völkischer Beobachter* for calling the party leaders 'November criminals', 'Jewish supporters' and 'riffraff'. In Munich, the Nazis had received a legal green light to say whatever they wanted.[28]

Hitler spoke publicly about Schlageter's execution at another Schlageter celebration in Munich on 10 June. This was organized by the patriotic associations, including the Nazi Party, and held on the Königsplatz in Munich to coincide with Schlageter's funeral service in Schönau. Speakers included Generals Erich Ludendorff and Karl von Kleinhenz, the former Munich police president, Ernst Pöhner, the former justice minister Christian Roth and several former officers. Press reports suggest that several thousand people attended the celebration. Following Ludendorff, the Protestant pastor Martin Joch promised that Schlageter's sacrifice would continue to live in German hearts. He ended his address, a mixture of political nationalism and religious prayer, with the plea: 'Lord help us! Lord, make us free!' Hermann Kriebel, the former chief of staff of the anti-revolutionary Bavarian Home Guard (Einwohnerwehr), who organized the demonstration, then called Schlageter a 'victim of the lust for power of inhumane enemies' and promised that they would one day take revenge for his death; he was interrupted by loud cheering.[29]

As Hitler started to speak at the end of the ceremony, he was greeted with loud cheers of 'Heil!' The death of a single German was not what upset Hitler, he said. He told the crowd of mourners that 'Hundreds of thousands like [Schlageter] died in the war'. Hitler claimed that what left him upset was that 'the German people didn't deserve his sacrifice!'

> The people of today are no longer truly worthy of the likes of Schlageter! For us, in whose ranks the dead man stood, Schlageter has a different meaning. His fate reminds us that we do not live in the deepest peace, that we do not live in peace and order, but in Germany's deadly struggle! . . . Schlageter's death must make us realize that freedom does not come through

protest or demonstrations, or through speeches, but only through deeds, through education to deeds! This single fanatic, Schlageter, is hated by the French more than ten thousand supporters of Ebert's calls for a united front! Our act of liberation will not come from a large front of weaklings. It will come from the fighting front of fanatics![30]

Hitler repeated the argument that there could be no real resistance against the French until there was a change in the leadership of the Reich:

First of all there must be such heroes at the head of the empire who can sweep the people along and incite them to resist. Because of a lack of such men we lost the war, and we are experiencing the same thing now. The spirit of resistance must be kindled from above! Only then will Schlageter's heroic death bear fruit. It is our duty to ensure this.

Hitler ended his quasi-religious address with a semi-prayer:

Lord God! We promise you that we will sacrifice ourselves for freedom to the last breath, therefore give us your blessing! In the spirit of resistance, there is no rest, no rest, until the day comes when it will roar through Germany. The people arise! The storm is breaking!

At the end of the demonstration, when Hitler finished speaking, there were more cheers of 'Heil!' and the crowd sang the German national anthem.[31]

A formal religious ceremony in memory of Schlageter was held later that day in the church of St Boniface nearby, where the Benedictine abbot Albanus Schachleiter, an early supporter of the Nazi movement, gave the funeral sermon. At the same ceremony, using the platform provided by the church, Kriebel announced:

The day is coming when we will take terrible revenge on France and on the traitors in our own country. Today there are only hundreds of thousands, soon there will be millions, who are crying out for the deed called for in Kleist's words: Beat them to death! The Last Judgement will not seek your reasoning![32]

From this point on, Schlageter featured regularly in Hitler's speeches during the summer and autumn of 1923. On 27 June, he condemned the 'betrayal' of 'our hero Schlageter'. On 8 July, in Ingolstadt in a two-and-a-half-hour speech in front of two thousand supporters, he reminded them of Schlageter's 'assassination' and claimed that, in the seven most recent cases where death sentences were handed down for active resistance, three recipients were 'also party comrades' (none of the sentences was ever carried out). At the start of September, a joint declaration of the patriotic associations, which Hitler signed, included the call for Germany's youth to join them and emulate Schlageter.[33]

Hitler may have suffered a major personal defeat in Munich on 1 May 1923, but the abrupt shift in his mood from extreme pessimism to unrealistic optimism would become a characteristic of his entire political career. In the depths of his depression in the summer of 1923, Schlageter's death offered Hitler not merely a rhetorical tool with which to mobilize his supporters, it represented something that he could believe in. Within weeks of the May Day failure, he wasn't just drumming up support for the coming nationalist leader who would destroy the republic, he was claiming the role for himself.

French soldiers march into Essen on 11 January 1923, the first day of the Ruhr occupation.

A French soldier guards coal, seized at the Westerholt mine.

The occupation of the Ruhr. A German civilian faces a French soldier, his bayonet drawn.

The execution of Albert Leo Schlageter by the occupying French forces on Golzheimer Heide, Düsseldorf, 26 May 1923.

A body lies at the edge of the tracks following a train bombing by German activists, Duisburg, 1923.

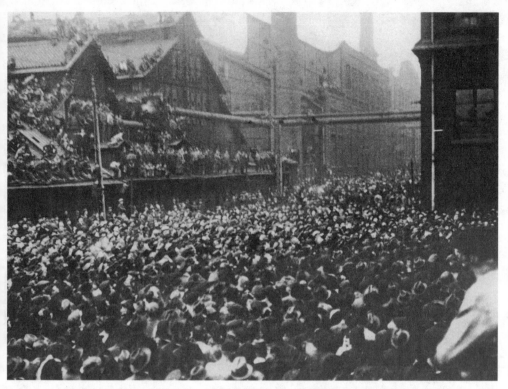

Protesting Krupp workers at the Essen plant, 31 March 1923. Shortly after this picture was taken, French soldiers opened fire on the crowd.

The funeral procession of the thirteen Krupp employees killed in the Essen shooting.

'Hitler's Shock Troops', Munich, November 1923.

Alfred Rosenberg (left) and Adolf Hitler watch the first stone being laid for a
memorial to the dead of the First World War, Munich, 4 November 1923.

Hyperinflation: children playing with worthless banknotes.

A two-trillion-mark note (two hundred million million) issued
in Berlin on 5 November 1923, the day antisemitic rioting
began in the city's Scheunenviertel.

The German Red Cross provides milk to children in Essen as part of the Ruhr Help campaign.

Queues for food in Berlin during the period of hyperinflation, summer 1923.

Gustav Stresemann surrounded by journalists, September 1923.

Rhineland separatists under the leadership of Josef Friedrich Matthes proclaim the existence of a republic of the Rhineland under the protection of French soldiers, 23 October 1923.

Street fighting on Düsseldorf's 'Bloody Sunday', 30 September 1923.

The Odeonsplatz, Munich, with the Feldherrnhalle in the background after
the failure of Hitler's putsch on 9 November 1923.

PERNET DR WEBER KRIEBEL LUDENDORFF HITLER RÖHM WAGNER
FRICK   BRÜCKNER

Facing accusations of treason and the attempted putsch, Ludendorff (centre)
and Hitler stand in front of the former war academy in Munich,
26 February 1924.

PART III

Summer 1923

10

The Year of the Zeros

There is no doubt that by the spring of 1923 Hitler had mastered the art of public speaking. But it wasn't just his rhetoric and performances that drew crowds to hear his message. By the time of the future Führer's thirty-fourth birthday, Germany was entering one of the most economically turbulent periods of modern European history.

At the start of April, just days before the Nazis' celebration of their leader's birth, Count Harry Kessler, a cosmopolitan German Europhile, predicted that Weimar Germany was on the verge of a 'financial catastrophe'. He feared that the economic situation facing the young democracy was 'more difficult and more dangerous than 1918', when the German Empire collapsed as a result of the combination of food shortages, starvation and military defeat.[1]

The cause of the problem was record-breaking inflation. It had surged almost continuously since the shock that followed Rathenau's murder. But the root of the problem went back to 1914. Before the First World War, the cornerstone of the international economy had been the gold standard: the idea that the value of every paper note in circulation had to be backed by an equivalent amount of gold or other precious metals held in reserve by a state's central bank. When it functioned properly, this system provided stability. Trade could flow across borders because it was safe to assume that foreign currencies had stable values. Within Germany, people could trust the value of the paper notes in their pockets, because they knew that they had the right to go to a bank and demand that they be given a piece of gold that matched its value.

When the war started in August 1914, the German central bank's fifty-seven-year-old president, Rudolf von Havenstein, who had held the top job since 1908, immediately decided that the gold standard had to go. At the time, the decision made sense. In the final days of July 1914, as Germans feared that a war was about to start, many rushed to banks to exercise their right to swap paper currency for gold. But even more importantly, the gold standard had to go because policy-makers like Havenstein recognized that the cost of war was too great to be funded through extra taxation or general state income. So they chose to print extra paper money. Unlike goldmarks, which had been backed by the value of gold, the newly printed paper marks rested solely on the public's faith in their value and, by extension, their faith in a German victory.

At the time the gold standard was abandoned in August 1914, men like Havenstein, who had the backing of the German Reichstag, expected that the war would end quickly and the public's faith would be repaid. But as the war dragged on the flood of new paper notes led to inflation. It surged in 1916 when German war costs soared as a result of the construction of a massive new German defensive line on the western front. But by then, Havenstein and others feared that reversing the decision would send a message to the general public that there could no longer be certainty of a German victory. So they printed more money to fund the war. But they did not remain passive either: to help maintain the belief that the bank would one day return to the gold standard, they hoarded almost all of the available precious metal in Germany, even asking the public to hand over their gold watches and jewellery.[2]

Printing extra money wasn't the only way to pay for the conflict. Like other states fighting the war, Germany also borrowed money long term. But unlike on the Allied side, where Britain and France sought loans from the United States, the German Empire borrowed from its own citizens. Between 1914 and 1918, it issued nine war bonds which were bought by members of the public using their savings. It was only in the final weeks of the war when interest in the ninth war bond plummeted that the system finally collapsed. Up until that point, the first eight war bonds had proved highly popular, as ordinary citizens believed that once Germany was victorious their war bonds would reward them with handsome profits.

In November 1918, when the war ended with defeat and revolution, the value of the German currency and the amount of printed money in circulation was unrecognizable compared to the situation in August 1914. Despite the revolution, Havenstein stayed in his job. For him and the rulers of the new republic, the goal was to wait for the right time to return to the gold standard and end the era of wartime inflation. It was obvious that this was necessary, but during the first year of the republic, few political leaders considered that it was a wise time to begin such a major course of fiscal correction, which was very likely to trigger social unrest. As the economy made the transition from wartime to peacetime, extra money in the form of newly printed notes was also a useful tool to fund new state welfare programmes, and to keep the economy on track so that returning soldiers could find new jobs, while existing workers retained their old ones. In this scenario, inflation quickly became a potent drug that successive Weimar governments could not wean themselves off. Best of all, inflation allowed the Weimar Republic to pay back the domestic debts that it inherited from the defeated German Empire. That meant ordinary savers lost out, but it quickly reduced Weimar Germany's internal debt, a move that was necessary as the victorious Allies' reparation demands intensified. It also benefited indebted German households and farms, as they could pay off their private debts with devalued currency.

The problem was that the same currency also had to be used for international financial exchange. Initially, inflation brought some benefits in this area too. The decreasing international value of the German currency made exports cheap. But the same situation also made it harder for German traders to pay for goods in foreign markets. Worse, the Weimar Republic had to pay its reparations and for this it needed a stronger, more valuable currency.

By the start of 1921, a series of minor reforms introduced since the end of the war appeared to have got German inflation back under control, only for the announcement of the London Ultimatum in May 1921 to trigger a new round of inflation and capital flight out of Germany. (Up to this point, some foreign speculators had been happy to buy cheap German marks because they expected their value to soar when the Germans finally decided to return to gold.) Now, restoring stability became Germany's financial priority. The night before he was murdered in June 1922, it formed the subject of Walther Rathenau's last conversation with the American ambassador to Germany. Less than six months later, as prices soared and the value of the mark against the dollar continued in free fall (the average monthly exchange rate of 317 marks per dollar in June 1922 fell to 7,589 per dollar in December 1922), Wirth's government had come no closer to agreeing a pathway to German stability.

For international financial experts looking at Germany, including economists like John Maynard Keynes, the main question was why the German central bank was not doing more to intervene and stabilize the value of its currency. After all, Germany might have left the gold standard, but it still had a hoard of gold and other precious metals that it could have used to steady the mark. But Havenstein strongly opposed such a move. For him, the bank's gold was the republic's financial bazooka, and he had no intention of firing it until he was certain that it would bring success. In the final months of 1922, when many economists thought it absolutely necessary, he feared that any such intervention could be rendered useless by unilateral French action. However, by doing nothing, Havenstein only increased the size of the challenge facing Germany in its fight to return to economic stability.

With the French and Belgian invasion of the Ruhr on 11 January 1923, the question of how to restore stability shifted decisively. Having used newly printed paper currency to fund the war, Cuno's government now adopted the same method to finance passive resistance, a decision that quickly turned the campaign into one of the most radical financial interventions made by any European state in the entire twentieth century. For the first six months of 1923, on average, the Weimar Republic spent 1 trillion marks a month on passive resistance. During the same timeframe it spent another 2.5 trillion marks in credits to businesses. This increased spending was necessary because Cuno's government in Berlin couldn't ask the workers of the Ruhr to lay down their tools and give up their wages just to frustrate the French and Belgians. It had to provide money to both workers and the industrial bosses to ensure their compliance. But with passive resistance shutting down the heartland of the German economy in the Ruhr, the only source of cash to fund this extra spending was newly printed money. The decision was the starting point for a new wave of accelerated inflation that made the inflationary addiction of the previous nine years suddenly look like the healthy consumption of a moderate drug.[3]

In Havenstein's defence, when this campaign started, the assumption was that it would be short-lived. Swept up in a moment of nationalist euphoria, he bet that the central bank had sufficient resources to prop up the value of the mark in international markets for as long as would be necessary for Germany to be politically victorious in the Ruhr. If the Ruhr occupation had lasted only a couple of weeks, his plan might have worked. But during the first weeks and months of the occupation, the radicalization that the occupation had generated on both sides meant that there could be no German reversal of its decision to finance passive resistance with printed money, even if those measures put the entire economy at risk. This was why Harry Kessler was so worried at the start of April 1923. With each passing week, he and other observers were increasingly gripped by the question: how much longer could the Reichsbank continue to support the exchange rate value of the mark and prevent its value from falling so far that it would wreak economic havoc throughout Germany?

On 18 April 1923, just two days before Hitler's thirty-fourth birthday, the answer came. That day was Havenstein's 'Black Wednesday', the point at which the bank realized that it had run out of resources to continue to support the value of the mark. The cause of Black Wednesday was hotly debated at the time. For a few days there had been an abnormal surge in demand for foreign currency in Berlin. On 13 April, Hugo Stinnes had bought 93,000 pounds sterling in a single transaction. This was approximately one-quarter of the total amount of sterling traded in Berlin on any given day. Stinnes later defended his purchase, pointing out that he only wanted it to be able to buy British coal for the German railways. But others accused him of wanting extra foreign currency in order to profit from the crisis. In the following days the surge in demand for foreign currency continued, causing a further fall in the value of the German mark. This was the point when the Reichsbank calculated that if it continued to try to counterbalance demand for dollars by spending its resources, it was just days away from having nothing left.

Havenstein was livid. He put the recent increased demand for dollars down to 'special interests' and speculators who simply didn't care about the 'well-being of the nation'. He was especially angry because, earlier in the year, he had tried to secure an emergency foreign currency loan from German industrial leaders, whose companies had built up savings held in foreign currency. But the industrial bosses turned him down, recognizing that using their holdings to help support the mark was a bad deal, especially when some of them wanted to use their foreign currency to purchase the assets of their struggling rivals. Havenstein complained that, 'in this time of Germany's most difficult struggle, even serious players in our economy' were driving up demand for dollars by purchasing more than they needed for their day-to-day business. He condemned their actions 'because they mean stabbing in the back, if not intentionally, the Reichsbank and all those engaged on the shared battle front for the sake of our politics and our economy'. But there was nothing he could do.[4]

With the end of the Reichsbank support action, the exchange value of the mark fell at an extraordinary rate. The numbers defy easy summary. Whereas the Reichsbank's support action had previously held the value of the dollar at a monthly average of under 25,000 marks, between mid-April and mid-May, and again between May and June of 1923, the dollar's value in Berlin doubled. On the first anniversary of Rathenau's murder on 24 June 1923, the value of a single dollar in Berlin reached 120,000 German marks – an extraordinary increase in the dollar's value compared to the 338 marks that it had been worth on the morning of Rathenau's death. As incredible as this was, it was only the beginning. During July, the average dollar-to-mark exchange rate in Berlin was 1 to 353,412 – an increase of nearly fourteen times the average price in April. By the end of August, the average exchange rate in Berlin had reached one dollar to 4.6 million marks. In September the dollar was worth 98.86 million marks, in October 25.2 billion and in November 2.1 trillion. In December 1923, the dollar hit the astronomical figure of 4.2 trillion.[5]

As the international value of the mark plummeted, the number of newly printed notes continued to increase dramatically. In July, for the first time, the state printers churned out 10-, 20- and 50-million-mark bills. They put the first 100-million-mark note into circulation in August and the first 500-million-mark note on 1 September. In November, the Reichsbank issued a 1-trillion-mark note.[6]

In all, around 10 billion banknotes were printed during this period: in August 1923, there were around 663 trillion marks in circulation. To put so many new notes into circulation at the height of the inflation, as many as thirty paper mills, 130 printing companies and 7,500 workers at the state printers were needed to manufacture the physical money. Their output became a symbol of the crisis: camera crews filmed trucks leaving printers containing new denominations of paper money in amounts unthinkable only days before and that would in turn become valueless as well. Just weeks after being printed, the useless notes were discarded. The sight of children playing with them in the streets became powerfully emblematic of everything that was going wrong with Germany's currency. The speed at which currency deflated meant that the price of a cup of coffee could change dramatically between the time it was ordered and the time it had to be paid for.[7]

Months before such extraordinary numbers became part of the everyday world of Germans, the German poor were already in trouble. The 1922 harvest had been a bad one and at the start of 1923, even before Havenstein's dam burst, many Germans were already facing starvation. In the Reichstag in mid-February, the president of the Ministry for Health, Franz Bumm, called upon Germans to open their eyes and see that the nation's children were going without 'underwear and other clothing, stockings and shoes'. But missing clothing was far from the worst problem facing children. In February 1923, 50 per cent of all German children were undernourished and diseases like diphtheria and tuberculosis were spreading rapidly, while state children's homes had to shut their doors because they had reached capacity. By then, it was already clear that the infant death rate was increasing, as was the number of miscarriages.[8]

Milk shortages were especially significant. Throughout February 1923, Berlin received just 300,000 litres of milk per day, one-quarter of the amount that the city received before the war, and only half of what Berlin's mayor, Gustav Böß, calculated the city needed to provide milk for children, pregnant women, breastfeeding mothers, the sick and the elderly. But even in this situation, when demand far outstripped supply, as much as 50,000 litres went unsold daily: ordinary Berliners desperate for milk could not afford it. The unsold milk was subsequently converted into butter and sold to hotels, where it was consumed by foreigners and Germans with access to foreign currency.[9]

Things were equally bad in Munich. One teacher reported that when she had a chance to offer the two poorest children in her class a hot daily breakfast provided by an American charity, twelve children applied for it and the decision as to who got fed and who went hungry had to be taken by the school doctor. In her words: 'The half-dressed children are a pitiful sight: you can count all their ribs, while their shoulder blades stick out almost like windmill blades; their chests are sunken, they have such skinny little arms.' She added:

> two children in my class gave off a terrible smell. I take them
> one by one to the side and say to them that they should tell
> their mother to wash their underwear, while talking to them
> about the importance of staying clean to stay healthy. The
> children replied to me: 'I've had my shirt on for a long time,
> I cannot take it off and change it because I only have one.'[10]

In the Ruhr, the situation was even worse. The occupiers had not set out to starve children. But once the campaign of passive resistance and the ensuing radicalization of the occupation took hold, the situation on the ground acquired a logic of its own. Control of imports, including food imports, and supply networks became key to control of the occupied region. The fight over the railways had an impact on who got fed and when during the crisis year. The combination of Degoutte's hostility and German resistance left some people in the Ruhr facing famine conditions.

In Essen, the shortages of milk were as bad as, if not worse than, in Berlin. According to newspapers, from the introduction of Degoutte's customs' zones which restricted economic exchange between the occupied Ruhr and unoccupied Germany, on 25 January until 19 February, the city, which required milk to feed '22,000 infants and 64,000 other children in urgent need', received only about 18,000 litres per day. In addition to shortages, the price of milk also jumped over the same timeframe due to inflation. Between those same dates, the price of fat increased over 400 per cent. For some of the poorest children, whose only point of contact with the medical establishment occurred within the framework of education, the occupiers' requisitioning of schools as military bases left them without access to doctors.[11]

Children were suffering from reduced resistance to measles and influenza; rickets were also a problem. Of those children whose schools remained open, in some districts as many as two-thirds were not receiving an adequate diet and one-third were chronically undernourished. As was the case elsewhere in Germany, the number of miscarriages increased. Many newborns were only breastfed for three months. The death rate among unweaned babies had increased by 15 per cent since the start of the year. Medicine prices were rising beyond the reach of many people and the number of hospital beds available to treat the sick was decreasing, following the French requisitioning of hospitals. In Essen, as many as 215 of the one thousand beds that were normally available were lost. As a consequence, sick people were being turned away or sent home prematurely, and patients with tuberculosis were put in beds alongside the uninfected, placing them at risk of catching this disease which spreads in the same way as colds or flu. In July, the regional president in Düsseldorf observed that the number of deprived people on the streets had increased. They were a constant reminder that the Ruhr occupation wasn't just a moment of German national humiliation, it was a public health crisis that continued to worsen as the year progressed.[12]

To alleviate the suffering of the population of the Ruhr, the Prussian minister for welfare together with other ministries and charities in Germany launched a national charity campaign: Ruhr Help. It called on Germans to donate money for the suffering population of the Ruhr. In the occupation zone, contributions to Ruhr Help were forbidden, as Degoutte viewed it as fundraising for passive resistance. Despite the attempts to fill the gaps created by the occupation with charity, the civilian population of the Ruhr continued to suffer. As the situation worsened, rather than bringing food in, a better solution appeared to be to get the children out.[13]

One of the first groups to leave arrived early on the morning of 15 February 1923 by train at Berlin's Friedrichstrasse station. The passengers included eighty children from the city of Essen between the ages of four and ten. After they got off the train they were given a small breakfast before they were taken to another station and put on a train heading towards their final destination: a children's home on the Baltic Sea. Their transport was organized by the Prussian state's newly created Central Office for Children's Aid in the Occupied Territory. By the end of the Ruhr crisis, more than 300,000 German child refugees would be evacuated from the occupied Ruhr, some to as far away as Denmark or Switzerland. Evacuation on this scale was necessary because, as officials in Hörde, a town to the south of Dortmund explicitly warned in March, without action a large number of the six thousand children in their district who were already suffering from acute malnutrition 'would certainly die'. The officials were not exaggerating. Between the start of the year and the summer of 1923, the death rate for unweaned babies increased by between 15 per cent and 33 per cent.[14]

During the evacuation campaign, the sickest and most deprived children, like those who left for Berlin on 14 February, were placed in state-owned children's homes. Those who were a little better off or in receipt of sponsorship from a charity went to stay on German farms. Even though families hosting 'Ruhr children' were not paid to do so, it was initially easy to find volunteers in unoccupied Germany to foster them. At the onset of the occupation, the people of the Ruhr were considered national heroes. Germans in the unoccupied territories saw it as their duty to care for their children. Among the more unique gestures, in Württemberg, Princess Zeil offered accommodation in her castle to eight girls aged between three and six, who would be taken care of by a nun. Other offers came from professional associations like the Association of Postal Workers, whose members in unoccupied Germany offered to provide accommodation to the children of postal workers in the Ruhr. The bulk of offers came from rural Germany. The Rural League estimated that it received as many as 500,000 offers to host children. This wasn't just altruism, however: teenage children from the Ruhr could also be a welcome source of free farm labour. But as more children had to be evacuated, the economic situation across the Reich worsened, leaving host families unable to afford to support children from the Ruhr.[15]

The mass evacuation led to harrowing scenes at stations as parents faced the reality that their children were leaving them for an unknown time. They watched as the children were given an identity card bearing their name and destination, and then boarded trains that carried them away from their families. Most parents didn't want to send their children away on long journeys. Some were concerned about their own fate as the occupied Ruhr became a childless zone. They thought that the presence of children had been a constraint on French brutality and worried that their absence would open the floodgates for further violence. They also didn't know when they would see their children again. The rules of the programme meant that parents could only visit their children in unoccupied Germany if the latter became seriously ill.[16]

Since these evacuations took place at the same time as the French interference in railway affairs, they were often affected by delays and chaos. The occupation forces also interfered with German telegraph and postal services, with the result that the food and water necessary for such journeys, which the German Red Cross aimed to provide, were often missing. Arrivals were also fraught. Host families in rural Germany reported making long journeys to receive children at railway stations only to discover that their guests from the Ruhr were not coming that day. More serious problems occurred when the host families were sent children of the wrong age or gender. Some rural families with boys were aghast when, against their wishes, they were sent working-class teenage girls. Considerable effort was made to avoid mixing Catholic children with Protestant families and vice versa. There is no information about whether measures were taken to protect children from violence and sexual abuse.[17]

Children had to bring clothing with them, as well as other items including ration card certificates, school books and a recent school report, not to mention enough food for the journeys, which were expected to last at least a day. Despite the best efforts of charities like Caritas and the German Red Cross, this requirement meant that the poorest children, those most in need of transport, were the least likely to have the necessary means to travel. The children of Recklinghausen provide an example of the problems the evacuation process created. On 20 February, the Welfare Office in Recklinghausen estimated that 90 per cent of the 800–1,000 children that it had planned to evacuate were at risk of exclusion from the programme because they did not have sufficient clothing. It appealed to the Central Office for Children's Aid for extra support. However, even though it received funding from the Ruhr Help campaign, the Central Office lacked the money necessary to pay for the children's evacuation.[18]

After it became obvious that the most vulnerable children could not afford to leave the Ruhr, the state-owned German railways company, the Reichsbahn, slashed transportation costs, and as many as 1,300 poor children from Recklinghausen made it to the town of Guben in Brandenburg, where they were hosted in a poor farming district. Almost all of the children from Recklinghausen turned up in rags; only a tiny number had a change of underwear. They also arrived with no educational materials. After that summer's rampant inflation, many of the host families simply did not have the resources to provide them with extra clothing or school books. Buying clothing could cost some foster families as much as 1 million marks. The charities and state organizations that they lobbied for funds came up short, and while doctors provided their services to the Ruhr children for free, the cost of medicines still rose sharply.[19]

Journeys back to the Ruhr were equally harrowing. The breakdown of transportation and communication systems left many children to return on their own. In September, an official in Dortmund complained:

Children have been found repeatedly on remote stations at night, crying and unescorted. We frequently have to find beds late in the evening for children still hours from home who have been picked up by first-aid teams and brought to us.[20]

Nor were children in the Ruhr the only ones suffering. Once the Reichsbank's support action ended, the price of food escalated at an extraordinary pace. It doubled between the end of April and the end of May. At the start of June, *Vorwärts* calculated that while the dollar was increasing in value at a rate of about 15 per cent a week, the price of food was increasing by 21 per cent and the cost of heating and lighting by 16 per cent. This was only the beginning. At the end of July, *Vorwärts* reported that in Berlin the price of a pound of margarine ranged between 120,000 and 140,000 marks, while a pound of low-quality meat was 100,000 marks. Between June and July, the cost-of-living index rose an unprecedented seven times in the space of just a few weeks, while in August, when it was available, the cheapest bread cost thousands of marks; in September, the price was in the millions and, from October, billions. Similarly, the price of a kilo of beef jumped from 440,000 marks at the start of August to almost 5 trillion in late November. For workers, the increase in food prices mean that their diet was restricted to boiled vegetables, and little fat.[21]

In April, the American consul in Cologne calculated that a family of four needed just under 110,000 marks a week to survive. By the start of June, *Vorwärts* reported that the same family of four would need 200,000 marks a week. By mid-August, the American consul put the survival figure at almost 21 million marks a week. Even though workers' wages were increased thanks to trade-union lobbying, culminating in the creation of an index linking wages to price increases at the start of September 1923, which helped shield some workers from the worst effects of price increases, no one was getting the kind of increases that would have been necessary to keep up. Already at the start of June, *Vorwärts* warned that the jump in prices meant 'untold misery for all manual and skilled workers, for all in receipt of fixed pensions' and 'mass deaths of the elderly and children'.[22]

Women suffered especially. When *Vorwärts* suggested in June that a family needed 200,000 marks a week to survive, one irate reader wrote to the newspaper to tell of her harrowing struggle to manage her household on her husband's wage of just over 50,000 marks a week. In one week, they had spent as much as 21,000 marks on gas. As the mother of a three-year-old, she was unable to leave the house to work and bring in a second wage and they never had enough money to buy sufficient food. She complained that they were always hungry and that their diet was limited to potatoes and little or no fat. She described the depression caused by the constant battle to survive, freely admitting that there were nights when she thought about leaving on the gas 'to put an end to this miserable existence of hunger'.[23]

Other women went further. In a year when suicide levels increased in Germany generally, women in the fifteen-to-thirty age bracket committed suicide at rates higher than young men of the same age, most likely because of the economic pressures they faced as a result of the labour market for traditional female jobs like house cleaning closing because middle-class families could no longer afford such luxuries. The increase in suicide was also attributed to the humiliation of queuing and coming home with insufficient food. By September 1923, women and children queued for up to twenty-four hours in Munich to have the chance to buy cheaply priced meat. In the same city in November, visitors to the food markets could see 'stunned and crying women'.[24]

Even though all forms of abortion were banned in Weimar Germany at this time, the number of abortions also increased alongside the hyperinflation. In April 1923, Willy Stammer, who lived in Dauborn in rural Hesse, brought his twenty-three-year-old girlfriend, Wilhelmine, to the local abortionist, Hermine Kastner. Later in the year, he returned with his sister, and again in December with the wife of a farmer for whom he occasionally worked. We know about Stammer because the abortionist was eventually arrested and sentenced to three years' imprisonment. During the trial, the judge noted that the vast majority of the forty-seven abortions with which she was charged took place 'during the time of severe inflation'. At one point, a man paid her 9 million marks, while others paid in kind, with Hermine Kastner receiving half a pound of butter and sausages, as well as on one occasion a jug of schnapps and a goldmark. For many women, it was the prospect of facing another mouth to feed at a time of food shortages and instability that pushed them towards the dangers of undergoing a back-street abortion, a practice that came with considerable risk to their health. Hermine Kastner was an exceptional case, in that none of the forty-seven women whom she faced trial for providing with abortions suffered injury at her hands. Social attitudes were changing too. Three years later, following heated debate, the criminal penalties for abortion were reduced and in 1927 the first liberalization of the abortion law took place to allow for abortions on medical grounds.[25]

In an article in *Vorwärts* at the start of July, a woman struggling with poverty described her life renting a single bedroom from another single woman, who slept in the kitchen. She explained the difficulties of trying to pay for food and the frustrations of not being able to afford lighting and heating. Even *Vorwärts*, which was not noted for its xenophobia, reported her anxiety that she feared her landlady might throw her out and replace her with a 'foreigner', whose access to foreign currency would give them greater purchasing power. Some such foreigners were attracted to visit Germany precisely because their possession of foreign currency could fuel a shopping bonanza and hedonistic lifestyle. In these conditions, the number of women working as prostitutes increased. Their visible presence on the streets even fed a new rumour that middle-class girls were being kidnapped and forced to work as prostitutes.[26]

Without a stable currency, farmers, who had lost their investment on the harvest because of the mark's collapse, hoarded food rather than sell it for paper money that would swiftly be rendered worthless. This was an important difference from the food crisis of the First World War, when the absence of food was caused by shortages and poor distribution. In 1923, food was available but the crisis was caused by consumers not being able to afford the prices that suppliers were willing to sell it for.

The shortages would have had an even worse impact on Germans' health but for the aid provided by foreign charities. At the end of the year, as he looked back on events, the newly appointed chancellor, Wilhelm Marx, remarked in his radio address to the German people that it was only thanks to the charity of the Danes, Dutch, Czechs, Swiss, Swedes, Norwegians and Germans abroad that many Germans would have something to eat at Christmas.[27]

The American Quakers played a key role. Even before the worst aspects of the 1923 food crisis became manifest, in January 1923, they decided to re-start direct aid operations in Europe's largest economy. It was a return to the situation that had existed in the immediate aftermath of the First World War, when the Quakers ran soup kitchens in Germany before withdrawing and making financial donations to German charities instead. In 1923, they felt that their presence was once again needed on the ground. The ensuing operation provided up to one million children a day with a meal of between 670 and 750 calories. The centres were usually located in schools. To get their Quaker soup, German children had to queue outside the distribution centre with their own utensils and bowls, and their ration was marked on a feeding card. They had to eat at the feeding centre to prevent them from taking it away to sell on the black market.[28]

The Quakers were the largest single donor organization in Germany from the United States, but there were others too. At the end of 1923, there were forty-three Swiss soup kitchens and eighty Swiss distribution centres in southern Germany. In the winter of 1923–4, they served just under two million meals. In addition to funding soup kitchens, ten Swiss towns paired with towns in the

German south to provide them with food and other aid, including children's clothing. By the end of 1923, the total weight of clothing, shoes, underwear and food donated to German children's homes from Switzerland reached 357,978 kilograms. By the end of 1925, the Swiss child transport system had brought at least 47,000 undernourished German children to Switzerland for recovery breaks. Since the Swiss and Americans, along with other providers of aid, had access to foreign currency, as the German mark collapsed across 1923, they could afford to pay for food where Germans couldn't.[29]

It was partially thanks to foreign aid that the fear of significant numbers of child deaths by starvation that was present at the start of the year was not borne out in reality. Information about the weight of German children highlights just how important this intervention proved. Thanks to foreign aid, the poorest German children received calories. Even though the nutritional crisis that took place in 1923 was so great that German children stopped growing at the expected rates, the most detailed statistics available suggest that the mean weight of German children was stable during 1923. The Quakers worked with German doctors to target undernourished children. The growth slowdown affected both boys and girls, but it was worse for girls. It was thanks to this crucial intervention in 1923 that, in 1924, as food supplies returned to normal, German children experienced 'catch-up growth', a term that nutritionists use to describe how children and young adults return to normal levels of growth after they have lived through famine conditions.[30]

Hyperinflation did not just leave people hungry. It also spread hatred and resentment through German society. Heightening the sense of unfairness was the fact that there were those who had access to foreign currency, or who simply enjoyed good fortune and managed to turn a profit from the crisis. In the middle of Germany's year of despair, Hugo Stinnes became Europe's richest man. He and others such as Otto Wolff, Friedrich Flick, Rudolf Karstadt, Hugo Herzfeld and Alfred Hugenberg were the 'Kings of Inflation'.[31] Some of them had access to dollar loans, others just won big on the stock market. Operating at levels beneath them, but benefiting for the same reasons, were a whole range of local

'Dollar Kings'. Families with relatives in the United States able to send dollars back home were able to flourish as those dollars grew precious. Other speculators simply got lucky. It felt like everyone in Germany had been dragged into some kind of turbo-casino where luck decided who won and who lost. In Berlin in February 1923, a police report estimated that as many as 200,000 people visited secret gambling clubs every day. The diaries of Victor Klemperer in the late summer capture the way that the usually astute and thoughtful scholar anxiously watched to see which of his colleagues and rivals had made big wins on the stock market. Each time somebody won, it felt like many more lost.[32]

The disparity between winners and losers created powerful resentments and divisions. The figure of the 'racketeer', the black-market dealer, was reviled across Germany. Antisemitism thrived: Jewish moneylenders were accused of hoarding currency and prof-iting from the crisis. City-dwellers walking to the countryside to forage for food for their starving children recalled enraged farmers telling mothers looking for milk to let their children 'drink water' or to 'eat stones'. In the starving cities, there were rumours of farmers profiting from the crisis to fill their rural houses with pianos and Oriental rugs.[33]

In this climate, the fifteen-year-old middle-class diarist Eva Weidner fantasized about violence. Her rage was caused by the increase in price of a cardigan she coveted which was now selling for 400 million marks. When her parents told her that she had to make do with her father's old cardigan 'dressed up as a sports jacket', she wrote: 'It is terrible. So many are starving, if only someone would murder Poincaré, him, the man who has murdered so many.' She was far from the only one to become obsessed with fantasies of revenge.[34]

With the value of money shifting at such a rapid pace, people's sense of time changed as well. Life became a race to spend freshly printed banknotes before the arrival of the next set of notes with even more zeros rendered them meaningless. Those who already despaired about the end of the monarchy and the creation of the republic were left with the sense that the world was accelerating away from them ever faster. For these traditionalists, money was supposed to hold value; it was something to be saved; something to be conserved carefully and spent only after due consideration. Middle- and upper-class girls were supposed to bring dowries that had been built up over many years to their marriages. All of these traditions and principles were swept away by hyperinflation. Images of children making paper aeroplanes out of worthless million-mark notes captured the way that something that had once been so central to people's sense of identity and status had now become worthless. Even decades later, German families passed down stories of how the wheelbarrows that they used to carry money were stolen, but that the notes piled in them were left behind by the thieves.

In an essay published in the *Berliner Illustrierte Zeitung* on 26 August 1923, Friedrich Kroner captured the 'overwrought nervousness' that characterized living through the end of money. He wrote how 'the number madness' which 'daily [drums] on the nerves' created an 'epidemic of fear, the most naked need' and 'queues of buyers long weaned from looking'.

> Yesterday rice was 80,000 marks a pound, today it is 160,000 marks, tomorrow may be twice as much . . . The piece of paper, the brand new banknote paper, still damp from printing, paid out this morning as a weekly wage, is rapidly depreciating in value on the way to the grocery store. The zeroes, the growing zeroes!

In all classes, the sense that others were living through good times or even just suffering less tore society apart.[35]

At the same time, the rates of petty crime, especially thefts and burglaries, increased dramatically. In 1913, police statistics record that 115,000 people were convicted of such crimes. Ten years later, the corresponding figure was 365,000, meaning that 1923 remains the year with the highest level of petty crime in modern German history. The explanation for this jump was not just social misery caused by hyperinflation: it was the sense of injustice that some people were winning that led others to abandon the idea that it was wrong to steal. For those struggling to survive on fixed incomes, like pensioners, the anger was partially driven by the belief that class rules had broken down and that their social inferiors had become their economic superiors.[36]

Academics suffered especially. Professor Louis Jacobsohn-Lask, an 'extraordinary associate professor' of more than twenty years' service at Berlin University, complained to the *Vorwärts* newspaper in August 1923 that for his teaching for the recently ended summer semester he received payment of an honorarium of a little under 1,200 marks. He threatened that if he was not paid more, he would throw the useless money at the feet of the Prussian minister for science, art and popular education. But his complaint got him nowhere. The university responded that he was a private lecturer (the equivalent of an adjunct professor today, contracted only to be paid for direct hours of work) and that his payment was linked to the tiny numbers of students who attended his course. In reply, Jacobsohn-Lask called it a 'screaming abuse', adding that it was unacceptable that private lecturers were now paid far less for their work than manual labourers.[37]

In December 1923, one man summed up the mood as follows:

> every estate blames the other, everyone sees an enemy in their fellow countryman. Everyone stands against everyone today and a spark is enough to ignite the revolution again. They will find many followers from decent circles of people who believe they are doing a good deed if they help hang a banker, a big merchant or even a farmer.[38]

The writer and thinker Elias Canetti later suggested that the period of hyperinflation 'had extreme consequences for all people, albeit not the same for everyone'.

> It was more than disorder which befell the people, it was like a daily explosion, something was left over from one thing, and it continued to affect the next day. I saw the effects not only

on a large scale, I saw them up close and undisguised in every member of the family; the smallest, most private, most personal event always had one and the same cause, the frantic movement of money.

All of this led him to conclude that, over the course of 1923, money had become 'a demon with a gigantic whip, lashing out at everything and reaching people down to their most private nooks and crannies'.[39]

Looking back from his exile in the United States in 1942, the German novelist and social critic Thomas Mann, who had been able to continue to pay his son's fees for boarding school during 1923 thanks to a monthly income of $25 from an American publisher, thought that there was a 'straight line' from the summer of 1923 to the Third Reich:

> The market woman who demanded in a dry tone 'one hundred billion' mark for a single egg, had lost during inflation her ability to be amazed at anything anymore. Since that time nothing was so mad or so atrocious that it could have caused any awe in people anymore . . . The millions who were then robbed of their wages and savings became the masses with whom Dr Goebbels was to operate . . . Having been robbed, the Germans became a nation of robbers.[40]

Mann's argument used to be part of a standard account that suggested that the period of hyperinflation destroyed the German middle class and by doing so paved the way for Hitler. Decades of painstaking work on the part of economic historians have shown that this argument is technically wrong. Many members of the middle class suffered despair and the loss of their livelihoods, but not everyone was financially ruined and those who paid off their mortgages with meaningless currency made gains during the crisis year. The winners and losers in this unique economic situation could often be the same person. A shop that lost income due to the economic collapse did not have to close its doors because the rent on its premises had fallen to almost nothing. Property owners hurting because of lost rental income due to rent controls might also be smiling because the rate of inflation allowed them to pay off the loan on the property that they were renting. Their creditors might lose on that loan, but they in turn might benefit on their own outstanding loans higher up the financial food chain. A business that saw its German income collapse, but which still traded internationally, could use its dollar income to pay off its outstanding domestic debts. But the losers really did lose. Pensioners on fixed incomes with no debts left to pay off struggled to survive. Suicide among the over-seventies, especially among men, jumped during 1923.[41]

Despite the mixed financial outcomes that hyperinflation produced, it undoubtedly was a moment of collective trauma for all Germans and especially for the German middle class. It not only devalued the German currency, but also national confidence in the value of money, with long-term psychological consequences. By the end of the summer, as the hyperinflation threatened to destroy the food supply for the winter of 1923–4, it was clear to smart-thinking people that the medicine had become the disease: the financial and economic crisis created by excessive printing of banknotes was greater than the political crisis caused by the invasion of the Ruhr. One of the most modern industrial societies was returning to the most primitive forms of economic exchange. Contemporaries didn't want worthless German marks: they wanted dollars, and if they couldn't have them, they preferred to exchange goods rather than currency if they could help it. Above all, they wanted stability, and increasing numbers of Germans blamed the republic for all that had gone wrong. In these circumstances, with each passing week, it was becoming more and more likely that the political consequences of accelerated inflation would include attempts to overthrow the state itself.

But throughout the summer of 1923, nationalism continued to trump such analysis. Months after it was obvious to more perceptive observers that they were both losing, Poincaré and Cuno remained determined to stay the course. Neither cared that the occupation had been an economic failure for both sides. It did not matter to Poincaré that, after ten months, France had obtained less coke and coal than it had during the ten *days* before the occupation. Equally disastrously, Cuno did not care that for the German Reich the cost of financing passive resistance was greater than its expenditure on reparations payments. Both leaders were determined to fight on. Poincaré knew that even if the conflict eventually brought down the economies of both countries, it would count as a French victory because Germany would go down first. That's why he refused all attempts at finding a mediated solution throughout the summer of 1923. He would only talk if the Germans ended passive resistance first, a decision Cuno wasn't willing to take as to do so would be both an admission of defeat and an admission that the strategy had been a blunder in the first place. Instead, Cuno preferred to sit tight, hoping that Britain and the United States would eventually come to Germany's aid and recognize that the French occupation put all of Europe's economic activity at risk. The printing of new notes to fund passive resistance would continue for as long as it took the British or Americans to intervene.

11

Waiting for Allies

With so much at stake, throughout 1923 Germany's best hopes were to be found in London. If the British government recognized that Germany was a victim of French aggression and that Poinaré's decisions put the entire European economy at risk, then Germans hoped that London would lead an international backlash against France that would eventually end the occupation. It was wishful thinking. But it wasn't entirely a pipe dream. Britain and France had sacrificed much on the battlefields of the First World War, but since the end of the conflict, despite remaining formal allies, they were far from united. When the Ruhr occupation began, the British took a stance that was summed up as 'benevolent neutrality', offering the French lukewarm but limited support. That was enough to give Cuno's government hope. Britain's lack of outright backing for the occupation meant that Germany's goal had to be to use the Ruhr crisis to convince the British to abandon the French and form a new alliance with Germany. In the most optimistic version of this future, the 1923 Ruhr crisis would end with the British reneging on the Treaty of Versailles and replacing it with a new British-German Treaty.

At the start of the occupation, such a possibility looked unrealistic, even fanciful. But as the year progressed, the prospect of British support for the German position started to look more likely. The first big sign that the British position might be about to change came on 20 April 1923, when British foreign secretary Lord Curzon gave a landmark speech in the House of Lords in which he stated that even though Britain was neutral, it could become a more active player in the conflict at any time. He even suggested promisingly that 'if Germany were to make an offer . . . an advance might be made'. Even if Curzon's speech came to nothing, it did signal a change in mood in London and raised hopes in Germany that it might be possible to alter the British position.

German hopes increased further at the end of May 1923 following a change in leadership in Downing Street. On 19 May 1923, the pro-French Conservative prime minister, Andrew Bonar Law, resigned. He had been unwell for weeks with the incurable throat cancer that would take his life five months later. Following his resignation, Curzon was expected to be his successor. But when senior politicians in the Conservative Party conspired against him, viewing both his politics and personality as unsuited to political success in a modern democracy, Curzon lost out on the job. Instead, the next prime minister was Stanley Baldwin, who had been one of the key players in Lloyd George's downfall the previous year. Unlike Curzon, Baldwin was less well-known in Germany. But his arrival in Downing Street still gave Germany some reason to hope that it might mean new policies towards Germany, even if others warned pessimistically that Poincaré could be the real winner as a result of the change. The pessimists initially proved correct. For the first few months of Baldwin's leadership, his strained relations with Curzon who, despite their rivalry, the new prime minister retained in the position of foreign secretary, meant that both men steered clear of igniting a new conflict over British policies towards the Ruhr occupation.[1]

Unsure of how Baldwin's government would work, just days after his appointment, Cuno's government set out to test the waters, making a diplomatic offer to end the crisis. This included an admission of German liability to pay reparations, new guarantees to ensure payments, permission for Allied inspections of German financial records and an agreement to submit the question of Germany's capacity to pay reparations to an international tribunal of experts. Berlin hoped that Cuno's chances of success would be increased by a change of public opinion in Britain. In contrast to the United States, which remained decidedly pro-French at this time, by the early summer, British public opinion was starting to move favourably towards the Germans. Even though die-hard anti-German publications such as the *Morning Post* remained 100 per cent behind France, others had shifted in a more pro-German direction. Both the *Manchester Guardian* and *The Times* warned that a more active British policy would be necessary to bring an end to the crisis in the Ruhr.[2]

The change in mood in Britain was partially caused by French violence towards German civilians in the Ruhr. Throughout the nineteenth and twentieth centuries, Britain was no stranger to using brutality to enforce its imperial power. But the 1923 crisis occurred at a particularly sensitive juncture. The First World War had decimated the British elite. In its immediate aftermath, many saw themselves as the rulers of a 'peaceable kingdom'. This left them with a strong sense that the violence of war, rather than Germany, was the real enemy and that it was their duty to prevent such a thing on such a scale from ever taking place again – the idea that future war should be avoided at all cost was the origins of what later became the policy of appeasement. This shift in thinking about war was well under way when the British public learnt of the first French atrocities in the Ruhr, which were the subject of daily reports in the British newspapers.[3]

British memory of the violence of the First World War now came back to aid Germany. At the start of that conflict, Britain's wartime leadership had argued that German atrocities committed against civilians in Belgium and France in 1914 necessitated Britain's participation in the war to combat such brutality. In 1923, with French and Belgian soldiers committing atrocities in Germany, the same kinds of justification were used to argue that it was necessary for Britain to intervene and stand up for German civilians during the occupation of the Ruhr. The Krupp works atrocity of 31 March 1923 was particularly important. In response *The Times* warned that France's desire to occupy the Ruhr permanently was dangerous, one of its correspondents reporting that, in at least ten cases, 'the bullets struck their victims from behind'. In a similar act of solidarity, the *Manchester Guardian* included an English-language translation of a German trade-union manifesto that condemned

the 'massacre' and warned against the creation of a 'military dictatorship in the Ruhr and Rhineland'. There was further empathy for
the German victims in *The Times*'s reporting on the Reichstag
memorial service. It described how at the end of the ceremony
Ebert left the presidential gallery to grip hands 'emotionally' with
the workers from Essen. *The Times* also included translations of
both Ebert's condemnation of the atrocity and Cuno's speech at
the same memorial service. Its readers read Ebert's words: 'Humane
feelings will everywhere be aroused by the dreadful outrage.'[4]

Mirroring the more pro-German voices found among those influ-
encing British public opinion, leading officials were also favouring
more pro-German positions. When Curzon heard that the Krupp
directors faced long periods of imprisonment after they were put on
trial by the French for their alleged role in the atrocity, he thought
that the 'sentences were absolutely barbarous'. When he learnt of
the expulsion of railway workers, Ralf Wigram, a junior official in the
Foreign Office, described the deportations as 'disgraceful'.[5]

As the situation in Germany worsened during the summer,
Foreign Office officials started to fear that France was determined
to provoke a German collapse. An angry Miles Lampson, the head
of the Central Department of the Foreign Office, observed on 22
June:

No one save France wants to see Germany in fragments and a
danger to Europe for years to come. It takes a Frenchman to
ignore the after-effects of what is going on in the Ruhr and the
Rhineland at this moment. It takes a Frenchman to perpetuate
the tradition of national hatred by perpetrating acts to those
regions which are little short of what the Germans did in time
of war.[6]

Frustrated by the lack of progress, at the end of June, Curzon
gave his officials permission to investigate policies that could be
more supportive of Germany. Britain was also facing pressure from
countries around the world to show leadership to bring the crisis
to an end. After almost three weeks of planning, Curzon made a

public declaration on 20 July. In it, he suggested that Britain would agree to France and Belgium's demand for an immediate end to passive resistance on two conditions: both countries would first agree to allow a group of international experts to examine formally Germany's capacity to pay reparations. The second was that once the German government agreed to end passive resistance, the French and Belgians would agree to withdraw their soldiers gradually from the occupied Ruhr.[7]

The French reply came on 30 July. It rejected Curzon's suggestion and made it very clear that Poincaré meant to hold out for total victory. At the time, although his support in the French Chamber of Deputies had decreased by around 180 votes since the highs of January, he still had a majority of around two hundred even if he was increasingly dependent on the right. Poincaré could remain firm because he had only been tested by British words; if the British backed them up with actions, the situation might change in unpredictable ways.[8]

In response, Curzon told the British cabinet that 'the French note indicated a determined opposition by the French Government to any immediate move in the direction of a settlement and an intention to prolong negotiations until Germany collapsed'. Eyre Crowe, permanent under-secretary of state at the Foreign Office, observed: 'It looks as if those were right who believe that M. Poincaré does not really desire a settlement, preferring to remain in the Ruhr and to see Germany reduced to impotence, as ends valuable in themselves.' Curzon now faced a new choice. He could accept Poincaré's outright rejection and return to a strategy of wait and see, or he could intervene by dramatically changing British foreign policy. In early August, he decided to go for the latter course. Cuno, who had been holding on in the hope of a British lifeline being extended, had already run out of time before Curzon issued his reply. Still, when it came, Curzon's decision would have profound consequences for the future of German democracy.[9]

By the middle of the summer, the future of Weimar democracy was looking increasingly bleak. Gustav Stresemann summed up the situation by describing Germany as 'dancing on a volcano' and 'facing a revolution'. In other times and places political elites have been guilty of exaggerating the fear of revolution to advance their interests, but in this case Stresemann could not be accused of overstating the danger. The shift in British opinion that took place in July occurred in parallel to ever-worsening economic and political conditions in Germany. For German Communists, the ongoing crisis appeared to be an unexpected golden opportunity to overthrow the Weimar Republic and turn Europe's largest economy into the continent's second major Communist state.[10]

With each week that the currency deteriorated in the late summer and early autumn, things looked increasingly promising for the would-be revolutionaries. The membership of the Communist Party was rising sharply: between September 1922 and September 1923, it jumped from just under 225,000 to around 295,000, while the number of local party branches increased from 2,500 to 3,300. By the end of July, encouraged by the international Communist strategists in Moscow, the time had come for Germany's Communists to make their first move. People weren't just starving, queuing and pushing around wheelbarrows full of money to pay for everyday goods. They were rioting. Often, workers rioted on payday, when they discovered that, after a week's work, even their indexed salary was not sufficient to buy anything. In other cases, the cause of rioting was not a lack of money to buy goods, but an absence of anything to buy as a result of growing shortages. After all, why would farmers or others sell their produce today, when the currency used to pay for it would be worthless tomorrow? Everywhere this occurred, Cuno got the blame. He was the chancellor, the man whose effigy was hung by workers who hated him for all of their woes.[11]

The strikes and riots that developed from this situation in late July, later known as the 'Cuno Strikes', quickly turned into a wave of violence in the streets. Police and citizen militias fought with protesting workers and Communist Party members, with both sides including many veterans of the First World War. There was increasing aggression on all sides and rioting often ended with exchanges of gunfire. In mid-August, the British ambassador, Lord D'Abernon, estimated that as many as two hundred people had lost their lives in the violence, which means that the violence of the barely remembered Cuno Strikes was responsible for around ten times as many fatalities as Hitler's putsch in November. In one example, in the town of Neuruppin, which is about 70 kilometres to the north-west of Berlin, fighting broke out between protesting workers, angry at the latest round of price increases, and members of the nationalist Bismarck Youth and property owners armed with rubber batons. During the fighting, the police opened fire, killing one protestor and injuring six more.[12]

Violence of this kind occurred across Germany. The number of people shot ranged from single individuals caught up in the cross-fire to groups of ten and more people, struck down when the police opened fire. Some of this violence took place in large German cities like Hamburg or Leipzig. But it also happened in sleepier middle-sized towns like Lübeck, Wittenberg, Breslau and Kulmbach. The violence was greater when the protests were led by Communists, whose tactics included violent attempts to seize police barracks or free prisoners. In one incident of this kind, as many as fifteen people were reported as having been shot in Cologne when a group of Communists allegedly tried to storm the police presidium. The violence wasn't just directed at the police and citizen militias. In Hüls, plunderers beat up a shop assistant so badly that she died of her injuries. In Zeitz, protestors stormed the local jail on 11 August. The next day they established a strike committee and formed a workers' militia. Soon afterwards, the police arrested the strike leadership, but during the ensuing stand-off between police and supporters of the strike, many of them Communists, the police opened fire and at least nine protestors were killed and many others injured. One police officer was injured in the arm.[13]

While conditions were deteriorating rapidly across Germany, the situation in the occupied Ruhr was particularly acute. In Gelsenkirchen, during the first two weeks of August, it was calculated by the local statistics office that the weekly cost of living for a family of four had jumped from 3,860,914 to 9,284,693 marks.

One local restaurant offered meals for the price of 800,000 marks per portion. *Vorwärts* reported that the situation in the Ruhr was so tense that there would only be calm if fresh food supplies arrived immediately. But with the French blocking the border, both food and money were in short supply. The result was more violent rioting. When workers plundered shops in Kettwig three people were killed, and there was yet more rioting in Dortmund, Recklinghausen and Bottrop. Three protestors lost their lives in Essen and over one hundred were injured when German police fired on rioters. Two people lost their lives in Oberhausen on 1 August, when a protesting crowd of five to six thousand workers refused to obey a command to disperse and the police responded with live fire. Another eight were injured.[14]

As the rioting continued, on 10 August 1923, the German Communist Party (the KPD) made its move. In the Reichstag, its four deputies matched their comrades' efforts in the streets with a motion of no confidence in Cuno. To accompany the motion, in Berlin, the Communists organized a strike at the Reich's printing works, a move designed to stop the printing of new paper bank-notes, which in the context of accelerated hyperinflation was an extremely dangerous act, aimed at intentionally worsening the shortages by reducing the supply of new money. Across Germany, the KPD's hotheads now went fully onto the offensive. They tried to claim that every single strike and working-class protest taking place in Germany, many of which had originally been organized by non-Communist trade unions or workers' councils, was happening under their leadership. They also mobilized regional networks to bring the workers out against the government. In Berlin on 11 August 1923, the KPD proclaimed a general strike, which was to continue until the fall of the Cuno government. The following day, the KPD called for the establishment of a national 'government of workers and peasants'.[15]

The Cuno Strikes looked increasingly like they might be about to become the first act in a revolutionary seizure of power. The situation appeared to be on a knife edge: there were riots in Hanover when a false rumour spread that female workers had been abused and shot by the police in the market that morning. They ended when the police dispersed the rioters, firing blank shots and marching on protestors using their rifle butts as batons. The Social Democratic *Vorwärts* accused the Communists of inciting the workers to violence, blaming the loss of life on the syndicalists who had called for 'direct action' such as 'the disarming of police officers, attacks on public buildings and on the state regulatory bodies'.[16]

Faced with the surge in violence from below and fears that worse was about to come, when the Social Democrats announced that they would no longer tolerate his government, Cuno resigned without much fuss on 11 August. Since the start of the year, he had grown tired of the job of chancellor and his energy had waned. His most important asset, his supposed good connections with America, had yielded nothing. As his conservative technocratic government came to an end, it was time for Germany's democrats to step up to defend the republic.

Cuno's replacement as chancellor was Gustav Stresemann, the forty-five-year-old head of the German People's Party (DVP), one of the few outstanding politicians of the Weimar Republic. Born in Berlin, Stresemann was first elected to the Reichstag in 1907, as a member of the National Liberal Party. Following the death of the party leader Ernst Bassermann in 1917, Stresemann took over the leadership. In November 1918, when the revolution swept away the old political system, Stresemann's natural political home might have been alongside Rathenau in the newly founded German Democratic Party, the heir to German political liberalism. But it didn't want him. At that time, Stresemann was considered too far to the right, thanks to his wartime support for the annexationist goals of the German nationalist right and for the campaign of unrestricted submarine warfare. During the winter of 1916–17 Stresemann had been among those in favour of restarting the latter even if it meant bringing the United States into the war on the Allied side. It was a choice that historian Alex Watson described as the 'worst decision of the war'.[17] But even after the war, Stresemann defended his record, saying that if it had been introduced six months earlier, it would have had far more beneficial results for Germany. He remained a supporter of an annexationist peace.[18]

Stresemann's exclusion from the German Democratic Party led him to found a new party, the German People's Party. It was to the right of the German Democratic Party and supported large business. In 1920, it made its major electoral breakthrough, bringing Stresemann to greater prominence in Weimar politics. His party included many politicians who did not openly support the Weimar Republic – many were disenchanted monarchists. But Stresemann was not. He was a nationalist in German foreign politics, but by the time he became chancellor he was also an avowed supporter of the republic. Commenting on his appointment, liberal journalist and supporter of Weimar democracy Theodor Wolff thought that few politicians had learnt more and changed more since the establishment of the republic.[19]

By the time he took on the chancellorship, Stresemann had a reputation as a clever speaker, and for several months it had been expected that he would replace Cuno. Stresemann himself described the expectation as a weight on his shoulders. Like Rathenau before him, he feared that the job might end with his murder. In a letter to his wife, Käte, he told her that to take up the job after Cuno was nothing less than 'political suicide'. But he was aware that he was the only candidate. Thinking about what would happen next left him facing 'sleepless nights'. From the moment that he accepted the role until his early death in 1929, Stresemann would stand up for German democracy and peaceful relations between France and Germany.[20]

Stresemann was the first leader of the pro-business German People's Party to become chancellor. Unlike Cuno's government, which functioned because the parties of the Reichstag were not willing to support a motion to remove him from office, Stresemann's government held a parliamentary majority. That point is worth dwelling on. Typically, historians have argued that the political crises of 1923 and the Weimar Republic's catastrophic failure to stop Nazism ten years later were a result of inherent weaknesses in the culture of German democracy. Some historians have even gone so far as to argue that because Cuno's government did not have a parliamentary majority (Cuno was not a member of a political party), it was a forerunner to the final governments of Weimar Germany, which also functioned without a majority and whose leaders were appointed by the president of the republic using his emergency powers. That comparison misses the point, however: in 1923, the Reichstag never lost control of the government. Once the largest party in the parliament decided that Cuno's technocratic government had served its purpose, it removed him from office. It was an example of the democratic system working as intended during a time of extraordinary crisis.

Stresemann was elected chancellor with the support of members of the pro-worker Social Democratic Party, his own pro-business German People's Party, the liberal bourgeois German Democratic Party (Rathenau's party) and the conservative Catholic Centre Party (Wirth's party). It was a coalition filled with division. The Social Democrats entered the coalition to protect workers' rights and save the republic, whereas the right wing of the German People's Party was there to protect the interests of business. Members of both parties hated each other. Consequently, when it came to vote on the new government, members of several coalition parties abstained and Stresemann ruled Germany initially with a majority of only nineteen.

The atmosphere in Stresemann's cabinet in August and September 1923 was defined by tension. The most obvious pathway to providing Germans with a functioning currency was to end passive resistance in the Ruhr immediately. But after eight months of suffering, this prospect was akin to re-signing the Versailles Treaty and accepting that the republic had been defeated by Poincaré. Nobody in the room wanted to do this, though everyone present was starting to recognize that it would have to be done.

The figures presented to the cabinet made it clear that drastic action was necessary to save German unity and democracy. As we saw, during the first six months of 1923, the Reich spent an average of 1 trillion marks a month funding passive resistance. In July 1923, that figure increased to 11.8 trillion on wages in the Ruhr, and a further 3.7 trillion on guarantees. In August, the care of orphans in the Ruhr cost 35 billion marks a week. When Stresemann took office, these astronomical figures were worsening by the day. At the time of his appointment, from 7 to 18 August passive resistance cost 180 trillion, whereas only 54 billion had been budgeted to pay for it. In the final week of August, it was expected to cost 150 trillion, most of which would be spent on paying wages.[21]

The figures were worse than the worst predictions. When the finance minister, Rudolf Hilferding, announced them to a meeting of party leaders on 22 August, he added that it was necessary for the government to wait for a 'foreign policy rescue'. But on the following day, 23 August, ten days after Stresemann's appointment as chancellor, Prussian minister president Otto Braun told the cabinet that the situation was 'actually worse than was previously thought. The German people have patiently endured everything so far because they have grown used to enduring over the past nine years.' He feared that without immediate measures the risk was that the German Reich would disintegrate. Carl Severing predicted that if they did not succeed in ending passive resistance in the immediate future, 'then Germany is irredeemably lost'. After he said this, minister for food and agriculture Hans Luther, who was not a member of any party but was closest to Stresemann's German People's Party, warned that an immediate end to passive resistance would also 'trigger countercurrents in Germany that could seriously endanger the existence of the Reich'. Johannes Fuchs, a Centre Party member and Rhineland politician, who was appointed minister in the newly created Ministry for the Occupied Territories, opposed an immediate end to passive resistance in favour of hanging on for a little longer, but summed up the cabinet's dilemma: 'Do we want to fight and risk chaos, or do we want to break off the fight and risk Germany being defeated?'[22]

The reason for hanging on was the British government. The first ten days of Stresemann's chancellorship mark the point where the crisis in Franco-British relations powerfully intersected with the crisis facing Germany's political leadership. It was Stresemann's misfortune that, two days before he became chancellor, on

11 August 1923, Britain's Ruhr policy appeared to offer Germany a breakthrough moment. Just as hyperinflation entered its most accelerated phase, the British sent a public diplomatic note to the French to state that in their view the occupation was illegal. The *Manchester Guardian*'s London correspondent called the note 'one of the most striking diplomatic documents published since the Armistice'. It was intended to convey that the Germans had the right to engage in passive resistance and that the illegal occupiers should indicate a path out of the crisis without making any further demands on the government of the illegally occupied country. Moreover, Curzon added that if France did not make a decisive move towards ending the conflict, Britain might be forced to renege on their alliance and enter into direct negotiations with the Germans.[23]

Curzon's note appeared to signal a major victory for Germany. Right at the start of Stresemann's chancellorship, the British provided him with the most important sign of international support for Germany's decision to launch the campaign of passive resistance. On 16 August 1923, the German ambassador in London, Friedrich Sthamer, informed the Foreign Ministry in Berlin that the differences between France and Britain were now too great to be overcome and that the end of the Entente would soon follow. The prospect was so good that Stresemann's initial response to the note was to stay calm and say nothing. He didn't want Germany to be accused of trying to put pressure on the British or interfere in their policy-making.[24]

Yet although it was a major victory, Curzon's note was also a diplomatic note and nothing more. Had it come several months earlier, the German government could have held out to see what its implications might be for the future course of passive resistance. But because it came only in August, Stresemann didn't really have the time to wait and see if the British threat to abandon France was truly serious.

The dilemma for Stresemann was that conditions in Germany required an immediate end to passive resistance, but the arrival of Curzon's note made that a political impossibility. Passive resistance had to continue at least until the Franco–British quarrel over the Ruhr entered its next act. On 23 August 1923, Stresemann even told his cabinet that he believed that Britain was working to isolate France and bring Belgium and Italy behind its policy.[25]

Unfortunately for him, although Curzon's note of 11 August seemed to promise that the German's dream of British intervention might come true, such optimism proved misplaced. The publication of Curzon's note was met with a strong pro-French backlash in Britain. Among the public, the backlash was led by veterans of the Entente politics of the last decade. On 15 August 1923, *The Times* published a letter by Valentine Chirol, its former Berlin correspondent, who had grown up in both France and Germany and spoke both languages fluently. His reasons for rejecting Curzon's note included the fact that he thought that the Weimar Republic was a 'democratic façade', and that Stresemann was 'one of the most violent pan-Germans and haters of England during the war'. Despite the fact that the *Daily Express* had recently claimed that Britain should clear out of the continent and 'give France a free road to work its will on Germany', Chirol condemned the British press for being more pro-German than it had been at any time since 1905. Among the cabinet, Lord Derby threatened Baldwin that he would resign if Britain did not support France.

In Chirol's view, which turned out to be correct, the British government's note threatening France with independent action to support Germany was nothing more than Curzon's 'preaching'. He damningly wrote:

> The British Note moves through a maze of frigid and often inaccurate criticism to a conclusion which, if it means anything, is tinged with even more unreality than the rest of it. Is it not time for us to return to realities?

He demanded that the British remember that France was in the Ruhr to uphold a treaty that Britain had signed, and that France's security concerns were largely a result of the British and American decision to renege on the security pact promised in Paris in 1919. In his final words in praise of the Entente, he called for British humility towards France:

> The Entente is not, and never has been, a boon conferred by us upon France which we might withhold from her without damage to ourselves as soon as we thought her undeserving of it. It has been a pact of common sacrifice and common salvation, and is still the one binding instrument by which we can ensure peace without jeopardizing the most vital and costly fruits of the war.[26]

A hostile French reply to Curzon's note came on 20 August. In it, Poincaré angrily rejected the British accusation that the occupation of the Ruhr was illegal, refused to concede to the idea of an independent assessment of Germany's capacity to pay and emphasized that there would be no staged withdrawal from the Ruhr. Faced with Poincaré's reply, the British Treasury argued that Britain should push ahead with independent arbitration. But the Foreign Office was already backtracking. After Lord Derby threatened to resign, Baldwin agreed that he should meet face to face with Poincaré to try to salvage the situation. But he also decided, with the support of Curzon, that the meeting should not take place immediately. To gain time, they used the excuse that they should discuss further action at the next Imperial Conference in the autumn, where the British government would take on the views of its dominions. Once this decision was made, while the German economy burned and Stresemann's cabinet faced up to the reality that the republic might not survive the winter, Baldwin left for his holidays on 25 August 1923. His destination was Aix-les-Bains, in southern France.[27]

Twenty-five days later, Baldwin stopped in Paris on his way back to London to meet with Poincaré face to face. At the end of their meeting, they issued a joint statement that suggested that Britain was firmly behind France's policy. In it, the two leaders promised to restore their countries' relationship to the way it had been during the days of Sir Edward Grey, when Britain went to war in August 1914 to support France. Baldwin also promised Poincaré that Britain would support France's right to reparations. If the French records of the meeting are correct, Baldwin even used the pejorative term 'le Boche' to describe who would be made to pay. In return for giving Poincaré everything he wanted, Baldwin got nothing. It was a case of an inexperienced British prime minister being schooled by the more senior French statesman – before the First World War, Poincaré had already been French prime minister when Baldwin was still a fledgling backbencher.[28]

The next day, the German chargé d'affaires in Paris told Stresemann that Germany had no longer any grounds to hope for British support in the Ruhr. The waiting was over. As a consequence of the British-French rapprochement, there could be no further argument about the right time to end passive resistance. Neither Baldwin nor Curzon paid a price for their indecision; Stresemann and the Germans did. On the day of his appointment as chancellor, the dollar-to-mark exchange rate in Berlin was 1 to 3,700,000. Forty-three days later, when the British finally removed the obstacle that their indecisive policy had created to ending passive resistance, the dollar-to-mark ratio was 1 to 121,000,000.[29]

Poincaré had played his hand perfectly. Both well informed about what was going on in Britain and a more effective negotiator than Baldwin, he knew that if France did not respond to the British note, the British would have to follow up with actions to give weight to their words. He gambled that they would not do so. At the time Curzon sent the note he had no intention of following through with actual measures that would make its threats reality, and told the British cabinet that a note containing such threatening words would be enough to move Poincaré to a new position. When Poincaré called his bluff, Britain was left with even less influence over French policy than before. Baldwin didn't even demand minor concessions to Germany; he gave Stresemann nothing and the end of passive resistance would come as a total victory for France.

The Weimar Republic had mobilized its population on nationalist grounds for nine months, only then to surrender after months of suffering and endurance. It was a terrible moment to be a pro-republican democrat. Some in London were aware of the extent to which British policy had helped cause the mess. As Austen Chamberlain wrote to his sister Ida on 22 September 1923:

> It seems to me that we are becoming the scold of Europe. We run about shaking our fists in people's faces, ascertaining that this must be altered and that that must stop. We get ourselves disliked and distrusted and misunderstood, and in the end we achieve nothing and relapse into humiliated silence or laboriously explain how pleased we are.[30]

PART IV

Autumn and Winter 1923

12

Separatism and the Future of the Rhineland

B y midsummer it was obvious that the 1923 crisis was not just a crisis of German politics and economics, it was a crisis of the European system of states. For France, the occupation was a costly burden that was not delivering its economic goals. For Germany, it had created the greatest moment of political and economic disruption since the end of the First World War. Money had ceased to function. Food shortages were unavoidable. When Stresemann finally ended the campaign on 26 September 1923, the decision announced that the disruption was about to reach a new peak. But it was also a message: if the republic could weather the worst of the storm, Stresemann would also eventually return Germany to normality. It was that prospect that gave Stresemann's announcement the character of a clarion call. For Weimar's opponents, the clock was suddenly ticking. They had to act now or forever regret that they had let the best opportunity to destroy the republic go to waste. For them, it was a 'now or never' moment. In October 1922, Mussolini had faced such a moment. In the weeks leading up to his appointment as prime minister, he knew that the time had come either to try to use force to obtain power or to recognize that he might never do so. Just one year later, German political extremists and fringe groups now faced the same moment of choice.

Just as Mussolini went for it in October 1922, or as Lenin had done in Russia five years earlier, in the autumn of 1923, three groups of political radicals did so almost simultaneously in Germany in a near three-month period of turmoil, from September to November 1923. Fascists and Communists tried to destroy the democracy and replace it with an ideologically driven authoritarian system of government, while political separatists did so by trying to tear the region of the Rhineland out of Germany altogether. On their own, each of these groups posed a serious threat to the future of Weimar democracy. But it was the near-simultaneity of their actions that really threatened the state. Their combined weight left Germany's democratic leaders facing up to the greatest moment of political pressure they had faced in their entire political careers. The future of Weimar democracy was on the line. Had any of the extremists been victorious, it is doubtful that Germany's first republic could have survived. Between them, their actions brought Germany to the brink of civil war.

The challenge posed by Rhineland separatism is the least well known. As we have seen, when the Versailles Treaty came into effect in January 1920, its terms included the Allied occupation of the Rhineland. France alone sent 95,000 soldiers into the region on the left bank of the Rhine. The Belgians and the British were there too. Together, the three occupying powers divided the region up into zones. It was from their zones that the French and Belgians launched their occupation of the Ruhr on 11 January 1923. When their soldiers marched into the Ruhr, they were met by crowds of protesting Germans singing 'The Watch on the Rhine'.

The song was a crucial part of the political and military identity of Germans in the late nineteenth and early twentieth centuries, and by singing it, German men were promising that they would defend the Rhine from French invasion, just as their fathers and grandfathers had done. But just as most Germans identified the river Rhine as one of the most important geographical boundaries defining German nationhood, a small number of the inhabitants of the Rhine region saw themselves as belonging to another nation entirely. They saw the occupation of the Rhineland after the First World War as an opportunity to break their region away from Germany once and for all.

This group did not think of themselves as Germans, but as Rhinelanders first and foremost. They were Catholics and claimed that German ethnic groups living in the Rhineland were racially different from those in Bavaria or Protestant-dominated Prussia. As early as November 1918, they had rallied behind the separatists' cry of 'Let's escape Berlin'. On 1 June 1919, Hans Adam Dorten, a lawyer who had fought in the First World War before turning to separatist politics in its immediate aftermath, proclaimed the existence of a republic in the Rhineland. But it was short-lived. Dorten's republic did not have the necessary support and it quickly fizzled out.

Later in 1919, Dorten downgraded his ambition to the creation of a new Rhenish state. Unlike the failed republic of the Rhineland that would have been completely independent from Weimar Germany, this Rhenish state was to exist as a new federal state and remain a part of the Weimar Republic but, like Bavaria, it would have its own federal political powers in areas like policing and education, and its own distinctive political culture. Even Konrad Adenauer, the future chancellor of West Germany, who was the mayor of Cologne from 1917 to 1933, was not entirely opposed to the idea. Had it been brought into formal existence, it would have been large enough to rival Prussia and Bavaria. But nothing came of the idea during the Weimar Republic – although it would later be the basis for the creation of what became the state of North Rhine-Westphalia, the largest of the German federal states to be created by the Allies after their victory in 1945.

In 1919, when the powers that decided on the contents of the peace treaty rejected the creation of an independent Rhenish state within the German system, as well as the idea of an entirely independent pro-French republic in the Rhineland, the separatists who supported a Rhenish state concentrated their efforts on propaganda. Their aim was to build their political movement to take advantage of the next political crisis that provided them with an opportunity to create a new state. In 1920, Josef Smeets, a former member of the left-wing Independent Socialist Party of Germany, who had founded a Rhineland League in autumn 1919, founded a new separatist organization based in Cologne called the Rhenish Republican People's Party. But despite its best efforts, this existed only as a discredited fringe group with few followers and a leadership riddled with personal rivalries. Smeets and Dorten personally hated each other.

The 1923 crisis offered the separatists an opportunity to put the future of their region at the heart of the struggle created by the occupation of the Ruhr. When the end of passive resistance gave France victory in that struggle, the separatists took up the challenge of their 'now or never' moment. Conditions were much changed from 1919: they now knew that they would gain more support from Paris for their efforts, and they hoped that British indifference would further help them to achieve their goals.

For Poincaré, if he could not annex the Ruhr outright, the next best option would be to create a new pro-French state in the Rhineland – possibly, but not necessarily, stretching eastwards to include the Ruhr. This had been a French policy at the Paris Peace Conference, but had not been realized because of British and American opposition. In 1923, Poincaré was less certain about what the British and Americans would do in the event of the establishment of a Republic of the Rhineland, but faced a 'now or never' moment of his own. Would he use the end of passive resistance to push for the realization of the French policy of 1919 and the creation of an independent but pro-French republic that would separate France from Germany and permanently weaken German economic power?

As Poincaré mulled over this decision in Paris, on the ground in the Rhineland the separatists who had been defeated in 1919 stepped up their efforts to present him with a *fait accompli*. On 29 September, a police spy recorded separatist leader Hans Adam Dorten announcing to a pro-separatist demonstration in Koblenz: 'We want to be free from all plunder, we want to be free from Germany, we want to be free from Prussia!' Before this, on 12 August, during a pro-separatist demonstration in Bonn, leaders had demanded the complete separation of the Rhineland from Germany, the formation of a government of the Rhineland, the creation of an independent Rhenish currency, international recognition for their new state and the beginning of separate negotiations with France. At these demonstrations, they argued that it was wrong that the Rhineland, with its distinct history and tradition, should belong to the state of Prussia, sharing a political home with the East Prussian Junkers, with whom they believed they had little in common. They claimed that their goal was to free the Rhineland 'from east and west' and that not all German 'tribes' must necessarily belong in the same state.[1]

At the end of September, Dorten told the French press that his aim was to include both Frankfurt and Essen in the new republic, and that its eastern border would run in a straight line between the cities. This was a bold statement. Neither was considered a part of the Rhine region: Essen was the coal capital of the Ruhr district, while Frankfurt was on the river Main, around 250 kilometres to Essen's south-east. But Dorten wanted Essen's coal and Frankfurt's trade, and hoped that his new state would even include the winemaking region of the Rhineland-Palatinate, Nassau and the former Grand Duchy of Hesse, one of the smaller German states that stretched to the north-east of the Rhine. Had he obtained this territory, the new republic would have had a population of around eleven million, compared to the Weimar Republic's total population of 60 million. A Rhenish militia would provide the new state with its first military force. Tellingly, it was first to be placed under the command of French and Belgian officers. The coal cities of Bochum and Dortmund in the Ruhr in the north, and the industrial city of Mannheim to the south of Frankfurt, were to be left in the Weimar Republic.[2]

It was only thanks to the exceptional conditions created by the 1923 crisis that a fantasist like Dorten, the leader of 'gangs of desperadoes', as the British consul in Cologne later called them, could come close to realizing his goals. At the start of August, the separatist newspaper *Das Freie Rheinland* had reached a daily print run of thirty thousand. Its readers included the losers in the 1923 crisis: unemployed workers, peasants and small farmers, as well as members of the lower middle classes who had lost out during the ongoing hyperinflation crisis. Even before the end of passive resistance, the separatist leaders were preaching that the people of the Rhineland were suffering more than Germans in the unoccupied territories. They argued that they bore the brunt of the occupation and that, when the time suited them, Germany's political leadership would abandon them.[3]

To take advantage of the worsening conditions, in the summer of 1923, the journalist and activist Josef Friedrich Matthes founded a new separatist organization, the Rhenish Independence League. Matthes, who was born in Würzburg in north Bavaria and had only moved to Düsseldorf in 1923, wanted to establish a separatist action committee in every village in the Rhineland and to unite the existing separatist organizations under his leadership. He could aspire to such ambitions because of his skills as a populist speaker and journalist. At the start of August, as many as six thousand people gathered to hear him speak at a concert hall in Düsseldorf. On 12 August, three thousand people turned up in Bonn to listen to his pro-separatist speeches. Responding to Matthes's growing popularity, on 15 August in Koblenz, Smeets and Dorten publicly agreed to work together. Matthes remained at a distance, however. He didn't want to be saddled with their debts, and his rivalry with Dorten continued. Despite the absence of a single leader, the separatist movement continued to gain momentum in September, with more pro-separatist demonstrations and parades in cities such as Trier, Bonn, Duisburg, Landau, Mainz and Mönchengladbach.[4]

When Stresemann received the French ambassador to Germany for the first time as German chancellor on 17 August, he told him:

> We were of the opinion that France intended to destroy Germany, or at least to destroy the unity of Germany, by wanting to separate the Rhineland from Germany, and that efforts in southern Germany aimed at separating Bavaria were also supported.

He warned the French ambassador that these policies would leave Germany unable to pay any reparations and that they would make it impossible for the German government to come to an agreement with France. In reply, the French ambassador told Stresemann that he profoundly regretted that Poincaré's policies had been so badly misunderstood in Germany.[5]

The French ambassador was lying. France had provided clandestine support to the separatists for several years. In 1920, the French provided them with more than 500,000 francs. In February 1921, they handed over 300,000 marks to support separatist candidates' campaigns for election to the Prussian parliament. Smeets and Dorten too were given French money. Initially, Smeets was given German marks from an office attached to Paul Tirard, the high commissioner in the Rhineland. But as the German currency's value worsened over the course of 1923, the French started to hand over francs instead. Smeets's newspaper, the *Rheinische Republik*, was financed almost entirely by this French money. Dorten's publication, the *Rheinischer Herold*, was also paid for by the French. In 1923, Dorten received around 15,000 francs per month. On 29 July, when he held a meeting at Koblenz to relaunch his party, the French gave him 10,000 francs to help pay for the occasion.[6] According to German police reports, at the beginning of September, Matthes is supposed to have received around 10 billion francs from Tirard. British records suggest that the separatists also later received French revolvers and ammunition. In July 1923, Poincaré summed up the French policy towards Dorten as follows: 'We must discourage neither his actions nor his efforts, especially since it is not impossible that his policy will ultimately lead to satisfactory results for us.'[7]

With the end of passive resistance, French support for separatism in the Rhineland increased. While some French military commanders on the ground in the Rhineland and Ruhr remained sceptical about the separatists, decision-makers in Paris started to dream that the long-held goal of an independent Rhineland might become a reality.

It was wishful thinking. Even after a summer of growth, the separatists were still a minority movement, with around 25,000–30,000 supporters. Moreover, the louder they amplified their message in towns and villages across the Rhineland, the more concerted the backlash against them became. Even during the crisis year, most people in the Rhineland still supported the Centre Party, which remained firmly committed to unity with the German Reich. Anti-separatist demonstrations took place and, on occasions, separatist speakers found themselves unable to speak because they were outnumbered by their opponents. But the backlash against them was not without consequences. It encouraged the separatists to claim that they needed weapons and military units to protect themselves and prevent attacks on their demonstrations. But they didn't just want weapons to protect themselves. They knew that if they were going to establish a Republic of the Rhineland, they would need to arm their followers and seize power. On 18 September, Dorten asked Tirard to arm the peasant supporters of separatism and to disarm the police. Even though Tirard refused, it was obvious to everyone that the situation was becoming exceptionally tense, with violence increasingly likely.[8]

The separatist leader Josef Smeets himself had almost been killed by an ultra-nationalist opponent in March 1923. While he was in his office with his brother-in-law, Smeets's sister opened the door to a young man in his early twenties, who told her that he wanted to buy newspapers but then proceeded to draw his pistol and fire a number of shots. Before Smeets's sister realized what was happening, her husband was dead. Smeets himself was shot in the head, but the bullet did not kill him. He was taken to hospital, where he underwent an operation and passed a number of days in a serious condition, before eventually recovering. The assassination attempt was the work of an unknown underground German nationalist group. While their use of violence may not have been popular among a majority in the Rhineland, their goal of maintaining Germany's unity was.[9]

With the end of passive resistance, the moment of action had arrived. The separatist leaders decided to organize a 'Rhenish Day' to take place in Düsseldorf on 30 September. The event was to be similar to the ultra-nationalists' 'German Day', with one key difference: it was to end with the proclamation of a Republic of the Rhineland. In the days before the event, German media reported that in addition to proclaiming the republic, the assembly would endorse its president and that Dorten had been assigned the job of envoy in Paris.[10]

To oppose the separatists' 'Rhenish Day', 40 kilometres to the south of Düsseldorf in Cologne, historically Düsseldorf's local rival city, the political parties of the Rhineland, with the support of trade unions and cultural organizations, staged an alternative pro-unity event to take place at a fairground on the same day. After the

Cologne male choir opened proceedings with a performance of the song 'German Greetings', the first speaker was the Centre Party's city councillor Peter Schaeven. He proudly told the assembled crowd that there were more people present and listening to him at that moment than there were supporters of the separatists across the entire Rhineland, and that they were there to celebrate the Rhineland's unity with the German Reich and to condemn Poincaré. He told them that the Rhineland belonged to Germany, the land of Schiller and Goethe, 'innumerable inventions' and 'God-gifted musicians'. As the crowd cheered, he condemned the separatists and the French, calling for the return of all those who had been deported by the occupying forces and the release of all prisoners. At the end of the rally, the assembly unanimously supported a strongly worded pro-Reich declaration, which was widely circulated in the German press. It warned against any attempt to deny the people of the Rhineland their right to self-determination. The Rhineland 'feels unshakably connected to the German fatherland. It will staunchly resist to the end any attempt to impose upon or interfere with its state affiliation.' Those who betrayed their fatherland 'in a subservient spirit to foreign rulers' had no place among the true Rhinelanders.[11]

The Centre Party claimed that this was the real 'mood' in the Rhineland. *Vorwärts* called the crowds that gathered in Cologne 'immense masses'. One nationalist newspaper stated that more than 100,000 people were in attendance, while another commented that the assembled crowd was so large that it could not fit into the fairground. Some even suggested that it was one of the largest demonstrations of its kind ever to take place. *Vorwärts* predicted that the attempt by 'French imperialism' to create an independent state in the Rhineland would fail due to the opposition of the pro-German working class and rhetorically asked how long the French would be able to keep Europe in a state of disquiet.[12]

While the demonstration in Cologne remained peaceful, in Düsseldorf the situation was tense. A week earlier, during the night of 22–3 September, two German police officers had been shot dead. Understandably, the Düsseldorf police were angered by the news that their colleagues had been gunned down in the course of their duties. Soon after, the perpetrators were identified as members of the Rhenish Independence League. They had allegedly participated in a meeting of special co-ordinators in Mönchengladbach, where they were heard agitating against the governments in Berlin and Prussia and cheering in favour of a Rhenish Republic. One of the men was supposed to have displayed his revolver to his drunken comrades.[13]

Even though the French commander in Düsseldorf, General Simon, forbade the city authorities from preventing the march from taking place, the Rhenish Day was still met with countermeasures. The driving force behind these was exiled district president Walther Grützner, whom Matthes despised and said he hoped would never return to Düsseldorf. Together with local parties and with the support of non-socialist and Christian workers', employees' and civil servants' organizations, Grützner called on the residents of Düsseldorf to stay at home. The idea was to turn Düsseldorf into a 'dead city' for the duration of the separatists' march. From 1 p.m., all streets, shops, bars and restaurants were to be entirely empty and the tram service was suspended. One reporter described how the effect of these measures meant that the city streets that were usually the busiest, including the Königsallee, were almost completely empty.[14]

More controversially, and perhaps deliberately linked to the plan to keep citizens off the streets, Grützner also instructed the Düsseldorf police to use force to disrupt the march. On 27 September, the lord mayor, Emil Köttgen, received an order, which was intercepted by French intelligence, instructing him to hit the separatist demonstration hard with everything available to him. It was an unambiguous call for state violence against the separatists, whom Grützner accused of 'high and national treason'.[15]

The order might have made political sense but it was ill-conceived. Even though the separatists were a small movement, on Rhenish Day itself the Düsseldorf police would be hopelessly outnumbered. On 30 September, out of a total police force of around 1,100 (a reduction of over 400) Düsseldorf's police commander Haas had around fifteen police officers, 450 'green' state police officers and 300 'blue' city police officers (the blue and green officers operated in the same area, but were nominally under different command structures). They were armed with a sabre, a revolver with sixteen to twenty bullets, and a rubber baton.[16]

These men were up against a far larger number of demonstrators. When the demonstration ended, contemporary assessments of the number of participants ranged from lower estimates of between eight and ten thousand to the organizers' suggestion that the figure was around thirty thousand. French officials put it at fifteen thousand, while the French media agency Havas suggested that it was forty thousand. There is greater clarity concerning the number of armed separatists in attendance. Reports agree that there were between fourteen hundred and two thousand.[17]

Knowing what was coming, the police commanders in Düsseldorf rejected Grützner's instructions. Carrying out his orders would only provoke a violent response on the part of the separatists and end in the intervention of the French military. In place of his plan, they therefore adopted a policy of intervening only if people or public buildings came under threat. They would let the separatists march, but they would not allow them to riot or beat people up. The police officers who took up positions in the streets did so with the permission of the French and they followed French instructions as to where they should be located. But many of them stayed out of sight in their police accommodation in the Mühlenstrasse, in the town hall and in the regional council.[18]

Between 11 a.m. and 1 p.m., the first separatists from outside Düsseldorf began to arrive. They were brought there in the trains of the Régie, the railway company established by the French as part of the occupation of the Ruhr, which made 12,500 seats available to support them. They also travelled for free, with some families taking the opportunity of a free trip to Düsseldorf. At 2 p.m., after the last Régie train arrived, the separatists formed a procession, including some two thousand members of the armed separatist security service. By the time the first Régie trains arrived in Düsseldorf, the violence had already begun. During the night before the demonstrations took place, separatists opened fire upon a police station. Another police station was fired on early on Sunday morning when up to sixty separatists stormed it and disarmed the officers, informing them that they had taken control of police duties. Large numbers of the separatists were reported as coming from Aachen, 80 kilometres to the south-west, near the border with France.[19]

But the skirmishes of the previous night were nothing compared to the fighting that followed. The 30th of September was quickly named 'Düsseldorf's Bloody Sunday'. By the time it was over gunfights had taken place between separatists and police in the city centre and in the area close to the main railway station. Altogether two hundred people were taken to hospital for treatment: seventy-four of them were seriously injured. At least ten died. These included one member of the city police and two members of the state police. Civilians in a park had fled for their lives when they were caught in the lines of fire. How the shooting started remains a controversial question.[20]

According to French official accounts, the demonstration was in full swing when, at around 3.45 p.m., a detachment of state police left the police barracks on Mühlenstrasse and opened fire on the separatists as soon as it encountered them. The state police were then joined by members of the city police, who also attacked the crowd. French observers later reported that up to two hundred armed men hunted down the separatist protestors, striking them with sabres and firing at them with revolvers, before following them into the neighbouring streets. French reports also suggest that the policemen attacking the separatists did not spare women and children, and that the armed separatists present were at first overwhelmed but that they ultimately responded with gunfire. According to the French historian Stanislas Jeannesson, once the French command had been alerted to the disturbance, French military soon arrived on the scene and restored order. Jeannesson suggests that, thanks to their interception of German communications, the French were fully aware that the German police would attack the demonstrators, but that they let the attack take place regardless.[21]

German accounts provide an altogether different explanation for the origins and course of the violence. They focus on the separatist 'shock troops'. When the first Régie trains arrived in Düsseldorf, they were welcomed by a crowd of a few hundred supporters. The separatists' shock troops then formed a 'closed procession' and made their way to Graf-Adolf-Platz, a central square, where Matthes addressed them. He criticized what he called the terror of the Prussian government and then declared: 'We have come to a peaceful rally today, but we are also men of action if need be.' At the end of his speech, he stated it was 'high time for an independent Rhineland'. At this point the shock troops made their way back to the main train station, where, following the arrival of more Régie trains, a far larger crowd of separatists had gathered. Together, they then formed marching columns and began to make their way through the empty city. The marchers at the side and head of the procession were reportedly armed with rubber batons and revolvers. A large number of green, white and red flags of the Rhenish Republic were visible. One newspaper correspondent described the strange situation where a large demonstration with several thousand participants marched through the city's empty streets, watched only by a few hundred people. He thought that those who turned out were largely 'curious', while the city itself felt like it was 'dead'.[22]

The demonstration was concentrated in the area around the Hindenburgwall, a major street in the centre of Düsseldorf close to the city's theatre and art gallery which was named after Germany's defensive position on the western front during the second half of the First World War, which was itself named after German military commander Paul von Hindenburg. There were curious, yet highly symbolic, scenes at the Bismarck Memorial, where demonstrators tried to hang the green, white and red flag of the separatist republic on the statue of the man who, more than anyone else, symbolized the unification of Germany. While this was taking place, Matthes was being driven around in a car. He stopped at the Kaiser Wilhelm Monument on the Hindenburgwall, where he announced that three speakers would address the crowd from different points. German newspaper correspondents claimed that at this point the first phys-ical violence took place. The *Berliner Tageblatt* correspondent noted that shock troops had started to use rubber batons to beat up bystanders who did not have cards demonstrating their membership of a separatist organization. The nationalist *Deutsche Allgemeine Zeitung* correspondent claimed that the separatists then started to disarm German police and also to threaten passers-by that they could hand them over to the French gendarmerie and have them deported. The same correspondent claimed that when two city police officers were disarmed, one of the separatists shouted: 'The first battle is won! Now the combat troops are to the fore and the weapons are out.'[23]

The blue city police watched these scenes from a short distance away, a few steps from the Bismarck Monument, close to the Mühlenstrasse. The *Berliner Tageblatt* correspondent claimed to have witnessed a man with a separatist armband draw his Browning pistol and fire in the Mühlenstrasse, killing a police officer. In German accounts of the violence, this was the first shot fired in Düsseldorf that day and the trigger for the gunfire that followed.[24]

The blue police received reinforcements from the green state police, who returned the separatists' fire. Panic followed. Some of the armed separatists took cover behind the columns of the theatre and fired back. Almost instantly the square was empty. The *Berliner Tageblatt* correspondent hid in a doorway. He saw a man shot dead just feet away from himself. The violence was only starting.[25]

According to German accounts, once the firing started, the separatists called upon the French for back-up against the police. When French cavalry and armoured cars appeared on the scene, the separatists reportedly welcomed them with cheers and great shouting. The French surrounded the German police and disarmed them. As soon as this happened, the separatists, who had previously fled the scene, now returned to take revenge. Several policemen were seriously injured and, according to some accounts, at least one was executed at this point.[26]

The violence increased in the ensuing chaos. Some of the worst incidents occurred in the court garden, a large park in the centre of Düsseldorf directly adjacent to the Hindenburgwall. During the afternoon, while the demonstrations were continuing, families had gathered as usual in the park. But once the firing started, some armed separatists thought that they had come under fire from snipers hiding there and started firing indiscriminately into the park, leaving at least sixty to seventy people injured, some of them seriously. 'It was a terrifying sight,' wrote the *Berliner Tageblatt* correspondent, who watched as 'women and children fainted, and the groans of the victims filled the air'. Several people tried to escape by swimming across the large pond in the middle of the park. The shootout lasted for around half an hour and extended into the Königsallee and the surrounding streets, as far as St John's Church.[27]

The injured included children. One journalist was shocked to see how a child who had been treated for wounds was being carried among the separatists. He presumed that it was with its mother. In an account published in a nationalist newspaper, 'two officials were tortured to death and . . . mutilated beyond recognition by the unrelentingly brutal crowd' in front of the French soldiers. Such accusations were a common trope of German accounts of enemy violence during and after the First World War.[28]

In a German trade-union report that was sent to Degoutte and quoted in the London *Times*, the separatists were blamed for having attacked the police with 'rubber-covered lead piping'. It described the 'outrages' perpetrated against the state police by separatists after the state police had been disarmed by the French. In one case, the separatists knocked a policeman to the ground and were in the process of 'brutally kicking and beating him with clubs' in front of French gendarmes who did nothing to intervene, when two French soldiers, members of a French Alpine Division, the Chasseurs Alpins, decided that they would intervene to end the brutality, driving the separatists away by threatening them with their rifles.[29]

One medical corps organized by the Social Democratic Party treated 117 injured. The French medical services were accused of going to the aid of the injured separatists. The local population was described as extremely hostile towards the French, whom they accused of disarming the German police, allowing the separatists to beat them badly and ignoring the plight of injured policemen, even when they were being kicked while lying on the ground. The *Berliner Tageblatt* called the French the 'protectors of the criminal rabble'. The separatists were accused of firing on disarmed German police, while the French cavalry were accused of striking the German police with their sabres. Later that day, as many as a thousand people protested against the separatists and the French in front of Düsseldorf town hall. By that time the city police chief Haas had been arrested by the French and a night-time curfew had been declared.[30]

In advance, the German press had reported that Rhenish Day was expected to end with the declaration of a Republic of the Rhineland. When it was over, the trade unions announced that they would respond to such a declaration with a general strike. The correspondent of *The Times* in Düsseldorf summed up the general mood in the city as one of horror. After speaking to people there, he claimed that even separatist supporters in the city thought that the police had behaved admirably and that the separatists had gone too far. The French decision to put German officials, including Haas, the town councillor for police affairs and two state police officers on trial was widely condemned. [31]

Even some French newspapers thought that the French support for German separatism was a mistake. They blamed Poincaré for getting caught up in something that he could not control. They worried that the lack of support among the population of the Rhineland could lead to an embarrassing end. For the French commanders in the Rhineland, the violence was an embarrassment too. In its aftermath they moved to distance themselves from the separatists and threatened that they wouldn't tolerate any repetition of the events in Düsseldorf. Their hostility on the ground pushed the separatists to concentrate their next efforts in the Belgian zone. But before the French military in the Rhineland could completely banish the separatists from their territory, Poincaré intervened once again in their favour. In October and

November, his decisions poured fuel on the fire of separatism and yet more lives were lost.[32]

Three weeks after Düsseldorf's Bloody Sunday, during the night of 20–1 October, the separatists finally proclaimed their republic. At around 4 a.m., in Aachen, in the heart of the Belgian zone, a few hundred separatists armed with pistols and cudgels seized control of public buildings, including the town hall, the finance department and the post office. This time the local police didn't oppose them. When local residents woke up on Sunday morning, they found the flag of the Republic of the Rhineland flying over their town. Walls in the centre of the town were covered by a proclamation declaring the existence of the Republic of the Rhineland. The putsch was organized by two local separatist leaders, the industrialist Leo Deckers and Dr Guthardt. At a demonstration organized by the 'provisional government', the speakers promised that the new republic would deliver food. It was expected that they would obtain fresh supplies from the Belgians and French. German accounts accused the Belgians of having prepared the way for the coup by deporting key trade-union figures, including the Christian miners' leading member of parliament Hasch, from Herzogenrath. In addition to the events in Aachen, public buildings were occupied in Bonn, Wiesbaden and Trier.[33]

The putsch soon expanded into towns in the French zone as well, though it met fierce resistance. On 22 and 23 October, as challenges to the authority of the republic occurred in Saxony and Bavaria, separatists took control of Saarburg, as well as occupying public buildings in Wiesbaden, Trier, Düren and Duisburg, drawing attacks by angry German nationalists. British observers noted that in some places the spontaneous resistance of locals, who were armed with sticks, had driven the separatists out of public buildings. In Koblenz, the same observers thought that the entire separatist putsch was spearheaded by only four hundred men. By 24 October, the putschists were holding on to just one public building in Aachen, and the attempt to seize control of Koblenz had come to an end. In its summary of events in the Rhineland, the *Berliner Tageblatt* reported that the separatists had largely been pushed back every-where they had attempted to seize power. There were simply too many people in the Rhineland who were determined to see them defeated.[34]

At first, Belgian soldiers remained neutral towards the separatists. Contrary to German suggestions that they had welcomed the sep-aratist putsch, the Belgians did not have a strategic interest in the emergence of an independent state in the Rhineland. However, their policy at first was to follow the French.[35] But everything changed on 24 October, when, just under a month after his victory on the issue of passive resistance, Poincaré made the decision to throw France's weight behind the separatists, initially pressuring the Belgians to go along with his policy, which was one of de facto recognition of a separatist government in the French zone.[36]

With the French behind them, the situation on the ground turned dramatically, but only briefly, in the separatists' favour, even if they could not count on the help of the French military. They occupied all public buildings in Koblenz on 25 October, while Régie trains helped to bring food and armed separatists to Aachen. The popu-lation that had resisted the separatists was now terrorized by their renewed strength. Watching this turn of events, Edward Thurstan, the British consul general at Cologne, was enraged. He viewed French support for the separatists at this time as a deliberate attempt to carve up Germany, and was horrified that the French government was supporting armed groups of separatists that he considered to be the worst kind of violent mob.[37]

Even before Poincaré announced his support for the separatists, the British had decided on their policy regarding separatist endeav-ours on 23 October: the planned Republic of the Rhineland would only gain control of the British zone of the occupied territory over the dead bodies of the British soldiers. The British military were given strict instructions to suppress any acts of separatist violence in the British zone. In addition to their military planning, the British also firmly decided that their political response would be to refuse to recognize any change to the status of the Rhineland that did not occur in accordance with the constitution of the Weimar

Republic. This was effectively an announcement that the British would support the German government, as it would be impossible to change the status of the Rhineland in Weimar's constitution without the support of the government in Berlin.

In a departure from their wavering and at times confused policy towards the Ruhr for much of 1923, the British now also decided to send the French a clear message, and prime minister Stanley Baldwin delivered a strong public speech in Plymouth on 25 October. It was intended to convey to the French that there was no division within the British cabinet on this issue: there could be no Republic of the Rhineland. Baldwin made it clear that the disintegration of Germany was unacceptable. The friendliest thing that he could say to the French was that the loss of the Rhineland would set back Germany's ability to pay reparations for years. Far more threateningly, he promised them that Britain could not 'contemplate the breaking-off of any part of Germany into a separate state, which would at once break the Treaty of Versailles'. On 30 October, the British ambassador in Paris, Lord Crewe, repeated Baldwin's message. He issued Poincaré with a formal British warning that the creation of a separate state from German territory would mean an end to the Treaty of Versailles.[38]

In response the French government denied that they had supported the separatists and told British diplomats that they must have been misled by German *agents provocateurs* trying to provoke discord between Britain and France. This incensed officials in the British Foreign Office, who had their own diplomats as well as military and intelligence agents on the ground in Germany and knew that their counterparts in the French diplomatic service were lying to their faces. Belgium, which never really wanted to see an independent Rhineland, quickly followed Britain's lead. With British backing, the Belgian military removed the last separatists from Aachen on 2 November and brought them to the French zone. By 9 November, the entire Belgian zone was free of all separatist influence.

Britain's support for Germany arrived just in time for Stresemann. A matter of days before he learnt that Britain would firmly oppose a new settlement in the Rhineland that went against his government's wishes, even Stresemann had conceded that the pressure was too great and that it might be desirable for negotiations to take place between politicians from the Rhineland and the French high commissioner. That concession came after discussions between Stresemann and representatives of business and politics from the Rhineland, including Adenauer, who thought that the best solution might be to allow the establishment of a Rhineland state but to keep it within the federation of German states. But once the British position was made clear, the proposals were quickly dropped.[39]

On the ground in the Rhineland, the outcome of the uprising now hinged on numbers, which did not favour the separatists. Even with French support, their highly localized 'power seizures' could only last for a short time. The violence of the separatists, and their willingness to plunder, enraged the population of the Rhineland, triggering an anti-separatist mobilization from below.

The endpoint for the Rhineland separatists came in the picturesque hills along the river Rhine known as the Siebengebirge or Seven Mountains, a tourist region around 100 kilometres to the west of the German-Belgian border about halfway between Bonn and Koblenz, where groups of men met secretly and decided to protect themselves and fight back. These men were German nationalists. They wanted their region to remain a part of Germany and they wanted to fight any separatists who claimed the right to seize their agricultural produce. They also held significant advantages over their opponents. Their villages were in the hills overlooking the Rhine, so they could see when the separatists' trucks were coming, and they knew the terrain more intimately than the separatists ever could.

On 15 November, two trucks of heavily armed separatists came into one of their villages, only to be met by gunfire. The shootout became known as the start of the battle of the Siebengebirge. In the ensuing ambush, twenty-three of thirty separatists were killed. The survivors returned with reinforcements to take revenge. Some reports suggest that as many as two thousand of them travelled along the Rhine to attack the Siebengebirge. When they got there, the fighting lasted for hours and more than seventy separatists were reported killed, with a further fifty taken as prisoner.[40] The violence was brutal. But, in the end, the separatists were defeated.

By the start of December, the separatist movement in the Rhineland had collapsed. When they attempted to hold a separatist meeting in Essen on 26 November, only the intervention of the French military protected them from a violent fate at the hands of angry crowds. Yet the French persisted, and astounded the British by supporting another independence movement before the year was over, this time to the south of the river Rhine, in Speyer in the Palatinate. Just as had happened in the autumn, this movement failed for lack of support.[41]

Poincaré's support for Rhineland separatism was a result of his ad hoc policy-making. Stubbornness had led him to hold out for total victory over the German campaign of passive resistance. But once Stresemann abandoned the campaign, Poincaré didn't really have a strategy for what to do next. The wisest move would have been to enter directly into negotiations with Stresemann. Britain and the United States would have been observers rather than participants, and a powerful France could have forced its conditions upon Germany. The German government would have had to accept them, and once they did so it would have been far harder for Britain and the United States to demand their reversal. Instead of going for this strategy, Poincaré chose hubris.

In the unstable conditions of October and November 1923, he hoped that by supporting the separatists he could realize the French dream of an independent Rhineland. Not only did he lose that battle but, in doing so, he squandered the chance his victory over passive resistance had given him to weaken the German state permanently. By the time the campaign of the separatists petered out, the international situation had entered a new stage: the British and Americans were ready for a political solution to both the Ruhr occupation crisis and the reparations crisis. Poincaré had wasted France's victory and Germany's future was now out of his hands.

13

'Soviet Saxony' and the Communist Threat

The separatists weren't the only extremist group to attempt to use the end of passive resistance to score a previously unimaginable victory. For Hitler's Nazis and Germany's Communists the clock was ticking too. Like the separatists, who were backed by France, the extremes of left and right could draw upon international support, while also modelling themselves on previous successes. Both Lenin and Mussolini had faced similar 'now or never' moments and seized them: Lenin took advantage of Russia's wartime crises in 1917 to take power over the disintegrating Russian Empire; Mussolini helped to bring about the collapse of state authority in Italy in the summer and autumn of 1922. Even though it is important to remember the way that international examples provided scripts for what the German extremists should do, ultimately, once Stresemann decided to to end passive resistance, the future of German democracy would be decided in the German federal states of Bavaria, Saxony and Thuringia.

Since the foundation of the Weimar Republic, the major regional political strife had stemmed from clashes between the pro-democratic north and the politically conservative south. The central German states of Thuringia and Saxony lay geographically between them. Though neither was as large or influential as their biggest neighbours to north and south, together their population was almost as large as that of Bavaria, Germany's second largest state. Unlike Prussia and Bavaria, they were left-wing states – Saxony was even known as 'Soviet Saxony'. In their industrial regions, in cities like

Chemnitz, the working class showed high levels of support for Communism. If the Communists were going to take power in Germany in 1923, these were the states where many people expected the revolution to start.

The centrality of their locations added to their importance. Thuringia and Saxony occupied the territory separating Bavaria from Prussia. If the Communists seized power in either or both, takeovers there could serve as the starting point for a Communist-led march north on Berlin. On the other hand, if the Communists took control over Thuringia or Saxony, it might also provide a pretext for the Bavarian right to march north to defeat Communism in the neighbouring states, before continuing on to Berlin to overthrow the republic in the ensuing chaos. Another alternative was that if the Bavarian nationalists marched north on Berlin, Saxony and Thuringia could become the first line in a red wall fighting to defend democracy. At the end of September 1923, no one could be certain which of these scenarios might come to pass. The only certainty was that Germany was closer to civil war than at any time in its recent history.

Initially, it looked like the republic's conservative-nationalist enemies in the south were preparing to make the first move. When news arrived that Stresemann had ended passive resistance, Bavaria's prime minister, Eugen von Knilling, declared a state of emergency in his state. He then handed over power to Gustav Ritter von Kahr, an antisemitic conservative monarchist who took the title of state commissioner for Bavaria. This effectively gave Kahr dictatorial powers. His position was created with the support of the chairman of the Bavarian People's Party (BVP), Heinrich Held, and the deposed crown prince of Bavaria, Rupprecht, who was hoping that the end of the crisis would see him restored to the throne as king of Bavaria, the position that his father had vacated during the revolution of November 1918. Unlike his father, who had lost favour during the war, Rupprecht had been a distinguished general and he remained among the more popular of the former German monarchs.[1]

Bavaria's conservative leadership argued that the suspension of

Bavarian democracy and appointment of Kahr were necessary to protect the existing structure of the state. They argued that, without political change at the top, the radical nationalist anti-republican forces that had gained strength in Bavaria during the previous nine months, including the Nazis, were likely to use force to try to achieve change from below. Knilling told Stresemann that Kahr would bring all 'patriotic' groups in Bavaria under his leadership and that the move was necessary because Bavaria was in a state of 'extraordinary excitement' and that it would prevent 'stupidities'. He also claimed that it was the best way to maintain 'peace' and promised that Kahr would demonstrate the 'fullest loyalty' and exercise a positive influence over 'the elements on the right in Bavaria'.[2]

In fact, Kahr represented one of the most significant threats to the existence of the Weimar Republic in October 1923. His goal was to destroy it. Together with Hans Ritter von Seißer, the head of the Bavarian state police, and Otto von Lossow, the commander of the Reichswehr in Bavaria, Kahr was intent on secretly exploring the possibility of joining forces with anti-republican conspirators in northern Germany to overthrow the democratic republic and replace it with a 'national dictatorship'. The head of the Bavarian government, in other words, was part of a network of conspirators intent on overthrowing the German government in Berlin and destroying the Weimar Republic itself.

For German supporters of democracy like Ebert and Stresemann, Kahr's appointment created extraordinary challenges. They faced the task of enforcing the republic's authority over an anti-republican government in Bavaria, while having to deal simultaneously with the threat posed by the Communists in Saxony and Thuringia, as well as the separatist movement in the Rhineland; at the same time, the value of the German currency continued to decrease at an incredible rate. Moreover, they had to remove the threats posed by both Communism and Nazism without provoking a civil war. In the end, the path they chose involved moving first against the Communists in Saxony and Thuringia, and hoping that this display of republican authority against the extreme left would be enough to derail the plans of right-wing putschists in Bavaria. It was a high-risk strategy.

As soon as he took up the position of Bavarian state commissioner, Kahr began to suppress his political opponents. He banned the sale of left-wing newspapers from outside Bavaria and broke off political relations with Saxony; formally ending the internal German diplomacy that allowed the federal states to maintain links, discuss issues of common importance and form barriers against Berlin. He also publicly criticized Stresemann and brought relations between Bavaria and the Reich to their lowest point since the foundation of the Weimar Republic. He ended the implementation of the Law for the Protection of the Republic in Bavaria (which had already been considerably watered down), and on 20 October, after Ebert and the chief of the army general staff, Hans von Seeckt, agreed to dismiss the commander of the Reichswehr in Bavaria, Lossow, and reinforce Seeckt and the Reichswehr's authority over Bavaria, Kahr responded by taking the 7th (Bavarian) Division of the Reichswehr, which was stationed in Bavaria, under his control and refused to recognize Lossow's dismissal.[3]

Kahr also actively promoted antisemitism. In his first public statement he declared that his actions would be motivated by 'extreme love of the Bavarian homeland, the German people and the greater German fatherland'. He promised to fulfil his 'patriotic duties', and warned that there would be no mercy for 'all acts hostile to the fatherland and any resistance to my orders'. In undertaking these measures, he added with knowing antisemitic intent that he expected to be able to rely upon 'all circles of German origin who want to serve our fatherland honestly as I do'.[4]

For Kahr's most vocal critics, the test of the republic's strength would be whether or not it could deal with his provocation. The Social Democratic *Münchener Post* announced that the Bavarian 'state of emergency' meant nothing less than 'a real Kahr dictatorship'. It observed that the 'way in which it came about outwardly adheres to constitutional provisions, but it is actually the realization of the long-announced "coup by stealth"'. In Munich, the *Vorwärts* correspondent was worried because Kahr was 'a fanatical enemy of social democracy'. He warned that he would use 'dictatorial measures' to attack the SPD and the trade unions, the Weimar Republic's strongest supporters in Bavaria. At the end of his report, the *Vorwärts* reporter pleaded that the republic's rulers in Berlin needed to respond with a show of force: 'Bavaria must know that it is part of the Reich, and that there is still power in the Reich!'[5]

The next day, Kahr proved the reporter's point. On the afternoon of Friday, 28 September, the SPD in Munich began to receive warnings from unnamed sources that the left was to be targeted that night. By way of response, they put in place a defensive guard of twenty men from the Social Democratic protection department at the offices of the Social Democratic newspaper, the *Münchener Post*. At around 9 p.m., the warnings turned out to be true. Several state police armoured cars and trucks turned up at a trade-union building, the offices of the *Münchener Post* and a bar frequented by the Social Democrats' protection department. Worryingly for all of Hitler's opponents in Bavaria, the collusion between his party and the police appeared to be on full display when the Nazi leader made sure that everyone could see him following the police trucks to the union offices in his personal car, driven by a chauffeur. It looked as though Hitler was personally directing affairs.

Once the police had completed their search of the union offices, they left. They had been unable to find the weapons they were looking for. The situation was far more tense at the *Münchener Post*. When the police arrived there, they blocked off the street and erected machine-gun posts, which they oriented towards the newspaper building. This time they could justify their actions. In a sealed-off room they found around forty infantry rifles, two light machine guns and a small number of hand grenades. Some of those present, who the Social Democratic reporters claimed were in the possession of gun licences, also had handguns, which the police seized. Supporters of the SPD claimed that these weapons were necessary to protect them in the event of an armed assault from Hitler's Fascists.

In the aftermath, the *Münchener Post* issued a statement to

Munich's workers, warning them that they should not provoke violence or provide the Allies with an excuse to expand the occupation beyond the Ruhr. Kahr responded too. He banned the Social Democrats' protection department. But by the time he made his move against them, Hitler and the patriotic leagues in Munich were already too angry with Kahr to take much notice.

Hitler was livid. On the night of 27 September, he had planned to speak at fourteen separate Nazi rallies in Munich. But following Kahr's appointment the day before, the rallies were banned. The *Völkischer Beobachter* responded with a tirade of hatred directed at Kahr. It claimed that he could not lead because he was not a 'real man' and went on: 'You can only stand unconditionally behind a leader . . . who you know will not collapse at crucial moments. Kahr collapsed several times.' The message was clear: only Hitler could lead the Bavarian movement for 'German Freedom', as Hitler called the Nazis at this time. The *Völkischer Beobachter* warned its supporters that Kahr would waste all of Hitler's accomplishments in growing the movement in Munich that year. But the personal invective targeted at him was insufficient for Kahr to ban the *Völkischer Beobachter*. His muted reaction was a telling indictment of his reluctance to deal with the Nazis from the very start of his rule as state commissioner.[6]

The shift to the right in Bavaria in the week that followed the end of passive resistance was mirrored by a shift to the left in Saxony and Thuringia at the same time. For Communists, this 'now or never' moment represented their best chance to force through a proletarian revolution since the end of the First World War. Even though the Cuno Strikes had fizzled out in mid-August, they had shown the level of anger among the German working class and left the leadership of the Communists in Germany hopeful that conditions were close to perfect for a new assault on Weimar democracy. The signs included increasing membership of the Communist Party and increased aggression among its membership. The example of Soviet Russia mattered too. Lenin had seized power in October 1917. Inspired by his example, in both Moscow and Germany, Communist strategists thought that 1923 was the ideal time for a

'German October'. At a key meeting in Moscow on 23 August, their watchword was 'now or never'. Their first target was the federal state of Saxony.

Mirroring the general strength of the left in Saxony, under the leadership of Erich Zeigner, the regional branch of the Social Democratic Party in the state was far more left-wing than the Social Democrats in Berlin. Zeigner was a firebrand. He only joined the party in November 1918 following the revolution. But in the climate of radical upheaval that continued in the republic's early years, Zeigner's advance was quick. In August 1921, he was appointed by another Social Democrat, Wilhelm Buck, as Saxony's justice minister. When Buck's minority government collapsed in March 1923, Zeigner received the support of both Social Democratic and Communist members of the Saxon regional parliament and was elected Saxon prime minister. He was thirty-seven years old. After his first speech in his new role, commentators on the political right accused him of siding with the French and called him a 'traitor'. Friedrich Ebert, the fifty-two-year-old president of the republic, was also unimpressed. Ebert thought that Zeigner was an inexperienced, politically naïve man who had risen too quickly through the ranks of the Social Democratic Party. Soon after, when they met for the first time, it was clear that Zeigner and Ebert hated each other.[7]

Throughout the summer of 1923, Zeigner remained an outspoken critic of Cuno and a thorn in the side of the more moderate Social Democrats. He was the kind of party leader who wasn't prepared to stay quiet and toe the party line. He declared passive resistance a failure, and he demanded that Cuno take action against right-wing Reichswehr officers. In a speech made on 16 June, he warned that the coming months would be extremely dangerous for Saxony, predicting that secret collaboration between Fascists and the Reichswehr in Bavaria would end with heavy fighting between them and the working class. A month later, he told a local newspaper that both his government and the government of Prussia had ample evidence of Reichswehr co-operation with the Nazis. In August 1923, the Reichswehr leadership was so annoyed with his public statements about its activities that it compiled a dossier of nineteen occasions on which he had been publicly critical of the Reichswehr between April and August.[8]

Just days after the establishment of Stresemann's grand coalition on 13 August 1923, Zeigner made even more enemies. In an interview with the *Vossische Zeitung*, he threatened both Ebert and war minister Otto Geßler. Ebert was a strong supporter of Geßler, whereas Zeigner wanted the latter sacked for failing to take action against secret co-operation between the Reichswehr and right-wing paramilitaries. At a crucial time in Germany's relations with the Allies, Zeigner threatened that if Ebert did not dismiss Geßler, he would reveal the contents of secret documents that proved that co-operation had taken place between the Reichswehr and right-wing paramilitary organizations that breached the terms of the Versailles Treaty. This was nothing short of sensational. Ebert refused to concede. When the two men met once again at the start of September, Ebert warned Zeigner that if the Saxon government could not guarantee 'peace and order', then the federal government would do it for them. Around the same time Stresemann called Zeigner 'a person who is not fully sane'.[9]

The biggest difference between centrist Social Democrats like Ebert and left-wing Social Democrats like Zeigner was their attitude towards Communism. For Ebert, German Communists were the Social Democrats' mortal enemies. Since the establishment of the Weimar Republic, German Communists had threatened his life and, at the peak of the violence of 1919, Ebert had fully supported Social Democratic co-operation with right-wing officers from the army or navy, including men like Hermann Ehrhardt, and the use of the harshest available force to suppress Communist rebels.[10]

Zeigner's attitude towards Communism was much more conciliatory. At the time when Ebert wanted the Social Democrats to support the inclusion of Hugo Stinnes in Stresemann's government and KPD supporters were calling for the death of Europe's richest man, Zeigner was prepared initially to govern with the tolerance of the Communist members of the Saxon regional parliament and later to form a coalition government with them. Zeigner couldn't understand Ebert's politics in the autumn of 1923. While Ebert thought that greater co-operation between the Social Democrats and the parties of the centre-right was the solution to the crisis, Zeigner thought that the Social Democratic Party was a revolutionary party and that the best way to protect the German working class from the danger of Hitler or other nationalists in Bavaria was to create a working-class 'people's front'. For him, the solution would be co-operation between the parties of the left, since the real enemy remained the parties of the 'bourgeoisie'.

For Zeigner's critics in the Social Democratic Party in Berlin and the German army, the most worrying development in the late summer of 1923 was his support for the creation of working-class paramilitaries, known as the Proletarian Hundreds. For their supporters, the Hundreds existed to defend democracy and the working class from the anti-republican violence of the right. As we have already seen, in Bavaria, and especially in Munich, in 1923, the Social Democrats had created an armed defensive group of men charged with protecting its assemblies and events from attacks by the Fascists. The Proletarian Hundreds were armed working-class militias on a far greater scale. Their supporters argued that their existence was necessary to fight for the protection of the republic in the event that Kahr or Hitler or both mobilized in Bavaria and tried to march through Saxony and Thuringia on their way to Berlin. In that case, the Proletarian Hundreds would slow their progress north, giving the republic's supporters more time to organize and prepare for its defence. But, for their critics, such arguments were merely a ruse. Men like Ebert were certain that the Hundreds were not being created to defend the republic – their existence was the first step in a Communist plan to destroy it.

They had good reason to harbour such fears. At the end of August, the Communist Party in Saxony received instructions from Moscow: it should no longer merely tolerate Zeigner's government in Saxony, but actively join the coalition. After doing so, Communist ministers' task would be to manipulate Zeigner to arm 50,000–60,000 workers. At a time when the Versailles Treaty limited the size of the German army to 100,000 men, such a sizable force could have destroyed Weimar democracy.[11]

The situation escalated further on 10 October 1923, when the Saxon Communists finally joined Zeigner's government. Three of them became ministers: Paul Böttcher became finance minister, Fritz Heckert economics minister and Heinrich Brandler took up the position of head of the State Chancellery. The only consolation for men like Stresemann was that Zeigner didn't give the Communists the Interior Ministry, which would have handed them control of police, but the constitution of his cabinet was sufficiently worrying for anti- and pro-republicans alike. The dust had barely settled on the news of these appointments when, less than a week later, a second Social Democratic-Communist coalition government emerged at the federal level, this time in Thuringia. There, the Social Democratic minority government led by August Frölich had lost a confidence vote on 11 September 1923 and was replaced by a new coalition that included Communists, with the Social Democrat Frölich remaining minister president.[12]

It was an extraordinary moment in German politics. The creation of Social Democratic-Communist coalitions in the central German federal states of Saxony and Thuringia occurred just as the fight between Bavaria and Berlin reached a new climax. Fears of a civil war grew by the day. The question was: how would the Reich government and leadership in Berlin respond?[13]

The republic had already attempted to oppose Kahr's Bavarian dictatorship by use of legal means and revealed its weakness in the process. Two weeks earlier, President Ebert and Chancellor Stresemann had declared a state of emergency across the entire German Reich. On paper, this placed power in the hands of war minister Geßler, who in turn put power in the hands of the commander of the German military, General Hans von Seeckt. That development should have had only one legal outcome: according to the constitution, the law of the federal government (the Reich) trumped the law of Bavaria, and so the state of emergency in the Reich should have overruled the state of emergency in Bavaria that had empowered Kahr. Stresemann and Ebert's measure, in other words, should have brought Kahr's rule to an end even before it had begun, with Lossow taking the reins of power in Bavaria and answering to Seeckt, who answered to Geßler, who answered to Stresemann.

But legal power and political power are different entities. Stresemann's cabinet had no way to enforce the Reich's state of emergency in Bavaria, and Lossow had no intention of meekly following Seeckt's orders. Stresemann's government was also fully aware that the only way to terminate Kahr's rule if he refused to obey was to mobilize the Reichswehr to enforce the Reich government's authority in Bavaria. The Reichswehr in Bavaria would very likely remain loyal to Kahr, and units of the Reichswehr from outside Bavaria would similarly be unlikely to disarm their Bavarian colleagues. More than three years after the failed Kapp Putsch in March 1920, when Seeckt allegedly said 'troops don't shoot at troops', the willingness of the army to fight and kill for the republic remained unproven.[14]

The republic's authority faced another test on 1 October, when Bruno Ernst Buchrucker, a member of the illegal Black Reichswehr, led a putsch in Küstrin, less than 100 kilometres to the east of Berlin. The coup was quickly put down, but there were some intense scenes as soldiers fired upon the putschists, killing and injuring a number of them. The news that four hundred men in total had participated in the attempted coup left Ebert shocked, while it also confirmed the suspicions of all of the Reichswehr's critics on the left, including Zeigner.[15]

Lacking a mandate to enforce its authority in Bavaria and apparently elsewhere, and facing challenges on multiple fronts, Stresemann's government was unable to survive the crisis. The threats to the republic's survival were proceeding at too fast a pace for parliament to meet to discuss what the state's response should be. The cabinet needed an enabling law, which would have given it the ability to rule without the support of parliament, but the introduction of such a law threatened to split the Social Democratic Party in two. A majority of its cabinet ministers supported the move. But they were opposed by a majority of the party's elected representatives in the Reichstag as well as the unions, who feared that the temporary suspension of parliamentary oversight would be used to destroy the social protections that the republic had guaranteed workers. They were especially worried that if it was introduced Hugo Stinnes's pro-business German People's Party would demand the abolition of the eight-hour working day.

After heated discussion, the Social Democratic Party cabinet members eventually agreed to support Stresemann's proposals, but when the party's parliamentary group shot them down, it spelled the end of Stresemann's government. On 3 October, only a week after it had made the decision to end passive resistance, Germany's first ever grand coalition was over. Stresemann had been chancellor for just fifty-one days. In his diary he described having to face up to the 'deepest depression'. He feared that he would only be remembered as the man who ended passive resistance.[16]

Except the grand coalition wasn't over. Three days later, in the words of *Vorwärts*, 'the new chancellor' was again Gustav Stresemann. Stinnes, Stresemann's great opponent within the German People's Party, had shown once again that his bullying tactics lacked political nuance. The powerful business leader had hoped that, once his cabinet fell, Stresemann would lose the position of party leader, shifting the German People's Party further to the right, and replacing the SPD in the governing coalition with Karl Helfferich's right-wing German National People's Party (DNVP). But this didn't happen. Stresemann retained the confidence of his party and remained leader. When the time came for a vote among the German People's Party deputies, Stinnes alone voted against him. Once Stresemann won the vote to stay as party leader, the DNVP refused to serve with him. Rathenau's party, the German Democratic Party, and the Catholic Centre Party also opposed joining a government with the DNVP. Once a new right-wing coalition was ruled out, it appeared that the only option was either for Stresemann to return with a Cuno-style minority government or new elections, something that could have had unforeseen consequences at the height of the republic's crisis.[17]

The situation looked drastic. Germany was on the verge of being a modern industrial country without a functional currency and without a government. It looked like the perfect time for anti-republican putschists to strike. But behind the scenes the leaders of the German Democratic Party and the Centre Party took the initiative. In long negotiations during the night of 5–6 October, a new agreement was reached. In response to the most crucial question for the Social Democratic Party a compromise had been found: the eight-hour working day would remain the norm, but exceptions could be made in certain crucial situations.[18]

On 6 October, Stresemann returned to the Reichstag. In a long speech he defended his record as chancellor. The biggest problem for his government was the 'foreign policy conditions'. Germany, he told the Reichstag, had to give up passive resistance because of 'financial exhaustion'. In Stresemann's words:

> As a nationalist, I believe that . . . the idea that the fortress has to surrender because it has no more provisions or because bringing in provisions presents the risk that the entire population will no longer be able to feed itself afterwards is nothing to be ashamed of, even if a nationalist mourns that things have reached such a state.

He argued that German democracy was not a failure. He placed the blame for its current predicament on the foreign policies of the victorious foreign powers and on the meddling politics of Germany's richest men. They continued to claim that they could do better, he warned. But each time a businessman joined the government, they, too, failed – a reference to Cuno and Stinnes. Underlining the uselessness of rhetorical appeals for nationalist sacrifice, he stressed that it was time for politicians to be brave and finally to 'fight against popular currents'. He asked if anyone calling for a dictator really believed that such a person would be able to achieve anything more against France, the strongest military power in the world. He even quoted the *Völkischer Beobachter*'s criticism of Seeckt and defended the Reichswehr.[19]

He insisted that the state of emergency was a necessary measure.

His government had to introduce it to prevent a march on Berlin from Bavaria. No German government had ever faced a worse situation. But Stresemann was certain that they could overcome it. In his final words:

> We must turn to the state and away from the parties, away from selfishess. The Reich is the only thing left to us in all the collapse we've seen. Preserving it now is the duty we have to fulfil not only in the present, but for all the generations that will come after![20]

On 13 October, the Reichstag finally voted on the enabling law, by which the Reichstag would grant the government extraordinary powers, especially in financial, economic and social areas. The constitution required that two-thirds of the Reichstag deputies be present and that two-thirds of them vote in its favour. If they failed to do so, Ebert was ready to dissolve parliament. Hoping to block the law, forty-three SPD deputies joined members of the Communist Party and the German National People's Party in abstaining. But Stresemann got the result he needed. Ebert's threat of new elections encouraged enough deputies to participate in the vote. Crucially, the enabling law, which was to last until 31 March 1924, reflected the need for political compromise: it included a clause that it would no longer remain in force if there was a change of government. The law would enable the defenders of democracy to save the republic, but it would cease to function if Stresemann's government collapsed and it was replaced by an anti-republican right-wing coalition.

The introduction of an enabling law at the high point of the crisis in 1923 deserves comment. Today, when most people think of an enabling law in the context of the Weimar Republic, they think of the spring of 1933 and the death of German democracy. At that time, Hitler, who had already been in office as chancellor since 30 January, sought an enabling law to dissolve the Reichstag. When he obtained it on 24 March 1933, it was a crucial step towards the legal establishment of his dictatorship. Ever since, some historians have argued that the possibility that the parliament could introduce enabling laws was a fundamental flaw in the Weimar Republic's constitution. According to this logic, if there was no mechanism to allow for its introduction, Hitler might not have been able to establish his dictatorship. In addition to its failure to recognize the brutal nature of the Nazis' determination to use force to rule, the same argument misses the point that in 1923 the enabling law had been a useful tool to protect the republic in a time of crisis, as the authors of the Weimar constitution intended it to be. In 1933, the problem was not the constitution, it was the determination of conservative political elites to use the crisis to destroy the democracy.[21]

Once they had secured the enabling law in 1923, Ebert and Stresemann chose Saxony as their first target for the re-establishment of the republic's authority. Even before, on 6 October 1923, war minister Geßler demanded that Zeigner cease attacking the Reichswehr or his government would be deposed. Geßler even threatened that he would resign if his demands were not met.[22] In Saxony, the Reichswehr general Müller hardly needed to wait for instructions from Berlin. In the wake of the creation of the Reich-level state of emergency during the night of 26–7 September, he was already technically in charge of the state of Saxony. On 13 October, three days after the KPD joined Zeigner's government, he used his emergency powers to ban the Proletarian Hundreds. The same day, Communist finance minister Paul Böttcher gave a speech to around five thousand Communist supporters at a rally in Leipzig's Zoological Gardens. In it, he criticized Müller's suppression of the Hundreds and demanded that the workers arm themselves for the coming struggle, which he predicted would end either with a White or Red dictatorship. The speech put Ebert under pressure. His previous concern about developments in Saxony had escalated to grim certainty that the time for action had come.[23]

On 16 October 1923, Müller moved to take the Saxon state police under his control. From this point on, they would answer to the Reichswehr. This decision meant that, within a week of the formation of a Social Democratic-Communist coalition under

Zeigner's leadership, the civilian politicians in Saxony no longer had any control over the police in their state. For the right wing of the German People's Party in Stresemann's government, Müller was taking the right steps. Reading reports of rioting, violence and Communist attacks going unanswered by Zeigner's government, they wanted Stresemann to take further action against Saxony. They wanted to see the Reichswehr march into Saxony and depose Zeigner's government.[24]

Zeigner and the Saxon Communists not only had the numbers in the Saxon parliament and a democratic mandate to rule, they also had allies in the new government in Thuringia – the only question was how they would use them to fight Müller's moves to restrict their power. On 21 October, four days before the anniversary of the Bolshevik October Revolution in 1917, the Communist Party called for a rally of their supporters in Chemnitz, one of the largest industrial cities in the east of Saxony. Müller didn't initially try to intervene. The organizers foresaw the rally as being a staging post for a German October revolution. At the rally they wanted to declare a general strike and the start of a workers' uprising, following the Russian model. Brandler was among the speakers. He told the Communists there that they had to stand up to the 'dictatorship of the army'. But the reaction was less than enthusiastic.

The crowds appeared to reject his calls for a working-class power seizure. Another SPD minister speaking at the same rally warned that if the Communists followed through with their threats, the Social Democratic-Communist coalition government in Saxony would collapse. The absence of cheers or enthusiasm caused the leadership to abandon their revolutionary plans. Since November 1918, Germany's Communists had launched too many failed uprisings to launch another one with little chance of success. They recognized that if they didn't even have a majority of workers behind them in 'Soviet Saxony', as their Red state was known, clearly the uprising would have no chance across the rest of Germany.[25]

One exception was Hamburg, the large port city in the German north. During the night of 22–3 October, armed Communists, reportedly members of the Proletarian Hundreds, attacked and took control of thirteen police stations on the outskirts of the city. Police reinforcements quickly restored control over ten of them, while fighting over the three remaining stations continued into the morning. At one stage, a police armoured car was destroyed and one police officer seriously injured. On 23 October, the WTB news agency reported that as many as 127 people had been injured in the violence, not including an unknown number of rebels. The first reports suggested that seven police officers had lost their lives and a further nineteen were 'severely wounded'. During the course of the day, the ambulances had to transport 108 people who had been injured and fourteen who were dead. The rebels were accused of continuing to snipe at police, even after the main fighting had come to an end. Historians have put the final death toll at twenty-four Communists and seventeen police.[26]

Social Democrats condemned the violence as self-defeating and dangerous. *Vorwärts*'s first report on the uprising called it 'criminal stupidity'. It warned that the KPD move would prolong the state of emergency across Germany and provide political justification for Kahr's claims that he was standing up to the 'Bolshevik North'. A few days later, still enraged, the newspaper proclaimed: 'The idiots who instigated the Hamburg putsch belong in the wax museum.'[27]

For General Müller, it mattered little that the Communists of Saxony had abandoned their plans. Before Stresemann's cabinet had given him the formal green light to do so, he ordered the Reichswehr into Saxony. On 23 October, Reichswehr soldiers occupied large cities including Dresden and Leipzig, as well as the towns of Meissen and Pirna. In Dresden, the Reichswehr's entry into the city took the form of a parade. Crowds formed to cheer the soldiers' arrival and, according to a *Berliner Tageblatt* telegram, when the soldiers marched past the state parliament, the deputies, including Social Democrats, gathered in the windows to salute them. In Plauen, the correspondent for the *Berliner Tageblatt* watched as soldiers from Württemberg and Baden entered the town with machine guns and armoured cars, taking up positions in front of public buildings including the town hall, train station and post office. Their commander took up office in the town hall. Though some gathered to express their disapproval at the soldiers' arrival, there was initially no violence against the Reichswehr. The occupiers did not return the favour, however, and in Pirna, 20 kilometres to the east of Dresden, Reichswehr soldiers fired shots at protestors assembled in the market. One demonstrator was killed and a further two were badly injured. Demonstrations against the Reichswehr followed in Zwickau, while in Annaberg-Buchholz as many as six hundred protestors occupied the town hall to prevent the Reichswehr from taking control of the building.[28]

There was more shooting when Müller's soldiers got to Chemnitz, and exchanges of gunfire between soldiers and workers in Freiberg that left twenty-three dead and thirty-one injured. The forces were unevenly matched, however, and, among those totals, only four soldiers suffered gunshot wounds. In mid-November, the *Dresdner Volkszeitung* reported that thirty-four people had died in all, and that the total number injured was between 110 and 130.[29]

On 27 October, Stresemann's government was forced to respond to what was already happening on the ground in Saxony. Müller's Reichswehr operation had started without a 'formal decision of the cabinet'. Opinion in the cabinet was still divided. In the end, after heated discussions, the federal government offered Zeigner a compromise: he could stay in power if he formed a new government that excluded the Communists. This compromise was necessary to keep the SPD in Stresemann's national government. They didn't like Zeigner any more than Ebert did, but they recognized that he had a democratic mandate and that the Reichswehr should not be allowed simply to choose who ran the state. But if Zeigner refused, then Geßler had the green light from Stresemann to name a commissioner to take control of Saxony until a new government could be formed there.[30]

Zeigner responded quickly. On 28 October, he appealed to the ideals of democracy: the Saxon parliament was the only body with the right to choose the government of Saxony. The democrats in the federal government did not agree. On 29 October, they deposed the Saxon government, declaring a formal 'Reich execution' against Saxony, opting to use their emergency powers to remove Zeigner's government in Saxony and replace it with a government of their own choosing, with the Reichswehr deployed to enforce the new government's authority on the ground. With Ebert's approval, Stresemann chose his German People's Party colleague Rudolf Heinze as Reichskommissar.[31]

The Saxon parliament was stripped of its powers, and Zeigner left his office surrounded by soldiers. He announced his resignation on 30 October. Exactly one month after Stresemann's government had criticized Knilling's decision to create a directorship in Bavaria, it had done the same thing in Saxony. Cautiously, the *Vossische Zeitung* warned: 'What has been done to the Saxons today can be done against any other German state tomorrow. Just imagine what the consequences would be if tomorrow a national German government thought it had to depose the Prussian government.'[32]

For Geßler, these events represented an opportunity to create a military dictatorship in Saxony. For those on the anti-republican right, the establishment of military rule in Saxony meant that a Mussolini-style march on Berlin would not start with a fight as the Bavarian putschists entered Saxony on their way north. Instead, the army on the streets of Saxony could join forces with the Bavarians and march on Berlin.

But Ebert and Stresemann foresaw the dangers of the situation and put a stop to this possibility before it could come into being. Three days after the Reich execution, thanks to their intervention behind the scenes, a Social Democratic minority government, which would not be opposed by the German Democratic Party, was formed. The new minister president was Alfred Fellisch, who had been economics minister in Zeigner's cabinet. On paper the situation had been restored to something similar to the situation that had existed earlier in the year. But the political price was enormous. Stresemann and Ebert had moved militarily against Saxony. Stresemann and Ebert had used emergency powers to remove Zeigner, a Social Democrat whom they both hated, and the Communists from government in Saxony. And they had not used the same powers to intervene in Bavaria.[33]

Stresemann had two reasons for declaring a Reich execution against the Saxon Communists. First, he was aware that he was seen as a man of the centre who preferred compromise over action. He wanted to show that he had the capacity to take 'energetic, clear action'. But, far more importantly, he wanted to take action against Saxony as a means of dealing with Bavaria. By removing the threat of the Communist Party in Saxony, he also removed the pretext for Kahr's mobilization against Berlin. For defenders of Stresemann and Ebert, the decision was a wise one: by removing the problem posed by the easier target – the left in Saxony – the federal government had prevented the need to undertake a similar Reich execution in Bavaria, which would have resulted in far greater violence than in Saxony.[34]

But the Social Democratic Party was shaken by the perception of hypocrisy that it had gone easy on the anti-republican right in Bavaria. Throughout the party, there was furious anger that a federal cabinet that included SPD ministers had supported such strong moves against an SPD-led government in the state of Saxony, while the same cabinet had taken no comparable measures against Kahr in Bavaria. Many Social Democrats were furious that the Social Democratic president of the republic, Friedrich Ebert, had helped to remove a Social Democrat from office in one federal state without undertaking similar measures against Bavaria. Some SPD members even accused Ebert of breaking the constitution. Worst of all, SPD members in Bavaria and beyond wanted to know why their party in Berlin had done so little to protect the Bavarian SPD from Kahr's moves to suppress it. At a time when they had organized an armed division to protect their members from assault at party meetings, they could not understand why Ebert and other senior figures in the party were prepared to tolerate Kahr. Faced with this pressure, the Social Democratic members of the cabinet now faced another 'now or never' moment. They issued an ultimatum to Stresemann: the state of emergency across the Reich must come to an end, but the federal government must also declare Bavaria to be in breach of the constitution and immediately take action there. In Saxony, the Reichswehr's role must be limited to 'auxiliary functions in the service of civil authorities and the dismissal of members of right-wing extremist organizations from the force'. Either Stresemann moved in the same way against Bavaria, or the Social Democrats would leave his government.[35]

Stresemann wanted to keep the Social Democrats in the cabinet. He knew that they were important allies in protecting the republic and that their participation in government provided the French, British and Americans with important evidence that the Weimar Republic was different from the German Empire that it had replaced in November 1918. But Stresemann also knew that the other coalition parties would not agree to the Social Democrats' demands, and he wanted to keep the state of emergency in existence. He also knew that if he kept the Social Democrats in government, he would provoke a split within his own party as well as in the Centre Party. Above all, regardless of Ebert's role in removing him from the Saxon government, Stresemann's coalition partners simply didn't want to be in government with a party whose members included Zeigner and which had just helped to bring the Communists into government in Saxony and Thuringia. There could be no compromise.[36]

On 2 November, the Social Democrats left the government. In their final cabinet meeting, interior minister Wilhelm Sollmann stated for a final time as a government member that the SPD could not agree to stay in the ruling coalition unless the Reich took action against Kahr's Bavaria. He noted that Geßler had not stated with absolute clarity that 'he would protect central Germany from the Fascists', and added that for them to stay in government, the Social Democrats would also want a clear statement challenging Kahr's antisemitism. Stresemann had previously told them that if his government agreed to the Social Democrats' demands, 'it would give the outward impression that the cabinet was in fact under a Marxist dictatorship'. The Social Democrats now stayed firm and left the government. At a meeting of the Social Democratic parliamentary members that afternoon, Robert Schmidt, who was quitting as vice-chancellor, told his party colleagues, 'Nothing else is possible for us now other than to go. Things will not be so bad for the party. The political consequences will be severe. History will judge us.'[37]

In the long term, Schmidt's prediction would come true. It would be June 1928, nearly five years later, before the Weimar Republic had another Social Democratic Party cabinet member. For the best years of the republic, the kind of politicians who would have strengthened the culture of Weimar democracy were not in a position to do so. But the Social Democrats did not have to wait the full five years before their absence from the cabinet could be clearly felt. Just days after they quit Stresemann's cabinet, the strategy of using a demonstration of the republic's authority in Saxony and Thuringia to send a message to Bavaria appeared to have unravelled entirely when Hitler's Nazis finally decided to make their move.

14

The Hitler Putsch

Even before Stresemann ended the campaign of passive resistance, it was widely predicted that Hitler would soon launch a putsch in Munich. By late summer, it was obvious that the May Day fiasco, when he had to tell his followers to stand down and hand back the weapons they had borrowed from the Reichswehr, had done little to damage his determination to use violence to destroy the republic. On 1–2 September 1923, he was in Nuremberg for another 'German Day' rally – the event that would later develop into the Nazi Party rallies of the 1930s. On this occasion, as many as 100,000 nationalists were reported as in attendance at the rally, where Hitler's talent as a speaker meant that he outshone even more established right-wing figures like General Erich Ludendorff who, alongside Hindenburg, was the chief commander of the German armies during the First World War and whose failed offensives in the spring and summer of 1918 bore the greatest strategic responsibility for Germany's defeat later that year. Hitler stood alongside Ludendorff, paramilitary leader Hermann Kriebel and Prince Ludwig Ferdinand of Bavaria as the assembled paramilitaries, including his SA, passed the podium. A journalist for the liberal and pro-democracy *Frankfurter Zeitung* who listened to Hitler's speech described how he 'thundered that, like the external conditions, the internal ones could only be changed by violent force'. If that wasn't clear enough, Hitler added that everyone who opposed them had to be 'crushed by force' and that none of their supporters 'should be afraid of having to make the heaviest of blood sacrifices'.[1]

The rally wasn't just a show of paramilitary strength and an occasion for Hitler to spread his violent rhetoric. It was also an important moment for the organization of Hitler's attempt to seize power just a few weeks later. During the rally, the SA, the Oberland League and the Reichsflagge, two like-minded paramilitary organizations that lacked a standout leader like Hitler, formed a new organization, which they called the German Combat League. Hitler was its political leader while the veteran paramilitary Kriebel was appointed its military head, and Hitler's adviser, the former diplomat Max Scheubner-Richter, its business manager.[2]

Following its foundation, its leadership issued a joint declaration which proclaimed that the new organization existed to fight against Germany's internal and external enemies, Marxism, Judaism, pacifism, the 'spirit of the Weimar constitution'. They also declared themselves opposed to former Chancellor Wirth's foreign policy of fulfilment (which had been abandoned since the start of the Ruhr occupation) and the hated 'parliamentary system with its dreary worship of the majority'. Their declaration specifically stated that the new organization was not a political party but that its members were 'fighters' 'ready to live and die for their fatherland'. The Combat League leaders called upon every German man who still had the 'spirit of the old front fighters of 1914' to join them. With such rhetoric, the new organization aimed to recruit war veterans and to prepare its membership to carry out violence. But it also tried to appeal to Germans who had been too young to fight in the war. Its message to 'German youth' was that they had to be 'ready to sacrifice themselves' and follow in the footsteps of Albert Leo Schlageter.[3]

The Nazis' newspaper, the *Völkischer Beobachter*, was delighted with the new organization. It argued that its existence proved that Germany was on its way to replace the Weimar Republic with a *Volksgemeinschaft*, the Nazi ideal of a spiritual community in which all Germans were united regardless of their religion, social status or geographical origins – a term that would become central to the regime's propaganda in the 1930s.[4]

This was extremely violent rhetoric, and it was only the beginning. Even before the end of passive resistance on 26 September

1923, Hitler's rhetoric had grown increasingly violent. He argued that Stresemann had betrayed the Ruhr and the small number of 'heroes' who risked their lives in the occupied region. Like other populist leaders, Hitler was quick to blame the media for German weakness. He told his followers that too few Germans realized the danger they faced because they read newspapers that were lying to them. On 5 September, at a Nazi Party rally in the Circus Krone in Munich, he outlandishly stated that because the media was lying to them, Germans did not know that in 'Soviet Saxony . . . fields were harvested by force, and that day after day private homes and farmsteads were plundered utterly, while school classes of young children who sang some folk song on a hike were beaten down with batons and sticks'. Instead of reporting on this, Hitler claimed that the 'bourgeois press' would only tell its readers about acts of violence that involved Jews. Instead of informing Germans about the 'Bolshevik acts that took place every day there', Hitler claimed that today, 'If by chance, a returning member of this meeting stepped on the foot of some Jew while boarding the tram', then the press would go after the 'swastika followers' – the dismissive term used by the pro-democratic press to dismiss Hitler's supporters – and not mention Bolshevik violence in Saxony.[5]

As he had done in the spring, at the same meeting he repeated the message that the victorious Allies were treating Germany no better than a colony that would soon collapse. When that occurred he wanted 'our movement' to 'become the bearers of the dictatorship of national reason, national energy, national brutality and determination'. Borrowing from the language of religious leaders, he promised that their movement would bring 'redemption' and that already 'millions could feel it'. Nazism was, in Hitler's words, 'almost like a new faith', and at this time there were only two possible futures: 'either Berlin marches and ends in Munich, or Munich marches and ends in Berlin!'[6]

Amidst the bombastic promises of violence, Hitler's calls for action in September and October also included a subtle change in tone. He started to speak more inclusively to his followers. Though always prone to speaking in terms of 'us and them', as the offensive approached he made more effort to speak about what 'we' were about to do. The subject of heroism became more prominent as he prepared his supporters to emulate the violent heroism of the past. On 12 September, he promised:

> In a few months, maybe weeks, the dice will roll in Germany too. We don't know how they will fall. We know only one thing: this movement has forged weapons for Germany upon which she will not stand defenceless and perish in this moment. We will take up the fight and are convinced: Victory must be ours! . . . What is looming today will be bigger than the world war! It will be fought on German soil for the whole world! There are only two options: either we become the sacrificial lamb or we become victors!

In the same speech he promised: 'Today Germany is no longer defenceless. In the deepest calamity, hundreds of thousands flock under one banner. If Germany is to live, we must be willing to lay down our lives.' Before this he had already glorified the idea of death for an ideal with the words: 'Happy are the fallen heroes. They still believed! And the only thing that keeps us survivors going, is and remains the burning longing to experience the day when the old flag rises again!'[7]

The announcement that passive resistance was over made Hitler even more radical. Even before it happened, he had already publicly predicted that Stresemann would abandon the Ruhr and betray the heroes who had died in its defence. Just hours after Stresemann's decision became public news, Hitler demanded that all members of the Nazi Party who were not yet members of the three organizations that joined forces in the German Combat League (the SA, Imperial Flag and Oberland paramilitary organizations) must join one of them within ten days or face expulsion from the party.[8]

A journalist from Britain's *Daily Mail* newspaper who interviewed Hitler at this time was amazed by his intensity. He wrote of how during their interview Hitler 'denounced' the decision to end passive resistance with 'intense violence'. In the journalist's words:

Speaking very rapidly and raising his voice as though he were addressing a mass meeting, he exclaimed: passive resistance should never have been abandoned. We blame the German Government for yielding to the French. It is clear that we could not have prevented the French from holding the Ruhr, but before we gave in every mine, every factory, and every furnace should have been destroyed. Poincaré should have had the deathly triumph which Napoleon had when he saw Moscow in flames.

At this point, the journalist inserted in his report that Hitler was so enraged as he spoke that it would have been 'useless' to interrupt him to ask how the inhabitants of the Ruhr would have lived after the destruction of the Ruhr region.[9]

As Hitler's rhetoric became more extreme and the economic situation in Munich worsened, the mood in the Bavarian capital grew increasingly tense. Hitler himself claimed that Germany needed a Mussolini, while the *Vorwärts* Munich correspondent claimed that the Nazis had a list of more than one hundred political leaders 'who are to be extracted and rendered harmless at the time of action in order to make counteraction more difficult'. It suggested that the list included the names of well-known Socialists and also many members of the bourgeoisie who were expected to oppose Hitler's plans for 'national cleansing'. To add to their opponents' fears that they would soon be arrested, at the end of September, one Nazi Stormtrooper division had even held a parade in honour of Stadelheim prison – the prison on the outskirts of Munich which had been used for leftist prisoners following the collapse of the Bavarian Soviet Republic in May 1919.[10]

Faced with this hostile future, at the end of September the *Vorwärts* Bavarian correspondent warned Social Democrats across Germany that the difference between Kahr and the patriots, on the one hand, and Hitler, Ludendorff and the *Völkischen* (ultra-nationalists), on the other, was that Kahr and his supporters wanted to wait until they thought that northern Germany was completely Bolshevized before striking against Weimar democracy, whereas Hitler and the nationalists were certain that the north was already completely Bolshevized and were therefore prepared to strike immediately.[11]

The *Vorwärts* correspondent's prediction that Kahr was waiting for events to change in northern Germany turned out to be only partially correct: Kahr wasn't waiting until north Germany was under the control of 'Bolsheviks', he was waiting for more powerful anti-republican forces in the north to strike first. Following his appointment as state commissioner for Bavaria, Kahr did enter into secret negotiations with anti-republican forces in northern Germany. But as he examined the chances of success, Kahr, who was supported by Lossow and Seißer, quickly decided that he was not prepared to lead the strike against Weimar democracy. Unlike Hitler and his radical allies in Munich, who were desperate to fire the first shots against the republic, Kahr only wanted to join in an anti-republican putsch once someone else started it in the north. When the Reichswehr chief of general staff Hans von Seeckt made it clear to him that his men would not disobey Stresemann by leading a counterrevolutionary putsch, Kahr toned down his ambitions and turned his back on the coup strategy.

That secret decision created a new dynamic in Bavarian politics. Hitler and Kahr had always been rivals. But Kahr's decision that Bavaria would not lead the anti-republican putsch as Hitler wanted now made them political enemies. Over the course of October, just as he attacked Stresemann and Cuno, Hitler now also blamed Kahr for cowardice and described his dictatorship as weak. In Bamberg on 7 October, he told his supporters that Kahr 'should have whipped up the people, he should have done more than ban all the left-wing press, he should have destroyed them, dispersed the government, arrested MPs responsible for the misfortune and marched on Berlin'.[12]

Just twelve days later, in another speech to the SA on 19 October, he promised his followers that they were at a 'turning point in German history' that would change the history of Europe and the world, and that it would not be long before the combat leagues struck. On 30 October, he told another Nazi Party assembly in Munich that it was time for Bavaria to lead the 'resistance' to

Weimar democracy and that the German question would only be solved when the swastika flag flew from Berlin's royal palace, before ending his speech with the words:

> There is no going back, we can only go forwards! The hour has come, we can all feel it. That's why we won't withdraw from this moment, but, like soldiers in the field, we will answer its command: get ready, German people, and march forward![13]

Those were fighting words. But by the time he uttered them, Hitler had already made a strategic error. The threat to Weimar democracy that was posed by separatism, Nazism and Communism had grown in strength because each fresh crisis compounded the effects of the others. Hitler should have recognized this and his movement should have struck at the peak of the crisis in October 1923, at the time of the Weimar government's decision to suspend the federal parliaments of Saxony and Thuringia. The 'now or never' moment was the final week of October. But Hitler missed his chance. Realizing their error, he and his entourage now decided to set the date for their putsch for the 11 November 1923, opting for symbolism over expedience. By launching their putsch on this date, the anniversary of the Armistice on the western front, the Nazis intended to gain the support of disgruntled war veterans and send a message that their movement would one day reverse the outcome of the First World War. Their plan was first to seize power in Munich, where they would establish a political directorate led by Hitler and Ludendorff. Once they had taken control of Bavaria, they intended to march on Berlin, hopefully gaining the support of right-wing anti-republican militias along the way. But as so often in Weimar's crisis year, events quickly overtook their plans.

Once he had decided against leading an anti-republican putsch from Bavaria, Kahr attempted to put the genie back into the bottle. His goal was to take support away from Hitler. He decided to replace action with a symbolic gesture. He began by scheduling a speech on the future of Bavarian politics for 8 November 1923. The date was chosen carefully. It was the fifth anniversary of Socialist

Kurt Eisner's revolution in Munich. For Bavarian opponents of Weimar democracy, it was one of the darkest days in their recent history. Once Hitler learnt of Kahr's event, with characteristic abruptness, he brought forward the day of the Nazi putsch from 11 to 8 November 1923. He wanted to steal Kahr's thunder and hijack his event, even though it gave him even less time to prepare.

Hitler's reasons for doing so are revealing of the nature of his movement at this time. Since the start of the year, it had grown in size and importance. But like all groups of radicals out to destroy a political system, it required momentum to keep it alive. After months of publicly declaring that violence was imminent, the Nazi leader and the leaders of the other Bavarian combat leagues could not walk away from that promise. If Hitler's speeches were to have any credibility in the future, he had to keep moving forwards towards the goal of overthrowing the state since the goal was what held his movement together and he feared that any attempt to put the brakes on would lead to the movement's disintegration. It was not the last time Hitler would gamble on action.

Kahr had chosen to give his speech in the Bürgerbräukeller, one of Bavaria's largest beer halls. Even though there were rumours that the Nazis might try to use violence to seize power, Kahr did not want a heavy police or military presence at the event – later giving rise to the suggestion that he may have wanted to make it easy for Hitler, a suggestion that cannot be proven with certainty. At 7.15 p.m., the Bürgerbräukeller had reached its capacity of three thousand and the doors had to be closed. The audience included many ordinary members of the public as well as the politically influential conservatives of Munich. Most of the Bavarian government was present, including the head of the Reichswehr in Bavaria, Lossow, and the head of the police, Seißer. The chief of the deposed Bavarian crown prince's cabinet, Karl Friedrich, Count von Soden, was also present – an important potential link to the former monarch. Alongside their boss, there were many senior police officers as well as influential bankers, businessmen and newspaper editors, although no subsequent account of events was written by a member of the political left, who stayed away from the event.[14]

While Kahr's audience were gathering in the Bürgerbräukeller, led by the Nazis, the combat leagues mobilized around 2,500 of their men. The main bulk assembled at the Löwenbräukeller, another of central Munich's largest beer halls. Shortly before 8 p.m., as many as 1,800 members of the Combat League had gathered in the Löwenbräukeller. While their leaders were expecting the putsch to take place that evening and were waiting for the order to come from Hitler at the Bürgerbräukeller, most did not know that anything had been planned. As they drank in the Löwenbräukeller, they listened to speeches by Hermann Esser, the former editor of the *Völkischer Beobachter* who had proclaimed Hitler the German Mussolini, and Ernst Röhm.

With the majority of his followers gathered elsewhere, Hitler arrived at the Bürgerbräukeller at around 8 p.m. His first act was to tell the police on the street outside that they should clear the crowds of onlookers so that they would not get in the way of the SA men who were about to arrive. Soon after, he was permitted to pass through the police cordon, where he took his place in the foyer, a full glass of beer in his hand. Shortly afterwards, the first trucks carrying SA men arrived outside. These would provide Hitler with the muscle necessary to launch the putsch.

Once they got there, a curious stand-off ensued. The SA men stayed in their trucks, while the few police who were guarding the event watched them, wondering what was going to happen next. The SA men had orders to wait until the Stoßtrupp-Hitler arrived. This elite group within the SA, which was directly answerable to Hitler, had been singled out to lead the coup. In June 1923, the police described its members as 'very radical' and noted that they had made it their duty 'to intensify the terror against the Jews'. Most were no older than twenty. They were commanded by Lieutenant Joseph Berchtold. They later formed the nucleus of the organization that became the SS.[15]

Once the Stoßtrupp-Hitler was ready, the SA men quickly surrounded the Bürgerbräukeller and took control of who was allowed to enter or leave. The police acquiesced as they did this. Inside the foyer, Hitler readied himself. With Göring in command of the SA men outside the building, Hitler now smashed his beer glass and made his way into the hall as Kahr was speaking. The next day's Wolff Telegraph Bureau report on what happened described his entry as follows:

> From the crowd of people that was milling about Hitler stood out, escorted by two heavily armed Nazis, who raised their pistols and demanded silence, as they pushed their way into the hall. When the silence was not forthcoming, the two Nazis fired revolver shots into the ceiling. Hitler then called out in a loud voice across the hall: 'We're not here to oppose Kahr!'[16]

In its report, the *Frankfurter Zeitung* described the shots as 'theatrical' and 'the only heroic action' that Hitler managed that evening.[17]

By the time Hitler reached the stage where Kahr was standing, the audience was in a state of alarm. Though uncertain of what precisely was going on, many in the crowd could see that armed men and a machine gun were now positioned at the entrance to the hall and that all the exits were blocked. There was no point in trying to leave. The first people who did so were turned back, some of them violently. Hitler would later claim that the machine gun was erected principally to announce the message that his putsch was under way. But there is no doubt that the putschists thus also had the capacity to open fire on the crowd at the beer hall. Behind the machine gun that the crowd could see, another covered the exit.[18]

At around 8.45 p.m., Hitler forced Kahr, Lossow and Seißer to follow him at gunpoint into a separate room. He promised that he would take personal responsibility for their safety. In the side room he is supposed to have apologized for humiliating them: 'Please forgive me for proceeding in this manner, but I had no other means. It is done now and cannot be undone.' Soon after he told them:

> I know that you gentlemen will find it difficult, but we must take this step; we shall have to make it easier for you gentlemen to make the break. Each one of us must take up the position

to which he is assigned; if he doesn't then he'll have no right to exist. You must fight with me, triumph with me, or die with me. If it all goes wrong, I have four bullets in my pistol, three for my collaborators and the last one for myself.[19]

In the main hall, the atmosphere remained tense. Many in the crowd shouted abuse at the putschists, insulting them by drawing parallels to coups in Latin America. Göring responded by taking to the stage and telling the audience to be quiet, reminding them that they still had their beer – an insult that only made matters worse. Hitler then returned to the main hall where he gave a speech that was later remembered as 'an oratorical masterpiece that would have done any actor proud'. Despite threatening violence, Hitler's use of nationalist anti-republican rhetoric gained him cheers and applause from the assembled audience.[20]

As Hitler called on the crowd to demand that Lossow, Kahr and Seißer join him and support the putsch, Ludendorff arrived, dressed in the full uniform of the Imperial German Army. There were cheers of 'Heil' as the former general walked through the beer hall. As the mood changed, Lossow was the first to give in and agree to support the putsch. Seißer soon followed, before Kahr agreed to 'take over directing Bavaria's fate as the placeholder of the monarchy'. This was enough for Hitler to believe that he had won over the three men to his cause.

Around an hour after Hitler had first entered the beer hall, he returned to the stage with the three men at his side, as well as Ludendorff. Kahr was the first to speak and told the audience that he was prepared to serve Bavaria as regent for the monarchy. As he spoke, witnesses recalled that his face was 'like a mask'. A delighted Hitler spoke next, declaring that he would be in charge of the policy of the new Reich government. He then shook hands with Kahr, in a gesture that sought to erase the memory of how he had only just forced Kahr to leave the main hall at gunpoint. Ludendorff then spoke, shamelessly pretending to be surprised by the course of events, even though he was one of the few people who did know that a putsch had been planned, before Lossow and

Seißer gave short addresses at Hitler's behest. Hitler would later say of this moment on stage together: 'We were all more deeply moved than rarely before.'[21]

The following day, the events were described as having occurred as follows:

Then a Staff officer of Hitler's soldiers stood in front of the assembly and declared: 'Today the national revolution begins. It is directed in no way against General State Commissioner von Kahr, who all of us admire. It is exclusively and solely directed against the Jewish government in Berlin (this sentence was met with loud cheers). We have taken this step, because we are convinced that the men at the top of the government of Germany, are men with whom we must make a strong break. The new government of Germany will be Hitler-Ludendorff-Pöhner, long live the new government!' In the hall following this announcement there was wild cheering. The assembly sang the German national anthem. Then Hitler appeared at the front of the assembly, after he got everyone to be quiet by firing a revolver shot. He told them: 'Five years ago today was the starting point for the greatest act of shame that brought unlimited misery to our race. Today after five years, it must be the day that the course of history changes (this was greeted by loud cheering). My suggestion is that the cabinet of Knilling is deposed (cheers of Bravo!). The Bavarian government will be formed from the state administrators (*Landesverweser*) and a minister president who has full dictatorial powers.'[22]

Though aspects of this account may be exaggerated, there is no doubt about the cheering: by the end of Hitler's performance in the beer hall, the crowd was on his side. The nationalist and later pro-Nazi historian, Karl Alexander von Müller, whose students included Hermann Göring, Baldur von Schirach and Rudolf Hess, later called Hitler's second speech 'a masterpiece'. He recalled that he had never experienced such a change of mood in a crowd, claiming that there was almost something like 'magic about it'.

He described the handshake between Hitler and Kahr on the stage of the beer hall as a kind of 'Rütli Scene', a reference to a fifteenth-century legend in which secret societies were formed by a sworn oath which was popularized by nationalists in the nineteenth century, including Schiller who included such a scene in his drama *Wilhelm Tell*.[23]

After they had achieved what they wanted, the putschists began to clear the hall. Before they let the audience go home, Hess stood on a chair and read out a list of names that included all the members of the Bavarian government who were present. Hitler himself had given the list to Hess, who added the names of the police president, Karl Mantel, and Count Graf Soden. There was little resistance from the crowd. After Hess read out their names, the men on Hitler's wanted list simply gave themselves up. Only the justice minister, Franz Gürtner, attempted to escape. They were first taken upstairs to a separate room and then to the villa of Julius F. Lehmann, the founder of a right-wing publishing house. They remained there until the following afternoon, when their guards fled. There was some violence as the rest of the audience dispersed from the beer hall. One man watched as a sixty-year-old with a white moustache was mishandled by armed men and thrown against a wall after he expressed disapproval at the course of events. By 10.30 p.m., the beer hall was empty. Only the putsch leaders and their troops remained.[24]

In the Löwenbräukeller at around 9 p.m., Ernst Röhm received the news that he had been hoping for: a message came from the Bürgerbräukeller to tell him that the putsch was under way. Röhm then announced to the assembled members of the Combat League that a new government had been formed and called on the men to march to the Bürgerbräukeller. One group from the Organization Oberland arrived there at around 10.45 p.m. Some of them quickly moved on to the Hofbräuhaus, making it their headquarters, and completing the occupation of the third of Munich's most famous beer halls. Others went to arms depots across the city where they acquired arms that had been hidden during the previous weeks and months.[25]

While some putschists got ready for a night of drinking, others set out to take over the city. To be successful they needed to gain control of military and police barracks, government buildings, railway stations and the press. By the early hours of 9 November 1923, almost all of their attempts had ended in failure. But not in bloodshed: when the putschists stood face to face with armed police or soldiers that night, neither side was willing to fire upon the other.

Crucial events took place at the Generalstaatkommissariat, the headquaters of Gustav von Kahr, the centre of political power in Munich. After a first attempt to seize the building failed, Ludendorff ordered Lieutenant Rossbach, a former Freikorps commander, to take the building, using wartime assault tactics if necessary. The men under Rossbach's command prepared to do so. They went as far as bringing a loaded field gun with them, with the intention of shelling the building, before the assault troops then charged into it. Rossbach even ordered his men to fix their bayonets and get ready for the assault. But the attack never took place.

As the men prepared themselves to fight, Rossbach got into conversation with Lieutenant Muxel of the police. Muxel was the father of a close friend of one of the putschists. He warned that Lossow, Seißer and Kahr had already backtracked on their promise to support the putsch in the beer hall. In the ensuing uncertainty, even as they faced off against each other at close range with loaded weapons and bayoneted rifles, neither side really wanted to open fire. Muxel eventually invited a small number of putschists into the building before an order from the commander of the Organization Oberland called them back and they abandoned their attempts to take the building.[26]

Separately, Röhm managed some limited success in his attempts to take control of the Regional Military Command. At about 10 p.m., he demanded entry to the building and managed to convince the sentries not to open fire on his men, most of whom had followed him there from the Löwenbräukeller. Once inside, his men began to occupy it, but they were only partially successful. Officers who opposed the putsch continued to use its telephone communications, which the putschists had not taken control of, to send messages out. But despite not taking full control, they occupied it in sufficient numbers for it to be the only place where shots had to be fired to remove the putschists the following day.

Later that night, when Röhm attempted to repeat the same tactic at the city commander's office (Stadtkommandantur), he was unsuccessful. In most cases, unlike at the Regional Military Command, the putschists' attempts to seize buildings were half-hearted and they failed to gain entry or convince the guards to join forces with them.[27]

There was more violence in store before the night was over. Once the crowd had left the Bürgerbräukeller, a number of men from the Stoßtrupp-Hitler went to the offices of the Social Democratic *Münchener Post* newspaper. Göring had ordered them to smash up the offices and destroy the printing presses, but they were stopped by police sent by Hitler, who very likely did not want the printing presses destroyed, having promised the facilities to Wilhelm Weiss, who hoped to produce copies of his nationalist right-wing magazine, *Heimatland*. The shock troops only left when a column of Landespolizei appeared.[28]

The violence against defenceless targets was in part a product of the failure of the putschists to secure any major objectives during the night of 8–9 November 1923. This left most of the state's military and police presence in Munich intact and ready to respond to the coup once the orders came. Between 2 and 3 a.m., Kahr, Seißer and Lossow issued a directive to radio stations. Soon after, they issued a proclamation on a poster which was displayed all over central Munich. Both stated their public commitment to defeating the putschists. Their about-turn came when they had escaped from the beer hall after Hitler had left and put Ludendorff in charge of their captivity. While in charge, Ludendorff had simply let them go, later claiming that he fully believed that they would keep their word, as he considered it unimaginable that a German military officer could lie to him. Scheubner-Richter's wife later recalled Ludendorff's shock two days later when his assumption turned out to have been so wrong. Even if Kahr, Seißer and Lossow had not been able to escape, it is unlikely that the putschists would have lasted much longer. Without the support of the Reichswehr, they were militarily too weak to obtain and hold on to power in Munich.

It was only in the early hours of 9 November, as the putschists realized that they were standing on the brink of defeat, that the putschist leadership decided upon the idea of marching into central Munich in a show of force. By mid-morning they had organized the columns, with the cadets from Munich's infantry school taking up the rear of the procession. The Nazis' best men were at the front: 150 or so men of Joseph Berchtold's Stoßtrupp-Hitler. The men of the Nazi Regiment Munich were beside them. The Organization Oberland was on the right-hand side. It had its own commander, but had joined forces with the Nazis to take power in Bavaria.

As the putschists moved through the streets, crowds formed to cheer them on. Some called out 'Heil!' The marchers were encouraged by antisemitic slogans. Some onlookers claimed that the republic only existed to protect the Jews. There was lots of singing. Both the marchers and the watching crowds shared a repertoire of nationalist and military songs that celebrated the greatness of the old Germany that had been destroyed by the revolution in 1918. As they reached the Residenzstrasse, the marchers sang the old military song 'O Germany in High Honour'. Hitler later claimed that 'the people were behind us'. But Munich was not yet his city. Other putschists remembered being mocked and insulted as they made their way through the streets.[29]

At the Ludwig Bridge, near the Müller public baths, the marchers came up against their first test: a company of armed state police who had been put on alert during the night. They were the state's first line of defence against civil disorder and part of a counter-offensive against the putschists. Their commander was Lieutenant Georg Höfler. He held the bridge with two infantry squads and one machine pistol. His men were probably strong enough to defeat Hitler's marchers if they really wanted to. Höfler later said that when the Nazi procession came in sight, his men's weapons were unloaded and that he was following a protocol designed to reduce the likelihood of unnecessary gunfire. But it is also true that many policemen sympathized with the nationalist goals of the demonstrators. Some Bavarian police commanders had even spent time during the previous twelve months training the paramilitaries they were now supposed to open fire on. Before a single one of them was ready to shoot, a bugle call sounded and the men of the Stoßtrupp-Hitler started running. They reached the armed policemen before any shots were fired. 'Don't shoot your comrades,' they cried. Passengers on a passing tram watched as Höfler's men were quickly outnumbered. The putschists seized their weapons, and some of them kicked and punched the disarmed policemen. The latter were then taken prisoner and led away to the putschists' headquarters in the Bürgerbräukeller. It was the marchers' first victory. Even though they had been on the back foot since the early hours of the morning, at that point it made them think that they might still be able to conquer Munich.

Minutes later they reached the Odeonsplatz. They were on their way to the Feldherrnhalle, a large mid-nineteenth-century neoclassical monument that honours the Bavarian army. Even though it was guarded by a larger group of state police, the timing favoured the putschists. Just a few minutes earlier, heavily armed machine-gun units of state police had left the square, rushing away towards the army museum at the Residenz Gardens where they thought they would soon be needed – it was the location of the military headquarters of Munich. The policemen who remained in the Odeonsplatz were armed with rifles. The square was also protected by an armoured car that belonged to the Reichswehr. From inside the car, Lieutenant Bruno Ritter von Hauenschild watched as the putschists and Nazi flag-bearers led by Hitler came into view. He saw the men at the front of the procession, most likely members of the Stoßtrupp-Hitler, move forward. He claimed that the Nazis had their bayonets drawn. Facing up to them, the state police held their rifles against their bodies, their rifle butts pointing away from them. They planned to use these to smash into and disperse the putschists. In their arms, they held night sticks, a type of police baton. They started moving towards the putschists. There was little question that the police would follow their orders and fight back.

But just as the police and the putschists appeared to be about to start to brawl, everything changed. The sound of a gunshot resonated for a second, before its place was taken by an explosion of firing. For thirty seconds to a minute, the police and the putschists fired upon each other. They shot to kill. In front of the doors of the Café Annast, the waiter Karl Kulm, who had come out to see what was going on, was struck by one of the bullets and died. Hauenschild claimed that his armoured car was hit at least five times. Some accounts suggest that machine guns were fired.

The fighting was over quickly. Two or three minutes after the first shot was fired, the only Nazis left in the Odeonsplatz were the dead and injured. The rest had fled. The state police held the square. Four of them lay dead, as did thirteen putschists. At least a further sixteen people were badly injured, including Göring, who had been shot in the leg. Hitler managed to escape into a side street, where he was rescued by a Nazi doctor before being arrested two days later.[30]

No one can say for certain who fired the first shot, whether machine guns were actually fired or whether members of the Stoßtrupp-Hitler really did advance with their bayonets drawn. State police lieutenant Michael Freiherr von Godin would claim that he was the target of the first bullet after rushing from the back of the nearby Feldherrnhalle to join in the attempt to block the putschists. He recalled seeing how his men were grabbed by the Nazis. Some of them had pistols held against their chests. As they fought back with their rifle butts and night sticks, Godin claimed that he beat away bayonet blows with the butt of his rifle. As he did so, he claimed that one of the Nazis suddenly drew a pistol beside him and fired a shot directly at him. The shot passed by his head, killing Sergeant Nikolaus Hollweg, who was directly behind him.

We cannot be entirely certain of the veracity of Godin's statement. He had reasons to exaggerate the threat posed by the Nazis as he had to provide a justification for his men firing on the demonstration. He may also have been confused or traumatized by the violence. Others claimed that the first shot was fired by a sniper in one of the nearby buildings, while the putschists blamed the police for starting the shooting. Afterwards they spread the lie that any policeman hit by bullets was a victim of his own colleagues' inaccurate firing.

Ludendorff had no need for excuses for his behaviour and remained in the Odeonsplatz amid the shooting. The most sympathetic accounts of his supporters suggest that he stood upright and marched through the hail of bullets, passing through police lines, and was later arrested. These accounts are probably an exaggeration: it is more likely that he was quickly arrested amid the confusion. By the time Hitler was arrested, Ludendorff was already a free man. His stature led him to be given an 'honourable release'. As Hitler fell into depression as he faced his cell, Ludendorff visited the wife of Scheubner-Richter to console her for the loss of her husband, who was shot dead as he linked arms with Hitler at the head of the march.

As the bodies turned cold in the Odeonsplatz, Sergeant Ertel of the 19th Infantry Regiment was waiting behind his machine gun. He was part of the operation to retake the Regional Military Command in the Schönfeldstrasse, the only military building in Munich that the putschists had managed to take over the previous night. Among the armed Nazis occupying the building was the twenty-three-year-old Heinrich Himmler. Ertel was in an isolated position, in one of the higher storeys of a building opposite the Regional Military Command with a direct view of its courtyard. His commander, Gerhard Böhm, had given him a strict order: he was only to open fire if the putschists fired first.

Böhm was under the command of General von Danner, who had responsibility for retaking the building. By the time he received his order, the duration of Röhm's occupation had already become an embarrassment to the army's authority. The Reichswehr were to lead the assault. They were to be supported by the state police. Danner's soldiers set out at 11.30 a.m. At the mouth of the Briennerstrasse, they set up heavy machine guns to cover the

Odeonsplatz and the Residenz. Heavily armed state police blocked off the Königinstrasse. Another company gathered in the courtyard beside the state library. Directly facing the Regional Military Command, a mortar company was at the ready. One of the putschists present later described this moment:

> Each of us is in his place in accordance with our oath. We tightened the chinstraps of our steel helmets and prepared to take up defensive positions. The Reichswehr advances towards us with armoured cars and artillery pieces, armed to the teeth. The buildings opposite the War Ministry are also occupied by the Reichswehr. Machine-gun barrels point at us. We have orders not to fire before the Reichswehr does.[31]

Ertel watched the same scene from his elevated position overlooking the courtyard. Suddenly, the putschists fired two shots. They hit two Reichswehr soldiers, who were injured but not killed. Ertel did not wait for further commands. He fired his machine gun, killing two putschists in the courtyard. This dramatically changed the mood among the remaining putschists. Most of them had not fought in the First World War; despite their claims to speak for the front generation, they were schoolboys or students during the conflict. Once they saw death, their brave words about fighting to the end were quickly forgotten. A section of the putschists swiftly began to surrender. They included men of the combat leagues, some of whom were older and did not want to die for a lost cause.

Their commander, Ernst Röhm, was not yet ready to surrender, however. He drew his pistol on his own men and forced some of them to remain at gunpoint. He was lucky. Just as it appeared that the putschists would be on the receiving end of a frontal assault, an officer of the Reichswehr brought him a message from Ludendorff, who was under arrest following the collapse of the march at the Feldherrnhalle. Ludendorff advised him to surrender. Röhm was offered generous terms. Previously, he had been told that if he surrendered, he would be arrested, but his men would be allowed to go home. He had rejected this offer. But after Ertel's bullets, he changed his mind and accepted these terms. Ertel's was the only direct gunfire unleashed between the Reichswehr and the putschists.[32]

By 1 p.m., the bulk of the marchers who had fled the Odeonsplatz had gathered on the Marienplatz, where they were arrested by trainee policemen without further loss of life. The remaining putschists were arrested soon after at the Bürgerbräukeller. By 3 p.m., Munich was entirely back in the hands of the police and Reichswehr. One of the policemen later recalled the speed with which the defeated putschists surrendered. But he also remembered the anger of the crowds. In the Maximilianstrasse, he listened as bystanders insulted the police for defeating the putschists, calling them 'defenders of the Jews! Betrayers of the Fatherland! Bloodhounds! Heil Hitler – Down with Kahr!' In the Odeonsplatz, in the aftermath of the gunfire, pro-putschist crowds shook their fists at them and threatened them with violence.[33]

In the immediate aftermath of the so-called Beer Hall Putsch, many supporters of the Weimar Republic mocked Hitler and his Combat League allies: they had shown that they were a rabble and not a serious fighting force. The putsch had shown what they already suspected: Hitler was a loudmouth, only capable of making populist promises that gained the support of the unthinking masses. His fighting forces, the SA and its Combat League allies, were nothing to be afraid of. The paramilitary organizations would only be a threat to the state if they could gain the support of the Reichswehr. In November 1923, that support was not forthcoming. On their own, they couldn't even win a fight with the Bavarian state police. Liberals and Social Democrats were far more annoyed by the Bavarian leaders, Kahr and Lossow, than they were by Hitler. They accused Bavaria's rulers of having allowed the situation to fester during the previous months to the point that an outsider like Hitler could think that he would have a chance of seizing power. This was their greatest crime. Few were concerned about Hitler personally; most considered him such an oddball that they felt no need to take him seriously as a political opponent. In the aftermath of his failed putsch, they expected him to disappear.

15

Taking It Out on the Jews

The defeat of the putsch was undoubtedly a victory for Weimar democracy. But in its immediate aftermath, the biggest winners were Germany's Jews. They had experienced the crisis of the Weimar Republic in the autumn of 1923 as a moment of terror. Jews were attacked in political discourse and physically assaulted in villages and in the streets and squares of towns and larger cities. Although worse was to come in the 1930s and '40s, this was the most dangerous antisemitic violence to take place in Germany up until that point in the twentieth century.

In Bavaria, these attacks were fuelled not just by the rhetoric of far-right agitators such as Hitler, but by government policies established by the likes of Gustav Ritter von Kahr. When he was appointed state commissioner, he not only used racist language that excluded Jews from the community of Germans, he also began the Bavarian state-led deportation of Jews. He did this in part to try to win supporters back from the Nazis. But it was also a measure that came naturally to him, as he had long been a politically active antisemite. On 5 October 1923, he issued a decree that ordered the deportation of foreigners who were found guilty of breaking the 'usury law'. This was a legal cover aimed at the deportation of Jews.

It wasn't the first time that Kahr had tried to deport Jews from Bavaria. As minister president from 1920–1, he had tried to put in place plans to deport all Jews who had arrived in Bavaria since 1914. That measure was aimed at removing so-called 'Eastern Jews', Jewish migrants from eastern Europe, whose numbers had increased during and following the First World War. But in 1921, Kahr's plans were stopped by the Bavarian parliament. With the powers that came with being appointed Bavaria's state commissioner, Kahr no longer needed to concern himself with opposition from parliament. On 13 October 1923, he signed new rules that allowed for the arrest of Jews as well as residence restrictions in Bavaria. On 17 October, he provided a more detailed explanation of his plans, including reasons for deporting families: 'Behaviour that is harmful to economic life is a sufficient ground to expel foreigners. If there is a reason to expel the head of the family, this expulsion can be extended to family members living in his household.' On 19 October, the district president for Upper Bavaria informed him in a report: 'dictatorship can only become popular through use of prison and the death penalty against those who are harmful to the population. The worn-out people currently have no higher goal in mind than the reduction of costs.' While Hitler was calling for 'Germany for the Germans', Kahr recognized that, at a time of acute housing shortages, it would be popular to deport Jews, seize their property and hand it over to Germans in Bavaria.[1]

The earliest records of searches of Jewish properties suggest that they started on 16 October and that the first deportations, including returning Polish citizens to Poland, followed the next day. Kahr personally signed every deportation order issued to Jewish families on that day. The deported families had to pay their own transportation costs, and even infants received deportation orders. According to a report compiled by the Reichskommissar for the supervision of public order, the first orders were issued to forty families in Munich, but it claimed that this figure quickly rose to 180 as a result of pressure from the *Völkischer Beobachter*. The same newspaper demanded that all property belonging to deported Jews be immediately seized. In reply, the Reichskommissar for the supervision of public order suggested that there were only four hundred Eastern Jewish (mostly stateless, Polish, Russian or Austrian) families in Munich and that any migrant who was actually involved in threats to public order had already been deported.[2]

The most common reason given for deportation was that 'those affected had immigrated in poor circumstances, but had become rich, as they understood how to enrich themselves during the deepest need of the German people'. For example, Bernhard Ass, together with his twenty-one-year-old daughter, Paula, and his thirteen-year-old son, Josef, both of whom were born in Munich, received a deportation order for this reason. He was the owner of a factory that employed two hundred people. He had no police record. Another business owner received a deportation order after he was denounced as a political supporter of the left. According to the report compiled by the Reichskommissar for the supervision of public order, one man received his deportation order just after his naturalization had been approved. Deportation orders were also issued to a Prussian and a Baden national. The Prussian citizen was from Ostrowo. He had been promoted during the war to the rank of junior officer and received both the Iron Cross and the Bavarian Military Merit Cross – Bavaria's main medal for bravery for enlisted soldiers. At the end of the war, he chose German citizenship (it is not clear from the surviving documentation why he received the Bavarian Military Merit Cross but became a Prussian citizen). The lawyer representing him was told that 'the state of emergency enables the expulsion of Reich Germans'. Another man had his deportation order rescinded after he was able to demonstrate that he was in possession of an Iron Cross, first class.[3]

Other reasons for deportation included having a police or criminal record. In some cases, officials searched through old documentation to find records of fines that had been issued fifteen to twenty years earlier to justify deportations. For example, the reasons for Adam M.'s deportation order were given as follows: 'It has been established that he does not obey police orders and does not have a good reputation.' In the case of a married couple from Bayreuth, the reasons for deportation were: 'It is suspected that the married couple, in conducting their commercial business, are taking advantage of the general economic crisis that has prevailed since the war in a way that is damaging to economic life.' In another case, a man received a deportation order because he was in possession of around 120 bottles of wine. The same man was accused of living with his lover, Anna S., in 'concubinage' in a house that he claimed to have acquired in 1922.[4]

This reference to a lover was one of several accusations that those who were to be deported were guilty of moral and sexual crimes – an ancient trope of European antisemitism. One Jewish man's deportation order included the statement that he had been fined 5 marks for sex crimes during the war and was now in possession of a luxury apartment and employed his own maid. Another man and his wife and their three children were condemned to deportation because he had been fined 250 marks in 1922 for not displaying a sign on his shop stating that it was a Jewish business. The same reason was given for the deportation of another man and his wife and their nine children from Nuremberg. According to Kahr, another man who traded scrap gold and pawned items deserved to be deported because he was 'not necessary to economic life'.[5]

On 24 October 1923, the report by the Reichskommissar for the supervision of public order stated that sixty prominent Jewish families in Munich were given a deadline of five days before their deportation and that many of them had been arrested and held in prison. The report confirmed that this was only the beginning and that plans were in place to 'act vigorously against the Jews'. Stresemann received this report on 25 October. On 29 October, German People's Party member Ernst Scholz confronted him about the latest antisemitic measures in Bavaria. When he replied, Stresemann failed to mention that he had received a detailed report on the deportations four days earlier. Instead, he told Scholz, 'this would not go on', and promised to investigate further. On the same day, interior minister Wilhelm Sollmann warned Stresemann that Kahr's policy towards Jews in Bavaria had resulted in a surge of internal German Jewish migration, including Jewish 'refugees' who were seeking protection in the occupied territories. He thought that these developments would damage Germany's international reputation. On 29 October, Stresemann received more details. This time they came from the Foreign Office. It reported that forty Eastern Jewish families in Munich had received deportation orders. Some of them were reported as having been residents in Munich for twenty to thirty years. The main grounds given for their deportation was that they had arrived in Bavaria poor but had 'since acquired a fortune at the expense of the Bavarian people'.[6]

Kahr was determined to proceed at all costs. He even refused to rescind his order when an appeal came from the Bavarian state minister for trade, industry and commerce. The Bavarian Association of Jewish Frontline Soldiers also objected, as did the Bavarian Industrialists Association, which protested 'in the name of the economy'. Even Munich's conservative Cardinal Faulhaber spoke out against the targeting of minorities in his sermon on 2 November 1923. Faulhaber also told Stresemann that the Catholic Church in Bavaria wanted to 'dismantle the hatred that runs rampant against our Israelite fellow citizens or other groups of people, without proof of guilt'. But the protest was ineffectual. Kahr told representatives of Munich's Jewish community: 'Should there be a relatively large number of Israelites among those expelled, the conclusion is obvious that violations of economic regulations have occurred frequently in these circles.'[7]

Kahr was a fanatical antisemite, and the deportations were a continuation of his failed policy as minister president in 1920–1. Back then he had not had the excuse of the Nazi movement to justify his policies, but in October 1923, it was obvious that Hitler was the reason for his rush to deport Jews. In the classic – and so often failed – manoeuvre of a politician who faces the threat of being outflanked, he moved further to the right, hoping to steal Hitler's thunder. This was why it was so important that the deportations be public knowledge. As an article in the *Weltbühne* published on 8 November put it: 'Herr Kahr does what Hitler has on his agenda, and that which they share. He expels the Jews.' Before that, Kahr's actions had been condemned by *Vorwärts* on 30 October:

The ideal of the *Völkischer Beobachter* and the Hitlerites, who don't want to rest until the last Social Democrat is hanged and the last Jew is beaten to death, has not yet been fully achieved. But the expulsion of the Jews, as in the Middle Ages, is in full swing.[8]

When Lossow and Kahr resigned in February 1924, the deportations continued. It was only after the resignation of Knilling, in July 1924, that they stopped. The legal basis for them, Kahr's October 1923 order, was only finally withdrawn in March 1925. The number of Jews deported has never been firmly established. Prior to 1914, Munich had a reputation for tolerance and liberalism towards its population of around ten thousand Jews. Part of the challenge in identifying how many deportations actually took place is that an unknown number of Jews chose to flee Bavaria before being deported. In some cases they might have taken flight for fear of being deported, but in many others it is likely that they left because of the expectation that Hitler would soon replace Kahr and that the start of his rule would be accompanied by a pogrom. A report prepared for the Reich Chancellery stated specifically that this was happening. Those who fled in this way could resettle in the other German states. As we have already seen, some went to the occupied territories. Most appear to have gone to Berlin.[9]

Kahr's antisemitism involved the forces of the state, but other types of antisemitism increased as the crisis worsened. Operating independently of the state, men wearing the uniforms of paramilitary organizations committed terrifying acts of violence. One of the worst examples took place during the night of 3–4 November, when a gang of twenty to thirty drunken men boisterously made their way through the village of Autenhausen, a rural hamlet in Upper Franconia on the banks of the river Kreck, close to the Bavaria–Thuringia border. The men were members of the Viking League and the Young German Order, two ethno-nationalist (*völkisch*) antisemitic organizations that had recently merged. They were led by Wolfgang Götze, a former officer cadet in the German navy, who was well connected in the world of right-wing conspiratorial politics. They were wearing uniforms and armed with pistols and bayonets. Götze hoped that his militia would soon join forces with Hitler and march on Berlin, but publicly their purpose was to protect the border of north Bavaria from invasive attacks by Thuringia's Communist Proletarian Hundreds.

They had spent the day engaged in drills before going drinking in a nearby village, just under 3 kilometres to the south. While drinking, they decided to go to Autenhausen to target the homes of the last two Jewish families in the village. In Autenhausen, their voices carried across the silence of the night. When some residents looked out to see what was going on, they told them to close their windows and turn off their lights. Some of the militia made threatening gestures.[10]

Once they arrived at the homes of brothers Emanuel and Adolf Gutmann, they surrounded the residences, before smashing in the windows and doors and forcing their way inside. One of the men announced: 'We are the true German race, we need money for our cause.' Quickly, they made Emanuel Gutmann open his safe. But this wasn't just an armed robbery. Once they finished ransacking the property, they took the brothers outside, leaving their terrified wives behind, and led them about 100 metres beyond the village. Then, in the darkness of the night, they stopped.

What followed was a kind of fake trial, which ended with a declaration that the Gutmanns were guilty of belonging to the true enemies of the German race. Götze's militia then debated their punishment: 'Should we shoot them?' 'Do we have shovels?' 'No. Should we hang them?' 'We have no rope.' In the end, the militia forced the brothers to lie on the ground and then attacked them with sticks, batons and bayonets. By this time, the brothers' heads were bleeding. Later it was claimed that the beating only stopped when the gang thought the Gutmanns were dead.[11]

But the brothers survived. After the gang left, they stood up and, supporting each other, made it back to their houses. Later that night, they fled with their wives, not stopping until they found help. A few days later, another group of men returned to the Gutmanns' unoccupied homes to steal their horses, cows, geese and ducks, as well as their beds, linen and clothing. It took the brothers

a few more weeks to recover physically, but they had clearly understood the message. In January 1924, Autenhausen, a village that
had been home to a small but thriving Jewish community since the
seventeenth century, lost its last Jewish residents.[12]

The assault on the Gutmanns should not be understood as an
isolated event, nor was it any less portentous for happening in a
rural village on the fringes of German political life. Since November
1918, the newspapers of the nationalist and conservative right had
blamed every German defeat upon the Jews. In the crisis months
of the second half of 1923, when passive resistance and hyperinflation joined the list of German national failures, an increasing
number of people were starting to believe them.

It wasn't just right-wing publishers who inspired antisemitism.
Fuelled by Kahr's antisemitic policies, as previously discussed, antisemitic language and activities became radicalized across Germany
during October 1923. In Nuremberg, an ethno-nationalist hotspot,
the antisemites used phrases such as 'Kill the Jews as if they were
dogs', 'Strangle the Jews', 'Build the gallows, hang them, protect
none of them!' and 'Blood must flow, Jewish blood'. At demonstrations of the radical right across Germany, the phrase 'Beat the Jews
to death' became increasingly common. The consequences of this
language went beyond intimidation of Germany's Jewish population.
In isolated rural hamlets, individual Jews were beaten up; in large
cities, antisemitic mobs hunted Jews through the streets.[13]

The way in which the hyperinflation crisis exacerbated pre-
existing antisemitic mentalities was on clear display in the East
Prussian town of Neidenburg in October 1923. At the start of the
month, just as German nationalists learnt of Stresemann's decision
to abandon passive resistance, a Jewish man, Leo Löwenstein, was
minding his own business walking across the market square, when
he suddenly heard someone shouting: 'There goes another Jewish
rascal.' Löwenstein ignored the insult and continued walking. But
a gang of fifteen to twenty antisemites were now pursuing him.
One of them cut across his path on a bicycle while the others
blocked the escape route behind him. Unable to run, he asked them
what he had done to deserve this treatment. The reply was: 'You

personally, nothing – it's your race.' It was the last thing he heard before they started punching him repeatedly in the face.[14]

Spurred on by the abandonment of passive resistance, there was more antisemitic violence in Neidenburg a few weeks later, on 27 October 1923. It occurred on the fringes of a large ethno-nationalist demonstration led by a former army lieutenant named Ehlert. Inspired by Hitler's language and brand of political theatre, Ehlert incited hatred amongst his followers with cries of: 'Heil! Jews Out! If Germany is to exist, the Jews must perish!' His supporters replied with cries of 'Heil! Jews out!' When the police arrived, Ehlert cursed at them, claiming that they were being paid by the Jews. There was violence on the fringes of the demonstration. One incident occurred when a Jewish man, Arnold Kratter, challenged one of the antisemites to a fight. Kratter's intention was to take on his adversary man-to-man in a boxing match, but once the protagonists reached a side street, a gang of Nazis attacked him. They spat on him and hit him with sticks, leaving him bleeding badly. Later that day, other Jewish residents were followed and attacked.[15]

There were further incidents of violence and intimidation in East Prussia, Thuringia, Bremen and Bavaria. In the town of Nördlingen, 70 kilometres to the north-west of Augsburg, groups of antisemites went on night marches which included stopping outside Jewish homes to sing antisemitic songs. In Beuthen on 5 October 1923, around six hundred people, many of whom were members of antisemitic organizations, went on a five-hour rampage against anyone who looked Jewish in the vicinity of the railway station. By the time they had finished, they had injured as many as twenty people, some of them seriously. The police eventually intervened to break up the riot, but they did not make any arrests. In Hamburg, the expectation of antisemitic violence led the banker Max Warburg to flee the city briefly (he had been told that his name was on the lips of antisemites in the city).[16]

Everywhere in Germany, Jews were being blamed for the country's economic collapse. In Thuringia, one newspaper, the *Landeszeitung*, published the dollar exchange rate with the subheading

'And the Jew triumphs'. In Gotha, swastikas were painted on buildings accompanied by the words 'Strike down the Jews'. In the same town, bricks were thrown at the synagogue's windows, smashing two of them during the night. In the Rhineland, Jews were accused of orchestrating the separatist movement. In Bremen, in the lead-up to local elections, a gang of Nazis attacked members of the Reich Association of Jewish Front Soldiers (though they later put out the fake news that the Jewish veterans had attacked the Nazis first). In all of these cases, the alignment of forces that made the violence possible was driven by the combination of local jealousies and pre-existing economic rivalries with the wider political language of antisemitism. In addition, the migration of eastern European Jews into Germany during a time of crisis added a new layer to traditional patterns of antisemitism. Above all, the Jews were accused of profiting from the hyperinflation crisis, and the forces of the state were too weak to be able to protect them (this would change from 1924 onwards when the state was much better placed to protect its Jewish citizens). As a consequence, October and November 1923 witnessed the most significant moment of antisemitic violence in twentieth-century Germany prior to the establishment of the Third Reich.[17]

The climax came in Berlin, where there were two days of antisemitic riots. The trouble began at lunchtime on 5 November. At 11 a.m., a large crowd of unemployed workers had gathered at the unemployment offices on the Alexanderstrasse. When they learnt that they would receive no payment because the office had run out of money, a rumour quickly spread that eastern European Jewish migrants living in the Scheunenviertel neighbourhood had hoarded all of the available money, planning to lend it back to Germans at exorbitant rates later on. Other rumours suggested that Jewish moneylenders would be willing to trade paper money for gold loan certificates.[18]

How these rumours spread has been much debated. At the time it was argued that they were deliberately put into circulation by mischievous antisemitic agitators, intent on steering Berlin's working class into the camp of the political right. If that was the case, no such agitators have ever been discovered and no one was ever prosecuted for such deliberate incitement. Instead, it is more likely that the idea that the rioters were controlled by professional anti-semitic agitators grew in popularity because it accomplished two crucial tasks. Firstly, it provided an easily understandable explanation for the outbreak of the rioting. Secondly, it allowed the political left – whose working-class supporters formed the bulk of the rioters – to blame the rioting on right-wing agitators, rather than admit that there was widespread antisemitism within the working class. Just as the Ruhr occupation altered the nature of working-class nationalism there, the effects of hyperinflation were changing working-class political identities in Berlin, a city that largely preferred to see itself as in the vanguard of Socialist and internationalist politics.

Regardless of what precisely triggered the rioting, once it started it was clear that Jews were under attack. The riot's epicentre was the Scheunenviertel, an area that was widely associated with eastern European Jews. As the *Vossische Zeitung* reported, once the rioting started, 'Every person on the streets who looked Jewish was surrounded by a screaming mob, struck to the ground and their clothes were stolen.' Rioters also broke into Jewish homes and destroyed or stole property, while some cried out, 'Beat the Jews to death' or 'Strip the Jews.' Tellingly, by dusk, many shop owners in the Scheunenviertel had painted the words 'Christian business' on their shop fronts.[19]

Berlin's Nazis did not let the riots go to waste. At dusk on 5 November 1923, they charged around the Friedrichstadt, a historic area of central Berlin not far from the Scheunenviertel. At the junction of Friedrichstrasse and Unter den Linden, just a few hundred metres from the Brandenburg Gate, Gendarmenmarkt square and Berlin Cathedral, they were spotted chasing after and intimidating anyone who they thought looked Jewish. Unlike the rioters in the much poorer Scheunenviertel, the Nazi 'rowdies' were led by well-dressed young men, probably student supporters of the Nazi Party drawn from the nearby university. Sometimes they left their activities at intimidation, but in other cases they dished out a beating to people who did not meet their definition of 'racial belonging'. With the police overstretched across the German capital, they could proceed as they wished. As far as is known, not a single bystander stood up to them.[20]

The rioting spread further across the city. In the well-off western district of Charlottenburg, butchers and bakers were looted. At the corner of Kantstrasse and Wilmersdorfer Strasse, also in the west of the city, at around midnight a large crowd forced cars to slow down and robbed their passengers. In central Berlin, on Invalidenstrasse and Grolmanstrasse, rioters targeted bakeries, a shoe store and a canned food shop. The next morning, there was more trouble along the arterial roads that link western Berlin with the city centre. Mobs of unemployed men appeared to be on their way to target the area around Wittenbergplatz, close to a number of department stores, including the famous Kaufhaus des Westens. Trucks carrying police rushed to prevent these flare-ups from gathering momentum. In the north of Berlin in Weißensee, a mob attacked the chief mourners at a Jewish funeral. The son of the deceased was knocked to the ground and badly beaten. His cousin, who was weakened by illness, was similarly mishandled.[21]

A special feature of this violent pogrom was the so-called 'Strip Commandos'. This was the term used by the press to capture the way in which groups of rioters would suddenly surround their victims and start to tear their clothes off, before then allowing their half-naked victims to go free, only then to chase them through the streets while an onlooking crowd loudly cheered them on. At the corner of Grenadierstrasse and Hirtenstrasse, one victim of this violent form of street theatre tried to escape by taking shelter inside a Jewish butcher's shop. The butcher and his son-in-law came out of their shop to protect him, armed with cleavers. In the vicious knife fight that followed, the younger man was stabbed, but he survived his injuries.[22]

The riots were not unexpected. One of the few things that gave the main Jewish political group, the Central Association of German Jews, cause for comfort in their aftermath was that their defensive plans had worked reasonably well. The association had a special section for war veterans, who had fought for Germany in the trenches of the First World War. As soon as they received the first reports that Jews were under attack, the veterans scrambled to defend their co-religionists. This was an important move: the assimilated German Jews who made up the membership of the association tended to distance themselves from more recent arrivals from eastern Europe – they even emphasized the differences between German and eastern European Jews in terms of culture and appearance. Because of those differences, many people did not expect them to rush to assist the Jewish migrants from eastern Europe. But once trouble kicked off, as many as twenty veterans rushed to help. They were armed with pistols and batons; some may even have been wearing their war medals.

When they got to the Scheunenviertel, the veterans were attacked by a group of more than one hundred antisemites in front of the famous Volksbühne theatre. Almost as soon as the fighting started, a shot was fired and a member of the mob was killed. Later an investigation discovered that the shot was most likely fired by someone in a building on the opposite side of the street. Their identity was never discovered. Nor was it established whether they were trying to help the Jewish war veterans or to incite the mob to finish them off.

Once the gunshot rang out, it looked as though the outnumbered Jewish war veterans might be beaten to death in the streets of Berlin. But just as the antisemitic crowd prepared to take revenge, large numbers of police arrived to stop the fighting.[23]

Rather than rescuing the Jewish war veterans, however, the police arrested them. In total, during the rioting, as many as two hundred Jews were brought to the police barracks in the Alexanderplatz. Many Jewish detainees were unhappy with their treatment. Some claimed that they were forced to stand with their hands over their heads. Others said that the police beat them. Dr Hugo Bernhardt, a Jewish doctor whose office was located close to the heart of the riots, was among them. He was horrified. He claimed that the first police officers on the scene ignored the plight of the Jews. After his arrest, he was mishandled and the police broke a bone in his right hand. In a telling interview with the *Vossische Zeitung* – despised by the antisemites as part of the 'Jewish Press' – he added:

> I was there [in the First World War] at the front for four years as a doctor, I was injured badly, I was awarded the Iron Cross, second and first class, and the Saxon *Ritter* [Knight's] Order. Conditions in Berlin do not give me the impression that I am living in a state governed by the rule of law.[24]

By the second day of the rioting the police had mobilized sufficient numbers to restore order. For the first time in Berlin's history, they used rubber truncheons to clear the crowds. The police commanders were under political pressure to end the rioting, having been told that if the riots continued, the army would be called in. While their men fought rioters in the streets, senior police officers defended the force's reputation in the press. They denied that the police had been slow to protect Jews and that the force had its own problem with antisemitism. The message was repeated again and again: the police did not tolerate antisemitism within its ranks.[25]

These claims were later shown to be untrue. While police intervention clearly saved the lives of some Jews during the rioting, in 1924 a court ruled that policemen had unlawfully struck members of the Reich Association of Jewish Front Soldiers with the butts of their rifles. The investigation also uncovered that the police were guilty of brutality against Jewish prisoners. The behaviour of three officers was so bad even in the context of the early Weimar Republic – when judicial leniency towards the forces of the state was the order of the day – that they were given custodial sentences and dismissed from the force. The same trial threw out the charges against the Central Association of German Jews, recognizing that its members had a right to defend themselves and their co-religionists.[26]

The Berlin riots were on a far greater scale than anything that happened in the towns and villages around Germany. Some contemporaries estimated that as many as ten thousand people had joined in the rioting. At least five hundred rioters were arrested.

There is no doubt that the riots were primarily of an antisemitic nature, but with more than 200,000 people unemployed and the price of a loaf of bread touching 140 billion marks, the timing of the riots was obviously to some extent connected to hunger and economic frustration.[27]

In their aftermath, the Central Association of German Jews was indignant:

> May the people pulling the strings behind this inhuman brutality take joy in their work, may the racist newspapers in Berlin try to clear their conscience, when they blame the violence on the 'vengeance of the starving people'. These terrible days have shown that in order to achieve their terrible goals, the racists leaders will not condemn every robbery and murder equally.

For the *Vossische Zeitung*, economic explanations were meaningless: 'It is an inflamed racist hatred, not hunger, that drives them to plunder. Every passer-by who looked Jewish was immediately tracked by young lads who got ready to rob them at the right moment.' To the left of the *Vossische Zeitung*, the Social Democratic newspaper *Vorwärts* was equally incensed. It published an article by Arthur Crispien, a Social Democratic member of parliament, that labelled the antisemites 'poor dupes'. In his words: 'Berlin has had its Jewish pogrom. Berlin has disgraced itself. A shame for a people that belongs to the most civilized in the world.'[28]

For the SPD, at issue was the question of who truly controlled the working class. For, even though many people blamed the rioting on the politically unorganized underclass that Karl Marx famously defined as the *Lumpenproletariat*, it was equally clear that many of the rioters belonged to the class of workers who were generally expected to march in the ranks of the Social Democrats. By way of response, in November 1923, the party organized twelve demonstrations in Berlin to protest against increasing antisemitism and threats to the unity of the Reich. It was a strong stand, but it was not enough. By the time of these party protests, the Social Democratic members of Stresemann's cabinet were already out of government, enraged by the Reich government's lack of action against Bavaria. On 2 November 1923, Wilhelm Sollmann, a fierce opponent of the Nazi Party who held the position of interior minister, told his cabinet colleagues that Kahr's policy of deporting Jews was like something from the 'Middle Ages'. He wanted it stopped and he wanted action to be taken against the antisemitic violence that had already taken place. Together with his colleague, Robert Schmidt, he accused Stresemann of doing nothing, but their concerns were ignored. The next day they resigned.[29]

There was more antisemitic violence in Munich during the failed Beer Hall Putsch of 8–9 November. As far as is known, only one German Jew, Ludwig Wassermann, a well-known member of the Central Association of German Jews in Munich, was in the Bürgerbräukeller when Hitler launched the coup. He was a politically conservative factory owner and a member of a lobby group that represented industry. Once the putsch began, Wassermann was taken hostage and held in the Bürgerbräukeller. Later, men from the Stoßtrupp-Hitler, led by Emil Maurice and Joseph Berchtold, went to the offices of the *Münchener Post*, which they searched for 'incriminating material'. They also tried to capture Erhard Auer, editor of the newspaper and leader of the Bavarian Social Democrats. They went to his home, but Auer, who had been warned by a member of the Reichswehr earlier that evening, had already gone into hiding. In place of Auer, his son-in-law, Karl Luber, was taken hostage. The Stoßtrupp-Hitler also vandalized Auer's property and threatened his wife, Sophie. Later that night, another group of SA men returned to Auer's home.[30]

Elsewhere that night, groups of around fifteen to twenty SA men carried out searches for Jews. They targeted restaurants and hotels that had 'Jewish-sounding' names. One of the first Jews they found was the tailor Martin Ambrunn, who lived in the well-off Bavariaring-Viertel area. They forced him to leave his home and wait outside in the street, while the SA men searched for more Jews in the same area. At around 3 a.m., Ambrunn was brought back to his wife and family to say goodbye to them. He was then led away before his captors suddenly decided to release him. When a mob of SA men came to his home, Eduard Kohn escaped by climbing down a drainpipe. As they searched for him, one SA man fired a shot into a large cabinet where he thought Kohn was hiding. In another incident, Justin Stein was taken hostage and brought to the Bürgerbräukeller. For a few hours he was held alongside Wassermann and Luber. At around 5 a.m., the three Jewish prisoners received a surprise visit. It was Hermann Göring. After inspecting them, Göring released all three. This probably reflected the haphazard nature of the putsch and the lack of planning that had gone into the putschists' anti-Jewish measures, rather than indicating any empathy with the prisoners – later the same morning Göring threatened that his men would execute all the other hostages they held.[31]

During the daylight hours of the morning of 9 November more searches were conducted for Jews. A group of men went to Bogenhausen, an area known as being home to rich Jews, where they searched for suitable prisoners. Their search consisted of such basic tactics as examining the names on doors and deciding to target people with 'Jewish-sounding' names. The seventy-four-year-old Isidor Bach, an elderly magistrate and member of the Central Association of German Jews, was among their victims. He was driven to the Hofbräuhaus and later to the Bürgerbräukeller. Julius Heilbronner was also taken hostage. In these two cases, the elderly men were accompanied by their daughters. Around the same time, another two men who were brought to the Bürgerbräukeller as Jewish prisoners were released when they were able to prove that they were not Jews. The engineer Jakob Guggenheim was also let go. His captors wanted to take him as a hostage, but they abandoned their efforts when they were confronted by his crying wife.[32]

The cases of violence during the failed Hitler putsch reveal a pattern. During the night of the coup, the Nazi mob had a clear sense that it was their duty to go after the 'Jews'. They knew that the Jews were their enemy and that the start of their regime meant that it was time to target them. But they did not have a list of prominent Jews in Munich and there was little or no systematic organization behind their anti-Jewish measures. It would be a further decade before such antisemitism from below would be led from above.[33]

The same pattern can be seen in all of the instances of antisemitic violence for which we have records in the autumn of 1923. The people who assaulted Jews, whether they were part of small groups, organized paramilitaries or participants in large-scale rioting, as was the case in Berlin's Scheunenviertel, had a political script that made it clear to them who was to blame for Germany's plight. But beyond Kahr's measures in the state of Bavaria, they did not have the organizational capacity systematically to target the Jews. The creation of such organizational capacity was a feature of Theodor von der Pfordten's constitution. Had the Nazi putsch been successful, it would have married the antisemitic violence from below with the antisemitic policies from above of men like Kahr. If Hitler's putsch had been successful, that marriage would have taken place in the winter of 1923–4 and not a decade later, in 1933.

The organizations that represented Germany's Jews in 1923 were fully aware of the dangers. They tried to lobby the federal government in Berlin and even Kahr and Knilling's government in Bavaria to intervene. Copies of the *CV-Zeitung* are found in the archival records of the Reich Chancellery. Deputations of Munich's Jews held meetings with both Knilling and Kahr. As we have seen, in their final contribution before they quit Stresemann's cabinet, the Social Democratic Party ministers demanded that he condemn Kahr's 'medieval expulsion of Jews'. But the responses to these demands for the Jews to be protected were far too weak.[34]

The backlash against antisemitism and anti-republican politics that had occurred after the murder of Walther Rathenau was not repeated in the months following Hitler's Beer Hall Putsch. The opponents of antisemitism did not follow through with strong legal measures against the racists. The 1923 crisis had created a 'now or never' moment for German opponents of antisemitism. Had they chosen to do so, the rulers of the republic could have refounded its authority and made Weimar a place that did not tolerate any form of antisemitic violence. But that never happened. Instead, underneath the surface of the return of prosperity that occurred from 1924 onwards, the visual and verbal tropes of antisemitism, which had grown in force since the end of the First World War and been radicalized during the republic's crisis year, remained powerful. In their moment of victory, the republic's leaders did not do enough to destroy them permanently.

Their inaction was aided by what the *Jüdische Echo* in November 1923 called the 'poisoning of public opinion'. As the pro-Zionism newspaper put it: 'The worst and most shameful thing about the flood of senseless and thoughtless hatred of Jews throughout all classes of the population is the lack of voices of reason and humanity on the part of the Christian population.' Too many people 'have been entirely silent and inactive against the year-long continuous antisemitic incitement to hatred that has been driven by lies and defamation'. They remained so.[35]

16

De-escalation and the
Triumph of Reason

A little over two weeks after the failed putsch, on 22 November 1923, Gustav Stresemann gave his last speech as German chancellor. He accused the putschists of betraying their fatherland and called the attempt to seize power in Bavaria 'a political adventure that was an unforgivably stupid thing to do'. An unstable Bavaria or a civil war on the border between Bavaria and Thuringia could have been used by Poincaré as a pretext to annex the Ruhr permanently in the name of maintaining order there. Stresemann warned of this danger as he condemned the Nazis, accusing them of risking the future of western Germany. To send a strong message that the Nazis were not real German patriots, he quoted the Munich journalist and writer Tim Klein:

> *You fought in the fog and the darkness,*
> *And your enemy, he lay defeated.*
> *But when you recognized the body at first light,*
> *It was your own fatherland.*

Stresemann blamed the French for the situation that had allowed both Communism and Nazism to thrive. In his words:

> If the French prime minister and French policy really wanted to secure stability in Germany on the basis of constitutional democracy, then their best policy would have been to remove the grounds for the development of extremes and radicalism in Germany.

Instead of removing those grounds, Stresemann argued that Poincaré had preferred to support German 'misery' and 'national humiliation'.[1]

It was a brilliant rhetorical performance, but it mattered little. The next day, he lost a vote of confidence in the Reichstag after motions calling for his removal were tabled by Helfferich's German National People's Party, the Social Democratic Party and the Communist Party. With their votes, and those of the Bavarian People's Party, the Weimar Republic lost its most accomplished chancellor. It was the logical outcome of the Social Democrats' decision to quit Stresemann's cabinet at the start of November, which led an angry Ebert to promise his party colleagues that, while the cause of their decision would be forgotten in six weeks, Germany 'will feel the consequences of your stupidity for ten years'.[2]

After Stresemann's fall, on 30 November he was succeeded by the Centre Party's Wilhelm Marx, who formed a new cabinet with no parliamentary majority that included no politicians of the left. Marx was a sixty-year-old judge from Cologne, known for his dour personality and willingness to compromise. His cabinet included ministers from the Centre Party, the German Democratic Party and the German People's Party, as well as Erich Emminger, a member of the Bavarian People's Party. Wisely, Marx insisted that Stresemann should remain as foreign minister – a generous move for a Centre Party politician to make towards Stresemann, whose critics in his own party, the German People's Party, were part of the reason he had lost his majority. Stresemann was isolated in his own party because of his willingness to work with the moderate left. Too many of his party's members hated everything about the Social Democrats and had no desire to share the middle ground with them. But even at this point in the crisis year, it is important to remember that it was a parliamentary decision to bring Stresemann down. Even following all of the tensions of the previous weeks, Seeckt's Reichswehr did not interfere or conspire in the process of forming a government. The 'now or never' moment for the republic's opponents was over.[3]

Marx would remain as chancellor until 15 December 1924. In

his maiden speech, he appealed for national unity and warned that
the economic situation facing the Reich necessitated urgent action
and that the country might still be only days away from collapse.
He promised the Reichstag: 'My struggle is against neither left nor
right, but against everyone who wants to use violence and force to
rob the German people of the last and best thing that it has left:
the unity of the nation.' When it came to the relationship between
the Reich and Bavaria, he promised that there would be no changes
to the constitution (which it would not have been possible for his
minority government to introduce anyway) but that in some areas,
where there had already been requests for greater powers for the
federal states, he would accept them.[4]

In addition to promising to bring about a reconciliation between
Bavaria and the Reich, Marx's cabinet actually included three
Bavarian ministers. Two of them, Otto Geßler and Eduard Hamm,
were members of the German Democratic Party. But it was the
appointment of Emminger as justice minister that was the real
signal of Marx's intentions. Emminger was a Bavarian conservative.
He was known for being the only Reichstag deputy who had publicly
spoken against widespread criticism of a Bavarian court's decision
to sentence Felix Fechenbach to eleven years' imprisonment for
treason. During the revolution of November 1918, Fechenbach had
been Kurt Eisner's right-hand man, but by the time his trial took
place in the summer of 1922, critics of the 'Fechenbach Affair' on
the moderate left argued that it only took place because of a right-
wing press campaign. In the words of the Social Democrats'
principal newspaper, *Vorwärts*, Emminger's appointment 'will weigh
heavily upon Marx's cabinet, and the political direction that he
represents will be the source of dangerous conflicts'. In an accurate
prediction of what was to come, it warned: 'That a cabinet of which
a representative of the Bavarian People's Party is a member won't
bring out large cannons to fire at Bavaria, is clear to everyone.'[5]
Marx never did lead a crusade against Bavaria. Instead, his policies
set the course for the conflict between the rebel state and the Reich
to end without the re-establishment of republican authority there.
Bavarian politics remained opposed to Weimar democracy, and

Munich and Nuremberg were the cells from which Nazism would re-emerge as a political force in the late 1920s.

Marx's government excluded Helfferich's German National People's Party. Though pleased to see the creation of a government that excluded the left, Helfferich and his party wanted no part in a cabinet that included Stresemann. Their hatred of Stresemann was linked to a broader set of recriminations that raged on the German right in the aftermath of the failed putsch.

By mid-December 1923, it was obvious to both conservative and *völkisch* nationalists that they had wasted the chance that the hyper-inflation crisis had offered to destroy the republic. The chairman of the United Patriotic Leagues of Germany went so far as publicly to blame Hitler for prematurely launching the putsch and dividing the republic's opponents. Just a few days later, *Vorwärts* argued: 'Nowhere is the hatred against each other greater than in the *völkisch* camp.' It was a

> witches' cauldron, a chaos, a mess, in which not a single person is satisfied. All of them want to see the creation of a dictatorship. All of them want to be the dictator. All of them think that the others are incapable of being the dictator. All of them think that the others are an embarrassing 'pest'.

Their opponents were so divided that the Social Democrats' main newspaper predicted that supporters of democracy in Germany could take a step back and relax as they watched the right-wing movement disintegrate of its own accord:

> These lads think that they can mock Social Democracy for its work to maintain German unity. But Social Democracy does not need to worry for a second that these forces will be able to avoid the fate that they deserve: their future is disintegration and decay.[6]

By the time those words appeared in print, Hitler had been in prison for exactly one month. The man who would later overcome the shame of the failed putsch and unite the *völkisch* and conservative nationalists behind his leadership had been arrested while in hiding on 11 November 1923. Just days after he had compared himself to Friedrich the Great, Luther and Wagner, Hitler's actual leadership during the putsch left him looking ridiculous. In the words of historian Larry Eugene Jones, his failure had 'thoroughly discredited the idea of a military coup among all but the most obtuse of Weimar's right-wing enemies'. When he arrived at Landsberg prison Hitler was extremely depressed and possibly even suicidal. He told prison psychologist Alois Maria Ott: 'I've had enough. I'm done. If I had a revolver, I'd use it.' He went on hunger strike for fourteen days. But as had occurred following the humiliation of 1 May 1923, and would recur during his future career as dictator, Hitler's psychology and ego allowed him gradually to convince himself that his defeat was actually the result of other people's failures. By mid-December, his visitors, including his half-sister, could describe his mood as improving. He also began to plot his defence at his trial.[7]

On 13 December, deputy state prosecutor Hans Ehard came to Landsberg to interview him. Thirty-four days after the putsch, Ehard had an experience that was not unlike that of the *Daily Mail* journalist on 2 October 1923, after Stresemann's decision to end the campaign of passive resistance. Hitler turned their interview into another monologue in which he repeated many of the points he customarily made during his speeches. He told Ehard that the putsch could not have been illegal because the regime that he wished to destroy was illegal. He threatened that he would deal with the charges he faced by calling on 'certain gentlemen' to act as witnesses. And he promised that when the time came for the trial he would fight like a 'wild cat' to discredit his enemies 'ruthlessly'.[8]

Hitler knew what he was doing. He had enough knowledge of anti-republican conspiracies in Bavaria to damage the reputations of Kahr, Lossow and Seißer, and, even more importantly, he could create an international scandal by exposing the Reichswehr's secret cooperation with Bavarian militias. Such a scandal would be even more explosive given that Hitler would confirm the truth behind the accusations made by men like Zeigner during the previous months.

Even though historians cannot be entirely certain what happened behind the scenes, it is most likely that Hitler's threats paved the way to a deal. The Law for the Protection of the Republic would play no role in his prosecution. The leader of a major anti-republican putsch would not face trial at the Court for the Protection of the Republic in Leipzig, where Rathenau's killers had been sentenced a year earlier. Instead, Hitler would be put on trial in a sympathetic Bavarian court. He was possibly even offered a lenient sentence in return for his political silence. So neither Theodor von der Pfordten's draft constitution, a crucial piece of evidence in what was supposed to be a trial for high treason, nor the violence against Jews and Social Democrats or the four members of the Landespolizei killed during the putsch, were mentioned during the proceedings. The courtroom became a political stage for Hitler to position himself as the conscience of anti-republican Germany. At the end of his trial, he said that the court could not condemn him:

> You may pronounce us 'guilty' a thousand times, but the goddess who presides over the eternal court of history will smile and tear up the charge of the public prosecutor, and smile and tear up the judgement of the court, for she will acquit us.[9]

On 1 April 1924, Hitler was sentenced to five years' 'fortress imprisonment'. The same sentence was handed down to Friedrich Weber, Hermann Kriebel and Ernst Pöhner. Five other accused received even shorter prison sentences while Ludendorff was acquitted. Despite the fact he was an Austrian citizen, the court rejected the case for Hitler's deportation on the grounds that his wartime service was sufficient to allow him to remain in Germany. In the ultra-conservative *Kreuzzeitung*, which was Hindenburg's favourite newspaper, right-wing editor and publicist Georg Foertsch declared: 'The sentence against Hitler, Pöhner, Kriebel and Weber is severe.'[10]

The pro-republican press was outraged. Its headlines included

'Germany's Justice Scandal', 'Mild Sentences for Treason' and 'A Catastrophe of Justice'. The *Berliner Volks-Zeitung* described Foertsch's claim as 'grotesque'. Summing up reactions to the sentencing, the paper concluded: 'The situation is clear: the right is celebrating, while the republic lowers its head in sorrow and shame.' In an observation quoted by other pro-republican newspapers, the Centre Party's *Germania* warned: 'The authority of the state and the people's sense of justice has been destroyed by this judgement.'[11]

When Hitler was released in December 1924, he immediately promised his followers that their struggle would start again. For the next four years he campaigned against the republic, without any major successes. In the German federal elections of May 1928, the Nazi Party received less than 3 per cent of the national vote and just twelve Reichstag seats, while the Social Democrats, under the leadership of Hermann Müller, returned to government with 153 Reichstag seats and just below 30 per cent of the national vote. It was only in 1929, following an electoral breakthrough in Baden, that the Nazi vote started rising continuously, reaching as high as 37.2 per cent of the vote in the regional elections in Oldenburg in May 1931. In the 1930 Reichstag election, they gained 18.3 per cent and established themselves as a national political force. Their re-emergence is a reminder that, just as Hitler and the anti-republican right failed to seize the 'now or never' moment to destroy German democracy in 1923, their opponents also failed to take their opportunity to destroy them permanently. The refusal to use the Law for the Protection of the Republic and to put Hitler on trial in Leipzig at the Court for the Protection of the Republic turned out to be one of the most costly errors in world history.

Just weeks after taking up the position of chancellor, Marx delivered an extraordinary Christmas message to the German people. He lamented that, because of the collapse of the German economy, many Germans would go without trees, candles and presents that year and that the government's only Christmas gift to them was going to be new taxes that would hurt them badly.[12] It was only thanks to the charity of other nations and German migrants who sent money and food back to Germany, Marx continued, that many Germans would have something to eat this Christmas at all. In the chancellor's words, Germany's middle class who

> could once celebrate Christmas without any worries has collapsed. In the families of many employees, workers and civil servants there will be no pure joy of Christmas this year because they have to face up to unemployment and a lack of trade. We are so poor, so poor . . . Never before has the number of Germans who cannot afford their daily bread been greater.

The cause of all this suffering was the occupation of the Ruhr: 'They cut off our arteries, they cut us off from our heart, the heart that pushes the economic and financial blood through the veins of our fatherland. An unspeakable chain of misery, pain and suffering began on this day.'[13]

A week later, on 31 December 1923, the journalist Erich Dombrowski echoed the chancellor's words:

> At the start of the year, measured against paper marks the dollar exchange rate was around 7,000, at the end of the year it stood at 4 trillion. Between these two shocking numbers there are hundreds of thousands of people whose economic existence lies in ruins, millions of unemployed and a shattered private and public economy. The difference between these two figures explains all of the Rhineland separatists' attempts at independence, all of the attempted putsches of the radical far right and the separatism of the peasants. It explains the rise of the Socialist-Communists in Saxony and Thuringia, and finally the cabinet and parliamentary crisis in the Reich.

Dombrowski predicted: 'our descendants will shrug their shoulders and sneer in contempt when they think about the nationalism and chauvinism of our times.'[14]

By the end of 1923, there were good grounds for Dombrowski's expectation that the hatred that had defined the political course of the year would not last. The German financial crisis had turned a corner. On 15 October, Stresemann's government agreed to the foundation of a new central bank, the Rentenbank, which was secured by a mortgage of agricultural land and industrial assets. The first notes of its new currency were issued on 15 November, just a week before Stresemann lost the confidence vote in the Reichstag. The Rentenmark was urgently needed: without a functioning currency, it was expected that farmers would hoard food and that Germans would starve during the winter of 1923–4. In his final speech as chancellor, Stresemann even warned that Germany was on the verge of a 'catastrophic famine'. In the middle of December, following a two-day conference on 13–14 December, the heated issue of the eight-hour working day was also resolved for the foreseeable future. Management, unions and the government agreed to the reintroduction of the ten-hour working day and the two-shift system in all areas where they had been in force before the war.[15]

Workers weren't the only ones facing hard times as a result of the crisis. To reduce costs, Stresemann's government had implemented a savage reduction in state spending: state employees' salaries were cut to 60 per cent of their pre-war levels and the jobs of up to 25 per cent of state employees were cut. Marx's government now continued the process in December 1923. On 7 and 19 December, finance minister Hans Luther introduced two emergency tax decrees. His goal was to increase dramatically the revenue coming into the Reich. The first decree was passed under Article 48, the second under the powers of the enabling act that was granted to Marx's government by the Reichstag on 8 December 1923, with the support of the SPD, whose parliamentarians were offered a role on oversight committees that ultimately played little role in events across the following months. To achieve his goal, Luther needed to find a way to collect taxes in a currency that was attached to the value of gold, rather than to the value of worthless paper marks. This made for an extraordinarily conflict-ridden process as taxes due for the year 1923 were based on prices that had been calculated in hyperinflated notes. Luther's officials overcame this challenge by using figures from 1922 and projections of what they thought would be due in 1924. The outcomes obviously left taxpayers frustrated. Some thought that they were being asked for too much, while others got away with the profits they had made during the hyperinflation crisis, even if Luther tried to claw back some of their gains with further special taxes in 1924.[16]

However politically unpopular Luther's measures were when they were announced, they worked. The emergency taxes first introduced in December 1923 put the state's finances back on track. Between December 1923 and January 1924, the percentage of the Reich's total revenue from corporation tax jumped from 0.17 per cent to 6.9 per cent. By March 1924, the books were balanced.[17] Farmers were among those who lost out. Even though they managed to use the effects of hyperinflation to reduce farm debt dramatically (by up to 80 per cent), they were so angry at the prospect of paying taxes in the new currency that they threatened to bring threshing machines, tractors and other farm equipment to the Wilhelmsplatz in central Berlin in order to demonstrate their dissatisfaction. But even the farmers' protests subsided. Luther himself later claimed that they realized that stabilization and the Rentenmark brought them more gains than losses.[18]

The price was worth it: even though the new Rentenmark notes continued to be printed, thus creating the possibility that they might quickly lose value as the number of notes in circulation increased, their value remained the same because confidence was returning. On 12 December 1923, *Vorwärts* announced to its readers that the 'time of the incredible, unbelievable price increases is over'. This was the 'miracle of the Rentenmark'. In 1924, this was followed by the introduction of the Reichsmark. Its arrival brought the era of currency turmoil to an end. Even before that, for some, the speed with which stability was restored brought its own sense of crisis: the sudden end to hyperinflation in the winter of 1923–4 was one of its most remarkable achievements. Almost as quickly as prices had begun accelerating out of control, the clock went back to ticking normally.[19]

The first steps of the German economic recovery were taken in a changed situation in international relations. The peak of the crisis in Germany in October and November 1923 coincided with a new alignment in London, Paris and Washington. This came down to Poincaré in part. He was the right man to lead France when it was a question of needing a stubborn ruler who would refuse to back down until Germany abandoned its policy of passive resistance. But once Stresemann's coalition gave him what he wanted, he had the wrong personality and decision-making capacity for what followed. He didn't have a plan for when Germany's government ended passive resistance. While he remained uncertain about what to do next, others moved faster and their decisions boxed him into a position from which the internationally isolated French prime minister, who was under increasing pressure at home, could not escape.[20]

Events in Britain were particularly important. As we have seen, for most of 1923 its policies were riddled with division and uncertainty. But in October and November, the situation in London changed in Germany's favour. The British position was no longer simply to oppose France's support for separatism. London now wanted an overall settlement of the entire 'German question'. On 5 October, the foreign secretary, Lord Curzon, gave another speech that was critical of French policy and infuriated Poincaré. But this time Curzon and his prime minister, Stanley Baldwin, spoke from the same page. The British foresaw two ways of reaching such a settlement: either an international conference involving all of the powers, or for the powers to agree on the creation of non-political committees of experts tasked with making new recommendations. British policy had moved towards supporting the creation of committees, and in the key weeks in October and November, Britain pressured France to accept one or both of its proposals; it knew that it was difficult for Poincaré to refuse both.[21]

London's renewed interest in a solution came in parallel to the return of American leadership. On 2 August 1923, the US president, Warren G. Harding, died. His place was taken by Calvin Coolidge, a Republican politician who first came to national attention for his role in suppressing strikes in Boston in 1919. In the weeks following his appointment, Europe appeared far from the agenda in

Washington. But once the new president was up and running in office, the US government began to re-examine its European policies. The end of passive resistance mattered in the United States too. For the first time since the occupation had begun, there was a clear shift in American public opinion in favour of Germany. To American observers, the news that passive resistance was over made it look like Germany had waved a white flag, while Poincaré decided to continue firing at them. Lloyd George also helped in this. In October, the former prime minister was touring America, giving speeches about his political career. When he spoke critically of France's Ruhr policy, the voice of Britain's wartime leader carried weight.

On 9 October, President Coolidge made an important speech in which he reasserted the United States' commitment to the December 1922 New Haven declaration, in which the US government announced its willingness to support the formation of an international committee of experts to examine the reparations question. In 1922, France had been sufficiently powerful for Poincaré to be able to ignore the declaration and to choose military occupation of the Ruhr. A year later, he was in a far weaker position. Both the British and the Americans now stepped up the pressure on the French prime minister. This time Poincaré was unable to hold out. At the end of October, he agreed in principle to the establishment of an international committee of experts. Most historians accept the argument of Marc Trachtenberg, who suggests that this about-face was really caused by Poincaré's uncertainty as to what he should do next. Despite some attempts to restore the direction of travel in France's favour – such as the French initiative of 13 November, which proposed that the reparations commission undertake a limited investigation into Germany's ability to pay – his government never recovered the initiative. Poincaré had wasted his victory.[22]

British domestic politics also helped Germany. On 25 October, Baldwin announced that he wanted to move towards a protectionist policy in international trade. To obtain public support for such a move, he called a general election for 6 December 1923. With

British politics focused on the vote, France's most effective supporters in London were unable to mobilize like-minded French loyalists against the emerging pro-German policies. The British delegate, John Bradbury, played a decisive role on the reparations commission, working behind the scenes to prepare the ground for a policy of creating two committees of investigation with wide terms of reference (France wanted them to be narrow). Under pressure from both Britain and the United States, Poincaré conceded that France would support their creation. There would be no international conference until they had completed their work. On 11 December 1923, after just over a month of exchanges across the Atlantic, Coolidge confirmed the participation of US experts in the new committees. They started their work in Paris in January 1924.[23]

The committees were known by the names of their chairpersons. British banker Reginald McKenna's committee had the job of reporting on what role German financial assets held outside Germany could play in future reparations payments. His committee was partially created to appease the French. Its existence made it look like there was an intention to go after Germany, tracing its every last possession anywhere in the world and forcing the Germans to sell it and send the proceeds back to Germany so they could contribute to the reparations effort. But in reality, behind the scenes, it was expected that its report would be inconclusive. The committee that really mattered was chaired by American banker Charles Dawes, a known Francophile from Chicago. Together with the other committee members, Owen Young, the chairman of both General Electric and the Radio Corporation of America, and Henry M. Robinson, a Californian banker and presidential advisor, Dawes would have a decisive impact on Germany's future.[24]

On 14 April 1924, when both committees submitted their reports, Dawes proposed a five-year reparations settlement financed by an American loan to Germany and a reduction of Germany's debt. Thereafter, the plan would be renegotiated. Under the Dawes plan, Germany would pay little for the first two years, before increasing its payments in the following years. But even with the increased amounts in the third, fourth and fifth years, the demands on Germany were modest. Crucially, the Dawes plan argued that reparations could only be paid once German economic unity was re-established. The plan ruled out any future French railway in the west (the Régie was effectively killed), as well as the imposition of separate taxes or customs duties or French participation in the Ruhr's industry. It was the most favourable offer that Germany had received since the clash over reparations had begun. With the American money flowing into Germany, the Weimar Republic could meet the demands of the Dawes plan almost in full.[25]

The Dawes plan was the mechanism on which the Weimar Republic's years of stabilization were based – the period of stability from 1924 until late 1929. In Washington, policy-makers felt that they had both promoted American interests and helped to depoliticize the reparations question. It seemed as if everyone had finally found the solutions they needed. At the time of its creation, the Dawes plan was not intended to set up a permanent flow of American finance into Germany. But no one was thinking about what might happen if an American crisis led to a sudden reversal of the direction of flow of American capital, as happened following the Wall Street Crash in October 1929, which led to the devastation of the German economy in 1930 during the Great Depression.[26]

By the summer of 1924, France was in no position to oppose the plan. As that year began, it had been France's turn to suffer a financial crisis. There was panic on the French stock exchange, and the value of the franc began to collapse. In response Poincaré tried to introduce new tax legislation. In the spring French state intervention in the market managed to reverse the fall in the value of the franc, but Poincaré's days were numbered. To help support the value of the franc, he had to accept a $100-million loan from the Americans, which left him with little room to reject the US-backed Dawes plan and opened him up to intense criticism from the French left, who lambasted his management of the country's finances. Nevertheless, he still tried to oppose Dawes. After the publication of the plan, he argued that Dawes and McKenna had been tasked with writing economic and not military reports and that they had no business stating that the military occupation of the Ruhr should end. The British were enraged.[27]

But Poincaré's ability to fight back against the new consensus in favour of stability was soon gone. On 11 May 1924, the French left was victorious in France's national elections and Poincaré lost the position of prime minister. He was replaced by Édouard Herriot, who was an open admirer of German culture. Herriot had written a biography of the German philosopher Immanuel Kant and he referred to him as well as Beethoven in his maiden speech. The British ambassador in Paris called him 'the exact opposite of Poincaré'.[28]

Herriot's goal was to withdraw French forces from the Ruhr as quickly as possible. He secretly promised the British that if the Germans agreed to the Dawes plan, France would immediately begin to withdraw soldiers from parts of the occupied region and the final withdrawal would take place one year after the ratification of the Dawes plan. Once the Reichstag approved the agreement on 29 August 1924, it was ratified in London the following day. On 6 September 1924, hundreds of thousands of Germans who had been expelled from the Ruhr were permitted to return. Three days later, on 9 September, the customs frontier between the occupied Ruhr and the rest of Germany was lifted and freedom of movement across the border was restored. On 13 September, expelled civil servants returned to work and, on 16 November, the unity of the German railway network in the west was restored. The last French soldiers left Düsseldorf without ceremony on 25 August 1925.[29]

Long before that, it had become obvious how little France had gained from the occupation of the Ruhr. In 1923, it received 263 million francs' worth of reparations. The previous year the figure had been 11.5 billion francs. The occupation's major achievement was not what Poincaré had intended: in failing, he had opened the door for his successors to pursue the politics of co-operation with Germany. Stresemann's close relationship with French foreign minister Aristide Briand, one of the forces for European optimism in the mid-1920s, was based on their shared rejection of Poincaré's politics. In 1926, Briand and Stresemann were joint recipients of the Nobel Peace Prize. Their key achievements included the 1925 Locarno Pact, which recognized Germany's western borders as permanent and in which both countries made a legal commitment never to return to war with each other.[30]

The Dawes plan, the Locarno Pact, Stresemann's excellent relationship with Briand and the domestic progress of the mid-1920s in Weimar Germany, when the republic left the years of its turbulent beginnings behind it: these are among the reasons why many historians of international relations argue that the Versailles Treaty was not responsible for the rise of Nazism and the destruction of the Weimar Republic. Instead, they argue that the 'Peacemakers' who gathered in Paris in 1919, to use the term adopted by historian Margaret MacMillan, a great-grandchild of David Lloyd George, made the best of the difficult circumstances they faced, creating a 'living document' that offered the potential for a successful revision in Germany's favour, as occurred after 1923.[31]

Their argument is not entirely wrong: when accountants add up what Germany actually paid before the Allied demands for reparations were abandoned altogether in 1932, the sums were well within the German economy's capacity to pay. The improvement in Franco-German relations under Stresemann and Briand in the mid-1920s was also real. Had it lasted, it could have become the foundation for a new era of economic and political co-operation in western Europe. The Versailles Treaty also did not cause Germans to vote for Hitler and choose extreme nationalism over internationalism and European co-operation. But what historians' defence of the Versailles Treaty fails to acknowledge sufficiently is that just as the 'living document' could move in Germany's favour, it could also move in the other direction. In 1923, Poincaré had tried to ensure that it did precisely that. His goal was to use France's superior military strength to exploit and control the economic resources of Europe's largest economy and most modern democracy. The idea that France was in the Ruhr merely to obtain reparations was obviously untrue. The 1923 crisis could have ended with the dismemberment of Germany. It was only in the final weeks of that year, after the cost of the international politics of punishment had revealed itself to be too high for all sides to pay, that there was sufficient support for a new politics of reconciliation. The Dawes plan could have come into being at the end of 1922, but it didn't because too many decision-makers were opposed to reconciliation at that point. This is why it is historically right to argue that throughout 1923 Germany was the victim of French aggression: once the invasion of the Ruhr began, German decision-makers faced a choice between conceding to Poincaré's demands and facing the potential dismemberment of the German state, and resisting the occupation through largely peaceful means. Both options came at the cost of major internal turbulence.

Of course, not all Germans were victims. Key figures in business, the Reichsbank and politics made poor policy decisions that worsened the situation for Germany. Others wanted to use the crisis to destroy the republic. But overall, the millions living in the Ruhr were victims. The women and girls who endured the occupational forces' sexual violence were victims. The many more who lived in fear that they would suffer under the occupation forces were victims. The families who lost their savings and incomes were victims. The children who starved were victims. Politically, Germany's republicans and democrats were also Poincaré's victims. Before the French and Belgian invasion, as the reaction to Rathenau's murder shows, they were slowly starting to fight back against the right-wing assaults and to give the republic greater legitimacy. But the events of 1923 left them in the same fight with one hand tied behind their backs: after all, how can democratic leaders build the legitimacy of a political system when a foreign power occupies its key industrial region and openly threatens its existence as a unified state, forcing hundreds of thousands of people to leave the Ruhr and setting in train the destruction of the currency and the impoverishment of hundreds of thousands more?

Throughout the 1923 crisis, this question mattered little to Poincaré. He wanted to punish Germany and he understood German complaints as fake claims of victimhood. Throughout the crisis year, he undoubtedly played the key role in the international system's abandonment of Weimar democracy. But the German democrats' plight was also the result of an indifferent America, the overambitious choices of Lloyd George, a pro-France Bonar Law and a wavering – but for a long time pro-France – Stanley Baldwin. All of them worked within the structures of international politics created in 1919 at the Paris Peace Conference, which led to a world of what the historian Michael Geyer has called 'blocked transnationalism' – a political moment when too many key decision-makers failed to recognize that the rulers of other states had legitimate grievances, when the linkages between developments in one state and developments in another were not fully understood or did not receive the attention they deserved. The events of 1923 and their legacies made the dangers of 'blocked transnationalism' obvious.[32]

The racist *völkisch* right had been defeated in 1923, but it was not destroyed. In 1926, Hans Grimm published the bestselling novel *Volk ohne Raum*, helping to popularize the idea that, as the title says, the Germans were 'a people without space'. Even though the Nazis remained a marginal force until they won electorally in Baden in 1929, they had learnt from the putsch. Hitler understood that he would never be able to take power without the support of the Reichswehr and the forces of the state. His strategy changed. After 1923, he knew that electoral successes were his best means of defeating his enemy. The calamity of the putsch mattered little to the people who later voted for the Nazis. All of this does not mean that there was a single pathway from the start of the republic to its end. But it does remind us that the republic's end did not occur in a historical vacuum either. The forces that destroyed it were able to mobilize ideas and political goals that had been simmering throughout its existence. In 1923, the democrats could defeat them; in 1933, they could not.

Paul von Hindenburg played a key role in that later crisis. In stark contrast to Friedrich Ebert, who used the emergency powers available to the president of the republic to help to save Weimar democracy in 1923, Hindenburg used the same powers to destroy it a decade later. The former field marshal was elected president of Weimar Germany following Ebert's untimely death in 1925. In the presidential election, which took place over two rounds, Hindenburg defeated Wilhelm Marx, the man who ended 1923 as chancellor of Germany, warning the Germans that they had never before been so poor. It was a close result: Hindenburg obtained 48.3 per cent of the vote and Marx 45.3 per cent. Would Hindenburg have won without the Ruhr crisis? That question is, of course, impossible to answer fully. But we can say with certainty that the crisis hindered the development of pro-democratic structures in Weimar Germany and that the ensuing economic collapse left many people disillusioned with the republic's achievements in the mid-1920s. It certainly helped Hindenburg. He won the election in 1925 thanks to the backing of the same coalition of voters that would later support the Nazis. For many of them, the solution to all of the republic's problems was to vote for a great man from Germany's past, a mythical general who appeared to represent a better time, when Germany was both respected and feared as an international military power. In 1925, they thought that Hindenburg was the man to restore Germany to greatness. In ever greater numbers from 1930 onwards, they thought that that man was Hitler.[33]

It is also undeniable that the 1923 crisis sapped pro-republican forces of some of their strength, and left too many workers, civil servants and ordinary people on the losing side of history: it left them angry about lost jobs and wages and about national humiliation. The currency's collapse left too many people feeling that they had suffered while others thrived. As Conan Fischer has argued, in the wake of the pain caused by the policy of passive resistance, 'the emotional connection between people and the new Republican order was as good as dead and buried'.[34]

But just as it is important to remember the negative legacy of 1923, we should not overestimate it. In 1923, the German currency died, but German democracy did not. At the end of the crisis year, German democrats stood tall. All four changes of federal government during 1923 had been a result of the interventions of the Reichstag. The Reichstag's power is a reflection that, while Weimar democracy was contested, it did have the strength to push back. Cuno was removed by a parliamentary vote. His rule was not something that foreshadowed the final three cabinets of the Weimar Republic which governed thanks to Hindenburg's presidial rule, as leading German historian Heinrich August Winkler has often suggested. It was instead an example of a democracy turning to a technocratic government in a time of economic crisis. The emergency enabling laws in 1923 were not forced upon the parliament – its members played crucial roles in determining their powers and in using this emergency measure as a means to protect the political order in a time of crisis, as the constitution intended. Seeckt's conspiratorial ambitions might provide ammunition to those who argue that the Reichswehr remained a 'state within a state', but when the time came for him to realize his dictatorial goals, he withdrew in the face of Ebert and Stresemann's democratic power. Even though Stresemann himself was not a committed democrat prior to the creation of the republic, his 1923 speeches made it clear time and again that both he and the audiences he spoke to appreciated the principles of democracy. The ideas behind the constitution had been part of German political culture for a lot longer than the constitution itself, which only came into being in August 1919. Those ideas included separation of powers, party formation, a free press, institutional memory of democratic traditions and decades of voting.

This is the most disturbing lesson of this book. Older accounts of the history of Weimar Germany have often portrayed it as a democracy without democrats, a place where the ideas and tradition of democracy were so weak that it was inevitable that it would succumb to some form of authoritarianism. Yet the more we learn about Weimar democracy, the more we realize that this view is misconceived.

The Weimar Republic was a young republic. But democratic ideas had been developing in Germany since the middle of the nineteenth century. There was more to the German Empire than militarism and the Kaiser. There was a strong voting culture and a strong movement to secure the democratic rights of German citizens. The ideal of democracy was not accepted by everyone, and many rejected it entirely, but it was part of the political culture nonetheless. Germany in the 1920s, in other words, had a long and strong tradition of democracy that both brought the republic into existence in 1918–19 and saved it in 1923. Of those two achievements, the democrats' victory at the end of 1923 was arguably their most important. In 1918–19, the old order's collapse made its replacement with a democratic system almost inevitable. When we think about the tradition of democracy and the failure of Weimar democracy, we realize that the democratic culture that was strong enough to win in 1923 was not strong enough to survive in 1933. Between those two points in time, its norms and processes were gradually eroded. It was that gradual erosion in the years before Hitler's appointment as chancellor on 30 January 1933 that facilitated the speed with which the Nazi dictatorship was created after that date.[35]

Today, the politics of the beer halls are still with us. The conventions and rallies of populist politicians and the digital beer halls of the present all bear some resemblance to Munich's beer halls in 1923. Just as the minorities that suffered at the hands of those radicalized by demagogues in 1923 deserved better protection by the state, today's minorities are deserving of protection from the digital warriors who inspire others to carry out their deeds now. When we think about Weimar's crisis year, it would be a political mistake if the crucial historical lesson went unheard: the politics of hatred can only function when violent and discriminatory speech acts go unpunished. Ultimately, politics in a democracy can only function when the system itself is respected and honoured.

Epilogue: 1933 and After

On the tenth anniversary of the Munich putsch, Hitler returned to the Bavarian capital to pay tribute to those who had died following him. That day, swastika flags were all but unavoidable in central Munich. The route that he had taken a decade earlier was lined now with marchers, large red swastika banners were draped from the streetlamps along the way and red Nazi banners stretched across the thoroughfares. At the Feldherrnhalle, there was a specially constructed black altar with a green memorial wreath, covered with laurel wreaths by members of the SS, SA and the Stahlhelm, the anti-republican First World War veterans' organization. In front of the altar, there were no fewer than 195 Nazi military flags.[1]

At about 12.30, the crowds gathered at the Odeonsplatz began to hear cheering from the direction of the Residenzstrasse, where participants had marched ten years earlier. Once again, Hitler led the procession, wearing a brown shirt as he had done in 1923. Göring and Kriebel walked beside him. When he reached the spot where Scheubner-Richter was shot and killed, Hitler stopped. A black flag at half-mast fluttered above him. The sound of trumpets greeted his pause, followed by a volley of artillery fire. Then there was silence. Everyone stood still as Hitler walked on his own to the eastern side of the Feldherrnhalle. He examined a newly created memorial covered with a black cloth. He then stood and saluted the 'old fighters' who marched past him. By 1933, the number of people who claimed to have been there alongside Hitler in 1923 had grown so large that it required a full thirty minutes for this part of the parade to cross the Odeonsplatz.

Since his trial in 1924, Hitler had carefully crafted a cult of the fallen that celebrated the sacrifice of those who died for his

movement on 9 November 1923. He dedicated his autobiograph-
ical 1924 manifesto *Mein Kampf* (*My Struggle*) to them. In his first
speech following his release from Landsberg prison in December
1924, he spoke of their sacrifice, as he promised his followers that
the 'struggle starts once again'. For the remainder of the Weimar
Republic, he and his comrades marked the anniversary of their
deaths. A part of their cult of the fallen involved the use of a relic:
the Blood Flag. Nazi legend had it that as one of the flag-bearers
fell to the ground after being shot on 9 November 1923, the swastika flag flying above him fell across his body, covering him and
soaking up his blood and the blood of the other fallen. Another
putschist is supposed to have rescued that flag and kept it safe. As
the Nazi movement grew in size, the Blood Flag became a crucial
icon. During the 1934 Nuremberg party rally, tens of thousands
watched it brought ceremoniously into contact with the movement's
other flags, so that every party member could march behind a
banner that had touched the Blood Flag which supposedly contained
the blood of the first 'martyrs' of the movement. The film director
Leni Riefenstahl captured the scene spectacularly in the only official film made about Hitler during the Third Reich, *Triumph of the
Will* (1935), which brought these scenes to an even larger audience.
For those who believed in this ceremony, it was incredibly powerful.

On 9 November 1933, after minister president Siebert awarded
him honorary citizenship of Bavaria, Hitler spoke about the meaning
of the Nazis' November dead. Newspapers record that he told the
assembled audience:

> Because the revolution of 1918 broke the laws of that time, they
> could not expect that we would accept their rules as laws. At that
> time, as men and political soldiers we declared war on them,
> determined to bring down the people responsible for November
> 1918, determined to bring them to justice one way or another.
> That's how we marched in November 1923, full of the belief
> that we could succeed in defeating those guilty of November
> 1918, in destroying the men who were guilty for the unspeakable
> suffering of our fatherland. At that time, fate decided otherwise.

A decade later, Hitler announced that the division that had once pitted the Nazis against the Reichswehr and Landespolizei no longer existed. On 9 November 1923, he claimed, they had all been 'tools of a higher power'. 'If our dead were to return to life today,' Hitler promised in 1933, 'they would shed tears of joy that the German army and the reawakened German people have once again become one.' As the cloth that covered the memorial fell, the audience sang the 'Horst Wessel Song', the Nazi Party's anthem celebrating a member of the SA who had died fighting the Communists in Berlin in 1930.[2]

The front of the memorial consisted of a large concrete block symbolizing a religious altar. Instead of a cross, above the altar there was a bronze swastika beneath a bronze Imperial Eagle. The text on the concrete block stated that the men who had lost their lives did so 'in the loyal belief that their race would one day rise again'. It faced directly onto the site where the gunshots were fired on 9 November 1923. The back of the monument carried the words 'And you were nevertheless victorious'. For the remainder of the Third Reich, two SS men stood guard in front of the memorial and anyone passing it was expected to raise their right arm and salute it.[3]

By the time of the twelfth anniversary of the putsch in 1935, Hitler was the undisputed Führer. The Reichswehr had accepted their new commander and his ambitious plans to restore Germany to greatness. Hitler's rivals within his own party had been done away with in the summer of 1934, during the so-called 'Night of the Long Knives', when he had his internal party rivals executed, including Röhm, one of the most important veterans of the putsch, and other opponents such as Kahr, who was murdered in Dachau concentration camp. In the aftermath of Röhm's murder in November 1934, the celebrations of the anniversary of the 1923 putsch were subdued. The re-enactment of the march from the Bürgerbräukeller to the Feldherrnhalle was shorter than it had been the previous year and Hitler did not join in.[4]

A year later, in 1935, the organizers of the commemoration restored the event to the central position it had held in Nazi mythology in

1933. The party's political headquarters had now moved from Munich to Berlin, but they wanted to emphasize the Bavarian capital's central role in the historic origins of Nazism. The first stage of their re-enactment began on the evening of 8 November, when the Bürgerbräukeller was teeming with bureaucrats and state officials, as well as representatives of the Wehrmacht and the families of the fallen. At 8.30 p.m., Hitler re-enacted his entry. Unlike twelve years before, when he had had to force his way through the crowd to reach the stage, this time Hitler shook hands as he made his way through the hall. Göring spoke first. He was followed by the Führer, whose speech was constantly interrupted by cheering. After he finished, the crowd sang the 'Horst Wessel Song' and the German national anthem. Outside in the streets there were more crowds, who greeted Hitler with cheers of 'Heil' wherever he went.[5]

The 1935 celebrations instrumentalized the bodies of the martyrs. At midday on 8 November, at three separate graveyards in Munich, the graves of the fifteen Nazi martyrs, plus that of the waiter Karl Kulm, were dug open. The family members of the dead watched as their relatives were exhumed and their bodies placed in new coffins – plain metal coffins – which were decorated by a dark red pall with a swastika in its centre. At the bottom of the swastika the name of each of the individual 'fallen' was visible in gold letters. It is most likely that the organizers of the event included Kulm among the exhumations because they wanted sixteen coffins so that there would be an even number on either side of their resting place in the specially constructed Temple of Honour.

That evening three separate processions brought the coffins into Munich in carriages pulled by six horses and accompanied by a guard of honour. On both sides of each procession, ten metres apart, SA men carried torches to light the way. The torches were the only source of light – the streetlights were turned off and public transport did not run for the duration of the ceremony. The sound of trumpets rang out to announce that the procession was approaching. As the coffins passed by, all of those present in the crowds raised their hands to give the Hitler salute. At 10 p.m., the three processions met in the Ludwigstrasse. The coffins were then taken together through the Victory Gate, a 21-metre-high three-arch memorial gate which was built in the 1840s to honour Bavarian soldiers returning from war.

The front of the procession reached the Feldherrnhalle at midnight. The Odeonsplatz and Feldherrnhalle were illuminated by more torches. As each coffin was carried into the hall, a new torch was lit. They were to remain there for the night. The entire display was watched by tens of thousands, including members of the Hitler Youth and League of German Girls. When Hitler arrived at the Feldherrnhalle, a spotlight lit up his car as it passed through the Victory Gate, whence it made its way through the cheering crowds. At the Feldherrnhalle, Hitler paused in front of each of the coffins, raising his arm individually to give the 'German greeting' to each of them. When he left the building, there was silence. Members of the SS and Hitler Youth took up their places as the guard of honour for the rest of the night. After Hitler and Rudolf Hess left the square, all of those who had marched behind the coffins paraded past them and the front of the Feldherrnhalle was lit up by spotlights.

The next day around noon, the 'old fighters', led by three men carrying the Blood Flag, once again set out from in front of the Bürgerbräukeller to retrace the steps they had taken on 9 November 1923. Hitler marched with them, in the middle at the front, as he had done in 1923. When Hitler reached the Feldherrnhalle, the coffins were brought out to join the procession as it continued to the Königsplatz, where a Temple of Honour had been specially built as their final resting place. At the Königsplatz, Munich's Gauleiter Wagner read the names of the dead, while the crowd answered, 'The risen one is here [*Hier der Wiedererstandenen*].' Following a further rendition of the German national anthem, Hitler went into the temple, where he paid his respects to each of the coffins individually. Until they were removed by the Americans in 1945, they would remain visible across the square, a permanent Nazi monument to the origins of Hitler's movement. Later, in the courtyard of the Regional Military Command, Himmler unveiled a memorial plaque for Casella and Faust, the two putschists shot dead in the building, which read: 'Through your blood Germany lives.'[6]

In 1935, tens of thousands of people participated in these events. The pro-Nazi press described them in glowing terms, arguing that what Munich had just experienced was like the burial of heroes in Valhalla. Another reporter claimed that the people watching were 'extremely serious and respectful'. The party's enthusiasm for its own spectacle should not be overestimated, however. The event was watched in secret by an observer for the Social Democratic Party, and a report was sent to the exiled party leadership in Prague. Had its author been discovered, they would have paid for their opposition with a period in a concentration camp, at the very least.[7]

The Social Democrats' observer recorded that, among the people of Munich in 1935, a wide range of opinions about the spectacle could be heard. According to the secret report, the most common response was: 'We have to let Hitler do that: he honours his dead, but the cost and effort are a little bit too much.' At the same time, public interest in the spectacle should not be underestimated or ignored either. The same observer noted depressingly:

The 9th of November was theatre the likes of which Munich has never seen. It must be admitted that the population participated in the events. For many people it was surely only curiosity that led them to attend. But the incredible power of the theatrics did not lack for effect. For the event on the evening of 8 November people were already standing in lines at midday, just to be able to watch a torchlit parade pass by in the distance. The masses were standing deep into the side streets, and it seemed like all of Munich was on its feet until well after midnight. It is not true when people say that the people did not participate in this piece of theatre. The participation is powerful. Everyone is amazed by the splendour unfolded by the Nazi Party.[8]

It wasn't just people in Munich who participated in the re-enactment of the putsch. With membership of the Nazi Party reaching five million by 1939, a huge number of Germans now became part of the official version of the party's history. Since the start of the Third Reich on 30 January 1933, there had been a never-ending wave of regime propaganda that celebrated the putsch. Re-enactments of the gunfire at the Feldherrnhalle took place in theatres across Germany. During the night of 8–9 November 1938, the speed of the pogrom was only possible because it occurred on the anniversary of the putsch, when an order from the party leadership in Munich immediately transformed a night of singing and drinking into a night of violence across the German Reich. Hundreds of synagogues were burned down. An unknown number of Jews were killed and tens of thousands arrested.

In Munich, the annual commemorative ritual continued until 1943. From that point on it was no longer possible for the Nazis and their supporters to gather on the Königsplatz because the square had been covered with camouflage in a vain effort to prevent Allied bombers from using it to identify their location above the city. When American forces entered Munich in 1945, they destroyed the Temple of Honour and reburied the coffins in the graveyards from which the bodies had been taken in November 1935.

The glorification of the putsch and its importance to the Third Reich are at the heart of the historical paradox of the Nazis' first attempt to seize power. When it happened, the putsch was so brief that its historical echo quickly went silent. After months of threatening the state with violent rhetoric, in November 1923, when his 'now or never' moment came, Hitler's attempt to seize power lasted around only twenty hours before ending in defeat at the hands of the Bavarian Landespolizei. At most, the putschists controlled a small number of buildings during those hours, and after their defeat there were those who celebrated the loss publicly. Just a few days after the putsch one Bavarian supporter of democracy, a sixteen-year-old girl, proudly walked through public spaces with a black, red and gold ribbon – the colours of the flag of the Weimar Republic, an important symbol of democracy – pinned to her chest.[9]

Her celebration is a reminder that there was no direct line from Hitler's defeat in 1923 to his victory a decade later. The speed with which German supporters of democracy forgot the putsch is a reminder that it was only after 1933 that the putsch's historical significance resounded inescapably through German politics, and only after the horrors of Nazism fully revealed themselves between 1939 and 1945 did it become a major event in the history of the European continent: a moment of fate for tens of millions of people who would lose their lives because of decisions taken by the putsch's leader in the following two decades. But when it happened during the year 1923, the putsch was not as important as the French occupation of the Ruhr and the ensuing economic collapse.

Photographs taken in Munich on 8 and 9 November 1923 are strongly revealing of that contrast. For Germans alive in 1923, the photographs of the putschists are images of anonymous young men, armed and determined to destroy Weimar democracy. It was only later that the anonymous faces became recognizable. In one photograph, there is a young, skinny man wearing rimmed spectacles. It is Heinrich Himmler, the future head of the SS and the architect of the Holocaust, one of the vilest humans to have ever existed. In another image, a thirty-year-old provincial journalist from the city of Nuremberg is giving a speech in central Munich at the Marienplatz. It is Julius Streicher, one of Nazi Germany's most important propagandists, a man whose success in spreading racist ideas through German society in the 1930s and 1940s helped to create the conditions for genocide.

In 1946, Streicher was one of ten men sentenced to death at the first of the Nuremberg trials. Six of the other Nazis who received the same sentence were veterans of the putsch. In November 1923, Hermann Göring marched alongside Hitler at the front of the procession. On 15 October 1946, Göring committed suicide, just hours before he was due to hang. The other veterans of the putsch who were sentenced to death were hanged later that night. The youngest of them in 1923 was the twenty-three-year-old Hans Frank, later known as the 'Butcher of Poland' for the crimes he committed during the Second World War, when in charge of the territory the Nazis called the General Government, which covered part of the former state of Poland. The concentration and death camp at Auschwitz, where well over one million people were murdered, was in his territory. Alfred Rosenberg, who hanged alongside him in 1946, was thirty years old during the 1923 putsch. Like Streicher, Rosenberg dedicated his life to spreading virulent antisemitism.

Two of those hanged in 1946 were not among the marchers on the morning of 9 November 1923. By the time they started marching, forty-six-year-old Wilhelm Frick was already under arrest. He had been sent to Munich's police headquarters during the night, where he was tasked with subverting the police response to the putsch. Had he been successful, he would have been appointed Munich's new police president. In 1933, Frick joined Göring as one of the two Nazi ministers in Hitler's first cabinet. During the first few months of the Third Reich, he played a key role in the establishment of the Nazi state, overseeing the dismissal of Jewish civil servants. Fritz Saukel was the only veteran of the 1923 putsch to be executed at Nuremberg who was not actually present in Munich on 8–9 November as he had been arrested on his way to the city. In 1946, he was hanged at Nuremberg for his role as organizer of the Nazis' forced labour programme.

It is because we know of the horrors of the regime that Hitler later created that the putsch overshadows all of the other political events to have taken place in the early Weimar Republic. It is the single event that ordinary people across the world are likely to have heard of in German political history before 1933. As we saw earlier, most famously, the Nobel Prize-winning German author Thomas Mann told an audience at Princeton University in 1942 (the year when the majority of the Holocaust's victims were murdered) that there was a straight line from the madness of 1923 to the madness of Nazism. Mann had good reason for doing so: he wanted to explain what had gone wrong in German history and he was determined to do everything he could to ensure that democracy would win.

But Mann's words from the 1940s overlook that just weeks after the putsch he had seen things differently. At Christmas 1923, he was part of an international coalition of artists who argued that they could lead Europe to a unified peace. By the time their words appeared in print, many in Germany had already forgotten Hitler. In the putsch's aftermath, German supporters of democracy were more preoccupied with Bavaria's conservative political establishment for failing to deal with him sooner than they were with Hitler. They had lived through a year of disruption and were beginning to see a path to stability on the other side.

Mann's earlier optimism is a reminder that in their moment of victory the supporters of Weimar democracy squandered their chance to destroy Nazism once and for all. The failure to insist on the punishment of the putschists according to the laws created for the protection of the republic was a terrible error. If anything, in their moment of victory democracy's supporters were too complacent. That complacency did not just allow the putschists to avoid punishment, it helped them secure a symbolic victory. They might not have seized power on 9 November 1923, but they had terrorized the state and their stories about the event became central to their political movement for the remainder of its existence.

Instead of removing the anti-democratic thread from the tapestry of modern German history, the victors of the 1923 crisis left it hanging on. Within a decade they became impotent when the forces they had defeated in 1923 returned to destroy them and the democracy that they cherished so dearly. The speed of democracy's unravelling in 1933 is a reminder that, when its norms are not supported and defended, with force if necessary, then democracy itself can disappear.

Acknowledgements

I am a historian of violent conflict in modern Europe. The starting point for my interest in this subject was my own childhood: I grew up in Dublin in the 1980s and '90s, a time and place in which news of political violence was a constant presence. Today I recognize that that world was defined by a mental border which allowed us to know that while we were close to the terrible violence of the Northern Ireland conflict, it was still distant from us. 'The North', where most of the killing took place, was a far-away place – a place that many people from 'The South' avoided. It was only when we travelled there to visit friends or family that we faced up to its proximity. Today, I have a distinct memory of crossing the 'Irish border', when I was just nine years old, in 1989. From the back seat, I watched as a British soldier instructed my father to get out of the family car and open the boot. As he always did, my father was wearing a shirt and tie – I would later learn that this was unusual, as was the fact that I never once heard my father swear. While my gentleman father followed the soldier's instructions, I thought that the soldier was on his own until I realized that a group of them were hiding in the bushes, trailing our car with their guns. This was not unusual. It remains a standard practice at military checkpoints.

Another memory exists alongside this one. In 1993 my mother and aunt brought me to O'Connell Street in the centre of Dublin to join in a demonstration condemning the violence of the IRA, the illegal organization responsible for more fatal violence in the Northern Ireland conflict than any other. That demonstration took place shortly after the IRA atrocity in the English town of

Warrington, where members of the IRA planted bombs in bins in a shopping district in order to target civilians. My memory of this event is vivid because one of the victims of the attack, Tim Parry, was just twelve years old, the same age as me. And like me, he also enjoyed football. The other victim, Johnathan Ball, was only three.

Less than a decade later, as an eighteen-year-old first-year student of history, I heard Tim Parry's father, Colin, speak bravely and eloquently about the loss of his son at a debate at Trinity College Dublin where everyone in the room knew that some of the other speakers had been a part of the organization that killed his son. By that time, I was old enough to know that I wanted to become a historian of violent conflict. I wanted to understand what makes people fight. But I also knew that I could not study the conflicts connected to the island where I had grown up. I needed to get away from familiar and repetitive conversations about the rights and wrongs of the violence of Ireland's first or second 'Troubles'. I knew then that I wanted to be an outsider historian: a historian who specializes in the study of a country other than that of their birth or upbringing. Germany was the obvious choice: the heart of the twentieth century's age of extremes.

That was the starting point for the journey that has led me to research and finish writing this book. It began in Trinity College Dublin, before continuing at the universities of Tübingen, Cambridge and the European University Institute in Florence. To all the academics and friends at those institutions who helped with my training and intellectual development as a historian, I offer my heartfelt thanks. The journey is too long for me to thank the many scholars individually, but it would be wrong not to offer a sincere word of admiration for the work of John Horne and Alan Kramer, two Dublin-based historians who transformed the study of European history on the island of Ireland. Alongside John and Alan, I would also like to thank my elder sister, the historian Heather Jones, for her support and example. It is with good reason that she is known among our common circles as the 'more successful one'. For conversations about the Weimar Republic and advice on developing an academic career, I would like to thank Anthony McElligott, formerly

Chair of History at the University of Limerick. I am also grateful and impressed by the work of my fellow historians more generally – I wish to express my admiration to all scholars of Weimar and the interwar period here in a way that cannot be done through the endnotes alone, and to acknowledge particularly the pioneering work of Conan Fischer and Elspeth O'Riordan. I would like to thank my former colleagues at the Ruhr University in Bochum, Germany, as well as at the Free University in Berlin, where I was fortunate to be a visiting scholar at Sebastian Conrad's Department of Global History.

Today I am proud to be able to call University College Dublin my academic home. Since I was first appointed as a postdoctoral fellow in 2012, I have benefited immensely from UCD's transformation into one of the leading centres for the study of war and political violence, as well as European history more generally. For their conversations, support, example and friendship, I am especially grateful to my colleagues in the School of History. Of them all, it would be wrong of me not to name and thank Robert Gerwarth and William Mulligan. They have both supported this project from its inception right down to reading and commenting on drafts of the final manuscript. Few people can be as fortunate to be able to call upon such distinguished colleagues for advice and encouragement.

In the time that I have worked at UCD, I have also had the privilege of getting to know around thirty so-called early-career researchers, most of whom have been based at the Centre for War Studies. Learning from them and enjoying their comradeship has been a delight, just as it has been a pleasure to see our 'Dublin school' stretch its wings and shape the way people think about the past and present in and beyond Ireland. Humanities research in Ireland is thriving in part thanks to the work of the Irish Research Council – Ireland's agency for funding excellent research in any discipline. Since I held my first award in 2012, I have benefited immensely from the council's support, most crucially in the form of a 2018 Irish Research Council Laureate Starting Grant. I hope this book shows what can be achieved when funding agencies give humanities researchers the time and space to undertake research as we see fit, contrary to the growing tendency to try to strait-jacket us into some one-size-fits-all approach that forgets that there are good reasons why our disciplines have different traditions.

This book exists in both English and German. The English edition provides more background for readers who are coming to the 1923 crisis for the first time. For their help and suggestions on both texts, in Berlin I would like to thank my German-language agent Barbara Wenner, as well as my editor Christian Seeger, and Kristin Rotter and the team at Propyläen and Ullstein books. I would also like to thank Nobert Juraschitz who did so much more than just translate. In London, I am extremely grateful to have Doug Young as an agent. My thanks are also due to Joe Zigmond at Basic Books UK and to Brian Distelberg at Basic Books in the USA. It is a great honour to join such a distinguished list in the United States and to be one of the first contributors to its UK sibling. For their editorial work I am especially grateful to Brandon Proia and Robert Shore. My thanks are also due to Caroline Westmore who oversaw the production of the manuscript with unrelenting attention to detail, support and enthusiasm. My thanks are due to the final proof-readers and fact checker. As always, any errors that remain are my own.

Finally, I am grateful to everyone who reads this book. I began the acknowledgements by referring to how my childhood experiences of violence helped shape my interest in the history of violence. It is therefore appropriate to end it with happier memories from the same time: Dublin is a literary city; its centre filled with bookstores each with their own individual character and charm. Crossing the thresholds of such places as a child was always a special moment, full of the anticipation that today we would come home with new books. Long may the magic of the bookstore continue to exist, and long may we support it instead of choosing the ease of online delivery from an anonymous warehouse.

This book is dedicated to Ulrike. With her in my life, I am no longer an outsider in Germany. Our sons Luke and Ben represent the best of both of our countries.

Picture Credits

Notes

Abbreviations

AA	Auswärtiges Amt (German Foreign Ministry Archive, Berlin)
BArch-Berlin	Bundesarchiv Berlin Lichterfelde (German Federal Archives, Berlin, Lichterfelde)
Bavarian Parliament	Stenographischer Bericht über die Verhandlungen des Bayerischen Landtags Vols 7–9 (Munich, 1922–4) (Stenographic Recordings of the Bavarian Parliament)
German Diary Archive	Deutsches Tagebucharchiv Emmendingen (German Diary Archive, Emmendingen)
JK	Jäckel, Eberhard, with Axel Kuhn (ed.), *Hitler: Sämtliche Aufzeichnungen 1905–1924* (Stuttgart, 1980) (Hitler, Complete Records, 1905–1924)
MAE	Ministère des Affaires Étrangères, Paris (French Foreign Ministry Archive)
Reichstag	Verhandlungen des Reichstages: Stenographische Berichte I. Wahlperiode 1920 (Vols 10–18) (Berlin, 1922–4) (Stenographic Records of the German Reichstag)
RK Stresemann	Akten der Reichskanzlei: Weimarer Republik: Die Kabinette Stresemann I und II, ed. Klaus Dietrich Erdmann and Martin Vogt, Vols 1 and 2, Boppard, 1978 (Cabinet Meeting Records for the Stresemann Governments)

SHD   Service Historique de la Défense, Vincennes
                       (French Military Archives, Paris)
StaF   Staatsarchiv Freiburg (Baden-Württemberg
                       State Archive, Freiburg)

Introduction: Germany 1923 – The Democracy That Did Not Die

1. Thomas Weber, *Becoming Hitler: The Making of a Nazi* (Oxford, 2017), 12.
2. Michael Brenner, *In Hitler's Munich: Jews, the Revolution, and the Rise of Nazism* (Princeton, 2022), 188.
3. Erich Dombrowski, 'New Year's Eve', *Berliner Tageblatt*, Nr 602, 31 December 1923, evening edition.
4. Jonathan Wright, *Gustav Stresemann* (Oxford, 2002), 246–7.
5. Harry Kessler, *In the Twenties: The Diaries of Harry Kessler* (New York, 1971), 7 April 1923, 229.
6. Martin Geyer, *Verkehrte Welt: Revolution, Inflation und Moderne: München 1914–1924* (Göttingen, 1998).
7. Ian Kershaw, *Hitler 1889–1936: Hubris* (London, 1999); Richard Evans, *The Coming of the Third Reich* (London, 2003); Niall Ferguson, 'Constraints and Room for Manoeuvre in the German Inflation of the Early 1920s', *Economic History Review*, 49:4 (1996), 635–66; Gerald D. Feldman, *The Great Disorder: Politics, Economics, and Society in the German Inflation 1914–1924* (New York, 1997); Martin Geyer, *Verkehrte Welt*.

Chapter 1: German Democracy Fights Back

1. Helene Kaiser's statement is from Martin Sabrow, *Der Rathenaumord: Rekonstruktion einer Verschwörung gegen die Republik von Weimar* (Munich, 1994), 88. Prozeller and Fischer's account as witnesses at the trial may also be read in 'Stubenrauch and the Spirit of Potsdam', *Vorwärts*, Nr 479, 10 October 1922, evening edition.
2. StaF 179/4, Nr 93, Bl.65–79, Judgement.
3. Sabrow, *Der Rathenaumord*, 108.
4. Ibid., 86–8.

5. Ibid., 92.

6. Ibid., 89–90.

7. Ibid., 91–2.

8. 'Techow's Uncle Speaks About the Deed', Day 4 of the Trial, *Vorwärts*, Nr 473, 6 October 1922, evening edition.

9. Sabrow, *Der Rathenaumord*, 98.

10. Ibid., 101–3.

11. BArch-Berlin NS26/1236 Akte Kern, Gisela Kern letter, 8 July 1936.

12. 'Helfferich as Provocator', *Vorwärts*, Nr 294, 24 June 1922, morning edition.

13. 'Tumultuous Scenes in the Parliaments: Violence in the Reichstag', *Berliner Tageblatt*, Nr 294, 24 June 1922, evening edition. See also 'Unprecedented Provocation in the Parliaments', *Vossische Zeitung*, Nr 296, 24 June 1922, evening edition.

14. Georg Bernhard, 'Who Will Protect the Republic', *Vossische Zeitung*, Nr 296, 24 June 1922, evening edition; Theodor Wolff, 'Walther Rathenau Murdered', *Berliner Tageblatt*, Nr 294, 24 June 1922, evening edition.

15. Reichstag, Session 234, 24 June 1922, 8035.

16. 'Long Live the Republic!', *Berliner Volks-Zeitung*, Nr 295, 25 June 1922, morning edition; Reichstag, Session 236, 25 June 1922, 8066; Otto Wels, 'Discussion of the Government's Statement', *Vorwärts*, 26 June 1922, special edition.

17. 'Rathenau's Last Journey', *Vorwärts*, Nr 298, 27 June 1922, morning edition; 'Organized Nationalist Assassination', *Bergarbeiter-Zeitung*, Nr 27, 3 July 1922; 'Get Out and Protest!', *Berliner Volks-Zeitung*, Nr 295, 25 June 1922, morning edition; 'The Parades of Demonstrators', *Freiheit*, Nr 256, 26 June 1922.

18. Harry Kessler, *Walther Rathenau: His Life and Work*, trans. W. D. Robson-Scott and Lawrence Hyde (New York, 1930), chapter XI.

19. 'Rathenau's Funeral', *Vorwärts*, 28 June 1922, special edition.

20. 'A Product of Fear', *Vorwärts*, Nr 298, 27 June 1922.

21. 'The Enemy is on the Right', *Vorwärts*, Nr 297, 26 June 1922, evening edition.

22. 'The Spirits Part', *CV-Zeitung*, Nr 10, 13 July 1922.

23. Dr Alfred Weiner, 'Is the Danger Over?', *CV-Zeitung*, Nr 10, 13 July 1922.

24. 'We Accuse! Rathenau, the Victim of German Ethno-nationalist Incitement to Hatred', *CV-Zeitung*, Nr 9, 30 June 1922; 'How They Incited Hatred Against Rathenau', *CV-Zeitung*, Nr 9, 30 June 1922; Dr Alfred Weiner, 'Is the Danger Over?', *CV-Zeitung*, Nr 10, 13 July 1922.
25. StaF F179/4 Nr 6/09, Judgement in the case against Heinrich Tillessen, 1947.

Chapter 2: The Future of French Power

1. On Wirth, see Heinrich Küppers, *Joseph Wirth: Parlamentarier, Minister und Kanzler der Weimarer Republik* (Stuttgart, 1997). More generally, the older study of Rudolf Morsey remains valuable: Rudolf Morsey, *Die Deutsche Zentrumspartei 1917–1923* (Düsseldorf, 1966).
2. Reichstag, Session 39, 12 May 1919, 1092–3.
3. Heinrich August Winkler, *Weimar 1918–1933: Die Geschichte der ersten deutschen Demokratie* (Munich, 1998), 155–61.
4. A. S. Hershey, 'German Reparations', *American Journal of International Law*, 15:3 (1921), 411–18.
5. Peter Krüger, *Die Aussenpolitik der Republik von Weimar* (Darmstadt, 1985), 132–49.
6. Shulamit Volkov, *Walther Rathenau: Weimar's Fallen Statesman* (New Haven and London, 2012), 193.
7. Ernst Schulin, 'Noch etwas zur Entstehung des Rapallo-Vertrages', in Hartmut von Hentig and August Nitschke (eds), *Was die Wirklichkeit lehrt: Golo Mann zum 70. Geburtstag* (Frankfurt, 1979), 177–202.
8. Carole Fink, *The Genoa Conference: European Diplomacy, 1921–1922* (Chapel Hill and London, 1984), 3–105.
9. Ibid.
10. Ibid., 152–3.
11. Hassan Malik, *Bankers and Bolsheviks: International Finance and the Russian Revolution* (Princeton, 2018).
12. Renata Bournazel, *Rapallo: Ein französisches Trauma* (Cologne, 1976), 79–112.
13. Fink, *The Genoa Conference*, 153–4.
14. Ibid.

15. Eva Ingeborg Fleischhauer, 'Rathenau in Rapallo: Eine notwendige Korrektur des Forschungsstandes', *Vierteljahrshefte für Zeitgeschichte* 54:3 (2006), 365–415; Horst Günther Linke, 'Der Weg nach Rapallo: Strategie und Taktik der deutschen und sowjetischen Außenpolitik', *Historische Zeitschrift* 264 (1997), 55–109.
16. Schulin, 'Noch etwas zur Entstehung des Rapallo-Vertrages'.
17. Ibid.
18. Ibid.
19. Conan Fischer, *The Ruhr Crisis 1923–24* (Oxford, 2003), 22.
20. Fink, *The Genoa Conference*, 175.
21. Ibid.
22. Walther Rathenau, *Cannes und Genua: Vier Reden zum Reparationsproblem* (Berlin, 1922), 28–9.
23. Kessler, *Walther Rathenau*, 339–40.
24. Bournazel, *Rapallo*, 160–209.
25. Ibid., 169–70; John F. V. Keiger, *Raymond Poincaré* (Cambridge, 1997), 287–90; Stanislas Jeannesson, *Poincaré, la France et la Ruhr (1922–1924): Histoire d'une occupation* (Strasbourg, 1998), 75–8.

Chapter 3: The Fascist Moment

1. For an introduction, see Richard Bosworth, *Mussolini* (London, 2002).
2. Giulia Albanese, *The March on Rome: Violence and the Rise of Italian Fascism*, trans. Sergio Knipe (London, 2019), 32; Mimmo Franzinelli, *Squadristi: Protagonisti e tecniche della violenza fascista* (Milan, 2003), 376; Dennis Mack-Smith, *Mussolini* (New York, 1982), 50–1.
3. Albanese, *The March on Rome*, 59.
4. Ibid., 64.
5. 'International Fascism: Rome-Berlin-Budapest', *Vorwärts*, Nr 515, 31 October 1922, evening edition.
6. Cited in 'The Bavarian Mussolini: The Organisation of "National Assault Troops"', *Vorwärts*, Nr 534, 11 November 1922, morning edition.
7. Walter Werner Pese, 'Hitler und Italien 1920–1926', *Vierteljahrshefte für Zeitgeschichte* 3:2 (1955), 113–26.
8. 'The German "Fascists"', *CV-Zeitung*, Nr 23, 16 November 1922.
9. 'Rathenau's Murderers Before the State Court: The first day – Incredible Interest', *Berliner Tageblatt*, Nr 446, 3 October 1922, evening edition. On the death sentence in Weimar Germany, see

Richard Evans, *Rituals of Retribution: Capital Punishment in Germany 1600–1987* (Oxford, 1996), 485–610, statistic here is on p. 915. 'Techow's Cross-examination', *Vorwärts*, Nr 470, 5 October 1922, evening edition.

10. 'The Testimonies of the Accused in the Rathenau Trial', Telegram from Our Special Correspondent, E. F., Leipzig, 3 October 1922, *Berliner Tageblatt*, Nr 447, 4 October 1922, morning edition.

11. 'The Lessons of the Rathenau Trial', *CV-Zeitung*, Nr 24, 19 October 1922; 'Under the Terror of Organization C.', *Vorwärts*, Nr 474, 7 October 1922, morning edition; 'The Good Boys', *Vorwärts*, Nr 228, 4 October 1922, evening edition.

12. 'Rathenau's Murderers Before the Court', *Vorwärts*, Nr 468, 4 October 1922, morning edition; 'The Nest of the German National Youth', *Vorwärts*, Nr 230, 6 October 1922, morning edition; 'Ludendorff Remains in the Dark', Leipzig, 9 October 1922, Exclusive Telegram, *Vorwärts*, Nr 477, 9 October 1922, evening edition.

13. 'The Prosecution Speech of the State Prosecutor', *Vorwärts*, Nr 482, 12 October 1922, morning edition; 'Lessons of the Rathenau Trial', *CV-Zeitung*, Nr 24, 19 October 1922; 'The Judgement in the Rathenau Trial', Telegram from Our Special Correspondent, E. F., Leipzig, 14 October 1922, *Berliner Tageblatt*, Nr 467, 15 October 1922, morning edition.

14. Ernst von Salomon, *The Outlaws*, trans. Ian F. D. Morrow (London, 1931). His 1951 semi-autobiographical novel that was intended to mock and reject the Allies' de-nazification process was even more successful in terms of attracting readers: Ernst von Salomon, *Der Fragebogen* (Hamburg, 1951).

15. 'The Judgement in the Rathenau Trial', *Vorwärts*, Nr 240, 15 October 1922, Sunday edition; 'The Press on the Rathenau Trial: Dissatisfaction on the Left and Right', *Berliner Tageblatt*, Nr 468, 16 October 1922, evening edition; 'Lessons of the Rathenau Trial', *CV-Zeitung*, Nr 24, 19 October 1922; Theodor Wolff, *Berliner Tageblatt*, Nr 468, 16 October 1922, evening edition; 'Judgement in the Rathenau Trial', Telegram from Our Special Correspondent, E. F., Leipzig, 14 October 1922, *Berliner Tageblatt*, Nr 467, 15 October 1922, morning edition.

16. Staatsarchiv Würzburg, 'State Prosecutor's Bill of Indictment at the District Court', 28 July 1923.

17. 'The *Völkische* Incitement to Hatred in the Main Triangle', *CV-Zeitung*, Nr 28, 16 November 1922.

18. Martin Sabrow, 'Die Judenhetzerin von Kitzingen', *Praxis Geschichte*, 2 (1992), 59–61; Elmar Schwinger, *Von Kitzingen nach Izbica: Aufstieg und Katastrophe der mainfränkischen, israelitischen Kultusgemeinde Kitzingen* (Kitzingen, 2009).

19. Sabrow, 'Die Judenhetzerin von Kitzingen', 60.

20. 'A Nazi (Hakenkreuz) Attempts to Murder a Jewish Passenger', *CV-Zeitung*, Nr 24, 19 October 1922.

21. 'The Bavarian Fascists', Augsburg, 16 October 1922, Exclusive Telegram, *Vorwärts*, Nr 490, 17 October 1922, morning edition.

22. 'The German Day in Coburg', *Vorwärts*, quoting *Deutsche Allgemeine Zeitung*, 24 October 1922.

23. Daniel Siemens, *Stormtroopers: A New History of Hitler's Brownshirts* (New Haven, 2017), 18; Kershaw, *Hitler 1889–1936*, 178–9; Peter Longerich, *Hitler: A Life*, trans. Jeremy Noakes and Lesley Sharpe (Oxford, 2019), 98–9.

24. 'On the Republic's Birthday', *Vorwärts*, Nr 261, 9 November 1922, morning edition.

25. Feldman, *The Great Disorder*, 487.

26. Ibid., 488.

27. Ibid., 483.

28. Heinrich August Winkler, *Von der Revolution zur Stabilisierung: Arbeiter und Arbeiterbewegung in der Weimarer Republik 1918–1924* (Berlin, 1984), 496–8.

29. 'Hugo Stinnes Declares War! No Stabilization of the Mark – 10-Hour Day', *Vorwärts*, Nr 532, 10 November 1922, morning edition; Feldman, *The Great Disorder*, 484.

30. Morsey, *Die Deutsche Zentrumspartei*, 457. Also cited in Küppers, *Joseph Wirth*, 191–2; 'The German Catholic Day', *Vossische Zeitung*, Nr 406, 28 August 1922, evening edition; 'The Catholic Day', Munich, 28 August 1922, Exclusive Telegram, *Vorwärts*, Nr 405, 28 August 1922, evening edition; Küppers, *Joseph Wirth*, 197.

31. Küppers, *Joseph Wirth*, 199.

Chapter 4: The Invasion of the Ruhr

1. 'Poincaré Awaits New German Offer', *New York Times*, 13 January 1923; Erich Dombrowski, 'A Journey Through the Ruhr District', *Berliner Tageblatt*, Nr 31, 19 January 1923, morning edition.

2. 'The Situation', *Berliner Tageblatt*, Nr 19, 12 January 1923, morning edition; Fischer, *The Ruhr Crisis*, 42.
3. Fischer, *The Ruhr Crisis*, 41–2; 'The Ruhr District Under French Military Rule', *Berliner Tageblatt*, Nr 19, 12 January 1923, morning edition; 'The Ruhr Occupation: 250,000 Men', Essen, 22 January 1923, Exclusive Telegram, *Vorwärts*, Nr 36, 23 January 1923, morning edition; Fischer, *The Ruhr Crisis*, 44–5, 47.
4. Quoted in Fischer, *The Ruhr Crisis*, 43; 'The Situation', *Berliner Tageblatt*, Nr 19, 12 January 1923, morning edition; Fischer, *The Ruhr Crisis*, 42; 'The Ruhr District Under French Military Rule', *Berliner Tageblatt*, Nr 19, 12 January 1923, morning edition.
5. Hans Spethmann, *Zwölf Jahre Ruhrbergbau: Aus seiner Geschichte von Kriegsanfang bis zum Franzosenabmarsch 1914 bis 1925*, Vol. III: *Der Ruhrkampf 1923 bis 1925 in seinen Leitlinien* (Berlin, 1925), 91; Fischer, *The Ruhr Crisis*, 43; 'The Victims from Bochum', *Berliner Tageblatt*, Nr 25, 16 January 1923, morning edition; 'Clashes and Demonstrations', Essen, 16 January 1923, WTB, *Vorwärts*, Nr 25, 16 January 1923; 'Peaceful Action', Bochum, 15 January 1922, Exclusive Telegram, *Vorwärts*, Nr 24, 16 January 1923, morning edition.
6. 'Clashes and Demonstrations', Essen, 16 January 1923, WTB, *Vorwärts*, Nr 25, 16 January 1923; 'Bloody Clashes in Bochum', Telegram from Our Correspondent, Bochum, 15 January 1923, *Berliner Tageblatt*, Nr 25, 16 January 1923, morning edition; 'It is Forbidden to Sing German Songs', Essen, 18 January 1923, WTB, *Berliner Tageblatt*, Nr 30, 18 January 1923, evening edition.
7. 'Peaceful Action', Bochum, 15 January 1923, Exclusive Telegram, *Vorwärts*, Nr 24, 16 January 1923, morning edition; 'A New Murder in the Ruhr District', Bochum, 20 January 1923, *Berliner Tageblatt*, Nr 34, 20 January 1923, evening edition.
8. 'Mine Owners Arrested', *Vorwärts*, Nr 33, 20 January 1923; 'Kowalskis Funeral', Langendreer, 23 January 1923, WTB, *Vorwärts*, Nr 19, 24 January 1923, morning edition; 'Murder in Langendreer', *Vorwärts*, Nr 35, 22 January 1923, evening edition.
9. 'The Langendreer Protest Sent Back', *Vorwärts*, Nr 37, 23 January 1923, evening edition; 'Poincaré and the Dead Man from Bochum', *Vorwärts*, Nr 36, 23 January 1923, morning edition.
10. Deutsches Bergbau-Museum Bochum, Bergbau-Archiv, 32/4364, quoted in Fischer, *The Ruhr Crisis*, 76; 'Another Victim of French

Brutality', *Berliner Tageblatt*, Nr 41, 25 January 1923, morning edition; 'New Bloody Deeds by the French: Revolver Shots and Stabbings', Telegram, Cologne, 23 January 1923, *Berliner Tageblatt*, Nr 38, 23 January 1923, evening edition; 'The Incident in Bochum', *Vorwärts*, Nr 29, 18 January 1923, evening edition; 'Peaceful Action', *Vorwärts*, Nr 37, 23 January 1923, evening edition.

11. SHD: 'Series A, Acts of Public Outrage Brought Against French Soldiers, N°1 to 57' (GR 19 NN 21A), 15, 23, 25.

12. Fischer, *The Ruhr Crisis*, 40–1; 'Poincaré's Triumph', Paris, 11 January 1923, *Vorwärts*, Nr 18, 12 January 1923, morning edition; 'The Situation', *Berliner Tageblatt*, Nr 19, 12 January 1923, morning edition.

13. Feldman, *The Great Disorder*, 445; Fischer, *The Ruhr Crisis*, 24.

14. Elspeth Y. O'Riordan, *Britain and the Ruhr Crisis* (New York, 2001), 11; Fischer, *The Ruhr Crisis*, 25; Stanislas Jeannesson, *Poincaré*, 95.

15. 'Statement of the Reich Foreign Minister: The Policy of Determined Moral Resistance', *Berliner Tageblatt*, Nr 32, 19 January 1923, evening edition.

16. Erich Dombrowski, 'Yesterday's Reichstag Session', *Berliner Tageblatt*, Nr 23, 14 January 1923, morning edition; Reichstag, Session 286, Sunday, 13 January 1923, 9431–2.

17. Reichstag, Session 286, Sunday, 13 January 1923, 9423.

18. 'In the National Interest! Why We Are Demonstrating on Our Own', *Vorwärts*, Nr 21, 13 January 1923.

19. 'Protest of the German People', *Berliner Tageblatt*, Nr 24, 15 January 1923, evening edition; 'National Day of Mourning in Munich', *Berliner Tageblatt*, Nr 24, 15 January 1923, evening edition.

20. 'Miners and French Tyranny', *Bergarbeiter Zeitung*, Nr 4, 27 January 1923.

21. 'In the National Interest! Why We Are Demonstrating on Our Own', *Vorwärts*, Nr 21, 13 January 1923; 'The Ruhr Occupation and Reparations: Berliners Support the Ruhr', *Vorwärts*, Nr 40, 25 January 1923, morning edition.

22. Theodor Wolff, *Berliner Tageblatt*, Nr 24, 15 January 1923, evening edition; Georg Bernhard, 'Poincaré or Europe', *Vossische Zeitung*, Nr 23, 14 January 1923, Sunday edition.

23. Erich Dombrowski, 'The Confiscation of the State Mines', *Berliner Tageblatt*, Nr 33, 20 January 1923, morning edition.

24. Erich Dombrowski, 'Six German Pit Representatives Arrested by the French', French headquarters, Essen, 20 January 1923, *Berliner Tageblatt*, Nr 34, 20 January 1923, evening edition.

25. 'List of the Martyrs: Arrested or Deported', *Berliner Tageblatt*, Nr 36, 22 January 1923, evening edition.

26. Fischer, *The Ruhr Crisis*, 54–5; 'An Appeal from the Government to Civil Servants', *Berliner Tageblatt*, Nr 33, 20 January 1923, morning edition; 'The First Arrests', Essen, 19 January 1923, WTB, *Vorwärts*, Nr 31, 19 January 1923, evening edition; Fischer, *The Ruhr Crisis*, 73.

27. 'Confiscation of the State Mines', *Berliner Tageblatt*, Nr 33, 20 January 1923, morning edition.

28. 'The First Arrests', Essen, 19 January 1923, WTB, *Vorwärts*, Nr 31, 19 January 1923, evening edition; 'Unions Demand the Release of Dr Schlutius', *Berliner Tageblatt*, Nr 33, 20 January 1923, morning edition; 'The First Arrests', Düsseldorf, 18 January 1923, WTB, *Vorwärts*, Nr 30, 19 January 1923, morning edition; 'The Demands of the Miners', *Vorwärts*, Nr 32, 21 January 1923.

29. Fischer, *The Ruhr Crisis*, 33, 54–5.

30. Ibid., 68–9; 'On the Eve of Action by All Miners: Intensified German Resistance', *Berliner Tageblatt*, Nr 34, 20 January 1923, evening edition; '65,000 Workers Demand Thyssen's Release', *Berliner Tageblatt*, Nr 35, 21 January 1923, morning edition; 'Release or Strike!', *Vorwärts*, Nr 34, 21 January 1923; 'The System of Moral Resistance', *Berliner Tageblatt*, Nr 37, 23 January 1923, morning edition.

31. Spethmann, *Zwölf Jahre Ruhrbergbau*, Vol. III, 89.

32. 'Those Without a Fatherland', *Vorwärts*, 22 January 1923, evening edition; Erich Dombrowski, 'At the Thyssen Works: August Thyssen and His Son Fritz', Mülheim, 22 January 1923, *Berliner Tageblatt*, Nr 38, 23 January 1923, evening edition.

33. 'The Speeches of the Defence Lawyers', Mainz, 24 January 1923, *Vossische Zeitung*, Nr 41, 25 January 1923, morning edition.

34. 'The Court Martial's Judgement Against the Industrialists', *Berliner Tageblatt*, Nr 41, 25 January 1923, morning edition.

35. Spethmann, *Zwölf Jahre Ruhrbergbau*, Vol. III, 105–6.

36. Jeannesson, *Poincaré*, 166, quoted in Fischer, *The Ruhr Crisis*, 71–3.

37. Spethmann, *Zwölf Jahre Ruhrbergbau*, Vol. III, 104; Reichstag, Session 311, 6 March 1923, 9950.

38. Reichstag, Session 291, 26 January 1923, 9516, 9527.
39. Reichstag, Session 291, 26 January 1923, 9529; 'The Workers'
Position', Elberfeld, 22 January 1923, Exclusive Telegram, *Vorwärts*,
Nr 36, 23 January 1923.
40. Zara Steiner, *The Lights That Failed: European International History
1919–1933* (Oxford, 2005), 223.

Chapter 5: Hitler's First Victory

1. JK, PND Bericht, 781–3. PND is short for Politischer Nachrich-
tendienst [des Polizeipräsidiums München]. It may be translated as
Political Intelligence Service [of the Munich Police Presidium].
2. Mark Jones, *Founding Weimar: Violence and the German Revolution of
1918–19* (Cambridge, 2016), 286–323.
3. JK, PND Bericht, 781; 'Nationalist Brass Music', *Vorwärts*, Nr 19, 12
January 1923, evening edition; Reichstag, Session 286, 13 January
1923, 9427. See also 'Reichstag and the Ruhr Occupation', *Vorwärts*,
Nr 22, 14 January 1923, morning edition; 'Steglitz and the Western
Suburbs', *Vorwärts*, Nr 23, 15 January 1923, evening edition.
4. JK, Munich, 15 January 1923, Speech at an NSDAP evening of
speeches, 791–3.
5. Ibid., 791–3, 792; JK, PND Bericht, 18 January 1923, 794–5; JK,
Munich, 25 January 1923, 'On the Party Conference 1923'.
6. JK, Nr 490, Munich, 20 February 1923, 'Speech to the National
Association of German Officers', *Völkischer Beobachter*, 22 February
1923; JK, 'Speech at an SA Assembly, Report from the *Münchener
Post* Newspaper', 8 March 1923, 843; Bavarian Landtag 186th public
session, 24 April 1923, 129–30; Ludwig Höllander, 'From the Dark
Days in Munich', *CV-Zeitung*, Nr 5, 1 February 1923.
7. BArch-Berlin NS26/365, NSDAP to the Police Directorate,
Munich, for permission to hold an assembly, 27 January 1923.
8. 'Police Protect Plunderers', Munich, 26 January 1923, Exclusive
Telegram, *Vorwärts*, Nr 44, 27 January 1923.
9. BArch-Berlin NS26/365 Nortz.
10. BArch-Berlin NS26/365, Ministry of the Interior to the Police
Directorate, Munich; BArch-Berlin NS26/365 Munich, 29 January
1923.
11. BArch-Berlin NS26/365, Munich, 29 January 1923.

12. 'From Eisner to Hitler', *CV-Zeitung*, Nr 6, 8 February 1923.

13. Kershaw, *Hitler 1889–1936*, 192; BArch-Berlin NS26/365; 'The Fascist Parallel Government', *Vorwärts*, Nr 53, 1 February 1923, evening edition.

14. R. Bauer, Hans G. Hockerts and Brigitte Schütz (eds), *München: 'Hauptstadt' der Bewegung: Bayerns Metropole und der Nationalsozialismus* (Wolfratshausen, 2002), 92.

15. 'Incidents in Munich', Munich, 15 January 1923, Exclusive Telegram, *Vorwärts*, Nr 23, 15 January 1923, evening edition.

16. BArch-Berlin NS26/386: National Socialist Party Conference, *Münchener Neueste Nachrichten*, Nr 27, 29 January 1923; JK, Munich, 28 January 1923, Speech at a Nazi Party Conference, 819–20.

17. BArch-Berlin NS26/386: National Socialist Party Conference, *Münchener Neueste Nachrichten*, Nr 27, 29 January 1923.

18. Ibid.

Chapter 6: The Escalation of Violence

1. AA, *Gewaltakte der französisch-belgischen Truppen im Ruhrgebiet* (Berlin, 1923), Nr 6121; Essen, 2 February 1923, WTB, *Vorwärts*, Nr 56, 3 February 1923, morning edition.

2. BArch-Berlin R708, Bl.524: The Mayor, Nr III 2165/22, Düsseldorf, 8 February 1923; 'On the Shooting of the Schoolgirl Anna Schiffer', report, 5 February 1923.

3. 'New Blood Victims of the Occupation', Essen, 2 February 1923, WTB, *Vorwärts*, Nr 56, 3 February 1923, morning edition, and Mainz, 2 February 1923, WTB, *Vorwärts*, Nr 56, 3 February 1923, morning edition; Erich Dombrowski, 'Bloody Incident in Gelsenkirchen', 12 February 1923, *Berliner Tageblatt*, 12 February 1923, evening edition.

4. Stanislas Jeannesson, 'Übergriffe der französischen Besatzungsmacht und deutsche Beschwerden', in Gerd Krumeich and Joachim Schröder (eds), *Der Schatten des Weltkriegs: Die Ruhrbesetzung 1923* (Essen, 2004), 210–11.

5. Fischer, *The Ruhr Crisis*, 92–109; 'No Ruhr Coal for Germany: Ban of Coal Imports', Paris, WTB, 1 February 1923, *Vorwärts*, Nr 53, 1 February 1923, evening edition; 'Comrade Grützner Deported', 19 February 1923, WTB, *Vorwärts*, Nr 83, 19 February 1923, evening

edition; 'Ministers Are to Be Arrested!', *Vorwärts*, Nr 89, 22 February 1923, evening edition.

6. 'New Blood Victims of the Occupation', Mainz, 2 February 1923, WTB, *Vorwärts*, Nr 56, 3 February 1923, morning edition; 'With Whips and Rifle Butts', Telegram from Our Correspondent, Bochum, 10 February 1923, *Berliner Tageblatt*, Nr 71, 11 February 1923, morning edition; Erich Dombrowski, 'The Rule of Violence in the Ruhr District', *Berliner Tageblatt*, Nr 29, 16 February 1923, morning edition; 'Poincaré's New Methods', *Vorwärts*, Nr 90, 23 February 1923, morning edition.

7. Erich Dombrowski, 'The Raging Soldateska', Essen, 12 February 1923, *Berliner Tageblatt*, Nr 73, 13 February 1923, morning edition. For similar comments on the French loss of nerve, see 'Acts of Violence and Reporting', *Vorwärts*, Nr 70, 11 February 1923; Erich Dombrowski, 'The Third Stage', Gelsenkirchen, *Berliner Tageblatt*, Nr 76, 14 February 1923, evening edition.

8. Jeannesson, 'Übergriffe der französische Besatzungsmacht und deutsche Beschwerden', 212.

9. SHD: GR 19 NN 201 File 4; BAarch-Berlin R708/30, Bl.249–50. Münster, 19 March 1923.

10. Michael Wildt, *Zerborstene Zeit: Deutsche Geschichte 1918–1945* (Munich, 2022), 159; Kershaw, *Hitler 1889–1936*, 431.

11. Fischer, *The Ruhr Crisis*, 96–7; 'Tanks Against Passers-by', Recklinghausen, 7 February 1923, Exclusive Telegram, *Vorwärts*, Nr 64, 8 February 1923, morning edition.

12. 'The Situation in Recklinghausen', *Vorwärts*, Nr 69, 10 February 1923, evening edition; 'Tanks Against Passers-by', Recklinghausen, 7 February 1923, Exclusive Telegram, *Vorwärts*, Nr 64, 8 February 1923, morning edition.

13. 'The Situation in Recklinghausen', *Vorwärts*, Nr 69, 10 February 1923, evening edition.

14. 'Ebert's Speech in Karlsruhe: Opposed to the Destruction of the Reich', *Vorwärts*, Nr 72, 13 February 1923, morning edition.

15. 'A Black Day for Bochum', *Vorwärts*, Nr 100, 1 March 1923, morning edition; 'The Essen Police Disarmed', *Vorwärts*, Nr 83, 19 February 1923, evening edition; 'Mass Arrests in Bochum', Bochum, 23 February 1923, Exclusive Telegram, *Vorwärts*, Nr 92, 24 February 1923, morning edition; 'Bochum and the Dicatorship of Terror', *Vorwärts*, Nr 96, 27 February 1923, morning edition.

16. Fischer, *The Ruhr Crisis*, 99–100.
17. 'Two Officers Murdered in Buer', *Vorwärts*, Nr 119, 12 March 1923, evening edition; 'Poincaré and Maginot's Acts of Revenge', Paris, WTB, 12 March 1923, *Vorwärts*, Nr 119, 12 March 1923, evening edition
18. Fischer, *The Ruhr Crisis*, 172; 'Harsh Reprisals, Buer, 12 March 1923, Exclusive Telegram, *Vorwärts*, Nr 120, 13 March 1923, morning edition; 'Murder in Buer', *Vorwärts*, Nr 130, 18 March 1923, Sunday edition.
19. 'The Horrific Deeds in Buer', Buer, 16 March 1923, Telegraph Union, *Vorwärts*, Nr 127, 16 March 1923, evening edition.
20. Annette Becker, 'Das Begräbnis des Leutnants Colpin in Lille am 21. März 1923', in Krumeich and Schröder (eds), *Der Schatten des Weltkriegs*, 257–63.
21. 'Ebert Addresses the Population of the Ruhr: The Assembly in Hamm', Hamm, 19 March 1923, Exclusive Telegram, *Vorwärts*, Nr 131, 19 March 1923, evening edition.
22. Klaus Wisotzky, 'Der "blutige Karsamstag" 1923 bei Krupp', in Krumeich and Schröder (eds), *Der Schatten des Weltkriegs*, 266.
23. Ibid., 267.
24. Ibid., 268.
25. Ibid., 268–9.
26. Cited in ibid., 269; 'Essen's Easter Sunday Tragedy', *Vorwärts*, Nr 154, 3 April 1923, evening edition.
27. Cited in Wisotzky, 'Der "blutige Karsamstag"', 272.
28. Ibid., 276–7; 'Essen's Easter Sunday Tragedy', *Vorwärts*, Nr 154, 3 April 1923, evening edition; 'Easter of Blood in the Ruhr District: 11 Dead – 32 Injured', Essen, 31 March 1923, WTB, *Vorwärts*, Nr 153, 1 April 1923, Sunday edition; Fischer, *The Ruhr Crisis*, 167.
29. Wisotzky, 'Der "blutige Karsamstag"', 279.
30. Hans Luther, *In Memoriam: Den Opfern des französischen Militarismus in Essen* (Berlin, 1923), 11–14.
31. Fischer, *The Ruhr Crisis*, 167.
32. Spethmann, *Zwölf Jahre Ruhrbergbau*, Vol. IV, 275; cited in Wisotzky, 'Der "blutige Karsamstag"', 281.

Chapter 7: Active Resistance

1. On Kölpin, see Julian Aulke, *Räume der Revolution: Kulturelle Verräumlichung in Politisierungsprozessen während der Revolution 1918–19* (Stuttgart, 2015), 203–19.
2. Mark A. Fraschka, *Franz Pfeffer von Salomon: Hitlers Vergessener Oberster SA-Führer* (Göttingen, 2016), 198.
3. Ibid., 203.
4. Gerd Krüger, '"Wir wachen und strafen!" Gewalt im Ruhrkampf von 1923', in Krumeich and Schröder (eds), *Der Schatten des Weltkriegs*, 238–9; Gerd Krüger, 'Das Unternehmen Wesel im Ruhrkampf von 1923', in Horst Schroeder and Gerd Krüger, *Realschule und Ruhrkampf: Beiträge zur Stadtgeschichte des 19. und 20. Jahrhunderts* (Wesel, 2002), 91–151.
5. Klaus Kemp, *Regiebahn: Reparationen, Besetzung, Ruhrkampf, Reichsbahn: Die Eisenbahnen im Rheinland und im Ruhrgebiet 1918–1930* (Freiburg, 2016), 139–45.
6. Fischer, *The Ruhr Crisis*, 107.
7. Ibid., 173–4.
8. Some sources also spell his name 'Synder'.
9. 'Sentenced to Death for Explosions: A Sabotage Process in a French Court Martial', Düsseldorf, 11 May 1923, WTB, *Vorwärts*, Nr 218, 11 May 1923, evening edition; Gerd Krüger, '"Wir wachen und strafen!"', 242.
10. Kemp, *Regiebahn*, 140; BArch-Berlin 8038/3, Bl.53–4; Jeannesson, *Poincaré*, 263. Contrast with Michael Ruck, *Die freien Gewerkschaften im Ruhrkampf 1923* (Cologne, 1986), 397–8.
11. BArch-Freiburg RH 53–6, Nr 55: Military District Command VI (Münster). 'The Struggle in the Ruhr (1923–1930). Report of the Explosive Commando Ringenberg-Graf Keller in Belgian Captivity'.
12. BArch-Berlin R708/32, Nr 4.
13. Quoted in Gerd Krüger, '"Wir wachen und strafen!"', 240.
14. Fischer, *The Ruhr Crisis*, 180; Fraschka, *Franz Pfeffer von Salomon*, 207.
15. '*Völkische* Dynamite Heroes: Party Printers in Münster Blown Into the Skies', Münster, 24 June 1923, Exclusive Telegram, *Vorwärts*, Nr 292, 25 June 1923, evening edition.
16. 'Ruhr Outrage: Bomb Exploded in a Train', *The Times*, 2 July 1923.
17. Fischer, *The Ruhr Crisis*, 176.

18. Ibid., 175–6.

19. 'Attack on a Belgian Holiday Train', *Vorwärts*, Nr 303, 1 July 1923, Sunday edition.

20. 'Reprisals After the Explosions', Cologne, 30 June 1923, WTB, *Vorwärts*, Nr 303, 1 July 1923, Sunday edition; 'Attack on a Belgian Holiday Train', *Vorwärts*, Nr 303, 1 July 1923; 'Sanctions for Duisburg', Duisburg, 30 June 1923, WTB, *Vorwärts*, Nr 304, 2 July 1923, evening edition; 'The Decisive Week', Paris, 2 July 1923, WTB, *Vorwärts*, Nr 304, 2 July 1923; 'Sanctions for Duisburg', Oberhausen, 1 July 1923, WTB, *Vorwärts*, Nr 304, 2 July 1923; 'Degoutte Orders a Blockade', *Vorwärts*, Nr 305, 3 July 1923, morning edition; '18 Fatal Victims of the Duisburg Catastrophe', Telegram from Our Correspondent, Ruhr, 2 July 1923, *Berliner Tageblatt*, Nr 306, 2 July 1923, evening edition; 'Dynamite', *Vossische Zeitung*, Nr 308, 2 July 1923, evening edition; Erich Dombrowski, 'The Regime of Horror on the Ruhr', *Berliner Tageblatt*, Nr 307, 3 July 1923, morning edition; Fischer, *The Ruhr Crisis*, 173.

21. 'Ruhr Sabotage: German Resentment of Vatican Order', Berlin, 6 July 1923, *The Times*, 7 July 1923; 'The Reich Government Protests Against Acts of Sabotage', *Vossische Zeitung*, Nr 317, 7 July 1923, morning edition. On Cuno's condemnation, see 'Attack on a Belgian Holiday Train', *Vorwärts*, Nr 303, 1 July 1923, Sunday edition; Jeannesson, *Poincaré*, 265.

22. Jeannesson, *Poincaré*, 265; 'Hand Grenade Explodes in Düsseldorf', *Vorwärts*, Nr 364, 6 August 1923, evening edition.

23. Jeannesson, *Poincaré*, 263.

24. Stefan Zwicker, *'Nationale Märtyrer': Albert Leo Schlageter und Julius Fučík – Heldenkult, Propaganda und Erinnerungskultur* (Paderborn, 2006), 56–7.

25. 'The Nationalist Ring of Spies', *Vorwärts*, Nr 281, 19 June 1923, morning edition.

26. Zwicker, *'Nationale Märtyrer'*, 59; 'Schlageter's Nachtgefährtin', *Der Abend – Spätausgabe des Vorwärts*, Nr 298, 26 June 1928.

27. Zwicker, *'Nationale Märtyrer'*, 61. On denials, see 'Die Abenteuer im Ruhrgebiet', *Der Abend – Spätausgabe des Vorwärts*, Nr 298, 26 June 1928.

28. Zwicker, *'Nationale Märtyrer'*, 61; 'Death Sentence in Düsseldorf: The Heinz Organizaton', *Vorwärts*, Nr 220, 12 May 1923, evening

edition. See also 'Death Sentence for Explosions: A Sabotage Process in Front of a French Court Martial', Düsseldorf, 11 May 1923, WTB, *Vorwärts*, Nr 218, 11 May 1923, evening edition.

29. Zwicker, *'Nationale Märtyrer'*, 65. The quotation is from BArch-Berlin R8038/9, Bl.50.
30. Zwicker, *'Nationale Märtyrer'*, 65–6.
31. BArch-Berlin R8035/10, Bl.38; Zwicker, *'Nationale Märtyrer'*, 91–3.
32. Quoted in Zwicker, *'Nationale Märtyrer'*, 72, 88.
33. Ibid., 68; BArch-Berlin R8039/2, Bl.54–5.
34. Zwicker, *'Nationale Märtyrer'*, 69.
35. 'Schlageter's Funeral: Nationalist and Anti-Republican Demonstrations', Elberfeld, 8 June 1923, Exclusive Telegram, *Vorwärts*, Nr 266, 9 June 1923, evening edition; *'Völkische* Dynamite Heroes: Party Printers in Münster Blown Into the Skies', Münster, 24 June 1923, Exclusive Telegram, *Vorwärts*, Nr 292, 25 June 1923, evening edition. Cited in Zwicker, *'Nationale Märtyrer'*, 70.
36. Cited in Zwicker, *'Nationale Märtyrer'*, 98, 108–9.
37. Cited in ibid., 71. He also called Schlageter a 'man who had been misled'; Jeannesson, *Poincaré*, 201, 263.
38. 'In Memory of Rathenau: Commemorations in the Reichstag and the Foreign Office', *Vorwärts*, Nr 292, 25 June 1923, evening edition; 'Property of the Reich: Rathenau's House', *Vorwärts*, Nr 290, 23 June 1923, evening edition; 'Rathenau's House: Taken Over By the Reich as a Foundation', *Vorwärts*, Nr 283, 20 June 1923, morning edition.

Chapter 8: The Occupiers' Revenge

1. BArch-Berlin R708/33, Bl.316–18.
2. Contrast the dismissal of this issue in Fischer, *The Ruhr Crisis*, 143–4.
3. MAE, La Courneuve 4-RG 170: MAE, Europe 1918–1929, Rive Gauche du Rhin, 170 (109CPCOM170), called a 'Memoir of Violent Acts Committed by the Occupation Troops' (September 1925–April 1928). This case is file 78, dated 22 September 1923; SHD GR19NN21A Files 35, 19, 7, 5.
4. SHD GR19 NN21A Files 47, 9, 18, 37; Jeannesson, 'Übergriffe', 223.

5. BArch-Berlin R708/34, Bl.5; ibid., R708/33, Bl.64.
6. AA, Nr 6121: *Gewaltakte der französisch-belgischen Truppen im Ruhrgebiet* (Berlin, 1923), Nr 67: 'The Moral Crimes of a Belgian Soldier Against German Woman S. (unmarried) on 4 February in Bottrop', 15–16; BArch-Berlin R708/34, Bl.149–50.
7. Bruno Cabanes, *La Victoire endeuillée: La sortie de guerre des soldats français, 1918–1920* (Paris, 2004), 99ff.
8. 'Bloody Clashes in Frankfurt', *Berliner Tageblatt*, Nr 160, 8 April 1920, morning edition; 'Clashes in Frankfurt', Frankfurt am Main, 7 April 1923, Exclusive Telegram, *Vorwärts*, Nr 179, 8 April 1920, morning edition.
9. MAE, La Courneuve 4-RG 170: MAE, Europe 1918–1929, Rive Gauche du Rhin, 170 (109CPCOM170).
10. Jeannesson, 'Übergriffe', 217.
11. Cited in ibid., 220.
12. AA, Nr 6121: *Gewaltakte der französisch-belgischen Truppen im Ruhrgebiet* (Berlin, 1923), Nr 68, 16–19, cit. 17.
13. Ibid., Nr 69, 22–3.
14. Ibid., 25.
15. SHD GR19 NN201 File 22.
16. Ibid. File 29.
17. SHD GR19 NN21A File 3.
18. Ibid. Files 2, 1.
19. Jeannesson, 'Übergriffe', 224; SHD GR19 NN201 Files 47, 9.
20. Jeannesson, 'Übergriffe', 222–3.
21. Cited in ibid., 220.
22. Gerd Krüger, '"Wir wachen und strafen!"', 248.
23. Ibid.
24. Ibid., 248–9.

Chapter 9: Hitler's First Defeat

1. Ian Kershaw, *The Hitler Myth: Image and Reality in the Third Reich* (Oxford, 2001). Cited in Ludolf Herbst, *Hitlers Charisma: Die Erfindung eines deutschen Messias* (Frankfurt, 2010), 125–66.
2. 'The Enemy Prepares for the Final Struggle', *CV-Zeitung*, Nr 17, 26 April 1923; 'German-*völkische* Celebrations', *CV-Zeitung*, Nr 17, 26 April 1923.

3. 'The Enemy Prepares for the Final Struggle', *CV-Zeitung*, Nr 17, 26 April 1923; 'German-*völkische* Celebrations', *CV-Zeitung*, Nr 17, 26 April 1923.

4. 'From Eisner to Hitler', *CV-Zeitung*, Nr 6, 8 February 1923; 'What is Going on in Bavaria?', *Vorwärts*, Nr 20, 13 January 1923, morning edition; 'The Bavarian "Unity-front": Kahr, Knilling, Ludendorff and Hitler', Munich, 8 January 1923, Telegraph Union, *Vorwärts*, Nr 11, 8 January 1923, evening edition.

5. Kershaw, *Hitler 1889–1936*, 649, note 74: JK, Nr 493, Munich, 26 February 1923, 'A German Student and Worker as Symbols of the German Future'. Speech at a Nazi Party, as reported by the *Münchener Post*, 28 February 1923, 841.

6. 'The Gospel of Hitler', *Münchener Post*, 23 April 1923, cited in Herbst, *Hitlers Charisma*, 148–9.

7. On the SA at this time see Daniel Siemens, *Stormtroopers: A New History of Hitler's Brownshirts* (New Haven, 2017), 19–20.

8. 'Bavarian "Emergency-police", Mr Schweyer and the *Völkischen* Associations', *Vorwärts*, Nr 150, 30 March 1923, morning edition.

9. 'The Assault on the *Münchener Post*: Foreigners, Hitler's Supporters and the Work-shy as Perpetrators', Munich, 2 March 1923 (wire service report), *Vorwärts*, Nr 103, 2 March 1923, evening edition.

10. 'National Socialist Breach of the Peace', Munich, 12 March 1923, Exclusive Telegram, *Vorwärts*, Nr 119, 12 March 1923, evening edition.

11. 'The Game of Civil War', Munich, 21 March 1923, Exclusive Telegram, *Vorwärts*, Nr 136, 22 March 1923, morning edition.

12. 'Stormtrooper Interpellation in Bavaria: Interior Minister Schweyer Against the State Court', Munich, 20 March 1923, Exclusive Telegram, *Vorwärts*, Nr 134, 21 March 1923, morning edition.

13. Bavarian Parliament, Public Session 186, 24 April 1923, 148.

14. 'Hitler's Greetings to Cuno', *CV-Zeitung*, Nr 13, 29 March 1923.

15. Bavarian Parliament, Public Session 186, 24 April 1923, 150–4.

16. 'The Invasion of the Ruhr and Hatred Against Jews', *CV-Zeitung*, Nr 11, 15 March 1923.

17. 'Anti-semitic Worries in the Ruhr District', *CV-Zeitung*, Nr 11, 15 March 1923.

18. 'Delegation of Bavarian Jews Meet Minister President von Knilling', *CV-Zeitung*, Nr 13, 29 March 1923.

19. JK, Nr 522, Munich, 30 April 1923, 'Points of Debate at a Meeting of the Working Groups of the Paramilitary Associations', 917.
20. 'The May War in Munich', *Vorwärts*, Nr 207, 4 May 1923, morning edition: JK, Nr 523, Munich, 1 May 1923, 'Speech to the SA'; Kershaw, *Hitler 1889–1936*, 195–7.
21. Kershaw, *Hitler 1889–1936*, 195–7.
22. Volker Ullrich, *Hitler: A Biography:* Vol. 1: *Ascent*, trans. Jefferson Chase (London, 2016), 162.
23. Ibid., 161.
24. Kershaw, *Hitler 1889–1936*, 197–8; Longerich, *Hitler*, 110–11.
25. 'Bavarian *französlinge*', Munich, 2 June 1923, Exclusive Telegram, *Vorwärts*, Nr 255, 3 June 1923, morning edition.
26. 'Tension in the Ruhr District', Elberfeld, 12 June 1923, Exclusive Telegram, *Vorwärts*, Nr 271, 13 June 1923, morning edition; 'On the Schlageter Case', *Vorwärts*, Nr 259, 6 June 1923.
27. 'Warning! Incitement for Severing to Commit Murder', *Vorwärts*, Nr 275, 15 June 1923, morning edition; Zwicker, *'Nationale Märtyrer'*, 72–3.
28. 'Hitler and Eckardt Against *"Vorwärts"*: Our Editor Receives a Fine of 40,000 Marks from a Munich Court', Munich, 18 June 1923, Exclusive Telegram, *Vorwärts*, Nr 281, 19 June 1923, morning edition.
29. Zwicker, *'Nationale Märtyrer'*, 90; 'Schlageter Celebrations in Munich', *Rosenheimer Anzeiger*, Nr 132, 11 June 1923.
30. 'Schlageter Celebrations in Munich', *Rosenheimer Anzeiger*, Nr 132, 11 June 1923; JK, Nr 534, Munich, 10 June 1923, 'Speech at an Assembly of the Patriotic Leagues', 12 June 1923, 934–5.
31. JK, Nr 534, Munich, 10 June 1923, 'Speech at an Assembly of the Patriotic Leagues', 12 June 1923, 934–5; 'Schlageter Celebrations in Munich', *Rosenheimer Anzeiger*, Nr 132, 11 June 1923.
32. Zwicker, *'Nationale Märtyrer'*, 112; 'Munich's Schlageter Celebrations', *Vorwärts*, Nr 272, 13 June 1923, evening edition.
33. JK, Nr 538, 940; JK, Nr 545, Ingolstadt, 8 July 1923, 'Speech to a Nazi-Assembly', 948; JK, Nr 546, Nuremberg, 2 September 1923, 'Appeal of the Patriotic Fighting Leagues', 990–1. As we have already seen, Luise Solmitz used the same quotation from Kleist in her diary following the occupation. She would later support Hitler and celebrate his appointment as German chancellor, see Kershaw, *Hitler 1889–1936*, 431–2.

Chapter 10: The Year of the Zeros

1. Kessler, *In the Twenties*, 7 April 1923, 229.
2. Feldman, *The Great Disorder*, 26–51.
3. Eberhard Kolb and Dirk Schumann, *Die Weimarer Republik* (Munich, 2009), 52; Feldman, *The Great Disorder*, 669; Ursula Büttner, *Weimar: Die überforderte Republik 1918–1922: Leistung und Versagen in Staat, Gesellschaft, Wirtschaft und Kultur* (Stuttgart, 2008), 178.
4. BArch-Berlin R43I/640, Bl.178–9: 'Protocol of a Meeting of the Central Committee'. Also cited in Feldman, *The Great Disorder*, 655.
5. 'Commemoration of the Rathenau Murder', *Vorwärts*, Nr 291, 24 June 1923, Sunday edition. The dollar reached 356 by 2 p.m. as the news of Rathenau's murder hit the markets: 'Rathenau's Death and the Stock Market', *Berliner Börsen Zeitung*, Nr 290, 24 June 1922. The average price in Berlin for June 1922 was 317.14: Bernd Widdig, *Culture and Inflation in Weimar Germany* (Berkeley, 2001), 36.
6. Widdig, *Culture and Inflation*, 45.
7. Ibid., 92.
8. 'National Education and Impoverishment', *Vorwärts*, Nr 86, 21 February 1923, morning edition.
9. Martin Geyer, *Verkehrte Welt*, 273; 'The Emergency in Berlin: An Account by Mayor Böß', *Vorwärts*, Nr 165, 10 April 1923, morning edition.
10. 'Our Life of Suffering: A Warning Cry for Help from Another Political Camp', *Vorwärts*, Nr 569, 6 December 1923, morning edition.
11. 'The Ruhr Occupation and Town Councils', *Vorwärts*, Nr 83, 19 February 1923, evening edition; 'National Education and Impoverishment', *Vorwärts*, Nr 86, 21 February 1923, morning edition.
12. Fischer, *The Ruhr Crisis*, 119; 'National Education and Impoverishment', *Vorwärts*, Nr 86, 21 February 1923, morning edition.
13. Fischer, *The Ruhr Crisis*, 120.
14. 'Children from the Ruhr Travel Through Berlin', *Vorwärts*, Nr 77, 15 February 1923, evening edition; 'Evacuation to the Countryside for Children from the Ruhr', *Vorwärts*, Nr 66, 9 February 1923, morning edition; Fischer, *The Ruhr Crisis*, 124; Conan Fischer,

'The Human Price of Reparations', in Conan Fischer and Alan Sharp (eds), *After the Versailles Treaty: Enforcement, Compliance, Contested Identities* (Basingstoke, 2007), 81–96.

15. Fischer, *The Ruhr Crisis*, 124.

16. Ibid., 117–35.

17. Ibid., 125–6.

18. Ibid., 122–3.

19. Ibid., 132.

20. Ibid.

21. 'Desperate Housewives', *Vorwärts*, Nr 353, 31 July 1923, morning edition; 'Increase Wages!', *Vorwärts*, Nr 255, 3 June 1923, Sunday edition; Feldman, *The Great Disorder*, 673; Martin Geyer, *Verkehrte Welt*, 319; Widdig, *Culture and Inflation*, 46.

22. Feldmann, *The Great Disorder*, 673; 'Increase Wages!', *Vorwärts*, Nr 255, 3 June 1923, Sunday edition.

23. 'Examination of a Worker's Budget', *Vorwärts*, Nr 263, 8 June 1923, morning edition.

24. Christian Goeschel, *Suicide in Nazi Germany* (Oxford, 2009), 15–19; Martin Geyer, *Verkehrte Welt*, 327.

25. Cornelie Usborne, *Cultures of Abortion in Weimar Germany* (New York, 2007), 164–5, 195.

26. 'Hopeless Starvation, by a Single Woman', *Vorwärts*, Nr 309, 5 July 1923, morning edition; Widdig, *Culture and Inflation*, 212; 'International Trafficking of Girls: Statements of Criminal Commissioner Kopp', *Vorwärts*, Nr 185, 21 April 1923, morning edition.

27. Mary Elisabeth Cox, *Hunger in War and Peace: Women and Children in Germany, 1914–1924* (Oxford, 2019), 326.

28. Ibid., 179.

29. Ibid., 293–4; '720 Million in Aid from Denmark', *Vorwärts*, Nr 64, 8 February 1923, morning edition.

30. Cox, *Hunger in War and Peace*, 326; Mary Elisabeth Cox, 'Hunger Games: Or How the Allied Blockade in the First World War Deprived German Children of Nutrition, and Allied Food Aid Subsequently Saved Them', *Economic History Review*, 68:2 (2015), 600–31.

31. See also Paul Ufermann, *Könige der Inflation* (Berlin, 1924).

32. Widdig, *Culture and Inflation*, 126.

33. Feldman, *The Great Disorder*, 702; Widdig, *Culture and Inflation*, 87.

34. German Diary Archive, 1804/1 Weidner Diary, 90–4.

35. Quoted in Widdig, *Culture and Inflation*, 44.

36. The figure is in ibid., 114. The comparison: Martin Geyer, *Verkehrte Welt*, 261.

37. 'Contempt for Intellectual Work', *Vorwärts*, Nr 384, 18 August 1923, evening edition.

38. Cited in Martin Geyer, *Verkehrte Welt*, 328.

39. Elias Canetti, *The Torch in my Ear*, trans. Joachim Neugroschel (London, 2011), 58–9.

40. Widdig, *Culture and Inflation*, 86, 10–11.

41. Evans, *The Coming of the Third Reich*, 103–17; Goeschel, *Suicide in Nazi Germany*, 16.

Chapter 11: Waiting for Allies

1. On Bonar Law, see Andrew Taylor, *Bonar Law* (London, 2006), 128. On mixed German responses, see 'Baldwin Prime Minister' and 'Henderson Above Baldwin', *Vorwärts*, Nr 235, 23 May 1923, morning edition; 'The Debate About the New Prime Minister', *Berliner Volks-Zeitung*, Nr 233, 23 May 1923, evening edition; 'Paris Satisfied by Baldwin's Appointment', Paris, Exclusive Telegram, *Deutsche Allgemeine Zeitung*, Nr 232, 23 May 1923, morning edition; 'French Sympathy for Baldwin', *Berliner Tageblatt*, Nr 233, 23 May 1923, evening edition.

2. Steiner, *The Lights That Failed*, 228; O'Riordan, *Britain and the Ruhr Crisis*, 54.

3. For examples of British newspaper reporting on the expulsions of railway workers from the Ruhr, see 'Ruhr Expulsions', *The Times*, 31 March 1923 (From Our Special Correspondent). See further, 'Bloodshed at Essen: Krupp Workers Fired On', *The Times*, 2 April 1923 (From Our Special Correspondent); 'Paris Defence of Shooting: Plea of German Provocation', Paris, 1 April 1923, *The Times*, 2 April 1923; 'French Grip on Ruhr: Sterner Punitive Measures', Düsseldorf, 9 April 1923, *The Times*, 10 April 1923; 'Prominent Germans Arrested', *The Times*, 11 April 1923.

4. John Horne and Alan Kramer, *German Atrocities 1914: A History of Denial* (New Haven, 2001), 366–400; 'French Ruhr Aims', From Our Own Correspondent, *The Times*, 31 March 1923; 'The Essen

Shooting', Essen, 2 April 1923, From Our Own Correspondent, *The Times*, 3 April 1923; 'German Indignation at the Massacre', Berlin, From Our Own Correspondent, *Manchester Guardian*, 6 April 1923; 'Dr Cuno's Funeral Oration: Reichstag Ceremony', From Our Own Correspondent, *The Times*, 11 April 1923; 'President Ebert's Message', Reuter, Berlin, 1 April 1923, *The Times*, 3 April 1923. See also 'German Protest Against Essen Shooting: Note to Allied Governments', Berlin, 4 April 1923, From Our Own Correspondent, *The Times*, 5 April 1923.

5. O'Riordan, *Britain and the Ruhr Crisis*, 75.

6. Ibid., 75–8; Lampson quotation, 78.

7. Ibid., 49.

8. Jeannesson, *Poincaré*, 208–22.

9. O'Riordan, *Britain and the Ruhr Crisis*, 79.

10. Wright, *Gustav Stresemann*, 211.

11. Winkler, *Weimar 1918–1933*, 200–1; 'An Emotional Mood in and Around Leipzig', *Vorwärts*, Nr 373, 11 August 1923, evening edition; 'Tension in the Ruhr District', Exclusive Telegram, *Vorwärts*, Nr 375, 14 August 1923, morning edition.

12. 'Events in Neuruppin', *Vorwärts*, Nr 356, 1 August 1923, evening edition.

13. 'Riots in the Reich', *Vorwärts*, Nr 375, 14 August 1923, morning edition; 'Tension in the Ruhr District', Exclusive Telegram, *Vorwärts*, Nr 375, 14 August 1923, morning edition; Dirk Schumann, *Political Violence in the Weimar Republic, 1918–1933: Fight for the Streets and Fear of Civil War*, trans. Thomas Dunlap (New York, 2009), 126.

14. 'The Frenzy of Rising Prices', Gelsenkirchen, 11 August 1923, WTB, *Vorwärts*, Nr 374, 12 August 1923, morning edition; 'The Victims of Incitement to Hatred', *Vorwärts*, Nr 378, 15 August 1923, evening edition; 'Riots in the Reich', *Vorwärts*, Nr 375, 14 August 1923, morning edition; 'Riots in Oberhausen', Oberhausen, 1 August 1923, WTB, *Vorwärts*, Nr 358, 2 August 1923, evening edition.

15. Schumann, *Political Violence in the Weimar Republic*, 124.

16. 'Riots in Krefeld', *Vorwärts*, Nr 373, 11 August 1923, evening edition; 'Riots in Hannover', *Vorwärts*, Nr 374, 12 August 1923, morning edition; 'The Victims of Incitement to Hatred', *Vorwärts*, Nr 378, 15 August 1923, evening edition.

17. Alex Watson, *Ring of Steel: Germany and Austria-Hungary in World War I – The People's War* (New York, 2014), 416.

18. Wright, *Gustav Stresemann*, 81.

19. 'Stresemann's Coalition Cabinet', *Berliner Tageblatt*, Nr 376, 13 August 1923, evening edition; 'The New Man', *Berliner Volks-Zeitung*, Nr 376, 13 August 1923, evening edition.

20. Wright, *Gustav Stresemann*, 210.

21. RK Stresemann, Vol. 1, Nr 14, 'Meeting of the Party Leaders', 57; RK Stresemann, Vol. 1, Nr 27, 'Meeting of the Economic Committee for the Occupied Territories', 28 August 1923, 132– 4, quotation on 134.

22. RK Stresemann, Vol. 1, Nr 14, 'Meeting of the Party Leaders', 22 August 1923, 58; RK Stresemann, Vol. 1, Nr 18, 'Cabinet Meeting of 23 August 1923', 75–83, quotation on 79; RK Stresemann, Vol. 1, Nr 18, 'Cabinet Meeting of 23August 1923', 80–1.

23. Friedrich Stampfer, 'Negotiations with France?', *Vorwärts*, Nr 356, 1 August 1923, evening edition; 'Britain States Her Case', London, Sunday Night, *Manchester Guardian*, 13 August 1923.

24. RK Stresemann, Vol. 1, Nr 8, 'Chancellor Stresemann's Notes on the Visit of Foreign Ambassadors on 17 August 1923', note 3, 18–19.

25. RK Stresemann, Vol. 1 Nr 18, 'Cabinet Meeting of 23 August 1923', 75–83, esp. 75.

26. 'The Entente: German Gambles on Disruption – To the Editor of *The Times*', *The Times*, 15 August 1923.

27. O'Riordan, *Britain and the Ruhr Crisis*, 90.

28. Jeannesson, *Poincaré*, 292–3; O'Riordan, *Britain and the Ruhr Crisis*, 97.

29. Jeannesson, *Poincaré*, 292–3; O'Riordan, *Britain and the Ruhr Crisis*, 97; 'Stresemann Forms His Cabinet', *Berliner Volks-Zeitung*, Nr 376, 13 August 1923, evening edition; '121,000,000 Dollars', *Berliner Volks-Zeitung*, Nr 450, 25 September 1923, evening edition.

30. O'Riordan, *Britain and the Ruhr Crisis*, 98.

Chapter 12: Separatism and the Future of the Rhineland

1. Quoted in Angelika Schnorrenberger, 'Der Düsseldorfer "Blutsonntag", 30. September 1923', in Krumeich and Schröder (eds), *Der Schatten des Weltkriegs*, 289–303, here 290; Jeannesson, *Poincaré*, 286.

2. 'Treasonous Dorten Speaks on the Republic of the Rhine', Paris, 30 September 1923, WTB, *Deutsche Allgemeine Zeitung*, Nr 454, 1 October 1923.

3. Schnorrenberger, 'Der Düsseldorfer "Blutsonntag"', 290.

4. Jeannesson, *Poincaré*, 285–6; Schnorrenberger, 'Der Düsseldorfer "Blutsonntag"', 290.

5. RK Stresemann, Vol. 1, Nr 8, 17 August 1923, 18–23, here 22.

6. Jeannesson, *Poincaré*, 287.

7. Schnorrenberger, 'Der Düsseldorfer "Blutsonntag"', 294. It has not been established if this money was actually paid; O'Riordan, *Britain and the Ruhr Crisis*, 112; citation in Jeannesson, *Poincaré*, 288.

8. 'The Centre Party and the Rhineland', *Germania*, Nr 270, 29 September 1923; Jeannesson, *Poincaré*, 319.

9. 'Attack on Smeets', Cologne, 17 March 1923, WTB, *Vorwärts*, Nr 130, 18 March 1923, morning edition; 'Attempt to Murder Smeets', Cologne, 19 March, WTB, *Vorwärts*, Nr 131, 19 March 1923, evening edition.

10. Jeannesson, *Poincaré*, 219; '"Rhenish Day"', Cologne, 28 September 1923, WTB, *Germania*, Nr 270, 29 September 1923.

11. 'The Rhineland's Commitment to the Unity of the Reich', Cologne, 1 October 1923, *Vossische Zeitung*, Nr 464, 1 October 1923, evening edition; 'Massive Anti-separatist Demonstration in Cologne: The Rhineland is Loyal to the Reich', Cologne, 30 September 1923, WTB, *Deutsche Allgemeine Zeitung*, Nr 454, 1 October 1923; 'The People of Cologne Swear Loyalty', Cologne, 1 October 1923, Telegraph Union, *Der oberschlesische Wanderer*, Nr 227, 1 October 1923.

12. 'Intransparent', *Germania*, Nr 272, 1 October 1923; 'In Hamborn as in Düsseldorf', *Vorwärts*, Nr 458, 1 October 1923, evening edition; 'Separatism on the Rhine', *Vorwärts*, Nr 457, 30 September 1923.

13. Schnorrenberger, 'Der Düsseldorfer "Blutsonntag"', 295; 'Uniformed Police Officer Shot', Düsseldorf, 24 September 1923, WTB, *Vorwärts*, Nr 447, 25 September 1923, morning edition.

14. Schnorrenberger, 'Der Düsseldorfer "Blutsonntag"', 292–4. See 'A "Dead Sunday" in Düsseldorf', Düsseldorf, 29 September 1923, WTB, *Germania*, Nr 270, 29 September 1923; 'Bloody Clashes in Düsseldorf', Düsseldorf, 1 October 1923, Telegram from Our Correspondent, *Berliner Tageblatt*, Nr 460, 1 October 1923, evening

edition; 'Bloody Sunday in Düsseldorf' (Report), *Deutsche Allgemeine Zeitung*, Nr 454, 1 October 1923.

15. Schnorrenberger, 'Der Düsseldorfer "Blutsonntag"', 296.

16. Ibid., 296–7.

17. Fourteen hundred Stormtroopers and thirty thousand demonstrators are in 'Bloody Clashes in Düsseldorf', Düsseldorf, 1 October 1923, Telegram from Our Correspondent, *Berliner Tageblatt*, Nr 460, 1 October 1923, evening edition. Twenty thousand is given in 'Bloody Sunday in Düsseldorf', *Deutsche Allgemeine Zeitung*, Nr 454, 1 October 1923, forty thousand in 'Havas Lies About Events', Paris, Telegraph Union, *Deutsche Allgemeine Zeitung*, Nr 454, 1 October 1923. Havas was the leading French news agency.

18. Schnorrenberger, 'Der Düsseldorfer "Blutsonntag"', 296.

19. Ibid., 291–7; 'The Düsseldorf Riot', From Our Special Correspondent, *The Times*, 6 October 1923; '10 Dead, 74 Badly Injured', Ruhr, 1 October 1923, Telegram from Our Correspondent, *Berliner Tageblatt*, Nr 460, 1 October 1923, evening edition.

20. '10 Dead, 74 Badly Injured', Ruhr, 1 October 1923, Telegram from Our Correspondent, *Berliner Tageblatt*, Nr 460, 1 October 1923, evening edition; 'The Victims of Düsseldorf', Elberfeld, 1 October 1923, Exclusive Telegram, *Vorwärts*, Nr 459, 2 October 1923, morning edition; 'Düsseldorf is Afraid', Düsseldorf, 1 October 1923, *Vossische Zeitung*, Nr 464, 1 October 1923, evening edition.

21. Jeannesson, *Poincaré*, 319.

22. 'Eyewitness Testimony', *Deutsche Allgemeine Zeitung*, Nr 454, 1 October 1923; 'The Fighting in Düsseldorf', Düsseldorf, 30 September 1923, *Vossische Zeitung*, Nr 464, 1 October 1923, evening edition.

23. 'Bloody Sunday in Düsseldorf', Exclusive Telegram, *Deutsche Allgemeine Zeitung*, Nr 454, 1 October 1923; 'Bloody Clashes in Düsseldorf', Düsseldorf, 1 October 1923, Telegram from Our Correspondent, *Berliner Tageblatt*, Nr 460, 1 October 1923, evening edition.

24. 'The Fighting in Düsseldorf', Düsseldorf, 30 September 1923, *Vossische Zeitung*, Nr 464, 1 October 1923, evening edition.

25. 'Bloody Clashes in Düsseldorf', Düsseldorf, 1 October 1923, Telegram from Our Correspondent, *Berliner Tageblatt*, Nr 460, 1 October 1923, evening edition. See also 'Bloody Sunday on the

Rhine: Separatists Attack Under French Protection', *Vorwärts*, Nr 458, 1 October 1923, evening edition.

26. 'Intransparent', *Germania*, Nr 272, 1 October 1923; 'Eyewitness Testimony', *Deutsche Allgemeine Zeitung*, Nr 454, 1 October 1923; '10 Dead, 74 Badly Injured', Ruhr, 1 October 1923, Telegram from Our Correspondent, *Berliner Tageblatt*, Nr 460, 1 October 1923, evening edition; 'The Victims of Düsseldorf', Elberfeld, 1 October 1923, Exclusive Telegram, *Vorwärts*, Nr 459, 2 October 1923, morning edition.

27. 'Düsseldorf is Afraid', Düsseldorf, 1 October 1923, *Vossische Zeitung*, Nr 464, 1 October 1923, evening edition.

28. '10 Dead, 74 Badly Injured', Ruhr, 1 October 1923, Telegram from our Correspondent, *Berliner Tageblatt*, Nr 460, 1 October 1923, evening edition; 'Eyewitness Testimony', *Deutsche Allgemeine Zeitung*, Nr 454, 1 October 1923.

29. 'Dissolution of Düsseldorf's Uniformed Police', Paris, 3 October 1923, Telegraph Union, *Vorwärts*, Nr 462, 3 October 1923, evening edition; 'The Düsseldorf Fighting: A Workers' Protest – From our Special Correspondent', *The Times*, 4 October 1923. See also '"Red Sunday" in Düsseldorf', *The Times*, 2 October 1923.

30. 'Events in Düsseldorf: Eyewitness Testimony', Düsseldorf, 1 October 1923, Telegram from Our Correspondent, *Berliner Tageblatt*, Nr 460, 1 October 1923, evening edition.

31. 'Bloody Sunday in Düsseldorf', Exclusive Report, *Deutsche Allgemeine Zeitung*, Nr 454, 1 October 1923; 'Rhenish Separatism', *Vorwärts*, Nr 457, 30 September 1923; 'Düsseldorf is Afraid', Düsseldorf, 1 October 1923, *Vossische Zeitung*, Nr 464, 1 October 1923, evening edition; 'The Dusseldorf Rioting: German Officials on Trial', Cologne, 4 October 1923, *The Times*, 5 October 1923.

32. 'France and the Separatists', Paris, 1 October 1923, *Vorwärts*, Nr 459, 2 October 1923, morning edition; Jeannesson, *Poincaré*, 320.

33. 'Republic of the "Rhineland"! Proclamation in Aachen', *Berliner Tageblatt*, Nr 43, 24 October 1923, weekly edition; 'Will the Reich Collapse?', *Berliner Tageblatt*, Nr 43, 24 October 1923, weekly edition.

34. O'Riordan, *Britain and the Ruhr Crisis*, 112; 'Separatists Defeated Almost Everywhere', *Berliner Tageblatt*, Nr 500, 24 October 1923, evening edition.

35. O'Riordan, *Britain and the Ruhr Crisis*, 112.
36. Jeannesson, *Poincaré*, 333.
37. O'Riordan, *Britain and the Ruhr Crisis*, 113.
38. Ibid., 114.
39. Wright, *Gustav Stresemann*, 233–8.
40. 'Fighting the Separatists', *Vorwärts*, Nr 550, 24 November 1923, evening edition.
41. O'Riordan, *Britain and the Ruhr Crisis*, 115–16.

Chapter 13: 'Soviet Saxony' and the Communist Threat

1. Wright, *Gustav Stresemann*, 220.
2. Reiner Pommerin, 'Die Ausweisung von "Ostjuden" aus Bayern 1923: Ein Beitrag zum Krisenjahr der Weimarer Republik', *Vierteljahrshefte für Zeitgeschichte*, 34:3 (1984), 311–40, 312; Winkler, *Weimar 1918–1933*, 210; 'State of Emergency Throughout Germany: The Executive Power of the Reichswehr Minister', *Vorwärts*, Nr 452, 27 September 1923, evening edition.
3. Wright, *Gustav Stresemann*, 235; Heinz Hürten, *Das Krisenjahr 1923: Militär- und Innenpolitik 1922–1924* (Düsseldorf, 1980), Nr 51, 96–7.
4. 'State of Emergency in Bavaria: Von Kahr Appointed General State Commissioner', *Vorwärts*, Nr 451, 27 September 1923, morning edition.
5. Pommerin, 'Die Ausweisung von "Ostjuden" aus Bayern 1923', 313; 'Ludendorff Revolution', 27 September 1923, Exclusive Telegram, *Vorwärts*, Nr 452, 27 September 1923, evening edition; 'State of Emergency in Bavaria: Von Kahr Appointed General State Commissioner', *Vorwärts*, Nr 451, 27 September 1923, morning edition.
6. 'Action Against the Munich Workers' Defence', Munich, 28 September 1923, Exclusive Telegram, *Vorwärts*, Nr 455, 29 September 1923, morning edition; 'Kahr's Crusade Against the Reich', Munich, 29 September 1923, Exclusive Telegram, *Vorwärts*, Nr 457, 30 September 1923, Sunday edition.
7. 'Incitement to Hatred Against Zeigner', *Vorwärts*, Nr 168, 11 April 1923, evening edition; Walter Mühlhausen, *Friedrich Ebert 1871– 1925: Reichspräsident der Weimarer Republik* (Bonn, 2006), 642.
8. Hürten, *Krisenjahr 1923*, Nr 29: List of Reichswehr Complaints

Against Saxon Minister President Zeigner, 63–5; Nr 51: Resolution of the Bavarian Government from 20 October 1923.

9. Mühlhausen, *Friedrich Ebert*, 645; 'Zeigner Against Geßler', Dresden, 14 August 1923, *Vossiche Zeitung*, Nr 383, 15 August 1923, morning edition; quoted in Mühlhausen, *Friedrich Ebert*, 655.

10. Jones, *Founding Weimar*, 225–6, 240, 245 and esp. 291–2.

11. Winkler, *Weimar 1918–1933*, 213–15.

12. Ibid., 224; Mühlhausen, *Friedrich Ebert*, 648.

13. Mühlhausen, *Friedrich Ebert*, 652.

14. Winkler, *Weimar 1918–1933*, 210–11.

15. 'The Right-Wing Putsch in Küstrin', *Vorwärts*, Nr 459, 2 October 1923, morning edition; Mühlhausen, *Friedrich Ebert*, 650.

16. Winkler, *Weimar 1918–1933*, 220; Wright, *Gustav Stresemann*, 222–3.

17. Feldman, *Hugo Stinnes*, 883–95.

18. Wright, *Gustav Stresemann*, 224–5.

19. Reichstag, Session 385, 6 October 1923, 11934–40.

20. Ibid.

21. Winkler, *Weimar 1918–1933*, 221–2; Wright, *Gustav Stresemann*, 226.

22. Wright, *Gustav Stresemann*, 234.

23. 'The Conflict Intensifies in Saxony', *Vorwärts*, Nr 487, 18 October 1923, morning edition; Mühlhausen, *Friedrich Ebert*, 653.

24. Mühlhausen, *Friedrich Ebert*, 649.

25. Winkler, *Weimar 1918–1933*, 225.

26. 'Communist Putsch in Hamburg', *Vorwärts*, Nr 496, 23 October 1923, evening edition; 'The Communist Putsch in Hamburg', Hamburg, 23 October 1923, midnight, Exclusive Telegram, *Vorwärts*, Nr 497, 24 October 1923, morning edition; Winkler, *Weimar 1918–1933*, 226.

27. 'Communist Putsch in Hamburg', *Vorwärts*, Nr 496, 23 October 1923, evening edition; 'The Insanity of Self-Destruction', *Vorwärts*, Nr 499, 25 October 1923, morning edition.

28. Mühlhausen, *Friedrich Ebert*, 657; 'Reichswehr Parade in Dresden', *Berliner Tageblatt*, Nr 499, 24 October 1923, morning edition; 'Events in Pirna and Annaberg', Plauen, 23 October 1923, *Berliner Tageblatt*, Nr 499, 24 October 1923, morning edition.

29. Mühlhausen, *Friedrich Ebert*, 657–8.

30. Ibid., 657.

31. Ibid., 662; RK Stresemann, Vol. 2, 868.

32. 'Law and Power', *Vossische Zeitung*, Nr 512, 29 October 1923, cited in Mühlhausen, *Friedrich Ebert*, 674.

33. Winkler, *Weimar 1918–1933*, 228; Mühlhausen, *Friedrich Ebert*, 667.

34. Wright, *Gustav Stresemann*, 239; RK Stresemann, Vol. 2, Cabinet minutes, 27 October 1923, 850.

35. Mühlhausen, *Friedrich Ebert*, 668; Winkler, *Weimar 1918–1933*, 229.

36. Wright, *Gustav Stresemann*, 243.

37. RK Stresemann, Vol. 2, Nr 215, 948–53; ibid., Nr 216, note 3, 954.

Chapter 14: The Hitler Putsch

1. JK, Nr 563, Nuremberg, 2 September 1923, 'Speech to a Nazi-Party Assembly', report from the *Frankfurter Zeitung*, 6 September 1923, 990.

2. Kershaw, *Hitler 1889–1936*, 198–9.

3. JK, Nr 564, Nuremberg, 2 September 1923, 'Appeal of the Patriotic Fighting Leagues', 990–2.

4. Ibid.

5. JK, Nr 566, Munich, 5 September 1923, 'Germany's Suffering from Wirth to Hilferding', 'Speech at a Nazi-Party Assembly', 998–1004.

6. Ibid., 1002.

7. JK, Nr 568, Munich, 12 September 1923, 'The Collapse of the November Republic and Our Movement's Mission', 'Speech to a Nazi-Party Assembly', report from the *Völkischen Beobachter*, 14 September 1923, 1007–13.

8. 'Hitler's Appeal: Preparation for the Attempted Coup', Munich, 26 September 1923, Telegraph Union, *Vorwärts*, Nr 450, 26 September 1923, evening edition.

9. JK, Nr 580, Munich, 2 October 1923, 'Interview with the *Daily Mail*', 1027.

10. 'On the Eve of the Hitler-Ludendorff Putsch', Munich, 26 September 1923, Exclusive Telegram, *Vorwärts*, Nr 451, 27 September 1923, morning edition.

11. 'State of Emergency in Bavaria: Von Kahr named General State Commissioner', *Vorwärts*, Nr 451, 27 September 1923, morning edition.

12. JK, Nr 581, Bamberg, 7 October 1923, 'Speech on German Day', 1028–9.

13. JK, Nr 586, Munich, 19 October 1923, 'Speech at an SA-Assembly', 1038–41, quoting report from the *Münchener Neueste Nachrichten*, 21 October 1923; JK, Nr 592, Munich, 30 October 1923, 'Speech at a Nazi-Party Assembly', 1047–51.

14. Harold J. Gordon, *Hitler and the Beer Hall Putsch* (Princeton, 1972), 282.

15. Dirk Walter, *Antisemitische Kriminalität und Gewalt: Judenfeindschaft in der Weimarer Republik* (Bonn, 1999), 121.

16. 'Nightmare in the *Bürgerbräu*', Munich, 9 November 1923, WTB, *Vorwärts*, Nr 526, 9 November 1923, evening edition.

17. 'Frankfurt, 10 November', *Frankfurter Zeitung*, Nr 837, 10 November 1923, evening edition.

18. Gordon, *Hitler and the Beer Hall Putsch*, 285.

19. Ibid., 286; Longerich, *Hitler*, 118.

20. Ullrich, *Hitler*, 149.

21. Ibid., 151.

22. "Nightmare in the *Bürgerbräu*', Munich, 9 November 1923, WTB, *Vorwärts*, Nr 526, 9 November 1923, evening edition. The use of the term *Verweser* is important to note. The same term was central to Theodor von der Pfordten's constitution of the new state.

23. Gordon, *Hitler and the Beer Hall Putsch*, 288.

24. Ullrich, *Hitler*, 151; Gordon, *Hitler and the Beer Hall Putsch*, 290.

25. Gordon, *Hitler and the Beer Hall Putsch*, 291.

26. Ibid., 307.

27. Ibid., 294–5.

28. Ibid., 308–9.

29. Ullrich, *Hitler*, 155; Kershaw, *Hitler 1889–1936*, 210–11.

30. 'Taking Care of the Putsch', *Frankfurter Zeitung*, Nr 837, 10 November 1923, evening edition.

31. Gordon, *Hitler and the Beer Hall Putsch*, 344–5.

32. Ibid., 347–8.

33. Ibid., 349–50.

Chapter 15: Taking It Out on the Jews

1. Reiner Pommerin, 'Die Ausweisung von "Ostjuden" aus Bayern 1923', 315–19; Gerald D. Feldman, 'Bayern und Sachsen in der Hyperinflation 1922/23', *Historische Zeitschrift*, 238:3 (1984), 569–609, here 607.

2. 'The Facts', *Das Jüdische Echo*, Nr 48, 30 November 1923; BArch Berlin, Bl.74: 'Berlin, 29 October 1923: Draft of the Reichs-Chancellery', L382124.

3. Pommerin, 'Die Ausweisung von "Ostjuden" aus Bayern 1923', 323. 'Report of an Eyewitness on the Deportation Measures Against Jews in Munich', 31 October 1923, in RK Stresemann, Vol. 2, Nr 211, 928; BArch-Berlin 43-1/2193, Bl.83–4 (part of 'Report of an Eyewitness from Munich'); BArch-Berlin 43-1/2193, Bl.69–70: Reich Commissioner for the Control of Public Order, Berlin, 30 October 1923, here Bl.70.

4. Pommerin, 'Die Ausweisung von "Ostjuden" aus Bayern 1923', 324.

5. Ibid.

6. Ibid., 315–16.

7. BArch-Berlin 43-1/2193, Bl.79 (part of 'Report of an Eyewitness from Munich'); Pommerin, 'Die Ausweisung von "Ostjuden" aus Bayern 1923', 325–6.

8. Quoted in Pommerin, 'Die Ausweisung von "Ostjuden" aus Bayern 1923', 335. Original is Martin Enker, 'Kahr, Hitler and the Jews', *Die Weltbühne*, Nr 45, 8 November 1923.

9. BArch-Berlin 43-1/2193, Bl.82 (part of 'Report of an Eyewitness from Munich').

10. 'The Deployment of Hitler's Guards', Coburg, 6 November 1923, Special Service of the *Vossische Zeitung*, *Vossische Zeitung*, Nr 527, 7 November 1923, morning edition; Walter, *Antisemitische Kriminalität*, 117. Some members of the group later claimed that participants in the raid were forced to join in – a claim that was made when they faced prosecution for this crime.

11. At least according to the report of the Jewish *CV-Zeitung*, which had reason to exaggerate the violence.

12. Walter, *Antisemitische Kriminalität*, 117. See 'Aus der Geschichte der jüdischen Gemeinden im deutschen Sprachraum', https://www.jüdische-gemeinden.de On Autenhausen see https://www.jüdische-gemeinden.de/index.php/gemeinden/a-b/287-autenhausen-oberfranken-bayern

13. 'Dark Days: Serious Rioting in Berlin and in the Reich', *CV-Zeitung*, Nrs 45–6, 23 November 1923; 'Anti-Jewish Rioting in Nuremberg', *Jüdische Rundschau*, Nr 95, 6 November 1923.

14. 'Neidenburger Idyll: German *Völkische* Hooligans Face Court', *CV-Zeitung*, Nr 5, 31 January 1924.

15. 'Neidenburg Jews' Attackers Appear in Court', *Jüdische Rundschau*, Nr 6, 22 January 1924.
16. Walter, *Antisemitische Kriminalität*, 116–18; 'Antisemitic Rioting in Beuthen', Breslau, 6 October 1923, Telegram from Our Correspondent, *Berliner Tageblatt*, Nr 471, 7 October 1923, morning edition; Feldman, *The Great Disorder*, 781.
17. 'Dark Days: Serious Rioting in Berlin and in the Reich', *CV-Zeitung*, Nrs 45–6, 23 November 1923.
18. The best account in English is David Clay Large, '"Out with the Ostjuden": The Scheunenviertel Riots in Berlin, November 1923', in Christhard Hoffmann, Werner Bergmann and Helmut Walser Smith (eds), *Exclusionary Violence: Antisemitic Riots in Modern German History* (Michigan, 2002), 123–40; 'Riots in the Centre of Berlin: Antisemitic Attacks', *CV-Zeitung*, Nr 525, 6 November 1923, morning edition.
19. 'Riots in the Centre of Berlin: Antisemitic Attacks', *CV-Zeitung*, Nr 525, 6 November 1923, morning edition. See also 'Major Incidents of Looting and Rioting in Berlin: The Activities of the Strip Commandos', *Berliner-Börsen Zeitung*, Nr 516, 6 November 1923, morning edition; 'The Attacks in Berlin', *CV-Zeitung*, Nr 525, 6 November 1923, morning edition; 'Major Incidents of Looting and Rioting in Berlin: The Activities of the "Strip Commandos"', *Germania*, Nr 308, 6 November 1923; Large, '"Out with the Ostjuden"', 131–5; Walter, *Antisemitische Kriminalität*, 153.
20. 'Mob Attacks in Friedrichstadt', *Vorwärts*, Nr 519, 6 November 1923, morning edition.
21. Large, '"Out with the Ostjuden"', 134; 'Attacks and Looting: A Turbulent Night: Police Respond With Full Force', *Vorwärts*, Nr 520, 6 November 1923, evening edition; 'Dark Days: Serious Rioting in Berlin and in the Reich', *CV-Zeitung*, Nrs 45–6, 23 November 1923.
22. 'Major Incidents of Looting and Rioting in Berlin: The Activities of the Strip Commandos', *Berliner-Börsen Zeitung*, Nr 516, 6 November 1923, morning edition.
23. Walter, *Antisemitische Kriminalität*, 152–3; Clay, '"Out with the Ostjuden"', 131.
24. Clay, '"Out with the Ostjuden"', 131; Landesarchiv Berlin Rep. 58, 2743, Judgement, City Court, Berlin, 18–20 June 1925, in Walter, *Antisemitische Kriminalität*, 297; 'Riots in the Centre of Berlin:

Antisemitic Attacks', *CV-Zeitung*, Nr 525, 6 November 1923, morning edition.

25. Walter, *Antisemitische Kriminalität*, 153.

26. Landesarchiv Berlin Rep. 58, 2743, Judgement, City Court, Berlin, 18–20 June 1925, in Walter, *Antisemitische Kriminalität*, 297.

27. The police later reported that, in total, between 3 and 7 November 1923 in Berlin, 55 clothes and shoe shops and 152 food stores were plundered. Of these, 146 were owned by Christians and 61 by Jews. Some historians take this as evidence that the motivation behind the rioters was only partially antisemitic. In this view, the riots were part-pogrom, part-bread riot. It is not entirely wrong to point out that Christian-owned businesses were also targeted. But it is important to remember that the targeting of businesses in an area primarily associated with Jews was an antisemitic act, *even if* the business owners in that district were not Jews themselves. Walter, *Antisemitische Kriminalität*, 153.

28. 'Dark Days: Serious Rioting in Berlin and in the Reich', *CV-Zeitung*, Nrs 45–6, 23 November 1923; 'Riots in the Centre of Berlin: Antisemitic Attacks', *Vossische Zeitung*, Nr 525, 6 November 1923, morning edition; Arthur Crispien, 'The Poor Cheated Ones!', *Vorwärts*, 8 November 1923; Walter, *Antisemitische Kriminalität*, 151.

29. 'Hatred of Jews and the Reaction', *Vorwärts*, 14 November 1923, evening edition; 'Against the Incitement to Hatred of the Jews', *Vorwärts*, 5 December 1923, evening edition; Walter, *Antisemitische Kriminalität*, 153–4.

30. Walter, *Antisemitische Kriminalität*, 122.

31. Ibid., 125–7.

32. Ibid., 133.

33. Ibid., 124.

34. Michael Brenner, *In Hitler's Munich: Jews, the Revolution, and the Rise of Nazism*, trans. Jeremiah Riemer (Princeton, 2022), 234, 238–42.

35. 'The Storm Tide of Hatred', *Das Jüdische Echo*, Nr 48, 30 November 1923.

Chapter 16: De-escalation and the Triumph of Reason

1. Reichstag, Session 392, 22 November 1923, 12180–5, quotations 12180, 12185, 12187.

2. Wright, *Gustav Stresemann*, 258.

3. Winkler, *Weimar 1918–1933*, 241; Büttner, *Weimar*, 207.

4. Reichstag, Session 394, 4 December 1923, 12296.

5. 'Marx's Cabinet', *Vorwärts*, Nr 561, 1 December 1923, morning edition.

6. Larry Eugene Jones, *The German Right, 1918–1930: Political Parties, Organized Interests, and Patriotic Associations in the Struggle Against Weimar Democracy* (Cambridge, 2020), 205–6; 'They Cannot Assert Themselves', *Vorwärts*, Nr 580, 12 December 1923, evening edition.

7. Ullrich, *Hitler*, 183; Larry Eugene Jones, *The German Right*, 207; Longerich, *Hitler*, 120.

8. Adolf Hitler, *Der Hitler-Prozess 1924: Wortlaut der Hauptverhandlung vor dem Volksgericht München*, Part 1 (Munich, 1997), 299–307; Ullrich, *Hitler*, 184; Longerich, *Hitler*, 121.

9. Kershaw, *Hitler 1889–1936*, 214–17; Longerich, *Hitler*, 125.

10. Longerich, *Hitler*, 125–6. The *Deutsche Allgemeine Zeitung* commentary was quoted in 'After the Munich Judgement', *Vossische Zeitung*, Nr 158, 2 April 1924, morning edition; 'After the Judgement: The Reverberations', *Berliner Volkszeitung*, Nr 158, 2 April 1924, morning edition.

11. 'After the Judgement: The Reverberations', *Berliner Volkszeitung*, Nr 158, 2 April 1924, morning edition; 'After the Munich Judgement', *Vossische Zeitung*, Nr 158, 2 April 1924, morning edition; 'Germany's Justice Disgrace', *Vorwärts*, Nr 158, 2 April 1924, evening edition.

12. Chancellor Marx, 'Christmas', *Germania*, Nr 352, 25 December 1923.

13. 'A Political Christmas Greeting from the Chancellor', Berlin, 25 December 1923, WTB, *Frankfurter Zeitung*, Nr 955, 27 December 1923, morning edition; 'Chancellor Marx on the Demands of the Hour', *Germania*, Nr 344, 17 December 1923.

14. Erich Dombrowski, 'New Year's Eve', *Berliner Tageblatt*, Nr 602, 31 December 1923, evening edition.

15. Adam Fergusson, *When Money Dies: The Nightmare of Deficit Spending, Devaluation, and Hyperinflation in Weimar Germany* (New York, 2010 edition), 207; Larry Eugene Jones, *The German Right*, 209.

16. Larry Eugene Jones, *The German Right*, 210; Wright, *Gustav Stresemann*, 229.

17. Fergusson, *When Money Dies*, 215–16.
18. Feldman, *The Great Disorder*, 815–16.
19. 'The Path to Recovery', *Vorwärts*, Nr 580, 12 December 1923, evening edition.
20. Keiger, *Raymond Poincaré*, 305.
21. O'Riordan, *Britain and the Ruhr Crisis*, 125.
22. Marc Trachtenberg, *Reparation in World Politics: France and European Economic Diplomacy, 1916–1923* (New York, 1980), 324–7.
23. O'Riordan, *Britain and the Ruhr Crisis*, 125–41.
24. Steiner, *The Lights That Failed*, 239.
25. Fischer, *The Ruhr Crisis*, 283.
26. Steiner, *The Lights That Failed*, 250.
27. Fischer, *The Ruhr Crisis*, 285.
28. Ibid., 284; Steiner, *The Lights That Failed*, 242.
29. Steiner, *The Lights That Failed*, 242; Fischer, *The Ruhr Crisis*, 288–9.
30. Keiger, *Raymond Poincaré*, 309–10; Fischer, *The Ruhr Crisis*, 276.
31. Margaret MacMillan, *Peacemakers: Six Months That Changed the World* (London, 2001), 493.
32. Michael Geyer, 'Zwischen Krieg und Nachkrieg – die deutsche Revolution 1918/19 im Zeichen blockierter Transnationalität', in Alexander Gallus (ed.), *Die vergessene Revolution von 1918/19* (Göttingen, 2010), 187–222, esp. 218–22.
33. Peter Fritzsche, *Rehearsals for Fascism: Populism and Political Mobilization in Weimar Germany* (Oxford, 1990), 155–65; Anna von der Goltz, *Hindenburg: Power, Myth and the Rise of the Nazis* (Oxford, 2009), 84–103.
34. Fischer, *The Ruhr Crisis*, 290.
35. Hedwig Richter, *Demokratie: Eine deutsche Affäre: Vom 18. Jahrhundert bis zur Gegenwart* (Munich, 2020), 152–207.

Epilogue: 1933 and After

1. 'The *Mahnmal*: The 10th Anniversary of 9 November 1923: Commemoration of the Dead at the Feldherrnhalle', Munich, 9 November 1933, *Berliner Morgenpost*, Nr 269, 10 November 1933. There is no English language equivalent of the German term *Mahnmal*. The closest terms are memorial or monument. However, the German term is drawn from the verb *mahnen* which means to

remind or warn. Hence, a *Mahnmal* is a memorial or monument that conveys a warning. Today it is usually associated with memorials to the victims of Nazism.

2. 'The Historical Procession: Celebrations to Unveil the *Mahnmal* – Hitler speaks to the Old Guard', Munich, 9 November 1933, Exclusive Telegram, *Vossische Zeitung*, Nr 529, 10 November 1933; 'The *Mahnmal*: The 10th Anniversary of 9 November 1923: Commemoration of the Dead at the Feldherrnhalle', Munich, 9 November 1933, *Berliner Morgenpost*, Nr 269, 10 November 1933.

3. Bauer, Hockerts and Schütz (eds), *München: 'Hauptstadt' der Bewegung*, 334–5.

4. Ibid.

5. 'The Führer with the Fighters from 1923', Munich, 9 November 1935, *Pommersche Zeitung*, Nr 132, 9 November 1935.

6. Bauer, Hockerts and Schütz (eds), *München: 'Hauptstadt' der Bewegung*, 335–7.

7. 'The Midnight Hour of Consecration', *Teltower Kreisblatt*, Nr 263, 9 November 1935; 'Midnight Act of Consecration at the Feldherrnhalle', *Sorauer Tageblatt*, Nr 263, 9–10 November 1935; 'Night-Time Honouring of the Dead Heroes', Munich, 9 November 1935, *Teltower Kreisblatt*, Nr 263, 9 November 1935. See also 'Honour the Old Fighters!', Munich, 9 November 1935, *Pommersche Zeitung*, Nr 132, 9 November 1935.

8. Deutschland-Berichte der Sozialdemokratischen Partei Deutschlands, Sopade, Vol. 2, 1935 (Prague, 1935), 5 December 1935, Nr 11, 2, A-17.

9. 'At Home With the Fascists', *Vorwärts*, Nr 536, 15 November 1923, evening edition.

Sources

Archives and Archival Documents

Akten der Reichskanzlei: Weimarer Republik: Die Kabinette Marx I
und II, edited by Karl Dietrich Erdmann, Hans Booms and Günther
Abramowski, Vols 1 and 2 (Boppard, 1973) (Cabinet Meeting
Records for the Marx Governments)

Akten der Reichskanzlei: Weimarer Republik: Die Kabinette
Stresemann I und II, edited by Klaus Dietrich Erdmann and Martin
Vogt, Vols 1 and 2 (Boppard, 1978) (Cabinet Meeting Records for
the Stresemann Governments)

Akten der Reichskanzlei: Weimarer Republik: Die Kabinette Wirth I und
II, ed. Klaus Dietrich Erdmann and Hans Booms, Vol. 2 (Boppard,
1973) (Cabinet Meeting Records for the Wirth Governments)

Auswärtiges Amt (German Foreign Ministry Archive, Berlin)

Bundesarchiv Berlin Lichterfelde (German Federal Archives, Berlin,
Lichterfelde)

Bundesarchiv Militär Archiv Freiburg im Breisgau (German Federal
Archives, Military Archive, Freiburg)

Deutsches Bergbau-Museum Bochum, Bergbau-Archiv (German
Mining Museum, Mining Archive, Bochum)

Deutsches Tagebucharchiv Emmendingen (German Diary Archive,
Emmendingen)

Deutschland-Berichte der Sozialdemokratischen Partei Deutschlands,
Sopade, Vol. 2, 1935 (Prague, 1935) (German Reports of the Social
Democratic Party of Germany [in exile])

Jäckel, Eberhard, with Axel Kuhn (ed.), *Hitler: Sämtliche Aufzeichnungen
1905–1924* (Stuttgart, 1980) (Hitler, Complete Records, 1905–1924)

Ministère des Affaires Étrangères, Paris (French Foreign Ministry
Archive)

Service Historique de la Défense, Vincennes (French Military Archives, Paris)

Staatsarchiv Freiburg (Baden Württemburg State Archive, Freiburg)

Staatsarchiv Würzburg (Bavarian State Archives, Würzburg)

Stenographischer Bericht über die Verhandlungen des Bayerischen Landtags, Vols 7–9 (Munich, 1922–4) (Stenographic Records of the Bavarian Parliament)

Verhandlungen des Reichstages: Stenographische Berichte I. Wahlperiode 1920, Vols 10–18 (Berlin, 1922–4) (Stenographic Records of the German Reichstag)

Newspapers

Bergarbeiter-Zeitung

Berliner Börsen-Zeitung

Berliner Morgenpost

Berliner Tageblatt

Berliner Volks-Zeitung

CV [Central-Verein]-Zeitung

Daily Mail

Deutsche Allgemeine Zeitung

Deutsche-Zeitung

Frankfurter Zeitung

Germania

Das Jüdische Echo

Jüdische Rundschau

Kreuzzeitung

Manchester Guardian

Morning Post

Der oberschlesische Wanderer

Pommersche Zeitung

Sorauer Tageblatt

Teltower Kreisblatt

The Times

Völkischer Beobachter

Vorwärts

Vossische Zeitung

Die Weltbühne

Selected Literature

Albanese, Giulia, *The March on Rome: Violence and the Rise of Italian Fascism*, trans. Sergio Knipe (London, 2019)

Andre, Daniela, 'Eleonore Baur – "Blutschwester Pia" oder "Engel von Dachau?"', in Marita Krauss (ed.), *Rechte Karrieren in München* (Munich, 2010), 166–85

Aulke, Julian, *Räume der Revolution: Kulturelle Verräumlichung in Politisierungsprozessen während der Revolution 1918–19* (Stuttgart, 2015)

Bauer, R., Hans G. Hockerts and Brigitte Schütz (eds), *München: 'Hauptstadt' der Bewegung: Bayerns Metropole und der Nationalsozialismus* (Wolfratshausen, 2002)

Becker, Annette, 'Das Begräbnis des Leutnants Colpin in Lille am 21. März 1923', in Gerd Krumeich and Joachim Schröder (eds), *Der Schatten des Weltkriegs: Die Ruhrbesetzung 1923* (Essen, 2004), 257–63

Bosworth, Richard, *Mussolini* (London, 2002)

Bournazel, Renata, *Rapallo: Ein französisches Trauma*, trans. H. Jany (Cologne, 1976)

Brenner, Michael, *In Hitler's Munich: Jews, the Revolution, and the Rise of Nazism*, trans. Jeremiah Riemer (Princeton, 2022)

Büttner, Ursula, *Weimar: Die überforderte Republik 1918–1933: Leistung und Versagen in Staat, Gesellschaft, Wirtschaft und Kultur* (Stuttgart, 2008)

Cabanes, Bruno, *La Victoire endeuillée: La sortie de guerre des soldats français, 1918–1920* (Paris, 2004)

Canetti, Elias, *The Torch in my Ear*, trans. Joachim Neugroschel (London, 2011)

Cox, Mary Elisabeth, 'Hunger Games: Or How the Allied Blockade in the First World War Deprived German Children of Nutrition, and Allied Food Aid Subsequently Saved Them', *Economic History Review*, 68:2 (2015), 600–31

——, *Hunger in War and Peace: Women and Children in Germany, 1914–1924* (Oxford, 2019)

Dale, Iain, *Conservative Party General Election Manifestos 1900–1997* (Basingstoke, 1999)

Duggan, Christopher, *The Force of Destiny: A History of Italy since 1796* (London, 2007)

Evans, Richard, *Rituals of Retribution: Capital Punishment in Germany 1600–1987* (Oxford, 1996)

——, *The Coming of the Third Reich: How the Nazis Destroyed Democracy and Seized Power in Germany* (London, 2004)

Feldman, Gerald D., 'Bayern und Sachsen in der Hyperinflation 1922/23', *Historische Zeitschrift*, 238:3 (1984), 569–609

——, *The Great Disorder: Politics, Economics, and Society in the German Inflation, 1914–1924* (Oxford, 1997)

——, *Hugo Stinnes: Biographie eines Industriellen 1870–1924* (Munich, 1998)

Ferguson, Niall, 'Keynes and the German Inflation', *English Historical Review*, 110:436 (1995), 368–91

——, 'Constraints and Room for Manoeuvre in the German Inflation of the Early 1920s', *Economic History Review*, 49:4 (1996), 635–66

Fergusson, Adam, *When Money Dies: The Nightmare of Deficit Spending, Devaluation, and Hyperinflation in Weimar Germany* (New York, 2010 edition)

Fink, Carole, *The Genoa Conference: European Diplomacy, 1921–1922* (Chapel Hill and London, 1984)

——, Axel Frohn and Jürgen Heideking (eds), *Genoa, Rapallo, and European Reconstruction in 1922* (Cambridge, 1991)

Fischer, Conan, *The Ruhr Crisis 1923–1924* (Oxford, 2003)

——, 'The Human Price of Reparations', in Conan Fischer and Alan Sharp (eds), *After the Versailles Treaty: Enforcement, Compliance, Contested Identities* (Basingstoke, 2007), 81–96

Fleischhauer, Eva Ingeborg, 'Rathenau in Rapallo: Eine notwendige Korrektur des Forschungsstandes', *Vierteljahrshefte für Zeitgeschichte*, 54:3 (2006), 365–415

Franzinelli, Mimmo, *Squadristi: Protagonisti e tecniche della violenza fascista* (Milan, 2003)

Fraschka, Mark A., *Franz Pfeffer von Salomon: Hitlers vergessener Oberster SA-Führer* (Göttingen, 2016)

Fritzsche, Peter, *Rehearsals for Fascism: Populism and Political Mobilization in Weimar Germany* (New York, 1990)

Geyer, Martin, *Verkehrte Welt: Revolution, Inflation und Moderne: München 1914–1924* (Göttingen, 1998)

Geyer, Michael, 'Zwischen Krieg und Nachkrieg – die deutsche

Revolution 1918/19 im Zeichen blockierter Transnationalität', in Alexander Gallus (ed.), *Die vergessene Revolution von 1918/19* (Göttingen, 2010), 187–222

Goeschel, Christian, *Suicide in Nazi Germany* (Oxford, 2009)

Goltz, Anna von der, *Hindenburg: Power, Myth and the Rise of the Nazis* (Oxford, 2009)

Gordon, Harold J., *Hitler and the Beer Hall Putsch* (Princeton, 1972)

Herbst, Ludolf, *Hitlers Charisma: Die Erfindung eines deutschen Messias* (Frankfurt, 2010)

Hershey, A. S., 'German Reparations', *American Journal of International Law*, 15:3 (1921), 411–18

Hitler, Adolf, *Wortlaut der Hauptverhandlung vor dem Volksgericht München I* (also: *Der Hitler-Prozess*, Part 1) (Munich, 1997)

Hofmann, Hanns Hubert, *Der Hitlerputsch: Krisenjahre deutscher Geschichte 1920–1924* (Munich, 1961)

Horne, John, and Alan Kramer, *German Atrocities 1914: A History of Denial* (New Haven, 2001)

Hueck, Ingo J., *Der Staatsgerichtshof zum Schutze der Republik* (Tübingen, 1993)

Hürten, Heinz, *Das Krisenjahr 1923: Militär- und Innenpolitik 1922–1924* (Düsseldorf, 1980)

Jeannesson, Stanislas, *Poincaré, la France et la Ruhr (1922–1924): Histoire d'une occupation* (Strasbourg, 1998)

——, 'Übergriffe der französischen Besatzungsmacht und deutsche Beschwerden', in Gerd Krumeich and Joachim Schröder (eds), *Der Schatten des Weltkriegs: Die Ruhrbesetzung 1923* (Essen, 2004), 207–32

Jones, Larry Eugene, *The German Right, 1918–1930: Political Parties, Organized Interests, and Patriotic Associations in the Struggle Against Weimar Democracy* (Cambridge, 2020)

Jones, Mark, *Founding Weimar: Violence and the German Revolution of 1918–19* (Cambridge, 2016)

——, *Am Anfang war Gewalt: Die deutsche Revolution 1918/19 und der Beginn der Weimarer Republik*, trans. Karl Heinz Siber (Berlin, 2017)

Keiger, John F. V., *Raymond Poincaré* (Cambridge, 1997)

Kemp, Klaus, *Regiebahn: Reparationen, Besetzung, Ruhrkampf, Reichsbahn: Die Eisenbahnen im Rheinland und im Ruhrgebiet 1918–1930* (Freiburg, 2016)

Kershaw, Ian, *Hitler 1889–1936: Hubris* (London, 1998)

——, *The Hitler Myth: Image and Reality in the Third Reich* (Oxford, 2001)

Kessler, Harry, *Walther Rathenau: His Life and Work*, trans. W. D. Robson-Scott and Lawrence Hyde (New York, 1930)

——, *In the Twenties: The Diaries of Harry Kessler*, trans. Charles Kessler (New York, 1971)

Keynes, John Maynard, *The Economic Consequences of the Peace* (London, 1919)

Kolb, Eberhard, and Dirk Schumann, *Die Weimarer Republik* (Munich, 2009)

Krüger, Gerd, 'Das Unternehmen Wesel im Ruhrkampf von 1923', in Horst Schroeder and Gerd Krüger (eds), *Realschule und Ruhrkampf: Beiträge zur Stadtgeschichte des 19. und 20. Jahrhunderts* (Wesel, 2002), 91–151

——, '"Wir wachen und strafen!" Gewalt im Ruhrkampf von 1923', in Gerd Krumeich and Joachim Schröder (eds), *Der Schatten des Weltkriegs: Die Ruhrbesetzung 1923* (Essen, 2004), 233–55

Krüger, Peter, *Die Aussenpolitik der Republik von Weimar* (Darmstadt, 1985)

Krumeich, Gerd, and Joachim Schröder (eds), *Der Schatten des Weltkriegs: Die Ruhrbesetzung 1923* (Essen, 2004)

Küppers, Heinrich, *Joseph Wirth: Parlamentarier, Minister und Kanzler der Weimarer Republik* (Stuttgart, 1996)

Large, David Clay, '"Out with the Ostjuden": The Scheunenviertel Riots in Berlin, November 1923', in Christhard Hoffmann, Werner Bergmann and Helmut Walser Smith (eds), *Exclusionary Violence: Antisemitic Riots in Modern German History* (Michigan, 2002), 123–40

Linke, Horst Günther, 'Der Weg nach Rapallo: Strategie und Taktik der deutschen und sowjetischen Außenpolitik', *Historische Zeitschrift*, 264 (1997), 55–109

Longerich, Peter, *Hitler: A Life*, trans. Jeremy Noakes and Lesley Sharpe (Oxford, 2019)

Luther, Hans, *In Memoriam: Den Opfern des französischen Militarismus in Essen* (Berlin, 1923)

McElligott, Anthony, *Rethinking the Weimar Republic: Authority and Authoritarianism 1916–1936* (London, 2014)

Mack-Smith, Dennis, *Mussolini* (New York, 1982)

MacMillan, Margaret, *Peacemakers: Six Months That Changed the World* (London, 2001)

Malik, Hassan, *Bankers and Bolsheviks: International Finance and the Russian Revolution* (Princeton, 2018)

Mann, Thomas, 'Erinnerungen aus der deutschen Inflation', in Mann, *Gesammelte Werke in zwölf Bänden*, Vol. 13: *Nachträge* (Frankfurt, 1974), 181–90

Morsey, Rudolf, *Die Deutsche Zentrumspartei 1917–1923* (Düsseldorf, 1966)

Mühlhausen, Walter, *Friedrich Ebert 1871–1925: Reichspräsident der Weimarer Republik* (Bonn, 2006)

Mulligan, William, *The Great War for Peace* (New Haven, 2014)

O'Riordan, Elspeth Y., *Britain and the Ruhr Crisis* (New York, 2001)

Pese, Walter Werner, 'Hitler und Italien 1920–1926', *Vierteljahrshefte für Zeitgeschichte*, 3:2 (1955), 113–26

Pommerin, Reiner, 'Die Ausweisung von "Ostjuden" aus Bayern 1923: Ein Beitrag zum Krisenjahr der Weimarer Republik', *Vierteljahrshefte für Zeitgeschichte*, 34:3 (1984), 311–40

Rathenau, Walther, *Cannes und Genua: Vier Reden zum Reparationsproblem* (Berlin, 1922)

Reichardt, Sven, *Faschistische Kampfbünde: Gewalt und Gemeinschaft im italienischen Squadrismus und in der deutschen SA* (Berlin, 2009)

Richter, Hedwig, *Demokratie: Eine deutsche Affäre: Vom 18. Jahrhundert bis zur Gegenwart* (Munich, 2020)

Ruck, Michael, *Die freien Gewerkschaften im Ruhrkampf 1923* (Cologne, 1986)

Sabrow, Martin, *Der Rathenaumord: Rekonstruktion einer Verschwörung gegen die Republik von Weimar* (Munich, 1994)

——, 'Die Judenhetzerin von Kitzingen', *Praxis Geschichte*, 2 (1992), 59–61

Salomon, Ernst von, *The Outlaws*, trans. Ian F. D. Morrow (London, 1931)

——, *Der Fragebogen* (Hamburg, 1951)

Schnorrenberger, Angelika, 'Der Düsseldorfer "Blutsonntag", 30. September 1923', in Gerd Krumeich and Joachim Schröder (eds), *Der Schatten des Weltkriegs: Die Ruhrbesetzung 1923* (Essen, 2004), 289–303

Schulin, Ernst, 'Noch etwas zur Entstehung des Rapallo-Vertrages', in Hartmut von Hentig and August Nitschke (eds), *Was die Wirklichkeit lehrt: Golo Mann zum 70. Geburtstag* (Frankfurt, 1979), 177–202

Schumann, Dirk, *Political Violence in the Weimar Republic, 1918–1933: Fight for the Streets and Fear of Civil War*, trans. Thomas Dunlap (New York, 2009)

Schwinger, Elmar, *Von Kitzingen nach Izbica: Aufstieg und Katastrophe der mainfränkischen, israelitischen Kultusgemeinde Kitzingen* (Kitzingen, 2009)

Siemens, Daniel, *Stormtroopers: A New History of Hitler's Brownshirts* (New Haven, 2017)

Spethmann, Hans, *Zwölf Jahre Ruhrbergbau: Aus seiner Geschichte von Kriegsanfang bis zum Franzosenabmarsch 1914 bis 1925*, Vol. III: *Der Ruhrkampf 1923 bis 1925 in seinen Leitlinien* (Berlin, 1929)

——, *Zwölf Jahre Ruhrbergbau: Aus seiner Geschichte von Kriegsanfang bis zum Franzosenabmarsch 1914 bis 1925*, Vol. IV: *Der Ruhrkampf 1923 bis 1925: Das Ringen um die Kohle* (Berlin, 1930)

Steiner, Zara, *The Lights That Failed: European International History 1919–1933* (Oxford, 2005)

Taylor, Andrew, *Bonar Law* (London, 2006)

Trachtenberg, Marc, *Reparation in World Politics. France and European Economic Diplomacy, 1916–1923* (New York, 1980)

Ufermann, Paul, *Könige der Inflation* (Berlin, 1924)

Ullrich, Volker, *Hitler: A Biography*: Vol. 1: *Ascent*, trans. Jefferson Chase (London, 2016)

Usborne, Cornelie, *Cultures of Abortion in Weimar Germany* (New York, 2007)

Volkov, Shulamit, *Walther Rathenau: Weimar's Fallen Statesman* (New Haven and London, 2012)

Walter, Dirk, *Antisemitische Kriminalität und Gewalt: Judenfeindschaft in der Weimarer Republik* (Bonn, 1999)

Watson, Alex, *Ring of Steel: Germany and Austria-Hungary in World War I – The People's War* (New York, 2014)

Weber, Thomas, *Becoming Hitler: The Making of a Nazi* (Oxford, 2017)

Widdig, Bernd, *Culture and Inflation in Weimar Germany* (Berkeley, 2001)

Wildt, Michael, *Zerborstene Zeit: Deutsche Geschichte 1918–1945* (Munich, 2022)

Winkler, Heinrich August, *Von der Revolution zur Stabilisierung: Arbeiter und Arbeiterbewegung in der Weimarer Republik 1918–1924* (Berlin, 1984)

——, *Weimar 1918–1933: Die Geschichte der ersten deutschen Demokratie* (Munich, 1993)

Wisotzky, Klaus, 'Der "blutige Karsamstag" 1923 bei Krupp', in Gerd Krumeich and Joachim Schröder (eds), *Der Schatten des Weltkriegs: Die Ruhrbesetzung 1923* (Essen, 2004), 265–88

Wright, Jonathan, *Gustav Stresemann: Weimar's Greatest Statesman* (Oxford, 2004)

Zwicker, Stefan, *'Nationale Märtyrer': Albert Leo Schlageter und Julius Fučík – Heldenkult, Propaganda und Erinnerungskultur* (Paderborn, 2006)

Index

Mark William Jones is assistant professor in history at University College Dublin. He holds a PhD from the European University Institute in Florence, Italy. The author of *Founding Weimar: Violence and the German Revolution of 1918–1919*, he lives in Dublin, Ireland.